TAX LAWS

Tax Laws

N.S. Zad

Price : ₹ 595

Law stated in this book is as amended upto 1st June, 2019

Published by :
Taxmann Publications (P.) Ltd.

Sales & Marketing :
59/32, New Rohtak Road, New Delhi-110 005 India
Phone : +91-11-45562222
Website : www.taxmann.com
E-mail : sales@taxmann.com

Regd. Office :
21/35, West Punjabi Bagh, New Delhi-110 026 India

Printed at :
Tan Prints (India) Pvt. Ltd.
44 Km. Mile Stone, National Highway, Rohtak Road
Village Rohad, Distt. Jhajjar (Haryana) India
E-mail : sales@tanprints.com

Disclaimer

Every effort has been made to avoid errors or omissions in this publication. In spite of this, errors may creep in. Any mistake, error or discrepancy noted may be brought to our notice which shall be taken care of in the next edition. It is notified that neither the publisher nor the author or seller will be responsible for any damage or loss of action to any one, of any kind, in any manner, therefrom. It is suggested that to avoid any doubt the reader should cross-check all the facts, law and contents of the publication with original Government publication or notifications.

For binding mistake, misprints or for missing pages, etc., the publisher's liability is limited to replacement within seven days of purchase by similar edition. All expenses in this connection are to be borne by the purchaser.

All disputes are subject to Delhi jurisdiction only.

Contents

PAGE

PART B : INDIRECT TAX (30 MARKS)

IMPORTANT NOTE:

- ***For CS Executive Old Syllabus Students:*** *All Chapters **except Chapter 19** are applicable for CS Executive Old Syllabus.*
- ***For CS Executive New Syllabus Students:*** Chapters 15 & 17 is not applicable for New Syllabus. In Chapter 16 questions relating to 'Settlement', 'Advance Ruling' are not in new syllabus hence can be ignored. Other questions however are relevant.

GRAPHS SHOWING CHAPTER-WISE WEIGHTAGE OF MARKS FOR PAST EXAMINATIONS

CHAPTER 1 : BASIC CONCEPTS

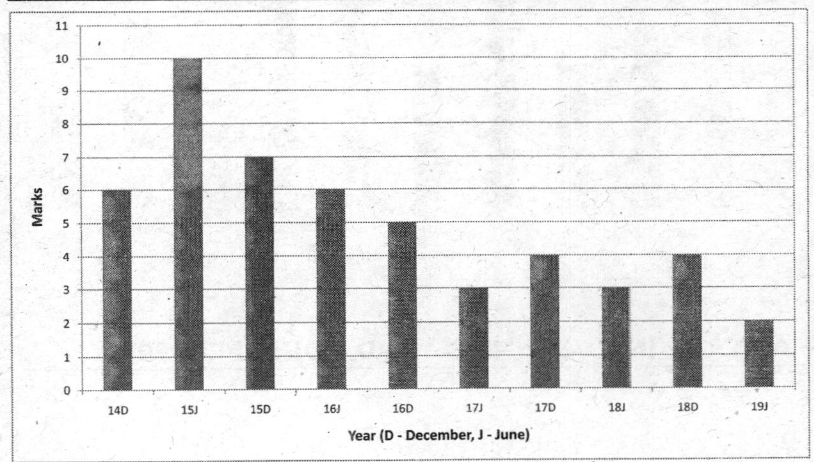

CHAPTER 2 : RESIDENTIAL STATUS

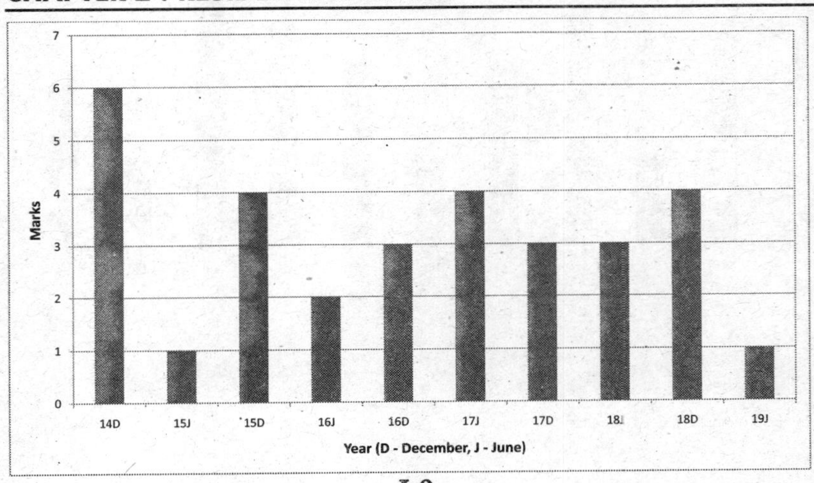

CHAPTER 3 : INCOME UNDER HEAD SALARIES

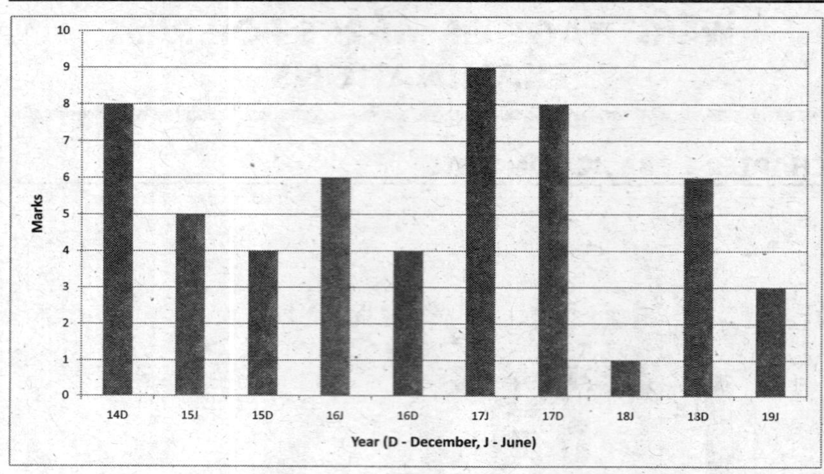

CHAPTER 4 : INCOME UNDER HEAD HOUSE PROPERTY

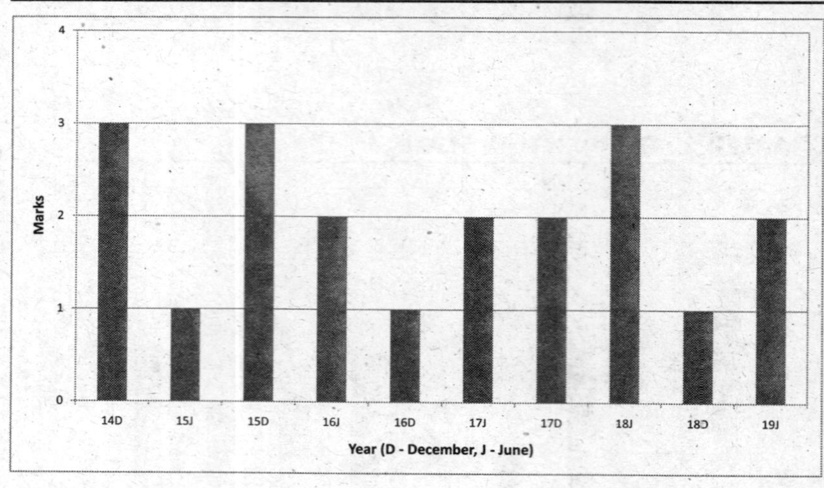

CHAPTER 5 : INCOME FROM BUSINESS OR PROFESSION

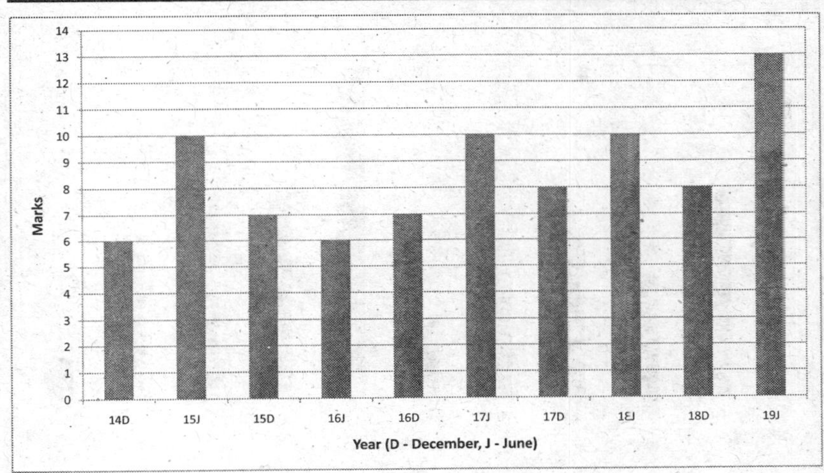

CHAPTER 6 : INCOME FROM CAPITAL GAIN

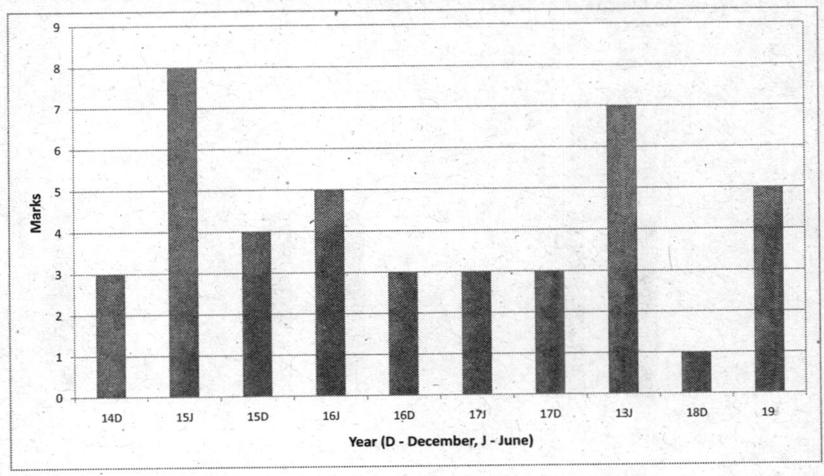

CHAPTER 7 : INCOME FROM OTHER SOURCES

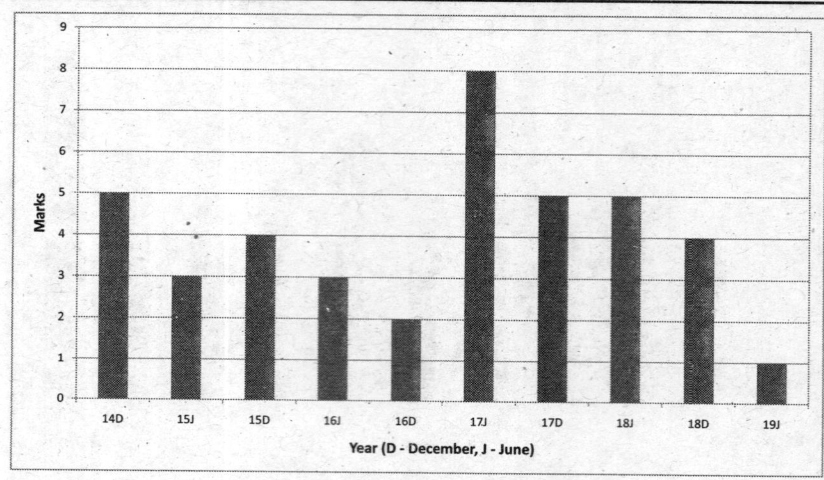

CHAPTER 8 : CLUBBING OF INCOMES

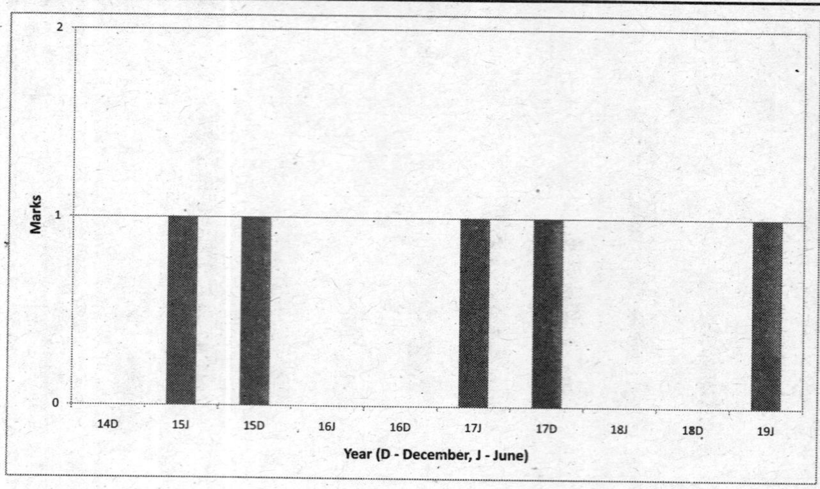

CHAPTER 9 : AGGREGATION OF INCOME AND SET-OFF OR CARRY FORWARD OF LOSS

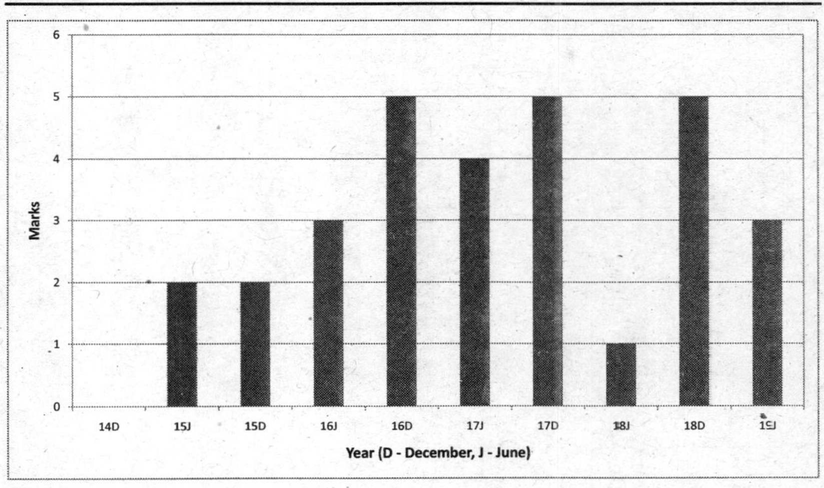

CHAPTER 10 : DEDUCTIONS FROM TOTAL INCOME

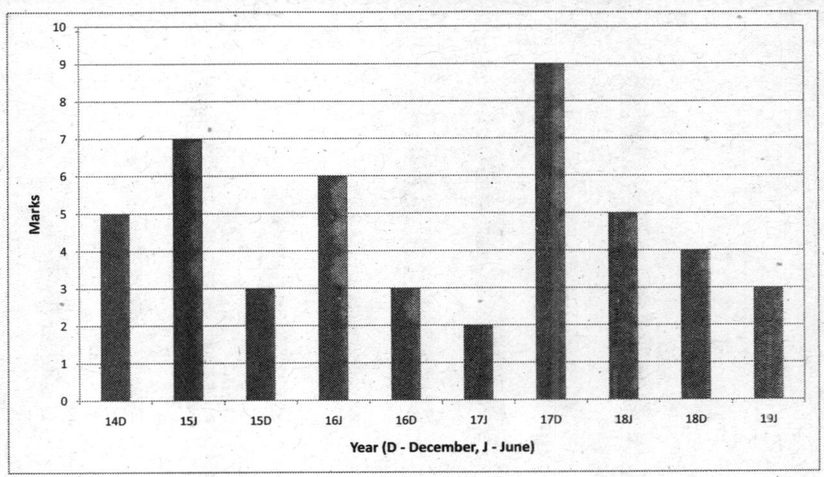

CHAPTER 11 : AGRICULTURAL INCOME & EXEMPTED INCOMES

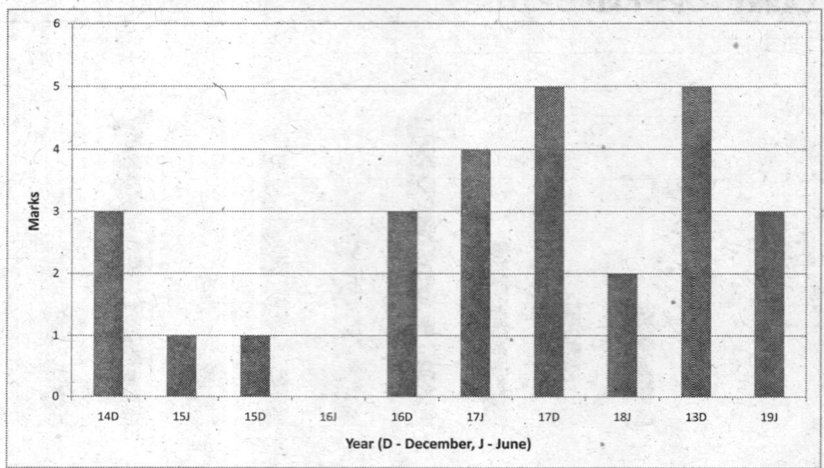

CHAPTER 12 : ASSESSMENT OF INDIVIDUAL, HUF, PARTNERSHIP FIRMS, TRUST, AOP, BOI & COMPANIES

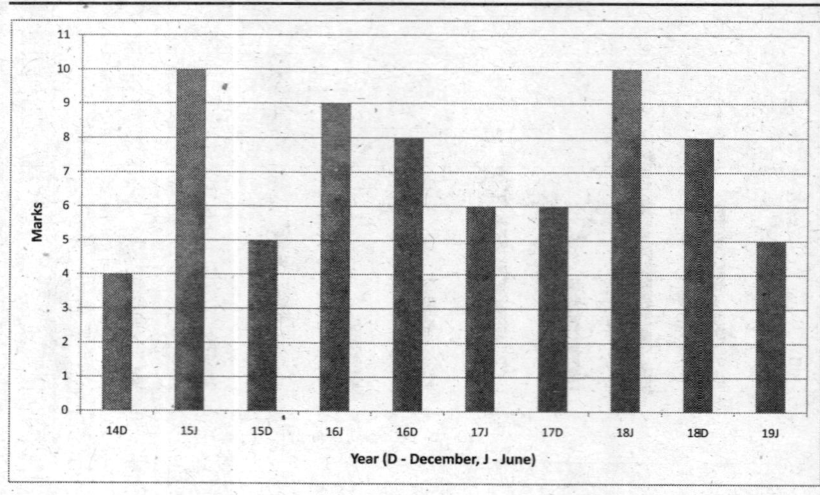

CHAPTER 13 : TDS, ADVANCE TAX, INTEREST PAYABLE BY/TO ASSESSEES

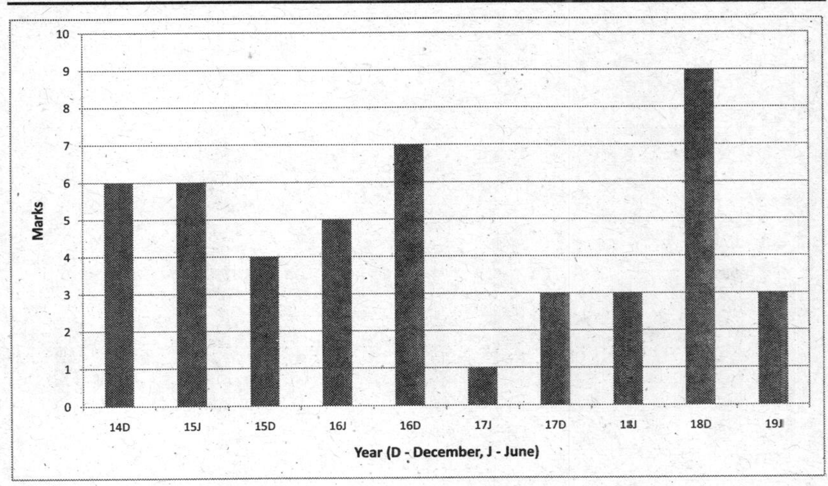

CHAPTER 14 : RETURN OF INCOME

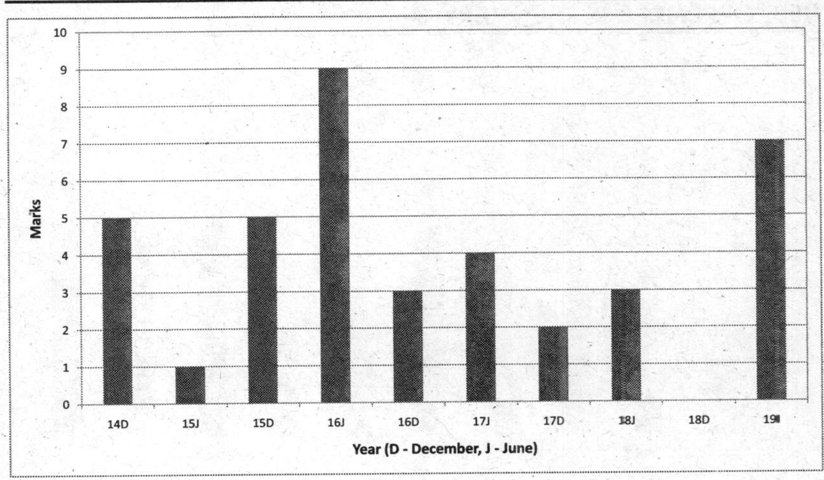

CHAPTER 15 : COMPUTATION OF TAX LIABILITY OF NON-RESIDENT ASSESSEES

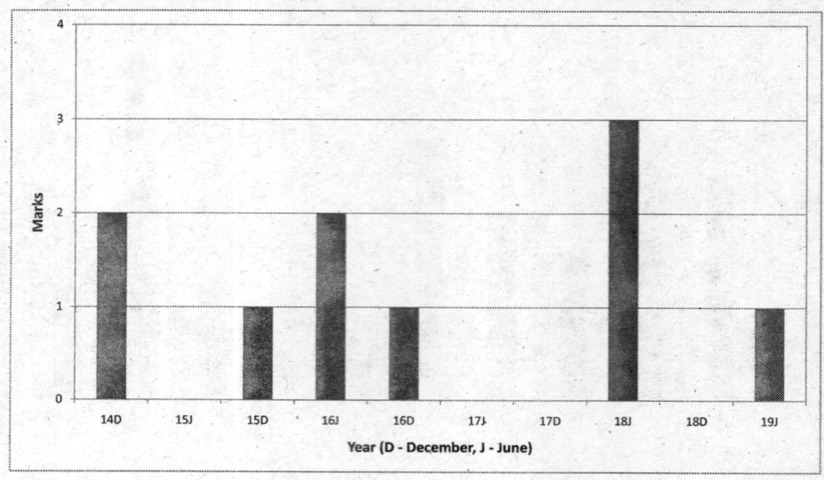

CHAPTER 16 : APPEALS, REVISIONS, SETTLEMENT, PENALTIES, OFFENCES & RECOVERY OF TAX

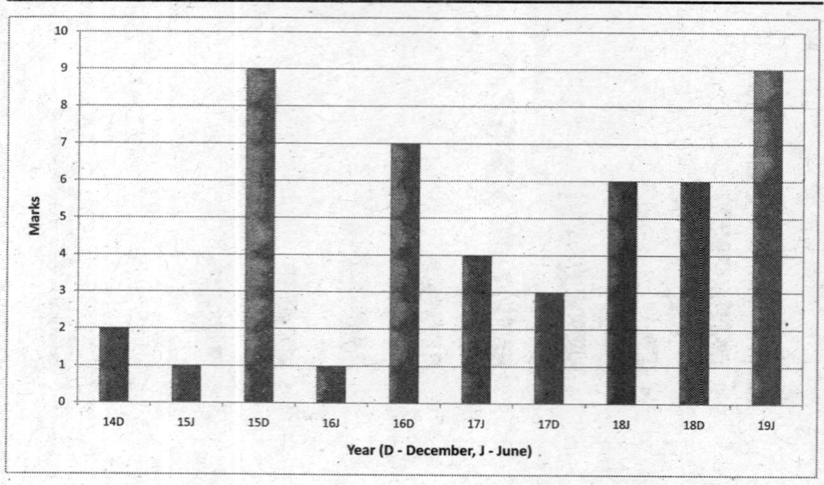

CHAPTER 17 : TAX PLANNING & MANAGEMENT, INTERNATIONAL TAXATION, ADVANCE RULING & GAAR

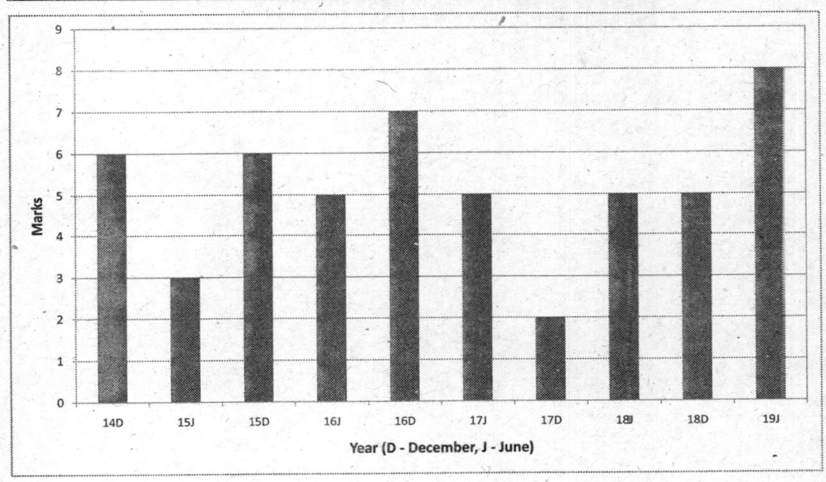

CHAPTER 18 : GOODS & SERVICES TAX LAW

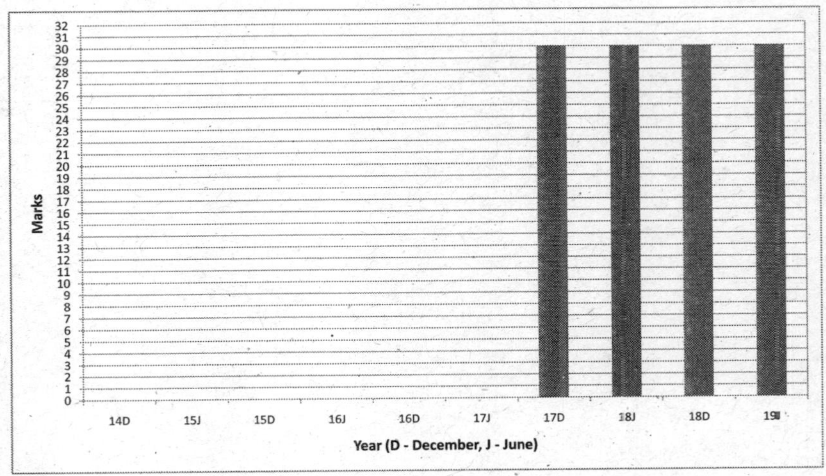

PART A

INCOME TAX (70 MARKS)

CHAPTER 1
BASIC CONCEPTS

MCQs ON THEORY

1. Power to impose tax on all income except agriculture income is with ____

(A) Central Government

(B) State Government

(C) Partly with Central and partly with State Government

(D) Local Authorities

2. Which of the following entry of Schedule VII of the Constitution of India gives the power to Central Government to impose tax on all income except agriculture income?

(A) Entry 72

(B) Entry 102

(C) Entry 82

(D) Entry 92

3. Power to impose income tax on agriculture income is with ______

(A) Central Government

(B) State Government

(C) Partly with Central and partly with State Government

(D) Municipal Corporation

4. The Income Tax Act, 1961 came into force on ______

(A) 1st April, 1962

(B) 1st March, 1962

(C) 1st April, 1961

(D) 15th August, 1961

5. The Income Tax Act, 1961 extends to ______

(A) Whole of India

(B) Whole of India including Jammu & Kashmir

(C) Whole of India excluding Jammu & Kashmir

(D) Whole of India excluding Jammu & Kashmir and union territories

6. The Income Tax Act, 1961 has total _____ schedules.

(A) X

(B) XII

(C) XIV

(D) XVII

7. Who has power to make the Rules under the Income Tax Act, 1961?

(1) Central Government

(2) CBDT

(3) CBEC

Select the correct answer from the options given below –

(A) (1) & (2)

(B) (1) only

(C) (1), (2) & (3)

(D) (2) only

8. Circulars issued by the CBDT are binding on ______

(i) Income tax authorities

(ii) Assessee

(iii) Income Tax Tribunal

(iv) Courts

Select the correct answer from the options given below –

(A) (i) and (ii)

(B) (iii) and (iv)

(C) (ii), (i) & (iii)

(D) (i) only

9. Supreme Court's decisions are binding on –

(*i*) Income tax authorities

(*ii*) Assessee

(*iii*) Income Tax Tribunal

(*iv*) High Courts

Select the correct answer from the options given below –

(A) (ii) only

(B) (i) & (ii) only

(C) (i), (ii) & (iii) only

(D) (i), (ii), (iii) & (iv)

10. Who present the Finance Bill in the Parliament?

(A) Prime Minister

(B) Speaker of Lok Sabha

(C) Minister of Finance

(D) Any of the above

11. Amendments made by Finance Act, 2018 generally become applicable from ______

(A) 1.4.2018

(B) 1.4.2019

(C) 1.6.2018

(D) 1.4.2020

12. PART I of the Finance Act, 2018 will deal with ______

(A) Rules for computation of net agriculture income

(B) Rates at which income tax to be levied on income for PY 2018-2019.

(C) Rates at which income tax to be levied on income for AY 2018-2019.

(D) Rate of TDS during the AY 2019-2020

13. Which of the following cannot be treated as person u/s 2(31) of the Income Tax Act, 1961?

(I) HUF

(II) AOP

(III) BOI

(IV) Artificial Juridical Person

Select the correct answer from the options given below –

(A) (IV) only

(B) (II) & (III) only

(C) (I), (II), (IV)

(D) None of the above

14. Which of the following formula is correct for "average rate of tax" as defined in section 2(10) of the Income Tax Act, 1961?

(A) $\text{Average rate of tax} = \dfrac{\text{Total income}}{\text{Tax on total income}} \times 100$

(B) $\text{Average rate of tax} = \dfrac{\text{Tax on total income}}{\text{Gross total income}} \times 100$

(C) $\text{Average rate of tax} = \dfrac{\text{Tax on total income}}{\text{Total income}} \times 100$

(D) $\text{Average rate of tax} = \dfrac{\text{Gross total income}}{\text{Tax on total income}} \times 100$

15. PART II of the Finance Act, 2018 will deal with ______

(A) Rate of TDS during the AY 2018-2019

(B) Rate of TDS during the AY 2019-2020

(C) Rate of TDS during the PY 2019-2020

(D) Rules for computation of net agriculture income

16. Which of the following is/are include in definition of 'Local Authority' as defined in Section 10 (20) of the Income Tax Act, 1961?

(a) Panchayat

(b) LLP

(c) Cantonment Board

(d) District Boards

(e) Municipal Committee

Select the correct answer from the options given below –

(A) (a), (c) & (e)

(B) (b), (e) & (a)

(C) (a), (c), (d) & (e)

(D) None of the above option is correct.

17. Sum received on maturity under the Keyman Insurance Policy __________ if the policy is taken in the name of an employee.

(A) is taxable as income under the head Profits and gains of business and profession

(B) is taxable as income from other sources

(C) is taxable as profits in lieu of salary u/s 17(3)

(D) is exempt from tax

18. PART III of the Finance Act, 2018 will deal with ______

(A) Rates for computing advance tax for the AY 2019-2020

(B) Rules for computation of net agriculture income

(C) Rates for computing advance tax for the AY 2018-2019

(D) Rate of TDS during the AY 2019-2020

19. Which of the following person can be treated as 'assessee' u/s 2(7) of the Income Tax Act, 1961?

(1) Any person in respect of whom proceeding has been taken

(2) Any person who is deemed to be an assessee

(3) Any person who fails to comply with duties imposed under the Act

(4) Any person against whom Assessing Officer has issued letter of enquiry

(A) (2) & (3)

(B) (4), (3) & (1)

(C) (3), (1) & (2)

(D) (1) only

20. As per section 2(29C) of the Income Tax Act, 1961, Maximum Marginal Rate (MMR) is the rate of income tax including surcharge, if any, applicable in relation to highest slab of income, specified in the Finance Act for the relevant year, in case of following persons, –

(I) An individual
(II) Co-operative Society
(III) An AOP
(IV) LLP
(V) BOI
(VI) Company

Select the correct answer from the options given below –

(A) (II), (IV) and (VI)
(B) (I), (III), (IV) & (V)
(C) (I) only
(D) (V), (III) & (I)

21. PART IV of the Finance Act, 2018 will deal with _____

(A) Rules for computation of net agriculture income
(B) Conditions for granting exemption in respect of agricultural income
(C) Rate of TDS during the AY 2019-2020
(D) Rates for computing advance tax for the AY 2019-2020

22. Which of the following statement is correct?

(i) Assessment year can be 12 months or less
(ii) Previous year must be of 12 months

Select the correct answer from the options given below –

(A) (ii) only
(B) Both (i) and (ii)
(C) (i) only
(D) Neither (i) nor (ii)

23. Maximum Marginal Rate (MMR) for AY 2019-2020 is ______

(A) 33.99%
(B) 35.535%

(C) 34.272%

(D) 35.88%

24. Mr. X set-up a business on 27.8.2018. Previous Year for him as per Income Tax Act, 1961 will be _____

(A) 1.4.2018 to 31.3.2019

(B) 27.8.2019 to 31.3.2020

(C) 1.4.2019 to 31.3.2020

(D) 27.8.2018 to 31.3.2019

25. For which of the following heads of income, the method of accounting employed by the assessee is irrelevant?

(a) Income from salary

(b) Income from house property

(c) Income from Profits and Gains of Business and Profession (PGBP)

(d) Income under the head capital gain

(e) Income from other sources

Select the correct answer from the options given below –

(A) (a), (c) & (e)

(B) (b), (d) & (a)

(C) (b) & (d)

(D) (e), (d), (a) & (c)

26. Section 68 of the Income Tax Act, 1961 deals with _____

(A) Taxability of unexplained investment

(B) Taxability of unexplained cash credit

(C) Taxability of unexplained expenditures

(D) Taxability of unexplained money

27. As per Section 2(32) of the Income Tax Act, 1961, an individual is said to have substantial interest in a concern if he or she is, at time during the previous year _____

(1) Beneficial owner of equity shares carrying 20% or more of the voting power in the company

(2) Entitled to appoint 1/5th or more directors in case of company

(3) Entitled to 20% or more of the profits such concern.

Select the correct answer from the options given below –

(A) (2) only

(B) (1) only

(C) (3) only

(D) (1) & (3) only

28. Match the following:

(1) Amount borrowed or repaid on hundi	(a) Section 69C
(2) Unexplained expenditures	(b) Section 69A
(3) Investment not fully disclosed	(c) Section 68
(4) Unexplained money	(d) Section 69
(5) Unexplained investment	(e) Section 69B
(6) Unexplained cash credit	(f) Section 69D

(A) (1) – (f), (2) – (a), (3) – (e), (4) – (c), (5) – (e), (6) – (d)

(B) (1) – (f), (2) – (b), (3) – (e), (4) – (a), (5) – (d), (6) – (c)

(C) (1) – (f), (2) – (a), (3) – (e), (4) – (b), (5) – (d), (6) – (c)

(D) (1) – (f), (2) – (b), (3) – (d), (4) – (a), (5) – (c), (6) – (e)

29. Rebate from tax on total income is available under ______

(A) Section 86A

(B) Section 88A

(C) Section 87A

(D) Section 85A

30. Income earned in previous year is taxable in assessment year. This is known as ....

(A) Assessment year rule

(B) Taxation rule

(C) Previous year rule

(D) Exception rule

31. Sum received on maturity under the Keyman Insurance Policy __________ if the policy matures in the hands of person carrying business and profession.

(A) is exempt from tax

(B) is taxable as profits in lieu of salary u/s 17(3)

(C) is taxable as income from other sources

(D) is taxable as income under the head Profits and gains of business and profession

32. Which of the following Sections contains exceptions to the previous year rule?

(A) Sections 152 to 156

(B) Sections 162 to 166

(C) Sections 172 to 176

(D) Sections 182 to 186

33. Under which of the following sections 'Relief' can be claimed from the total tax payable?

(A) Under Sections 86, 89, 90A & 91

(B) Under Sections 85, 86, 89A & 90

(C) Under Sections 86, 87, 90A & 92

(D) Under Sections 84, 88, 89A & 91A

34. Which of the following is correct slab of income tax for resident person having age of 32 years?

	Income	**Rate**
(A)	Up to ₹ 3,50,000	Nil
	Next ₹ 1,50,000	5%
	Next ₹ 5,00,000	20%
	Balance	30%
	Income	**Rate**
(B)	Up to ₹ 2,00,000	Nil
	Next ₹ 3,00,000	5%
	Next ₹ 5,00,000	20%

Balance	30%

Income	Rate
(C) Up to ₹ 1,50,000	Nil
Next ₹ 3,50,000	5%
Next ₹ 5,00,000	20%
Balance	30%

Income	Rate
(D) Up to ₹ 2,50,000	Nil
Next ₹ 2,50,000	5%
Next ₹ 5,00,000	20%
Balance	30%

35. As per section 172 of the Income Tax Act, 1961, where such a ship carries passengers, livestock, mail or goods shipped at a port in India, ______of the amount paid or payable on account of such carriage to the owner or the charterer or to any person on his behalf, whether that amount is paid or payable in or out of India, shall be deemed to be income accruing in India to the owner or charterer on account of such carriage.

(A) 10.5%
(B) 5.5%
(C) 7.5%
(D) 8.5%

36. Sum received on maturity under the Keyman Insurance Policy __________ if the policy is taken in the name of any other person other than employer or employee.

(A) is exempt from tax
(B) is taxable as profits in lieu of salary u/s 17(3)
(C) is taxable as income from other sources
(D) is taxable as income under the head profits & gains of business & profession

37. Which of the following is correct slab of income tax for non-resident person having age of 62 years?

	Income	Rate
(A)	Up to ₹ 3,00,000	Nil
	Next ₹ 2,00,000	5%
	Next ₹ 5,00,000	20%
	Balance	30%

	Income	Rate
(B)	Up to ₹ 2,00,000	Nil
	Next ₹ 3,00,000	5%
	Next ₹ 5,00,000	20%
	Balance	30%

	Income	Rate
(C)	Up to ₹ 5,00,000	Nil
	Next ₹ 5,00,000	20%
	Balance	30%

	Income	Rate
(D)	Up to ₹ 2,50,000	Nil
	Next ₹ 2,50,000	5%
	Next ₹ 5,00,000	20%
	Balance	30%

38. In case of individual assessee, the amount of income tax shall be increased by surcharge of _____ if the total income exceeds _____

(A) 12%; ₹ 1 Crore

(B) 10%; 1 Crore but do not exceed ₹ 10 Crore

(C) 10%; ₹ 10 Crore

(D) 10%; ₹ 50 lakhs but do not exceed ₹ 1 Crore

39. Which of the following sections deals with the taxation of income under the head 'salary'?

(A) Section 15 to Section 17

(B) Section 14 to Section 18

(C) Section 15 to Section 20

(D) Section 16 to Section 18

40. There are _____ heads of income as per section 14 of the Income Tax Act, 1961.

(A) Four

(B) Three

(C) Six

(D) Five

41. LTCG is chargeable to tax at special rate under ______

(A) Section 112AA

(B) Section 111AB

(C) Section 112

(D) Section 111

42. Match the following:

(1) Assessment of persons leaving India	(a) Section 174A
(2) Assessment of persons likely to transfer property to avoid tax	(b) Section172
(3) Shipping business of non-residents	(c) Section 176
(4) Assessment of AOPs or BOIs or artificial juridical person formed for a particular event or purpose	(d) Section 173
(5) Discontinued business	(e) Section 175
	(f) Section 174

(A) (1) – (f), (2) – (e), (3) – (c), (4) – (a), (5) – (b)

(B) (1) – (f), (2) – (e), (3) – (d), (4) – (c), (5) – (a)

(C) (1) – (e), (2) – (f), (3) – (b), (4) – (d), (5) – (c)

(D) (1) – (f), (2) – (e), (3) – (b), (4) – (a), (5) – (c)

43. STCG from the sale of listed securities is chargeable to tax at special rate under ______

(A) Section 111AA

(B) Section 112

(C) Section 115BB

(D) Section 111A

44. Which of the following is correct slab of income tax for resident person having age of 82 years?

(A)

Income	**Rate**
Up to ₹ 3,00,000	Nil
Next ₹ 2,00,000	5%
Next ₹ 5,00,000	20%
Balance	30%

(B)

Income	**Rate**
Up to ₹ 2,00,000	Nil
Next ₹ 3,00,000	5%
Next ₹ 5,00,000	20%
Balance	30%

(C)

Income	**Rate**
Up to ₹ 5,00,000	Nil
Next ₹ 5,00,000	20%
Balance	30%

(D)

Income	**Rate**
Up to ₹ 2,50,000	Nil
Next ₹ 2,50,000	5%
Next ₹ 5,00,000	20%
Balance	30%

45. Which of the following statement is correct?

(1) Illegal incomes are taxable in the same manner as legal income.

(2) Even fictitious incomes are liable to income tax.

Select the correct answer from the options given below –

(A) (2) only

(B) Both (1) and (2)

(C) (1) only

(D) Neither (1) nor (2)

46. Which of the following sections deals with the taxation of income under the head 'income from house property'?

(A) Section 21 to Section 28

(B) Section 22 to Section 27

(C) Section 23 to Section 28

(D) Section 12 to Section 16

47. Winning from lottery, crossword puzzles, races, card games etc. is chargeable to tax at special rate under ______

(A) Section 111BD

(B) Section 115BB

(C) Section 115AA

(D) Section 111BB

48. Rebate under Section 87A of the Income Tax Act, 1961 is available if the total income does not exceed ______

(A) ₹ 2,50,000

(B) ₹ 5,00,000

(C) ₹ 3,50,000

(D) ₹ 10,00,000

49. Which of the following sections deals with the taxation of income under the head 'income from capital gain'?

(A) Section 40 to Section 50A

(B) Section 45 to Section 60A

(C) Section 55 to Section 65A

(D) Section 45 to Section 55A

50. In case of co-operative society which of the following is correct income tax slab?

(A)

Income	**Rate**
Up to ₹ 2,50,000	Nil
Next ₹ 2,50,000	5%
Next ₹ 5,00,000	20%
Balance	30%

(B) Income	Rate
Up to ₹ 1,00,000	5%
Next ₹ 1,00,000	20%
Balance	30%

(C) Income	Rate
Up to ₹ 50,000	5%
Next ₹ 50,000	20%
Balance	30%

(D) Income	Rate
Up to ₹ 10,000	10%
Next ₹ 10,000	20%
Balance	30%

51. For which of the following assessee no income tax is chargeable, if the total income does not exceed ₹ 2,50,000?

(*i*) Resident individual
(*ii*) HUF
(*iii*) Non-resident individual
(*iv*) AOP
(*v*) LLP
(*vi*) BOI
(*vii*) Co-operative society
(*viii*) Artificial juridical person

Select the correct answer from the options given below –

(A) (i) & (ii) only
(B) (i), (ii), (iii), (iv) & (vi) only
(C) (i), (ii) & (iii) only
(D) (i), (ii), (iii), (iv), (vi) & (viii) only

52. Which of the following sections deals with the taxation of income under the head 'Income from other sources'?

(A) Section 56 to Section 59

(B) Section 55 to Section 60

(C) Section 57 to Section 58

(D) Section 55 to Section 65

53. To which of the following assessee(s) tax rate of 30% is applicable?

(I) HUF

(II) Domestic Company having turnover above ₹ 250 Crore since PY 2016-2017

(III) Partnership Firms

(IV) Foreign Companies

(V) LLP

(VI) Artificial Juridical Persons

Select the correct answer from the options given below –

(A) (I) & (VI)

(B) (VII), (IV), (I)

(C) (V), (III), & (II)

(D) (II), (III), (IV) & (V)

54. In case of domestic companies, the amount of income tax shall be increased by surcharge of _____ if the total income exceeds ₹ 1 Crore but does not exceed ₹ 10 Crore.

(A) 10%

(B) 7%

(C) 5%

(D) 12%

55. Which of the following sections deals with the taxation of income under the head 'Income from profit and gains of business and profession'?

(A) Section 28 to Section 45AAB

(B) Section 29 to Section 46DC

(C) Section 28 to Section 44DB

(D) Section 30 to Section 44DB

56. Under which of the following heads of income, the income has to be computed in accordance with either cash or mercantile system of accounting regularly followed by the assessee?

a. Income from other sources

b. Income from salary

c. Income from PGBP

d. Income from capital gain

e. Income from house property.

Select the correct answer from the options given below –

(A) a, b, e

(B) b, c, d

(C) a, c

(D) c, a, b, d

57. In case of foreign companies, the amount of income tax shall be increased by surcharge of ______ if the total income exceeds ₹ 1 Crore but does not exceed ₹ 10 Crore.

(A) 5%

(B) 7%

(C) 2%

(D) 12%

58. An employee instructs his employer to pay ₹ 5,000 to a charity out of his total salary due of ₹ 50,000.

₹ 5,000 paid to charity by the employer by deducting from total salary due is .....

(A) Diversion of income

(B) Application of income

(C) Not a income at all

(D) None of the above

59. In case of domestic companies, the amount of income tax shall be increased by surcharge of ______ if the total income exceeds ₹ 10 Crore.

(A) 5%

(B) 12.36%

(C) 7%

(D) 12%

60. In case of foreign companies, the amount of income tax shall be increased by surcharge of _____ if the total income exceeds ₹ 10 Crore.

(A) 5.15%

(B) 7%

(C) 5%

(D) 12%

61. XYZ & Co. is a partnership firm consisting of father and three sons. The partnership deed provided that after the death of father, the business shall be continued by his sons, subject to condition that the firm shall pay 30% of the profit to their mother. If firm pay 30% profit after the death of father _____

(A) It is application of income and liable to tax

(B) It is diversion of income not liable to tax

(C) It is application of income and not liable to tax

(D) It is diversion of income and liable to tax

62. Which of the following type of receipt is liable to tax?

(i) Capital receipts

(ii) Revenue receipts

Select the correct answer from the options given below –

(A) Both (i) and (ii)

(B) (ii) only

(C) (i) but not (ii)

(D) Neither (i) nor (ii)

63. The definition of income as given in Section 2(24) of the Income Tax Act, 1961 is _______ type of definition.

(A) Exhaustive

(B) Exclusive

(C) Inclusive

(D) Partly exhaustive & partly inclusive

64. Compensation received for loss of earning is a ________

(A) Capital receipt

(B) Revenue receipt

(C) Deferred revenue receipt

(D) Not a receipt at all.

65. Which of the following statement is FALSE?

(1) Capital receipts are taxable unless expressly exempted.

(2) Revenue receipts are exempt from tax unless expressly taxed.

Select the correct answer from the options given below –

(A) (2) only

(B) Both (1) and (2)

(C) (1) only

(D) Neither (1) nor (2)

ANSWERS:

1.	(A)	2.	(C)	3.	(B)	4.	(A)	5.	(B)	6.	(C)	7.	(D)
8.	(D)	9.	(D)	10.	(C)	11.	(B)	12.	(C)	13.	(D)	14.	(C)
15.	(B)	16.	(C)	17.	(C)	18.	(A)	19.	(C)	20.	(D)	21.	(A)
22.	(D)	23.	(D)	24.	(D)	25.	(B)	26.	(B)	27.	(D)	28.	(C)
29.	(C)	30.	(C)	31.	(D)	32.	(C)	33.	(A)	34.	(D)	35.	(C)
36.	(C)	37.	(D)	38.	(D)	39.	(A)	40.	(D)	41.	(C)	42.	(D)
43.	(D)	44.	(C)	45.	(C)	46.	(B)	47.	(B)	48.	(C)	49.	(D)
50.	(D)	51.	(D)	52.	(A)	53.	(C)	54.	(B)	55.	(C)	56.	(C)
57.	(C)	58.	(B)	59.	(D)	60.	(C)	61.	(B)	62.	(A)	63.	(C)
64.	(B)	65.	(B)										

PAST EXAMINATION MCQs

1. Dec 2014: As per Section 2(31), the following is not included in the definition of 'person' —

(A) An individual

(B) A hindu undivided family

(C) A company

(D) A minor

2. Dec 2014: The tax exemption limit for a resident senior citizen is —

(A) Up to ₹ 2,00,000

(B) Up to ₹ 5,00,000

(C) Up to ₹ 1,80,000

(D) Up to ₹ 3,00,000

3. Dec 2014: AB & Co. received ₹ 2,00,000 as compensation from CD & Co. for premature termination of contract of agency. Amount so received is —

(A) Capital receipt and taxable

(B) Capital receipt and not taxable

(C) Revenue receipt and taxable

(D) Revenue receipt and not taxable

4. Dec 2014: For a domestic company whose turnover never been above ₹ 250 Crore, the minimum amount of total income liable for surcharge and the rate of surcharge applicable therein are —

(A) ₹ 10 Crore and 10% respectively

(B) ₹ 1 Crore and 7% respectively

(C) ₹ 1 Crore and 12% respectively

(D) ₹ 10 Crore and 5% respectively

5. Dec 2014: According to Section 2(24) definition of 'income' is —

(A) Inclusive

(B) Exhaustive

(C) Exclusive

(D) Descriptive

6. Dec 2014: An assessee, being an individual resident in India, is entitled to a deduction, from the amount of income-tax on his total income which is chargeable for an assessment year, of an amount equal to 100% of such income-tax or a lesser amount. The maximum amount of total income qualifying for such deduction and the maximum amount of deduction so available is —

(A) ₹ 3.5 lakh and ₹ 2,500 respectively

(B) ₹ 5 lakh and ₹ 2,500 respectively

(C) ₹ 5 lakh and ₹ 5,000 respectively

(D) ₹ 3.5 lakh and ₹ 5,000 respectively

7. June 2015: The year in which the income is earned is known as —

(A) Previous year

(B) Financial year

(C) Both (A) and (B)

(D) None of the above

8. June 2015: For the PY 2018-2019, taxable income of A Ltd., a domestic company is ₹ 10,86,920. Its turnover for PY 2016-2017 was below ₹ 250 Crore. Its tax liability would be —

(A) ₹ 2,79,880

(B) ₹ 4,47,811

(C) ₹ 3,35,860

(D) ₹ 2,82,600

9. June 2015: The total income of Atul, a resident individual, is ₹ 2,90,000. The rebate allowable u/s 87A would be —

(A) ₹ 2,500

(B) Nil

(C) ₹ 2,000

(D) ₹ 5,000

10. June 2015: 'Income' u/s 2(24) includes —

(*i*) The profits and gains of a banking business carried on by a co-operative society with its members.

(*ii*) Any advance money forfeited in the course of negotiations for transfer of capital asset.

Choose the correct option with reference to the above statements —

(A) Both (i) and (ii)

(B) Only (i)

(C) Only (ii)

(D) Neither (i) nor (ii)

11. June 2015: Lalit, a resident individual of 81 years works as a consultant. If his taxable income is ₹ 5,20,000, the tax payable by him would be —

(A) ₹ 22,660

(B) ₹ 4,120

(C) ₹ 2,080

(D) ₹ 4,160

12. Dec 2015: A new business was set-up on 1st July, 2018 and trading activity was commenced from 1st September, 2018, the previous year would be the period commencing from —

(A) 1st April, 2018 to 31st March, 2019

(B) 1st July, 2018 to 31st March, 2019

(C) 1st September, 2018 to 31st March, 2019

(D) 1st October, 2018 to 31st March, 2019

13. Dec 2015: X Marine Lines Inc., a Singapore company engaged in shipping business collected ₹ 150 lakhs towards carrying goods from Chennai Port. Its presumptive income chargeable to tax in India would be —

(A) ₹ 15 lakhs

(B) ₹ 11.25 lakhs

(C) ₹ 12 lakhs

(D) Nil

14. Dec 2015: HSK, an LLP had taken keyman insurance policy on the life of its managing partner. The policy got matured on 13th September, 2018 and an amount of ₹ 75 lakh was paid by the insurers to the managing partner. The amount so received on maturity of the policy by the managing partner is —

(A) Fully exempt u/s 10(10D)

(B) 50% of ₹ 75 lakh exempt

(C) ₹ 75 lakh taxable

(D) ₹ 25 lakh exempt and ₹ 50 lakh taxable.

15. June 2016: Raghu traced a missing girl by spending ₹ 20,000. For this, he was awarded with a sum of ₹ 1,20,000. In this case the award is taxable to the extent of ₹ —

(A) 1,00,000

(B) 1,20,000

(C) 1,15,000

(D) Nil

16. June 2016: Raman & Co., a partnership firm, received ₹ 5,00,000 from an insurance company under keyman insurance policy consequent to demise of partner Pramod. The amount of premium ₹ 2,30,000 paid earlier was claimed as deduction under Section 37 by the firm. The amount received from the insurance company is —

(A) Tax-free under section 10(10D)

(B) Fully taxable as income

(C) ₹ 2,70,000 is taxable

(D) ₹ 2,30,000 is taxable

17. June 2016: Metro Ltd., a domestic company, is assessed with a total income of ₹ 11.25 Crore. The surcharge payable by the company shall be at the rate of —

(A) 2%

(B) 5%

(C) 10%

(D) 12%

18. June 2016: Dr. Ashok commenced medical practice on 1st September 2018. The previous year for the profession for the assessment year 2019-2020 would be —

(A) 1st April 2018 to 31st March 2019

(B) 1st September 2018 to 31st March 2019

(C) 1st June 2018 to 31st March 2019

(D) 1st September 2018 to 31st January 2019

19. Dec 2016: Under the Income Tax Act, 1961 the term 'assessee' means a person –

(A) Who is an assessee in default

(B) From whom tax is due

(C) Against whom any proceeding under the Act has been taken

(D) All of the above

20. Dec 2016: Normal rates of income-tax are prescribed in the –

(A) Income-tax Act, 1961

(B) Income-tax Rules, 1962

(C) Finance Act of the current year

(D) CBDT circulars

21. Dec 2016: Arul Industries got waiver of Goods & Services Tax (GST) of ₹ 2,20,000 for the financial year 2018-2019. The amount of waiver is —

(A) Exempt income

(B) Capital receipt

(C) Revenue receipt

(D) None of the above

22. June 2017: Maruti & Co. is an AOP consisting of 4 members with equal share. None of the member has income exceeding the taxable limit. The total income of the AOP is ₹ 5 lakhs. The income-tax liability of the AOP would be:

(A) ₹ 12,880

(B) ₹ 77,250

(C) ₹ 13,000

(D) ₹ 20,600

23. Dec 2017: A municipal committee legally entitled to manage and control a municipal fund is chargeable to income-tax in the status of:

(A) Individual

(B) Association of persons

(C) Local authority

(D) Artificial juridical person

24. Dec 2017: A domestic company has total income of ₹ 120 lakhs. The rate of surcharge is applicable on income-tax would be:

(A) 2%

(B) 5%

(C) 7%

(D) 2%

25. Dec 2017: Mr. Ganapathy a resident individual received ₹ 12 lakhs during the financial year 2018-2019 by way of dividend from domestic companies. The companies have paid dividend distribution tax under Section 115-O on the dividend declared. The applicable rate of tax on such dividend income would be:

(A) 10.3%

(B) 30.9%

(C) Nil

(D) 15.45%

26. Dec 2017: The tax rate applicable for a non-resident engaged in shipping business in India shall be:

(A) 5%

(B) 7.5%

(C) 10%

(D) 20%

27. Dec 2017: A domestic company whose turnover for the previous year 2015-2016 ₹ 420 Crore; for previous year 2016-2017 ₹ 80 Crore and for previous year 2017-2018 ₹ 120 Crore. Its total income (computed) for the assessment year 2019-2020 is ₹ 30 Crores. The rate of income tax applicable for such company (without cess) would be:

(A) 30%

(B) 40%

(C) 29%

(D) 25%

ANSWERS:

1.	(D)	2.	(D)	3.	(C)	4.	(B)	5.	(A)	6.	(A)	7.	(A)
8.	(D)	9.	(C)	10.	(A)	11.	(D)	12.	(B)	13.	(B)	14.	(C)
15.	(B)	16.	(B)	17.	(D)	18.	(B)	19.	(D)	20.	(C)	21.	(C)
22.	(C)	23.	(C)	24.	(C)	25.	(A)	26.	(**)	27.	(D)		

***** MCQ is wrongly drafted. For further clarification please see the hints.***

HINTS FOR PAST EXAMINATION MCQs

22.

On first 2,50,000		Nil
On next 2,50,000	@ 5%	12,500
		12,500
(+) Education cess	@ 4%	500
Net tax		13,000

Note: Rebate u/s 87A is not available to AOP.

26.

Shipping business of non-residents [Section 172]: 7.5% of freight to owner or charter shall be deemed to be total income and taxable at 40% *plus* surcharge *plus* education cess.

Thus, 7.5% rate is used to calculate deemed income and not tax and hence question itself is wrong.

CHAPTER 2

RESIDENTIAL STATUS

MCQs ON THEORY

1. How residential status is classified in India?

(A) Citizen, Not ordinary citizen, Non-citizen

(B) Resident, Not-ordinary resident, Non-citizen

(C) Ordinary resident, Not-ordinary resident, Non-resident

(D) Any of the above

2. There are two basic conditions given in Income Tax Act, 1961 to determine whether the individual is resident or not. How many condition(s) should be fulfilled by the individual in order to call resident?

(A) Both the basic condition

(B) Any one of the basic condition

(C) First basic condition

(D) Second basic condition

3. Section 5 of the Income Tax Act, 1961 deals with _____

(A) Determination of residential status

(B) Scope of total income

(C) Additional conditions to be fulfilled for determining residential status

(D) Income deemed to be received

4. Which of the following basic condition is/are correct?

(1) He must be India for 180 days or more

(2) He must be in India for 60 days or more or 365 days in last 4 years.

Select the correct answer from the options given below -

(A) Both (1) and (2)

(B) (1) only

(C) (2) only

(D) Neither (1) nor (2)

5. The total income of any previous year of a person who is a resident includes all income from whatever source derived which—

(A) is received or is deemed to be received in India in such year by or on behalf of such person

(B) accrues or arises or is deemed to accrue or arise to him in India during such year

(C) accrues or arises to him outside India during such year

(D) all of the above

6. If a person is resident in India for 182 days or more, he may be ______

(A) Resident

(B) Not-ordinary resident

(C) Non-resident

(D) (A) or (B)

7. In the case of a person not ordinarily resident in India, the ______ shall not be so included.

(A) income which is derived from a business controlled in or a profession set up in India

(B) income which accrues or arises to him outside India

(C) income which accrues or arises to him in India

(D) all of the above

8. Which of the following section deals with "income deemed to be received"?

(A) Section 6

(B) Section 7

(C) Section 8

(D) Section 9

9. If an individual do not fulfil both the basic conditions, he is called as ______

(A) Not-ordinary resident

(B) Non-citizen

(C) Non-domiciled

(D) Non-resident

10. The total income of any previous year of a person who is a non-resident includes all income from whatever source derived which -

(A) is received or is deemed to be received in India in such year by or on behalf of such person or accrues or arises or is deemed to accrue or arise to him in India during such year

(B) is received or is deemed to be received outside India in such year by or on behalf of such person or accrues or arises or is deemed to accrue or arise to him outside India during such year

(C) both (A) and (B)

(D) neither (A) nor (B)

11. Which of the following basic condition is/are correct?

(1) He must be India for 182 days or more

(2) He must be in India for 60 days or more AND 365 days or more in last 4 years.

Select the correct answer from the options given below -

(A) Both (1) and (2)

(B) Neither (1) nor (2)

(C) (1) only

(D) (2) only

12. Which of the following section deals with "income deemed to accrue or arise in India"?

(A) Section 10

(B) Section 8

(C) Section 9

(D) Section 11

13. Which of the following income is taxable in the hands of person who is ordinary resident?

(A) Income which accrues outside India but received in India.

(B) Income received outside India but which accrues in India.

(C) Both (A) and (B)

(D) Neither (A) nor (B)

14. As per *Explanation* to Section 6(1), the period of 60 days specified in Section 6(1) dealing with second basic condition is substituted by ________ in certain circumstances.

(A) 180 days

(B) 190 days

(C) 182 days

(D) 365 days

15. Which of the following statement is true (✓) or false (×)?

(a) Once a person is a resident in a previous year, he shall be deemed to be resident for subsequent year also.

(b) A resident in India cannot become resident in any other country for the same assessment year.

(c) A foreign company is always non-resident in India.

(d) Salary payable by Government of India to an Indian citizen for services rendered outside India is not taxable in India.

Select the correct answer from the options given below -

	(a)	(b)	(c)	(d)
(A)	✓	×	✓	×
(B)	×	✓	×	✓
(C)	✓	✓	✓	✓
(D)	×	×	×	×

16. In which of the following case, as per *Explanation* to Section 6(1), the period of 60 days specified in Section 6(1) dealing with second basic condition is substituted by 182 days.

(I) Person resident in India, leaves India during the previous year for employment purpose

(II) Person resident in India, leaves India during the previous year as a member of crew of an Indian ship.

(III) Person resident outside India who is citizen of India comes on visit to India in previous year.

Select the correct answer from the options given below -

(A) (I) only

(B) (I) and (II) only

(C) (I), (II) and (III)

(D) None of the above

17. Which of the following type of income is taxable in the hands of person who is ORDINARY RESIDENT?

(*i*) Income received or is deemed to be received in India.

(*ii*) Income which accrues or arises or is deemed to accrue or arise in India.

(*iii*) Income received in India from business situated outside India but controlled from India.

(*iv*) Income received in India from any source (other than business income) situated outside India.

(*v*) Income which accrue or arise outside India and received outside India during the preceding previous year and remitted to India during the current previous year.

Select the correct answer from the options given below -

	(i)	**(ii)**	**(iii)**	**(iv)**	**(v)**
(A)	✓	✓	✓	✓	✓
(B)	✓	✓	✓	✓	×
(C)	✓	✓	✓	×	×
(D)	✓	✓	×	×	×

18. To which of the following type of person, the period of 60 days specified in second basic condition will be substituted by 182 days?

(A) Indian Citizen

(B) Person of Indian Origin

(C) Both (A) and (B)

(D) Neither (A) nor (B)

19. Which of the following income(s) shall be deemed to be received in the previous year as per Section 7 of the Income Tax Act, 1961?

(I) Annual accretion in the previous year to the balance at the credit of an employee participating in a recognized provident fund, to the extent provided in Rule 6 of Part A of the Fourth Schedule

(II) Contribution made, by the Central Government or any other employer in the previous year, to the account of an employee under a pension scheme referred to in Section 80CCD

Select the correct answer from the options given below -

(A) Both (I) & (II)

(B) Neither (I) nor (II)

(C) (II) only

(D) (I) only

20. The facility to substitute period of 182 days in second basic condition instead of 60 days is available to __________, who leaves India during the previous year for employment purpose

(A) Indian Citizen

(B) Person of Indian origin

(C) Both (A) and (B)

(D) Neither (A) nor (B)

21. In which of the following case, Royalty paid outside India will be taxable in India?

I. Income by way of royalty payable by a person who is a resident where the royalty is payable in respect of any right, property or information used or services utilized for the purposes of a business carried on by such person outside India.

II. Income by way of royalty payable by a person who is non-resident, where the royalty is payable in respect of any right, property or information used or services utilized for the purposes of a business or profession carried on by such person in India.

III. Income by way of royalty payable by the Government.

Select the correct answer from the options given below -

(A) I & III

(B) II & III

(C) II only

(D) I, II & III

22. Which of the following day is included (✓) or excluded (×) while counting the number of days stay in India?

(i) The day of arrival

(ii) The day of departure

Select the correct answer from the options given below -

	(i)	(ii)
(A)	×	✓
(B)	×	×
(C)	✓	×
(D)	✓	✓

23. Activities that not to constitute business connection in India are specified in _____

(A) Section 9

(B) Section 9A

(C) Section 10

(D) Section 8A

24. Which of the following statement is correct in relation to determination of residential status of an individual?

1. The period of stay is compulsorily required to active and continuous.
2. Where an individual is in India for a part of the day for less than 12 hours out of 24 hours, he will be considered to be not stayed in India.
3. An Indian citizen is always treated as resident in India.

Select the correct answer from the options given below -

(A) (1) & (2)

(B) (2) & (3)

(C) (1) & (3)

(D) None of the above

25. Which of the following shall be deemed to accrue or arise in India?

(A) Income by way of interest payable by the Government to non-resident.

(B) Income by way of interest payable by a person who is a resident where the interest is payable in respect of any debt incurred, or moneys borrowed and used, for the purposes of a business in India

(C) Income by way of interest payable a person who is a non-resident, where the interest is payable in respect of any debt incurred, or moneys borrowed and used, for the purposes of a business or profession carried on by such person outside India

(D) (A) and (B)

26. When an individual be regarded as "Not-ordinary Resident"?

(A) If he fulfils one of the basic condition and none of the additional condition.

(B) If he fulfils both basic condition and both additional condition.

(C) If he does not fulfil any of the basic condition but fulfils one of the additional condition.

(D) If he fulfils one of the basic condition and one of the additional condition.

27. Which of the following type of income is taxable in the hands of person who is NOT-ORDINARY RESIDENT?

(*i*) Income received or is deemed to be received in India.

(*ii*) Income which accrues or arises or is deemed to accrue or arise in India.

(*iii*) Income received in India from business situated outside India but controlled from India.

(*iv*) Income received in India from any source (other than business income) situated outside India.

(*v*) Income which accrue or arise outside India and received outside India during the preceding previous year and remitted to India during the current previous year.

Select the correct answer from the options given below -

	(*i*)	(*ii*)	(*iii*)	(*iv*)	(*v*)
(A)	✓	✓	✓	✓	✓
(B)	✓	✓	✓	✓	×
(C)	✓	✓	✓	×	×
(D)	✓	✓	×	×	×

28. Which of the following shall be deemed to accrue or arise in India?

(1) Income earned by non-resident engaged in the business of running a news agency or of publishing newspapers, magazines or journals from activities which are confined to the collection of news and views in India for transmission out of India

(2) Income earned by non-resident engaged in purchase of goods in India for the purpose of export.

(3) Income from operations which are confined to the shooting of any cinematograph film in India.

Select the correct answer from the options given below -

(A) (1), (2) & (3)

(B) (1) & (3)

(C) (2) & (1)

(D) None of the (1), (2) & (3)

29. A person is said to be not-ordinary resident in India if such person has been -

(A) a non-resident in India in any 9 years out of the total 10 years preceding the previous year.

(B) in India for a period of 729 days or less during the 7 years preceding the previous year.

(C) Neither (A) nor (B)

(D) Either (A) or (B) or Both (A) & (B)

30. Which of the following statement is/are incorrect?

1. Income accruing or arising outside India shall not be deemed to be received in India within the meaning of Section 5 by reason only of the fact that it is taken into account in a balance sheet prepared in India.
2. Income which has been included in the total income of a person on the basis that it has accrued or arisen or is deemed to have accrued or arisen to him shall not again be so included on the basis that it is received or deemed to be received by him in India.

Select the correct answer from the options given below -

(A) 2 only

(B) 1 only

(C) Both 1 and 2

(D) Neither 1 nor 2

31. A person is said to be ordinary resident in India if such person has been -

(A) Resident in India for 2 years out of the total 10 years preceding the previous year

(B) in India for a period of 730 days or more during the 7 years preceding the previous year.

(C) Both (A) and (B)

(D) Either (A) or (B)

32. Where the fees for technical services are payable in respect of services utilized in a business or profession carried on by person outside India or for the purposes of making or earning any income from any source outside India ____

(A) shall be deemed to be received in India

(B) shall be deemed to accrue or arise in India

(C) shall be not be deemed to accrue or arise in India

(D) shall be deemed to accrue or arise in India but not taxable in India.

33. When person will be considered as non-resident?

(A) If he fulfils both the additional conditions.

(B) If he do not fulfil any one of the additional conditions.

(C) If he fulfils any one of the basic conditions but do not fulfil both additional conditions.

(D) If he do not fulfil both basic conditions.

34. The word "business connection" has been explained in ______

(A) *Explanation* to Section 9(1)(i)

(B) *Explanation* to Section 8(1)(i)

(C) *Explanation* to Section 9(2)(ii)

(D) *Explanation* to Section 8(1)(ii)

35. In which of the following case HUF said to be resident in India?

(*a*) If the control and management of its affairs is wholly situated in India.

(*b*) If the control and management of its affairs is wholly situated outside India.

(*c*) If the control and management of its affairs is partly situated in India.

Select the correct answer from the options given below -

(A) (a) or (b)

(B) (b) or (c)

(C) (a) or (c)

(D) None of the above

36. Which of the following type of income is taxable in the hands of person who is NON-RESIDENT?

(*i*) Income received or is deemed to be received in India.

(*ii*) Income which accrues or arises or is deemed to accrue or arise in India.

(*iii*) Income received outside India from business situated outside India but controlled from India.

(*iv*) Income received in India from any source (other than business income) situated outside India.

(*v*) Income which accrue or arise outside India and received outside India during the preceding previous year and remitted to India during the current previous year.

Select the correct answer from the options given below -

	(*i*)	(*ii*)	(*iii*)	(*iv*)	(*v*)
(A)	✓	✓	✓	✓	✓
(B)	✓	✓	✓	✓	×
(C)	✓	✓	✓	×	×
(D)	✓	✓	×	×	×

37. In which of the following case HUF said to be non-resident in India?

(*i*) If the control and management of its affairs is wholly situated outside India.

(*ii*) If the control and management of its affairs is partly situated outside India.

Select the correct answer from the options given below -

(A) (ii) only

(B) (i) only

(C) Both (i) and (ii)

(D) Either (i) or (ii)

38. In order to determine whether HUF is not-ordinary resident -

(A) Additional conditions have to be checked for all adult male members of the family

(B) Additional conditions have to be checked for the KARTA of the family.

(C) HUF can never be not-ordinary resident, hence there is no need to check additional condition for any one.

(D) None of the above

39. A partnership firm is said to be resident in India -

(A) If business is controlled from India for more than 182 days or more.

(B) If business is controlled from India for more than 182 days or more AND all partners are in India for more than 365 days or more in 4 years preceding the previous year.

(C) If the control and management of its affairs is situated partly in India.

(D) If all the partners fulfils the both basic conditions and any one of the additional condition.

40. A company is said to be resident in India ______

1. If it is Indian company
2. If its place of effective management, in that year, is in India.

Select the correct answer from the options given below -

(A) 1 only

(B) 2 only

(C) Both 1 and 2

(D) Either 1 or 2

41. Which of the following company is said to be resident in India?

a. An Indian company having business situated wholly outside India.

b. A foreign company having its effective management in India.

c. A subsidiary company registered in India having holding company situated outside India and fully controlled by the holding company from outside India.

Select the correct answer from the options given below -

(A) a only

(B) a & b only

(C) c only

(D) a, b & c

42. Dividend payable by an Indian company outside India is ______

(A) Exempt in the hands of recipient.

(B) Taxable in the hands of the recipient.

(C) Not taxable at all

(D) Taxable in the hands of the company and exempt in the hands of the recipient.

43. Total income of a person is determined on the basis of his ________

(A) Citizenship

(B) Residential status

(C) Both (A) and (B)

(D) Neither (A) nor (B)

44. Residential status is determined for ___

(A) Accounting year

(B) Financial year

(C) Previous year

(D) Assessment year

PRACTICAL MCQs

45. Ram left India on 1.10.2018 for a pleasure trip to USA and return to India on 5.4.2019. Before 1.10.2018 Ram had never been out of India. Ram is _____ for the PY 2018-2019.

(A) Ordinary resident

(B) Not-ordinary resident

(C) Non-resident

(D) None of the above

46. Mr. Laxman was working with X Ltd. as Finance Manager cum Company Secretary. During the year he was sent by company to USA for official work on 15.7.2018. He returns back on 5.4.2019. His stay in India during last 4 years is as follows:

Year	*Stay in India*
2017-2018	108
2016-2017	47

2015-2016	83
2014-2015	119

Mr. Laxman is ______ for the PY 2018-2019.

(A) Resident and ordinary resident

(B) Resident but not-ordinary resident

(C) Non-resident

(D) None of the above

47. A person receives ₹ 2 lakh as income from business in India which was controlled from France. It will be taxable in the hands of that person, if he is _____

(A) Resident and ordinary resident

(B) Resident but not-ordinary resident

(C) Non-resident

(D) All of the above

48. Mr. Tom a resident of Australia, visit 100 days each year since 2006-2007 to India. Mr. Tom is ______ for the PY 2018-2019.

(A) Ordinary resident

(B) Not ordinary resident

(C) Non-resident

(D) Non-resident citizen

49. Rafiq is a citizen of Bangladesh. His grandmother was born in Dhaka in year 1940. Rafiq came to India for the first time since 1981 on 5.10.2018 for visit of 190 days. Mr. Rafiq is ______ for the PY 2018-2019.

(A) Non-resident

(B) Not-ordinary resident

(C) Resident and ordinary resident

(D) Resident

50. A person receives ₹ 5 lakh as income from business in France which was controlled from Kanpur (India). It will be taxable in the hands of that person, if he is _____

(1) Resident and ordinary resident

(2) Non-resident

(3) Resident but not-ordinary resident

Select the correct answer from the options given below -

(A) (1) & (2)

(B) (2) & (3)

(C) (1) & (3)

(D) (1), (2) & (3)

51. In PY 2018-2019, a sailor has remained on a ship for 183 days outside the territorial water of India. He is ______ for the PY 2018-2019.

(A) Ordinary resident

(B) Not-ordinary resident

(C) Non-resident

(D) All of the above

52. A person receives pension in Sri Lanka of ₹ 2,51,000 for services rendered in India. It will be taxable in the hands of that person, if he is _____

(1) Non-resident

(2) Resident and ordinary resident

(3) Resident but not-ordinary resident

Select the correct answer from the options given below -

(A) (3) & (2)

(B) (1), (3) & (2)

(C) (2) & (1)

(D) (1) & (3)

53. Mr. Rohit an Indian Citizen left India on 22.9.2018 for the first time to work as an officer of a company in Germany. Rohit's residential status for AY 2019-2020 is ___

(A) Ordinary resident

(B) Not-ordinary resident

(C) Non-resident

(D) None of the above

54. Interest on UK Government bond accrued for the year 2018-2019 is ₹ 40 lakhs and out of it 25% is directly received in India. Depending upon residential status, how it will be taxed?

Choose the correct option given below.

	Ordinary Resident	*Not-ordinary resident*	*Non-Resident*
(A)	40 lakhs	40 lakhs	40 lakhs
(B)	10 lakhs	10 lakhs	10 lakhs
(C)	40 lakhs	10 lakhs	10 lakhs
(D)	40 lakhs	Not taxable	Not taxable

55. Teji, a citizen of India, is an export manager of XYZ Ltd. since 1.5.2014. He has been regularly visiting USA for export promotion. He spent the following days in USA during the last 5 years.

Previous year ended	*No. of days spent in USA*
31.3.2019	295
31.3.2018	310
31.3.2017	270
31.3.2016	150
31.3.2015	320

Determine the residential status of Teji assuming that prior to 1.5.2014 he had never travelled abroad.

(A) Non-resident

(B) Not-ordinary resident

(C) Resident and ordinary resident

(D) Resident

56. Rent from house in London, accrued in London and received in London will be ______

(A) Taxable in the hands person whether he is ordinary resident, not-ordinary resident or non-resident.

(B) Taxable in the hands person if he is ordinary resident or not-ordinary resident.

(C) Taxable in the hands person if he is ordinary resident only.

(D) Taxable in the hands person if he is not-ordinary resident or non-resident.

57. A, Russian national comes to India for the first time during year 2014-2015. During the financial years 2014-2015, 2015-2016, 2016-2017, 2017-2018 and 2018-2019, he was in India for 65 days, 60 days, 80 days, 160 days and 70 days respectively. Determine his residential status.

(A) Non-resident

(B) Ordinary resident

(C) Resident

(D) Not-ordinary resident

58. Past un-taxed profit of ₹ 1 lakh brought to India during the previous year will be ____

(A) Taxable in the hands person if he is ordinary resident or not-ordinary resident

(B) Taxable in the hands person if he is ordinary resident only.

(C) Taxable in the hands person whether he is ordinary resident, not-ordinary resident or non-resident.

(D) Not be taxable in the hand of any person whether he is ordinary resident, not-ordinary resident or non-resident

59. Sunny, a non-resident, residing in New York since 2001, came back to India on 19.2.2017 for the permanent settlement in India. Residential status of Sunny for PY 2018-2019 will be ________

(A) Resident

(B) Non-resident

(C) Not-ordinary resident

(D) Ordinary resident

60. An individual earned profit of ₹ 15 lakh on sale of shares in Indian company and received in Germany. This profit will be ______

(A) Exempt in the hands of person whether he is ordinary resident, not-ordinary resident or non-resident.

(B) Taxable in the hands person if he is not-ordinary resident or non-resident.

(C) Taxable in the hands person if he is ordinary resident or not-ordinary resident.

(D) Taxable in the hands person whether he is ordinary resident, not-ordinary resident or non-resident.

61. Mr. Dilip, Karta of HUF, claims that business HUF is transacted from Nepal and all the policy decision are taken there. Mr. Dilip has not visited India since year 2002. Other male members of HUF are however resident in India. Residential status of HUF for the AY 2019-2020 is ______

(A) Resident

(B) Not-ordinary resident

(C) Non-resident

(D) Ordinary resident

62. An individual earned dividend of ₹ 7.5 lakhs from Japanese Company and received in Japan. Such dividend will be ______

(A) Taxable in the hands person whether he is ordinary resident, not-ordinary resident or non-resident.

(B) Exempt in the hands of person whether he is ordinary resident, not-ordinary resident or non-resident.

(C) Taxable in the hands person if he is not-ordinary resident or non-resident.

(D) Taxable in the hands person if he is ordinary resident only.

63. Titanic Inc. incorporated in USA. Its key management and commercial decisions are taken in Board Meetings held in Ooty at Tamilnadu for the PY 2018-2019. Titanic Inc. is ____ for the AY 2019-2020.

(A) Resident

(B) Non-resident

(C) Not-ordinary resident

(D) None of the above

64. Mrs. Laxmi earned dividend from PR Ltd., an Indian Company. Dividend earned is _______

(A) Taxable in hands of Mrs. Laxmi if she is ordinary resident.

(B) Taxable in hands of Mrs. Laxmi if she is ordinary resident or not-ordinary resident.

(C) Taxable in hands of Mrs. Laxmi whether she is ordinary resident, not-ordinary resident or non-resident.

(D) Exempt in the hands of person whether he is ordinary resident, not-ordinary resident or non-resident.

65. Reliance Ltd. is company incorporated in India. Its key management and commercial decisions are taken in Board Meetings held in London for the PY 2018-2019. Reliance Ltd. is ____ for the AY 2019-2020.

(A) Non-resident

(B) Not-ordinary resident

(C) Resident

(D) None of the above

ANSWERS:

1.	(C)	**2.**	(B)	**3.**	(B)	**4.**	(D)	**5.**	(D)	**6.**	(D)	**7.**	(B)
8.	(B)	**9.**	(D)	**10.**	(A)	**11.**	(A)	**12.**	(C)	**13.**	(C)	**14.**	(C)
15.	(D)	**16.**	(C)	**17.**	(B)	**18.**	(C)	**19.**	(A)	**20.**	(A)	**21.**	(B)
22.	(D)	**23.**	(B)	**24.**	(D)	**25.**	(D)	**26.**	(D)	**27.**	(C)	**28.**	(D)
29.	(D)	**30.**	(D)	**31.**	(C)	**32.**	(C)	**33.**	(D)	**34.**	(A)	**35.**	(C)
36.	(D)	**37.**	(B)	**38.**	(B)	**39.**	(C)	**40.**	(D)	**41.**	(D)	**42.**	(D)
43.	(B)	**44.**	(C)	**45.**	(A)	**46.**	(A)	**47.**	(C)	**48.**	(B)	**49.**	(A)
50.	(C)	**51.**	(A)	**52.**	(B)	**53.**	(C)	**54.**	(C)	**55.**	(C)	**56.**	(C)
57.	(D)	**58.**	(D)	**59.**	(C)	**60.**	(D)	**61.**	(C)	**62.**	(D)	**63.**	(A)
64.	(D)	**65.**	(C)										

PAST EXAMINATION MCQs

1. Dec 2014: The following additional conditions are to be satisfied by a person to be resident and ordinarily resident in India —

(A) He is a resident in at least any two out of the ten previous years immediately preceding the relevant previous year

(B) He has been in India for 730 days or more during the seven previous years immediately preceding the relevant previous year

(C) Both (A) and (B) of above

(D) None of the above.

2. Dec 2014: X, an Indian citizen, who is living in Delhi since 1984, left for Japan on 1st July, 2018 for employment. He came back to India on 2nd January, 2019 on a visit and stayed for 4 months. His residential status for the AY 2019-2020 would be —

(A) Resident and ordinarily resident

(B) Not ordinarily resident

(C) Non resident

(D) Resident

3. Dec 2014: Abhay earns the following income during the previous year ended 31st March, 2019:

Interest on U.K. Development Bonds (1/4th being received in India): ₹ 2,00,000; profits on sale of a building in India but received in Holland: ₹ 2,00,000.

The income liable to tax for the AY 2019-2020 if Abhay is resident and not ordinarily resident in India, is —

(A) ₹ 2,50,000

(B) ₹ 4,00,000

(C) ₹ 2,00,000

(D) ₹ 50,000

4. Dec 2014: If Karta is resident and ordinarily resident in India but control and management of HUF is situated partly outside India in the previous year, the HUF is —

(A) Resident and ordinarily resident

(B) Not ordinarily resident

(C) Non resident

(D) Resident

5. Dec 2014: Atul is a foreign citizen. His father was born in Delhi in 1954 and mother was born in England in 1953. His grandfather was born in Delhi in 1925. Atul visited India to see Taj Mahal and visit other historical places. He came to India on 1st November, 2018 for 200 days. He has never come to India before. His residential status for AY 2019-2020 will be —

(A) Non-resident in India

(B) Not ordinarily resident in India

(C) Resident in India

(D) None of the above

6. June 2015: Paresh, a software engineer at ABC Ltd. left India on 10th August, 2018 for the treatment of his wife. For income-tax purpose, his residential status for the AY 2019-2020 will be —

(A) Resident

(B) Non-resident

(C) Not ordinarily resident

(D) Cannot be determined from the given information

7. Dec 2015: Residential status of an Indian company is resident and ordinarily resident for the year —

(A) If the entire control and management is wholly in India

(B) If part of the control and management is in India

(C) Regardless of the place of control and management

(D) If it is listed on recognised stock exchange.

8. Dec 2015: HUF of Ashwin consisting of himself, his wife and 2 sons is assessed to income-tax. The residential status of HUF would be non-resident, when —

(A) The management and control of its affairs is wholly in India

(B) The management and control of its affairs is wholly outside India

(C) The status of karta is non-resident for that year

(D) When majority of the members are non-residents.

9. Dec 2015: Ram who was born and brought up in India left for employment in Dubai on 20th August, 2018. His residential status in respect of the AY 2019-2020 would be —

(A) Resident and ordinarily resident

(B) Non-resident

(C) Not ordinarily resident

(D) None of the above

10. Dec 2015: Income of non-resident when attributed from operations in India relating to the following is taxable in India:

(1) Profits of business

(2) Fee for technical services

(3) Royalty

(4) Income from house property in India

Select the correct answer from the options given below —

(A) (1) and (4)

(B) (1), (3) and (4)

(C) (1) and (3)

(D) (1), (2), (3) and (4)

11. June 2016: Arun, a non-resident of India celebrated his 80th birthday on 10th October 2018. If his total income for the previous year is ₹ 6,00,000 his income-tax liability for the previous year 2018-2019 is —

(A) ₹ 33,800

(B) ₹ 41,200

(C) ₹ 33,475

(D) Nil

12. June 2016: Alpha Ltd. is an Indian company. It carries its business in Delhi and London. Total control and management of the company is situated in London. More than 85% of its business income is from the business in England. If so, its residential status will be —

(A) Resident

(B) Non-resident

(C) Not ordinarily resident

(D) Foreign company

13. Dec 2016: A company incorporated outside India having its place of effective management situated in India in the previous year will be treated as -

(A) Resident

(B) Not ordinarily resident

(C) Non-resident

(D) None of the above

14. Dec 2016: Ritesh, an Indian citizen, left India for U.K. on 1st September, 2018 to take up a job there. His residential status for the assessment year 2019-2020 would be —

(A) Residential and ordinarily resident

(B) Not ordinarily resident

(C) Non-resident

(D) None of the above

15. Dec 2016: Satish brought into India, in the previous year, past untaxed income which was earned in U.K. The income will be taxable if Satish is —

(A) An ordinarily resident

(B) A not ordinarily resident

(C) A non-resident

(D) None of the above

16. June 2017: Mr. Rajiv, born and brought up in India left for employment in Belgium on 15.10.2018. He has never gone out of India, previously. What is his residential status for the assessment year 2019-2020?

(A) Non-resident

(B) Not ordinarily resident

(C) Resident

(D) Indian citizen

17. June 2017: Mr. Ramji (age 55) is Karta of HUF doing textile business at Nagur. Mr. Ramji is residing in Dubai for the past 10 years and visited India for 20 days every year for filing the income tax return of HUF. His two major sons take care of the day to day affairs of the business in India. The residential status of HUF for the assessment year 2019-2020 is:

(A) Non-resident

(B) Resident

(C) Not ordinarily resident

(D) None of the above

18. June 2017: When a capital asset located in India is sold by a non-resident to another non-resident at a place outside India, the capital gain is taxable:

(A) at the place of transferor

(B) at the place of transferee

(C) at the place of location of asset

(D) at the place of both transferor and transferee

19. June 2017: Thomas Inc. of Australia borrowed money from various companies in Australia for doing business in India by name ANS Co. Ltd., Mumbai. Thomas Inc. paid interest of ₹ 500 lakhs (converted) to various lenders. The amount of interest paid:

(A) has accrued in India

(B) is exempt from tax

(C) does not accrue in India

(D) is taxable in Australia

20. Dec 2017: Mr. Alok Chatterjee born and brought up in India since 1971, left for Singapore on; 10.10.2018 for the purpose of employment. His residential status would be:

(A) Resident

(B) Not ordinarily resident

(C) Non-resident

(D) None of the above

21. Dec 2017: In the case of an individual being not ordinarily resident the following income is chargeable to tax:

(A) Business income accruing outside India

(B) Property income accruing outside India

(C) Income accruing outside India if it is derived from a business controlled in India

(D) Interest income accruing outside India

22. Dec 2017: Mr. Ajay (age 40) resident of India earned agricultural income of ₹ 1 lakh from land situated in Sri Lanka. His total income in India amounts to ₹ 7 lakhs. The tax liability would be:

(A) ₹ 77,250

(B) ₹ 75,400

(C) ₹ 74,675

(D) ₹ 56,650

ANSWERS:

1.	(C)	**2.**	(C)	**3.**	(A)	**4.**	(A)	**5.**	(A)	**6.**	(A)	**7.**	(C)
8.	(B)	**9.**	(B)	**10.**	(D)	**11.**	(A)	**12.**	(A)	**13.**	(A)	**14.**	(C)
15.	(D)	**16.**	(C)	**17.**	(A)	**18.**	(C)	**19.**	(A)	**20.**	(A)	**21.**	(C)
22.	(B)												

HINTS FOR PRACTICAL MCQs

45. Stay of Ram from 1.4.2018 to 1.10.2018 is 184 days. Thus, Ram fulfils both the basic conditions as well as both the additional conditions; hence Ram is ordinary resident.

46. Stay of Laxman from 1.4.2018 to 15.7.2018 is 106 days. He does not fulfils first and second condition; hence Laxman is non-resident.

Common hint for 47, 50, 52 & 56, 58, 60, 62, 64.

Incomes are taxable in the hands of a person depending upon this residential status as show below:

Particulars	Ordinary Resident	Non-ordinary Resident	Non-Resident
Income received or deemed to be received in India whether earned in India or elsewhere.	✓	✓	✓

Particulars	Ordinary Resident	Non-ordinary Resident	Non-Resident
Income which accrues or arises in India or deemed to accrue or arises in India during the previous year, whether received in India or elsewhere.	✓	✓	✓
Income which accrues or arises outside India from a business controlled from India.	✓	✓	×
Income which accrues or arises outside India from any other source (other than business income)	✓	×	×
Income of earlier years remitted to India during the previous year.	✓	×	×

48. ***Step 1: Calculate stay during current PY.***

Stay in PY 2018-2019 = 100 days

Step 2: Calculate stay in last 4 PY

Previous year ended	*No. of days spent in India*
31.3.2018	100
31.3.2017	100
31.3.2016	100
31.3.2015	100
	400

Step 3: Check basic conditions

He is in India for 182 days or more	×
He is in India for 60 days or more AND 365 days in last 4 previous year	✓

If he fulfils one or both basic conditions he is resident. Once he is resident we have to check additional condition to determine whether he is ordinary resident or not-ordinary resident.

Step 4: Determine status for last 10 years.

No.	Year	Stay	Stay in last 4 PY	Status
1	2017-2018	100	400	R
2	2016-2017	100	400	R
3	2015-2016	100	400	R
4	2014-2015	100	400	R
5	2013-2014	100	400	R
6	2012-2013	100	400	R
7	2011-2012	100	400	R
8	2010-2011	100	400	R
9	2009-2010	100	300	NR
10	2008-2009	100	200	NR
11	2007-2008	100	100	NR
12	2006-2007	100		
13	2005-2006	-		
14	2004-2005	-		
15	2003-2004	-		

Step 5: Check additional conditions

He is resident in India in for at least 2 years in last 10 previous year	✓
He stays in India for 730 or more in last 7 previous year	×

He fulfils both the additional conditions; he is ordinary resident, if not, he will be not-ordinary resident.

In other words a person will be not-ordinary resident in following cases

- If he do not fulfil both the additional conditions
- If he fulfil only one additional condition.

Thus, in given case Mr. Tom is not-ordinary resident.

49. Stay of Rafiq from 5.10.2018 to 31.3.2019 is less than 182 days. Further he is a person of Indian origin and hence in second basic condition 182 days will be substituted for 60 days. He does not fulfil both basic conditions; hence, he is non-resident.

51. A sailor fulfils first basic condition; hence he is resident. In absence of data of last 10 years it can be safely be assumed that he is resident all those year and hence fulfils both additional conditions and thus he is ordinary resident.

53. Rohit does not fulfil first basic conditions. He also does not fulfil second basic condition as period of 182 days will be substituted for him instead of 60 days as he has gone for employment purpose. Thus, he is non-resident.

54.

Particulars	OR	NOR	NR
Interest on UK Government bond			
- Directly received in India	10,00,000	10,00,000	10,00,000
- Accrued there and received there	30,00,000	-	-
	40,00,000	10,00,000	10,00,000

55. ***Step 1: Calculate stay during current PY.***

Stay in PY 2018-2019 = 70 days

Step 2: Calculate stay in last 4 PY

Previous year ended	*No. of days sent in USA*	*No. of days spent in India*
31.3.2018	310	55
31.3.2017	270	95
31.3.2016**	150	216
31.3.2015	320	45
		411

** Leap year

Step 3: Check basic conditions

He is in India for 182 days or more	×
He is in India for 60 days or more AND 365 days in last 4 previous year	✓

Since, Teji fulfil one of the basic conditions; hence he is resident.

Step 4: Determine status for last 10 years.

No.	Year	Stay	Stay in last 4 PY	Status
1	2017-2018	55	721	NR
2	2016-2017	95	992	R
3	2015-2016	216	1,141	R
4	2014-2015	45	1,461	NR
5	2013-2014	365	1,461	R
6	2012-2013	366	1,461	R
7	2011-2012	365	1,461	R
8	2010-2011	365	1,461	R
9	2009-2010	365	1,461	R
10	2008-2009	366	1,461	R
11	2007-2008	365	1,461	R
12	2006-2007	365		
13	2005-2006	365		
14	2004-2005	366		
15	2003-2004	365		

Step 5: Check additional conditions

He is resident in India for at least 2 years in last 10 previous year	✓
He stays in India for 730 or more in last 7 previous year	✓

He fulfils both the additional conditions; hence he is ordinary resident.

57. ***Step 1: Calculate stay during current PY.***

Stay in PY 2018-2019 = 70 days

Step 2: Calculate stay in last 4 PY

Previous year ended	*No. of days spent in India*
31.3.2018	160
31.3.2017	80
31.3.2016	60
31.3.2015	65
	365

Step 3: Check basic conditions

He is in India for 182 days or more	×
He is in India for 60 days or more AND 365 days in last 4 previous year	✓

Since, he fulfils one of the basic conditions he is resident.

Step 4: Determine status for last 10 years.

No.	Year	Stay	Stay in last 4 PY	Status
1	2017-2018	160	205	NR
2	2016-2017	80	125	NR
3	2015-2016	60	65	NR
4	2014-2015	65	-	NR
5	2013-2014	-	-	NR
6	2012-2013	-	-	NR
7	2011-2012	-	-	NR
8	2010-2011	-	-	NR
9	2009-2010	-	-	NR
10	2008-2009	-	-	NR
11	2007-2008	-	-	NR
12	2006-2007	-		
13	2005-2006	-		
14	2004-2005	-		
15	2003-2004	-		

Step 5: Check additional conditions

He is resident in India for at least 2 years in last 10 previous year	×
He stays in India for 730 or more in last 7 previous year	×

He does not fulfils both the additional conditions; hence, he is not-ordinary resident

59. ***Step 1: Calculate stay during current PY.***

Stay in PY 2018-2019 = 365 days

Step 2: Calculate stay in last 4 PY

Previous year ended	*No. of days spent in India*
31.3.2018	365
31.3.2017	41
31.3.2016	-
31.3.2015	-
	406

Step 3: Check basic conditions

He is in India for 182 days or more	✓
He is in India for 60 days or more AND 365 days in last 4 previous year	✓

Since, he fulfils both the basic conditions he is resident.

Step 4: Determine status for last 10 years.

No.	Year	Stay	Stay in last 4 PY	Status
1	2017-2018	365	41	R
2	2016-2017	41	-	NR
3	2015-2016	-	-	NR
4	2014-2015	-	-	NR
5	2013-2014	-	-	NR
6	2012-2013	-	-	NR
7	2011-2012	-	-	NR
8	2010-2011	-	-	NR
9	2009-2010	-	-	NR
10	2008-2009	-	-	NR
11	2007-2008	-	-	NR
12	2006-2007	-		
13	2005-2006	-		
14	2004-2005	-		
15	2003-2004	-		

Step 5: Check additional conditions

He is resident in India for at least 2 years in last 10 previous year	×
He stays in India for 730 or more in last 7 previous year	×

He does not fulfils both the additional conditions; hence, he is not-ordinary resident

61. If the business of the HUF wholly controlled from outside India, it is non-resident. Thus, stay of Karta is immaterial. *(If HUF is resident, additional conditions are required to be checked for Karta to determine whether HUF is 'ordinary resident' or 'not-ordinary resident.)*

63. A company is resident in India in following cases:

- It is a company registered in India.
- In case of foreign company if its effective place of management is in India.

Titanic Inc. has taken all key management and commercial decisions in Board Meetings held in Ooty at Tamilnadu. Thus, its effective place of management is in India and it is resident in India.

65. An Indian company is always resident in India irrespective of the fact of its effective place of management.

HINTS FOR PAST EXAMINATION MCQs

2. Total stay of Mr. X in India = 30 + 31 + 30 + 30 + 29 + 31 = 180 days.

X does not fulfil first basic condition. He is Indian citizen and gone out of India for employment purpose and hence in second condition period of 182 days will be substituted for 60 days and thus he also does not fulfil second basic condition; hence X is non-resident.

3. 1/4th of 2,00,000 + 2,00,000 = 2,50,000.

5. Total stay of Atul up to 31.3.2018 = 30 + 31 + 31 + 28 + 31 = 151 days

Atul does not fulfil first basic condition. He is person of Indian origin and hence in second condition period of 182 days will be substituted for 60 days and thus he also does not fulfil second basic condition; hence Atul is non-resident.

11. *Calculation of tax liability of Arun (non-resident, age 80):*

On first	2,50,000		Nil
On next	2,50,000	@ 5%	12,500
On next	1,00,000	@ 20%	20,000
	6,00,000		32,500
(+) Education Cess @ 4%			1,300
Total tax			33,800

Note: *Irrespective of age of non-resident, tax will be calculated as per first slab. Benefit of age is available to resident assessee only and not to non-residents.*

13. An Indian company is always resident in India even though most of its control & management is situated outside India.

14.

He is in India for 182 days or more	×
He is in India for 182 days or more AND 365 days in last 4 previous year	×

Since none of the basic condition is fulfilled Ritesh is non-resident.

16. Stay in current previous year = 198 days

He is in India for 182 days or more	✓
He is in India for 182 days or more AND 365 days in last 4 previous year	✓

Since, Rajiv fulfil both basic conditions; hence he is resident.

He also fulfils both additional conditions; hence is Ordinary Resident.

17. HUF is treated as resident in India if the control and management of its affairs is situated wholly or partly in India.

To determine whether HUF is ordinary resident or not-ordinary resident additional condition has to be checked for Karta of HUF.

Since, Mr. Rajiv do not fulfil both additional condition HUF is Not Ordinary Resident.

20. Stay in India for current previous year = 184 days. Since, Mr. Alok fulfils both the basic condition as well as both additional conditions he is ordinary resident in India.

22. Agricultural income outside India is not treated as 'agricultural income' as per Section 2(1A). Thus, such income will come under regular slab.

On first	2,50,000		Nil
On next	2,50,000	@ 5%	12,500
On balance	3,00,000	@ 20%	60,000
	8,00,000		72,500
(+) Education cess @ 4%			2,900
			75,400

CHAPTER 3

INCOME FROM SALARY

MCQs ON THEORY

1. Which of the following sections deals with the provisions relating to salary under the Income Tax Act, 1961?

(A) Sections 14, 15 & 16

(B) Sections 15 to 20

(C) Sections 16, 17, 18 & 19

(D) Sections 15, 16 & 17

2. An income under the head salary is taxable ______

(A) If there exist "contract for service" between person who makes the payment and person who receives the payment.

(B) If there exist principle and agent relationship between two person.

(C) If and only if there exists an employer and employee relationship

(D) All of the above

3. Salary is taxable on _____

(1) Due basis

(2) Received basis

Select the correct answer from the options given below –

(A) (2) only

(B) (1) only

(C) (1) or (2) whichever is later

(D) (1) or (2) whichever is earlier

4. Which of the following relationship is/are essential in order to tax a particular income under the head "Salary"?

(1) Employer and employee
(2) Principal and agent
(3) Master and servant
(4) Contractor and contractee

Select the correct answer from the options given below –

(A) (2), (3) & (4)
(B) (1), (3) & (4)
(C) (1) & (3)
(D) (4) & (2)

5. *Statement I:*

Salary received by MP's & MLA's is taxable under the head "Salary".

Statement II:

Salary received by judges of Court is chargeable to tax under the head "Salary".

Select the correct answer from the options given below –

(A) Statement I is true while Statement II is false.
(B) Statement I is false while Statement II is true.
(C) Both statements are false
(D) Both statements are true.

6. HRA is exempt to the extend specified in –

(A) Section 10(13A)
(B) Section 10(12B)
(C) Section 10(10F)
(D) Section 10(12AB)

7. Deduction in respect of entertainment allowance is available to _______

(a) Government employee
(b) Employees of local authority
(c) Employees of statutory corporation

Select the correct answer from the options given below –

(A) (a), (b) & (c)

(B) (b) & (c) only

(C) (a) & (b) only

(D) (a) only

8. *Assertion (A):*

The retainership fee received by an Advocate General from Central Government cannot be taxed under the head salary.

Reason (R):

Advocate General is not employee of Central Government and hence retainership fee received by him will be treated as professional income.

Select the correct answer from the options given below –

(A) Both A and R are true and R is correct explanation of A.

(B) Both A and R are true but R is not correct explanation of A.

(C) A is true but R is false.

(D) A is false but R is true.

9. Entertainment allowance is –

(A) Exempted under Section 16(ii)

(B) Allowed to be deducted under Section 16(ii)

(C) Exempted under Section 16(iii)

(D) Allowed to be deducted under Section 16(iii)

10. Pay and allowances received by the Chief Minister of the State is ______

(A) Exempt from tax

(B) Chargeable to tax but deduction can be claimed in respect of entire salary and allowance

(C) Chargeable to tax under the head "Salary"

(D) Chargeable to tax under the head "Income from other sources"

11. Which of the following is correct deduction for entertainment allowance?

(A) *Least of the following:*

(*a*) Actual amount spent

(*b*) ₹ 5,000 p.m.

(*c*) 20% × (Basic + DA)

(B) *Highest of the following:*

(*a*) Actual amount received

(*b*) ₹ 5,000

(*c*) 20% of basic salary

(C) *Least of the following:*

(*a*) Actual amount received

(*b*) ₹ 5,000

(*c*) 20% × (Basic + DA)

(D) *Least of the following:*

(*a*) Actual amount received

(*b*) ₹ 5,000

(*c*) 20% of basic salary

12. *Statement P:*

Salary received by partners from the firm is taxable under the head salary.

Statement Q:

Arrear of salary is taxable on due or received whichever is earlier.

Select the correct answer from the options given below –

(A) P and Q both are true

(B) P and Q both are false

(C) Q is correct but not P

(D) P is correct but not Q

13. Maximum deduction available for professional tax is _____

(A) ₹ 5,000

(B) Entire amount paid as professional tax

(C) ₹ 2,500

(D) There is no limit at all

14. "Salary" is defined in ______ under the Income Tax Act, 1961.

(A) Section 16(2)

(B) Section 18(1)

(C) Section 19(3)

(D) Section 17(1)

15. Deduction in respect of HRA u/s 10(13A) is available to the ______

(A) Government employees

(B) Employees of statutory corporations

(C) Private sector employees

(D) All of the above

16. Which of the following is included in "Salary" as defined in Section 17(1) of the Income Tax Act, 1961?

I. Annuity and pension

II. Annual accretion to the balance of Recognized Provident Fund.

III. Income from investment made out of salary income.

IV. Contribution made by Central Government to account of an employee under a pension scheme referred to in Section 80CCD.

Select the correct answer from the options given below –

(A) I, III & IV

(B) II, IV & I

(C) III & II only

(D) I, II, III & IV

17. Which of the following is correct deduction for HRA if person leaves in Delhi?

(A) *Least of the following:*

(*a*) Actual amount spent

(*b*) Rent paid – 20% of salary

(*c*) 40% of salary

Where,

Salary = Basic + DA (*if it enters into retirement benefit*)

(B) *Highest of the following:*

(*a*) Actual amount received

(*b*) Rent paid – 10% of salary

(*c*) 50% of basic salary

Where,

Salary = Basic + Taxable allowances

(C) *Least of the following:*

(*a*) Actual amount received

(*b*) Rent paid – 10% of salary

(*c*) 40% of basic salary

Where,

Salary = Basic + DA (*if it enters into retirement benefit*)

(D) *Least of the following:*

(*a*) Actual amount received

(*b*) Rent paid – 10% of salary

(*c*) 50% of basic salary

Where,

Salary = Basic + DA (*if it enters into retirement benefit*)

18. The term 'perquisite' is defined in _____

(A) Section 17(3)

(B) Section 15(2)

(C) Section 16(3)

(D) Section 17(2)

19. Children education allowance is exempt to the extent of –

(A) 1,200 p.a. for two child

(B) 100 p.m. for two child

(C) 300 p.m. for three child

(D) 100 p.m. per child for two child

20. When employee receives certain amount of salary for specified period, it know as _____

(A) Graded pay scale

(B) Tax-free salary

(C) Fixed pay scale

(D) Foregoing of salary

21. Deduction in respect of employment tax is available _____ of the Income Tax Act, 1961.

(A) u/s 16(iii)

(B) u/s 15(ii)

(C) u/s 16(ii)

(D) u/s 17(iii)

22. *Statement X:*

Tax free salary means the employer takes the burden of tax which is to be paid on the salary of the employee.

Statement Y:

In such case total salary of employee will be salary earned plus tax paid by the employer on salary.

Select the correct answer from the options given below –

(A) Both statement are false

(B) Both statement are true

(C) X is true but Y is false

(D) Y is true but X is false

23. Computation of exempted HRA depends on –

(I) HRA Received

(II) Rent paid

(III) Employment agreement

(IV) Salary of employee

(V) Nature of agreement with landlord

(VI) Place of rented house

Select the correct answer from the options given below –

(A) (I), (II), (V) & (VI)

(B) (III), (I), (VI) & (V)

(C) (VI), (IV), (II) & (I)

(D) (III), (I), (VI) & (I)

24. Which of the following is NOT included in "Salary" as defined in Section 17(1) of the Income Tax Act, 1961?

1. Payment in respect of leave not availed of.
2. Profit in lieu of salary
3. Loan against salary
4. Advance salary

Select the correct answer from the options given below –

(A) 1 & 2

(B) 2, 3 & 1

(C) 4 & 3

(D) 3 only

25. Which of the following allowance is/are fully taxable?

(*i*) Dearness allowance

(*ii*) City compensatory allowance

(*iii*) Medical allowance

(*iv*) Tiffin Allowance

Select the correct answer from the options given below –

(A) (i), (ii) & (iii)

(B) (ii), (iii) & (iv)

(C) (i) and (ii) only

(D) (i), (ii), (iii) & (iv)

26. Hostel expenditure allowance is exempt to the extent of –

(A) 300 p.m. for two child

(B) 600 p.m. for three child

(C) 300 p.m. per child for two child

(D) 3,600 p.a. for two child

27. When employee receives salary before it becomes due on receipt basis it is known as ____

(A) Loan against salary and it is not taxable

(B) Loan against salary and it is taxable under the head salary

(C) Advance against salary and it is taxable under the head salary

(D) Advance against salary and it is not taxable

28. Identify which of the following statement is correct (✓) and which is incorrect (×).

(*i*) Commission received on fixed percentage basis comes in ambit of salary.

(*ii*) Salary accrued to non-resident outside India and received outside India but remitted to India when he renders service in India to his employer is taxable in India.

(*iii*) Salary, pension received from UNO is exempt.

(*iv*) Maximum deduction for entertainment allowance for all type of employees is ₹ 5,000.

Select the correct answer from the options given below –

	(*i*)	**(*ii*)**	**(*iii*)**	**(*iv*)**
(A)	✓	×	✓	×
(B)	×	✓	×	✓
(C)	✓	✓	✓	✓
(D)	×	×	×	×

29. Which of the following allowance is/are fully exempt?

1. Servant allowance
2. Project allowance
3. Overtime allowance
4. Warden allowance

Select the correct answer from the options given below –

(A) 1 & 3

(B) 2 & 4

(C) 1, 2, 3 & 4

(D) None of the above

30. _______ means that the employee waives his salary after it becomes due or accrues him.

(A) Surrender of salary

(B) Foregoing of salary

(C) Both (A) and (B)

(D) None of the above

31. The term 'perquisite' as defined in Section 17(3) is of _____ type.

(A) Exhaustive

(B) Exclusive

(C) Inclusive

(D) Comprehensive

32. Which of the following allowance is exempt to the extent of amount expended for the purpose for which it is given?

(*a*) Warden allowance

(*b*) Family allowance

(*c*) Transport allowance

(*d*) Tribal Area allowance

Select the correct answer from the options given below –

(A) (c) & (d)

(B) (b) & (a)

(C) (a), (c) & (d)

(D) None of the above

33. *Assertion (A):*

Surrender of salary by employee to the employer is taxable in the hands of employee.

Reason (*R*):

Though surrender of salary is taxable in the hands of employee but surrender of salary to the Central Government under the Voluntary Surrender of Salaries (Exemption from Taxation) Act, 1961 shall be exempt.

Select the correct answer from the options given below –

(A) Both A and R are correct but R is not correct explanation of A

(B) Both statement are incorrect

(C) A is correct but not R

(D) Both A and R are correct and R is correct explanation of A

34. Which of the following is/are included in "Accommodation" as per Explanation to Section 17(2) read with Rule 3 of the Income Tax Rules, 1962.

1. House
2. Hotel
3. Flat
4. Mobile home
5. Farmhouse
6. Ship
7. Guesthouse
8. Caravan

Select the correct answer from the options given below –

(A) 5, 3, 1 & 7

(B) 7, 2, 4, 6 & 1

(C) 4, 2, 8, 1, 7 & 3

(D) 6, 8, 4, 1, 5, 3, 2 & 7

35. Transport allowance to the employees of transport system is exempt to the extent of –

(A) ₹ 3,200 in case of blind or orthopedically handicapped employees

(B) 60% of such allowance or ₹ 15,000 p.m. whichever is less

(C) ₹ 3,600 in case of blind or orthopedically handicapped employees

(D) 70% of such allowance or ₹ 10,000 p.m. whichever is less

36. Match the following:

I. Contract for service	1. Taxable salary
II. Paper setter/invigilator	2. Exempt.
III. Surrender of salary to government	3. Business income
IV. Remuneration received by Judges	4. Not an employee

Select the correct answer from the options given below –

	I	II	III	IV
(A)	4	3	2	1
(B)	4	3	1	2
(C)	3	4	1	2
(D)	3	4	2	1

37. Which of the following can be treated as "specified employee" within the meaning of Section 17(2)(*iii*) of the Income Tax Act, 1961?

(A) An employee who is director

(B) An employee who has substantial interest

(C) An employee whose monetary payment exceeds ₹ 50,000

(D) All of the above

38. Which of the following allowance is exempt to the extent of amount expended for the purpose for which it is given?

(1) Travelling allowance

(2) Transport allowance

Select the correct answer from the options given below –

(A) (2) only

(B) Both (1) and (2)

(C) (1) only

(D) Neither (1) nor (2)

39. If a person resident in India renders service outside India for his employer, then _____

(A) Salary is exempt if it is received outside India when employee stays outside India.

(B) Salary is not exempt but allowances and perquisites received outside India will be exempt u/s 10(7)

(C) Neither salary nor allowances or perquisites received outside India will not be exempt and it is income taxable under the head salary and employee is liable to pay tax on it.

(D) Employer is allowed under the Income Tax Act, 1961 to pay tax on salary received outside India by the employee.

40. What is the value of Rent Free Accommodation provided to the Government Employee?

(A) Lower of – Actual rent paid by the Government or 15% of salary.

(B) Actual amount reimbursed by Government for the rent paid by the employee for hiring the house.

(C) License fee determined by the Government as reduced by the rent actually paid by the employee

(D) 15% of salary if the population of city where accommodation is provided exceeds 25 lakhs

41. When employee get annual increment on his salary, it known as _____

(A) Foregoing of salary

(B) Fixed pay scale

(C) Tax-free salary

(D) Graded pay scale

42. Tribal area allowance is exempt to the extent of –

(A) ₹ 200 p.m.

(B) ₹ 800 p.m.

(C) ₹ 2,000 p.a.

(D) ₹ 600 p.a.

43. Which of the following allowance is exempt to the extent of amount expended for the purpose for which it is given?

(*i*) Uniform allowance

(*ii*) Daily allowance

Select the correct answer from the options given below –

(A) (i) only

(B) Both (i) and (ii)

(C) (ii) only

(D) Neither (i) nor (ii)

44. Perquisite of car is taxable for –

(A) Non-Government employees

(B) Government employees

(C) Specified employees

(D) All of the above

45. Which of the following allowance(s) is/are wholly exempt?

a. Allowances to High Court Judges

b. Allowances to employees of UNO

c. Allowances to employees of space research organization

d. Allowances to employees of RBI

e. Allowances to employees of Tribunals

Select the correct answer from the options given below –

(A) a, c, d & e

(B) b, c, d & e

(C) a, b & d

(D) a & b

46. If the Company registered under the Companies Act, 2013 provides house to its employee by taking on rent, the value of such accommodation for income tax purpose has to be taken –

(A) Actual rent paid by the employer as reduced by the rent actually paid by the employee plus 10% p.a. of the cost of furniture provided plus hire charges paid for furniture taken on hire.

(B) 15% of salary as reduced by the rent actually paid by the employee plus 10% p.a. of the cost of furniture provided plus hire charges paid for furniture taken on hire.

(C) Higher of actual rent paid by the employer or 15% of salary as reduced by the rent actually paid by the employee plus 10% p.a. of the cost of furniture provided plus hire charges paid for furniture taken on hire.

(D) Lower of actual rent paid by the employer or 15% of salary as reduced by the rent actually paid by the employee plus 10% p.a. of the cost of furniture provided plus hire charges paid for furniture taken on hire.

47. When motor car having cubic capacity not exceeding 1.6 litres is owned or hired by the employer and given to the employee for private use only, the value of motor car taxable in the hands of employee will be –

(A) ₹ 1,800 p.m. for motor car and ₹ 900 p.m. for the driver

(B) ₹ 2,400 p.m. for motor car and ₹ 900 p.m. for the driver

(C) Amount incurred by the employer plus driver's salary plus 10% p.a. of actual cost of car or actual hire charges less amount recovered from the employee.

(D) [Amount incurred by the employer] less [₹ 1,800 p.m. for motor car and ₹ 900 p.m. for the driver]

48. While computing the limit of ₹ 50,000 to determine whether an employee is a specified employee or not, which of the following is/are excluded or deducted?

1. All monetary payments
2. All non-monetary benefits
3. Deduction u/ss 80C to 80U
4. Monetary payment exempt u/s 10
5. Deduction u/s 16

Select the correct answer from the options given below –

(A) 3, 1 & 5

(B) 5, 4 and 2

(C) 3, 2 & 4

(D) 4, 2 & 5

49. For the purpose of claiming exemption for leave travel concession u/s 10(5) family includes –

(*a*) Spouse

(*b*) Dependant major son

(*c*) Independent minor daughter

(*d*) Dependant grandmother

Select the correct answer from the options given below –

(A) (a), (b) & (d)

(B) (a), (b) & (c)

(C) (a), (c) & (d)

(D) (a) & (c) only

50. If the employers provides the accommodation to the employee in a hotel then ______

(A) It is not taxable in the hands of employee as it is specifically exempted

(B) It is taxable in the hands of employee to the extent of higher of (i) actual charges paid or (ii) 24% of salary as reduced by the amount recovered by the employer

(C) It is taxable in the hands of employee to the extent of lower of (i) actual charges paid or (ii) 20% of salary as reduced by the amount recovered by the employer

(D) It is taxable in the hands of employee to the extent of lower of (i) actual charges paid or (ii) 24% of salary as reduced by the amount recovered by the employer

51. Transport allowance to the employees of any organization (*other than employees of transport system*) is exempt to the extent of –

(A) 70% of such allowance or ₹ 10,000 p.m. whichever is less

(B) ₹ 3,200 in case of blind or orthopedically handicapped employees

(C) 60% of such allowance or ₹ 15,000 p.m. whichever is less

(D) ₹ 3,600 in case of blind or orthopedically handicapped employees

52. Underground allowance is exempt to the extent of –

(A) ₹ 8,000 p.a.

(B) ₹ 1,200 p.m.

(C) ₹ 800 p.m.

(D) ₹ 900 p.m.

53. When motor car having cubic capacity not exceeding 1.6 litres is owned or hired by the employer and given to the employee partly for private use and partly for official use and expenses of running and maintenance are born by the employer, the value of motor car taxable in the hands of employee will be –

(A) [Amount incurred by the employer] less [₹ 1,800 p.m. for motor car and ₹ 900 p.m. for the driver]

(B) Amount incurred by the employer plus driver's salary plus 10% p.a. of actual cost of car or actual hire charges less amount recovered from the employee.

(C) ₹ 1,800 p.m. for motor car and ₹ 900 p.m. for the driver

(D) ₹ 2,400 p.m. for motor car and ₹ 900 p.m. for the driver

54. Which of the following allowance(*s*) is/are wholly exempt?

i. Sumptuary allowance to judges of Supreme Court

ii. Allowances to Indian Citizen who is government employee and rendering services outside India

Select the correct answer from the options given below –

(A) ii only

(B) i only

(C) neither i nor ii

(D) both i and ii

55. Which of the following allowance is exempt to the extent of amount expended for the purpose for which it is given?

(I) Research allowance

(II) Underground allowance

Select the correct answer from the options given below –

(A) (I) only

(B) Neither (I) nor (II)

(C) Both (I) and (II)

(D) (II) only

56. Which of the following statement is/are true in relation to transport facility provided to the employee by the transport organization?

(A) It is taxable at ₹ 1,600 p.m./₹ 3,200 in case of blind or orthopedically handicapped employees

(B) It is taxable at 70% of cost of such facility or ₹ 10,000 p.m. whichever is less

(C) It is taxable at amount charged from general public less amount recovered from the employee.

(D) Not taxable at all.

57. In respect of leave travel concession, if the journey is performed by air, exemption up the amount not exceeding _____ is available.

(A) Economy fare of national carrier of shortest route

(B) First class fare of national carrier by shortest route

(C) First class AC rail fare by shortest route.

(D) Any of the above at the choice of assessee

58. Which of the following is included in "Salary" for the purpose of valuation of RFA?

1. Basic salary
2. Portion of dearness allowance not included for retirement benefit
3. Allowances less exempted portion
4. Perquisite specified in Section 17(2)
5. Bonus
6. Lump sum payment received at the time of retirement
7. Commission
8. Fees
9. Employers contribution in excess of 12%
10. Monetary payments

Select the correct answer from the options given below –

(A) 5, 8, 3, 1, 10, 2 & 7

(B) 1 to 10 all except 4 & 9

(C) Except 2, 4, 6 & 9 all other are included

(D) 10, 3, 9, 7, 8, 5 & 1

59. Identify the allowances that are exempt to the extent of amount expended for the purpose for which it is given?

i. Helper allowance
ii. Transport allowance
iii. Research allowance
iv. Conveyance allowance
v. Tribal Area allowance
vi. Uniform allowance
vii. Daily allowance
viii. Underground allowance

Select the correct answer from the options given below –

	i	*ii*	*iii*	*iv*	*v*	*vi*	*vii*	*viii*
(A)	✓	×	✓	×	×	✓	×	✓
(B)	×	✓	×	✓	✓	×	✓	×
(C)	✓	×	✓	✓	×	✓	✓	×
(D)	×	✓	✓	✓	✓	×	×	✓

60. As per the current applicable law, if the assessee desires to claim exemption for leave travel concession and having three children and out of them last two children are twins born after year 1999 then he can claim exemption in respect of –

(A) Two children

(B) Three children

(C) One child

(D) None of the above

61. The medical facility provided to the employee by the employer engaged in hospital service profession

(A) Is exempt if medical treatment is given to the employee

(B) Is exempt if medical treatment is given to any member of employees family

(C) Both (A) and (B)

(D) None of the above

62. Which of the following type of rent free accommodation is exempt?

(A) Hotel accommodation less than 30 days say for 25 days

(B) Accommodation of temporary nature in remote area

(C) Both (A) and (B)

(D) (A) but not (B)

63. Exemption in respect of retrenchment compensation is available –

(A) u/s 10(10B)

(B) u/s 10(10AB)

(C) u/s 10(10BB)

(D) u/s 10(10C)

64. Any sum paid by the employer in respect of an expenditure incurred by an employee on his medical treatment of any of his family member is exempt up to ___

(A) ₹ 20,000

(B) Nil

(C) ₹ 15,000

(D) ₹ 25,000

65. If the sweeper, watchman, gardener is provided by the company to specified employee –

(A) It shall be fully exempt in the hands of employee.

(B) It shall be taxable in the hands of employee at such value as Assessing Officer think fit.

(C) Salary paid to such person by the employer will be taxable whether employer recovers anything from the employee or not

(D) Salary paid to such person by the employer less amount recovered from the employee will be taxable.

66. Maximum deduction for retrenchment compensation u/s 10 (10B) is –

(A) ₹ 5,00,000

(B) ₹ 10,00,000

(C) ₹ 3,00,000

(D) ₹ 15,00,000

67. Which of the following medical facility is exempt?

(1) Treatment in government hospital approved by Chief Commissioner

(2) Treatment of prescribed disease in a hospital approved by Chief Commissioner

(3) Health insurance premium paid by the employer

(4) Health insurance premium reimbursed by the employer

Select the correct answer from the options given below –

(A) (2), (3), (1) & (4)

(B) (2) & (3)

(C) (2) & (4)

(D) (1), (2) & (3)

68. Gratuity is wholly exempt in the hands of _____

(*a*) Employees of Statutory Corporations

(*b*) Employees of Local Authority

(*c*) Employees of Central Government

(*d*) Employees of State Government

Select the correct answer from the options given below –

(A) (b) & (c)

(B) (b), (c) & (d)

(C) (c) only

(D) (c) & (d)

69. For the purpose of valuation of interest free or concessional loans made available to the employee or any member of his household, which of the following rate has to be considered?

(A) Rate charged by RBI for similar purpose as on 1st day of relevant previous year.

(B) Rate charged by SBI for similar purpose as on last day of relevant previous year.

(C) Rate charged by RBI for similar purpose as on last day of relevant previous year.

(D) Rate charged by SBI for similar purpose as on 1st day of relevant previous year.

70. Leave encashment is wholly exempt in the hands of –

1. Central Government employees
2. Employees of Local Authority
3. State Government employees
4. Employees of Statutory Corporation

Select the correct answer from the options given below –

(A) 3, 2 & 1

(B) 4, 2, 1 & 3

(C) 3 & 1

(D) 1, 2 & 4

71. Exemption in respect of compensation received for voluntary retirement or separation is available –

(A) u/s 10(10D)

(B) u/s 10(10C)

(C) u/s 10(10B)

(D) u/s 10(10E)

72. If the hotel accommodation is provided to the employee on account of transfer from one place to another place for a period not exceeding 15 days, then –

(A) It is taxable in the hands of employee; lower of actual charges or 24% of salary less any amount recovered from the employee.

(B) Value of such perquisite shall be taken as NIL.

(C) Value of such perquisite shall be taken actual charges paid by the employer without any kind of deduction.

(D) None of the above is correct as information given is insufficient.

73. Maximum deduction for gratuity for the employees covered under the Payment of Gratuity Act, 1972 is –

(A) ₹ 10,00,000

(B) ₹ 20,00,000

(C) ₹ 15,00,000

(D) ₹ 40,00,000

74. While calculating the value of benefit arising out of transfer of computers and electronic gadget rate of depreciation has to be taken at –

(A) 50% under WDV Method

(B) 20% under WDV Method

(C) 50% under SLM Method

(D) 10% under SLM Method

75. Maximum exemption for compensation received for voluntary retirement separation is –

(A) ₹ 10,00,000

(B) ₹ 3,00,000

(C) ₹ 5,00,000

(D) ₹ 15,00,000

76. Exemption in respect of leave encashment is available if such leave encashment is received ____

(1) After retirement

(2) After resignation

(3) During continuance of service.

Select the correct answer from the options given below –

(A) (1) & (2) only

(B) (2) & (3) only

(C) (1) & (3) only

(D) (3) only

77. In case of double accommodation i.e. where on account of transfer of employee from one place to another place, the employee is provided with accommodation at the new place while retaining the accommodation at the other place, the value of perquisite shall be for first 90 days –

(A) Aggregate value of both accommodation determined as per relevant Rules of the Income Tax Rules, 1962.

(B) Value of that accommodation whose value is lower computed as the Income Tax Rules, 1962 has to be taken.

(C) Value of that accommodation whose value is higher computed as the Income Tax Rules, 1962 has to be taken.

(D) Average value accommodations computed as the Income Tax Rules, 1962 has to be taken.

78. Which of the following statement is correct?

(A) In case of RPF, employees contribution in excess of 12% of salary is taxable.

(B) In case of URPF, deduction u/s 80C is available.

(C) In case of SPF, employees contribution is taxable.

(D) All of the above

79. While calculating the exempted gratuity for the employees covered under the Payment of Gratuity Act, 1972, meaning of salary is taken –

(A) Salary = Basic salary

(B) Salary = Basic salary + DA (all)

(C) Salary = Basic salary + DA (to the extent it from part of retirement benefit) + percentage wise fixed commission on turnover

(D) Salary = Basic salary + DA (all) + percentage wise fixed commission on turnover + All taxable allowances

80. Club facility provided to an employee or any member of his household is –

(A) Taxable in the hands of employee and value of benefit is actual expenditure incurred less amount recovered from the employee

(B) Exempt if the expenditure is incurred wholly for business purpose

(C) Both (A) and (B)

(D) None of the above

81. If leave encashment is received during the continuity of service –

(I) It is fully taxable and no exemption is available

(II) Relief u/s 89 can be claimed

Select the correct answer from the options given below –

(A) (I) only

(B) (II) only

(C) Both (I) and (II)

(D) Neither (I) nor (II)

82. Which of the following statement is correct in relation to approved superannuation fund?

(A) Employer's contribution in excess of ₹ 1.5 lakh is taxable.

(B) Employees contribution is taxable

(C) Deduction in respect of employee's contribution is available u/s 80C.

(D) All of the above

83. If the company engaged in manufacturing of food article provides "gas facility" to the employee then what is taxable value of such perquisite in the hands of employee –

(A) Manufacturing cost p. u. × Number of units consumed by the employee

(B) Amount paid by the employer

(C) ₹ 500 p. m.

(D) ₹ 200 p. m.

84. When leave encashment is received by employee from more than one employer in the same previous year, then _____

(A) Exemption per employer of ₹ 1,50,000 is available

(B) Exemption per employer of ₹ 3,00,000 is available

(C) The aggregate quantum of exemption must not exceed the limit of ₹ 3,00,000 in that year.

(D) The aggregate quantum of exemption must not exceed the limit of ₹ 10,00,000 in that year.

85. If the individual (*covered under Payment of Gratuity Act*) receives gratuity from four employers then maximum amount exempted as gratuity is –

(A) ₹ 2,50,000 per employer and ₹ 10,00,000 in aggregate

(B) ₹ 3,00,000 per employer and ₹ 12,00,000 in aggregate

(C) ₹ 10,00,000 per employer and ₹ 40,00,000 in aggregate

(D) Total amount of exemption claimed in that previous year shall not exceed ₹ 20,00,000.

86. If employee has received arrear of salary or advance salary, he can claim relief –

(A) u/s 88

(B) u/s 89

(C) u/s 89A

(D) u/s 88A

87. Any sum paid by an employer in respect of expenditure incurred on medical treatment of an employee or any of his family members in respect of disease or ailments prescribed in _____ in a approved hospital is exempt.

(A) Rule 4A

(B) Rule 2AA

(C) Rule 3A

(D) Rule 4AA

88. If employee has already claimed exemption in respect of leave encashment in earlier year, then –

(A) Fresh limit of ₹ 3,00,000 is applicable when he again receives leave encashment from other employer

(B) The limit of ₹ 3,00,000 will be reduced by the amount of leave encashment received earlier.

(C) The limit of ₹ 3,00,000 will be reduced by the amount of exemption claimed earlier.

(D) The limit of ₹ 3,00,000 will be reduced by the amount of leave encashment received earlier or the amount of exemption claimed earlier whichever is less.

89. Which of the following is/are included in the meaning of salary for the purpose of valuation of rent free accommodation?

1. Bonus
2. Fixed commission
3. Commission fixed percentage on turnover
4. Facility of gas, electricity etc.

Select the correct answer from the options given below –

(A) 1 & 3

(B) 1 & 2

(C) 1, 2 & 3

(D) 2, 3 & 4

90. Gratuity received by employee covered under the Payment of Gratuity Act, 1972 while in employment ____

(A) Then least of the following is exempted

(1) Amount received

(2) Last salary × 15/26 × Completed year of service

(3) ₹ 20,00,000

(B) is fully exempt

(C) Then least of the following is exempted

(1) Amount received

(2) Average salary × 1/2 × Completed year of service

(3) ₹ 20,00,000

(D) is fully taxable

91. Which of the following is/are included in the meaning of 'family' for the purpose of valuation of medical facility?

(*a*) Spouse
(*b*) Major son not dependant
(*c*) Married daughter
(*d*) Dependant mother
(*e*) Brother not dependant

Select the correct answer from the options given below –

(A) (a) & (d)
(B) (c), (b), (a) & (d)
(C) (d), (e), (b) & (a)
(D) (a), (b) & (d)

92. _____ will not be taxable.

(A) Leave salary received by widow/legal heirs of the assessee, who dies during the employment.
(B) Leave salary received by the family of Government employee
(C) Both (A) and (B)
(D) Neither (A) nor (B)

93. Which of the following interest free or concessional loan facility is/are exempt?

(I) Where the amount of loan does not exceed ₹ 15,000
(II) Loan given for treatment of disease specified in Rule 3A

Select the correct answer from the options given below –

(A) Neither (I) nor (II)
(B) (II) only
(C) (I) only
(D) Both (I) and (II)

94. Exemption in respect of leave encashment is available –

(A) u/s 10(10AA)
(B) u/s 10(10AB)
(C) u/s 10(10AC)
(D) u/s 10(10BB)

95. Commuted pension received is wholly exempt in the hands of –

(*i*) Employees of Statutory Corporations

(*ii*) State Government employees

(*iii*) Employees of Local Authority

(*iv*) Central Government employees

Select the correct answer from the options given below –

(A) (ii) & (iv)

(B) (ii), (iii) & (iv)

(C) (i), (iii) & (iv)

(D) (i), (ii), (iii) & (iv)

96. Which of the following is/are included in the meaning of salary for the purpose of valuation of rent free accommodation?

(I) Entertainment allowance

(II) Arrear of salary

(III) Entertainment allowance after allowing deduction u/s 16 (ii)

(IV) Advance salary

Select the correct answer from the options given below –

(A) (III) only

(B) (I), (II) & (III)

(C) (I) only

(D) (II), (III) & (IV)

97. Maximum exemption in respect of leave encashment is –

(A) ₹ 3,00,000

(B) ₹ 5,00,000

(C) ₹ 10,00,000

(D) ₹ 15,00,000

98. A person working in private sector enterprises can be claim exemption in respect of commuted pension up to –

(A) 1/2 of the commuted value of pension if receives gratuity also.

(B) 1/3rd of the commuted value of pension if does not receive gratuity.

(C) 1/2 of the commuted value of pension if does not receive gratuity.

(D) 1/4th of the commuted value of pension if does not receive gratuity.

99. Meal facility is exempt up to –

(A) ₹ 25 per meal

(B) ₹ 50 per day

(C) ₹ 75 per meal

(D) ₹ 50 per meal

100. Which of the following is/are included in the meaning of 'family' for the purpose of valuation of medical facility?

(*i*) Father (not dependant)

(*ii*) Dependant grand son

(*iii*) Grandmother (dependant)

(*iv*) Major son (not dependant)

Select the correct answer from the options given below –

(A) (iv) only

(B) (i), (ii) & (iii)

(C) (ii) & (iv)

(D) None of the above

101. Uncommuted value of pension received is taxable in the hands of –

(A) Government employees

(B) Non-government employees

(C) Employees of Statutory Corporation

(D) All of the above

102. Which of the following food facility is/are exempt?

1. Tea or snacks provided after working hours
2. Food or non-alcoholic beverages provided during working hours in off shore installation.

Select the correct answer from the options given below –

(A) 2 only

(B) Neither 1 nor 2

(C) 1 only

(D) Both 1 and 2

103. While calculating the exempted gratuity for the employees not covered under the Payment of Gratuity Act, 1972, meaning of salary is taken –

(A) Salary = Basic salary

(B) Salary = Basic salary + DA (all) + percentage wise fixed commission on turnover

(C) Salary = Basic salary + DA (to the extent if form part of retirement benefit) + percentage wise fixed commission on turnover

(D) Salary = Basic salary + DA (all) + percentage wise fixed commission on turnover + All taxable allowances

104. Exemption in respect of leave travel concession is available –

(A) u/s 10(5)

(B) u/s 10(6)

(C) u/s 10(7)

(D) u/s 10(8)

105. While calculating the value of benefit arising out of transfer of motor car rate of depreciation has to be taken at –

(A) 20% under SLM Method

(B) 50% under SLM Method

(C) 20% under WDV Method

(D) 50% under WDV Method

106. The term "profit in lieu of salary" is defined in –

(A) Section 17(3)

(B) Section 18(2)

(C) Section 16(2A)

(D) Section 15(ia)

107. While calculating the exempted leave encashment, meaning of salary is taken –

(A) Salary = Basic salary + DA (all) + percentage wise fixed commission on turnover

(B) Salary = Basic salary

(C) Salary = Basic salary + DA (all) + percentage wise fixed commission on turnover + All taxable allowances

(D) Salary = Basic salary + DA (to the extent it form part of retirement benefit) + percentage wise fixed commission on turnover

108. In case of double accommodation i.e. where on account of transfer of employee from one place to another place, the employee is provided with accommodation at the new place while retaining the accommodation at the other place, the value of perquisite shall be for after 90 days –

(A) Value of that accommodation whose value is lower computed as the Income Tax Rules, 1962 has to be taken.

(B) Average value accommodations computed as the Income Tax Rules, 1962 has to be taken.

(C) Aggregate value of both accommodation determined as per relevant Rules of the Income Tax Rules, 1962.

(D) Value of that accommodation whose value is higher computed as the Income Tax Rules, 1962 has to be taken.

109. Which of the following pension is fully exempt –

(A) Pension received from UNO

(B) Commuted pension received from pension fund established by LIC

(C) Commuted pension received from pension fund established by approved insurer

(D) All of the above

110. Any sum paid by an employer in respect of expenditure incurred on medical treatment of an employee or any of his family member in respect of disease or ailments prescribed in Rule 3A is exempt if treatment is done in –

(*a*) Any hospital

(*b*) Government hospital

(*c*) Approved hospital

Select the correct answer from the options given below –

(A) (b) & (c)

(B) (a) only

(C) (a), (b) & (c)

(D) (c) only

111. While computing value of benefit from the sale of movable asset under the head income from salary, depreciation is –

(A) Deducted from cost of assets for every completed year and part of year is treated as fully year.

(B) Deducted from cost of assets for every completed year and part of year is treated as fully year if number of month exceeds 6 months.

(C) Deducted from cost of assets for every completed year and any fraction of year will be ignored even if it is more than 6 months.

(D) None of the above

112. While calculating the value of benefit arising out of transfer of any assets (*other than motor car computers and electronic gadget*) rate of depreciation has to be taken at –

(A) 10% under SLM Method

(B) 20% under SLM Method

(C) 20% under WDV Method

(D) 10% under WDV Method

113. Exemption in respect of gratuity is available __ of the Income Tax Act, 1961.

(A) u/s 10(10A)

(B) u/s 10(15)

(C) u/s 10(10)

(D) u/s 10(12)

114. Match the following:

List I (*Nature of payment*)	*List II* (*Exempt Amount*)
I. Gratuity	1. Fully taxable
II. Leave encashment	2. ₹ 1,50,000
III. Voluntary retirement	3. Fully exempt
IV. Approved superannuation fund	4. ₹ 15,00,000
V. Uncommitted pension	5. ₹ 20,00,000
	6. ₹ 3,00,000
	7. ₹ 5,00,000

Select the correct answer from the options given below –

	I	II	III	IV	V
(A)	5	7	6	2	1
(B)	5	6	7	2	1
(C)	5	6	7	1	2
(D)	5	7	6	1	2

PRACTICAL MCQs

115. State which of the following income are chargeable to tax under the head income from salary?

(1) Javed works as servant for Mr. Aktar and Mr. Aktar pays him monthly remuneration for his service ₹ 25,000.

(2) Ram and Ravan forms a partnership and it agreed that both will receive salary of ₹ 1,00,000 per month.

(3) Mrs. Laxmi is an employee of Ravindranath Tagore College and she receives ₹ 5,00,000 from a university for setting paper of Advanced Accounting.

(4) Mr. Prakash Bapat an elected MLA from State of Maharashtra get salary of ₹ 1,50,000 p.m.

Select the correct answer from the options given below –

(A) (1) and (4)

(B) (3), (2) and (1)

(C) (4), (2) & (4)

(D) (1) only

116. Satara Hospital Ltd. provides medical facility to its one of employee. Estimated value of benefit of such facility is ₹ 40,000. However, the company recovered ₹ 10,000 from the employee by way of deduction from salary. Taxable value of medical facility = ?

(A) ₹ 30,000

(B) ₹ 40,000

(C) Nil

(D) Nil, if employee is not a specified employee.

117. Miss Utkarsha employed in Hi-Fi Ltd. In the grade of 20,000-500-25,000-1,000-40,000-1,500-60,000 on 1.7.2005. Her gross salary for the AY 2019-2020 –

(A) ₹ 3,09,000

(B) ₹ 3,21,000

(C) ₹ 2,97,000

(D) ₹ 3,12,000

118. Free education was provided to the two children of the employee namely Raghav and Ruchira in a school maintained and owned by the company. The cost of such education for Raghav is ₹ 1,200 and for Ruchira ₹ 900 per month. No amount was recovered by the company for such education facility from the employee. Taxable value of benefit of education facility = ?

(A) ₹ 25,200

(B) ₹ 14,400

(C) Nil

(D) ₹ 10,800

119. Bala was employed by the company on 1st April, 2018 at a basic salary of ₹ 37,500 p.m. The company provided movable assets such as television, refrigerator, air-conditioner at the residence of Bala from 1st July 2018. The actual cost of such asset provided to the company is ₹ 1,10,000. The company recovered ₹ 4,500 from the Bala by way of deduction from salary. Taxable value of use of benefit from movable asset is –

(A) Nil

(B) ₹ 6,500

(C) ₹ 3,750

(D) ₹ 11,000

120. Kapil is employed in Amazon Ltd. He receives tax free salary of ₹ 3,00,000 for the year and Amazon Ltd. Pay a tax on salary ₹ 3,090. Kapil also deposit ₹ 1,00,000 in public provident fund during the year. Total income of Kapil –

(A) ₹ 3,03,090

(B) ₹ 4,05,000

(C) ₹ 1,95,000

(D) ₹ 2,03,090

121. Mr. Raja avails the benefit of leave travel concession and went by air (economy class) on a holiday on 24.1.2019 along with his wife and three children i.e. son aged 6 years and twin daughters of 2 years age. Total cost of tickets reimbursed by his employer was ₹ 1,00,000 (₹ 55,000 for 2 adults and ₹ 45,000 for three children). Taxable value of LTC = ?

(A) Nil

(B) ₹ 55,000

(C) ₹ 15,000

(D) ₹ 45,000

122. X received retrenchment compensation of ₹ 10,00,000 after 29 years & 7 months service. At the time of retirement his basic salary was ₹ 20,000 p.m.; DA ₹ 5,000 p.m. Compute taxable retrenchment compensation –

(A) ₹ 4,32,692

(B) ₹ 5,67,308

(C) ₹ 6,35,486

(D) ₹ 4,98,077

123. Vaibhav is an employee of Big Ltd. Since year 2013 whose salary has been increased from ₹ 40,000 p.m. to 50,000 p.m. w.e.f. 1st July 2018. The salary becomes due on the first day of next month. Taxable salary of Vaibhav for AY 2019-2020 –

(A) ₹ 5,60,000

(B) ₹ 5,70,000

(C) ₹ 4,80,000

(D) ₹ 6,00,000

124. T is a member of Recognized Provided Fund (RPF). His basic pays is ₹ 10,000 p.m. DA is ₹ 5,000 p.m. (60% is included in pension). His employer contributes 15% of salary to Recognized Provided Fund. Taxable Contribution to Recognized Provided Fund –

(A) ₹ 23,400

(B) ₹ 4,680

(C) ₹ 390

(D) ₹ 8,580

125. Tanushri whose basic salary is ₹ 25,000 per month is provided a motor car by her company of 1400cc to be use for private purpose only. Other details of car are as follows:

Cost of the car	6,00,000
Expenses of running of car	18,800
Expenses on maintenance	22,000
Drivers salary	2,000 p.m.

The company depreciates the car @ 15% p.a. on WDV basis. The company recovered ₹ 1,600 p.m. from the Tanushri towards the use of car.

Taxable value of perquisite of motor car –

(A) ₹ 32,400

(B) ₹ 1,05,600

(C) ₹ 1,24,800

(D) ₹ 39,600

126. Ram Trivedi, an Indian Citizen, is posted in the Indian High Commission at London. His basic pay is ₹ 1,40,000 p.m. and overseas allowance ₹ 40,000. Besides, he is entitled to airfare for going from and coming to India and also free use of Government's car (1.8 liter) with driver at London. Gross salary of Ram for AY 2019-2020 –

(A) ₹ 16,80,000

(B) ₹ 21,60,000

(C) ₹ 21,79,200

(D) ₹ 21,85,200

127. Mr. Z whose basic salary is ₹ 48,755 p.m. is provided a motor car by his company of 1600cc to be uses for *partly for official purpose and partly for private purpose.* Other details of car are as follows:

Cost of car to the company	4,00,000
Expenses of running of car	12,375
Expenses on maintenance	28,425
Drivers salary	2,000 p.m.

The company depreciates the car @ 15% p.a. on WDV basis. The company recovered ₹ 750 p.m. from the Mr. Z towards the use of car.

Taxable value of perquisite of motor car –

(A) ₹ 23,400

(B) ₹ 86,800

(C) ₹ 32,400

(D) ₹ 9,0000

128. Q is a member of Unrecognized Provided Fund (URPF). His basic pays is ₹ 10,000 p.m. DA is ₹ 5,000 p.m. His employer contributes 15% of salary to Unrecognized Provided Fund. Taxable Contribution to Unrecognized Provided Fund –

(A) Not taxable when contribution is made.

(B) ₹ 5,400

(C) ₹ 450

(D) ₹ 9,900

129. Rani is employed by XYZ Ltd. on basic salary of ₹ 75,000 p.m. DA is 60% of basic (out of which 40% is included for retirement benefit). Her employer contributes 16% of salary to RPF and Rani also makes similar contribution. Deduction available to Rani under Section 80C is –

(A) ₹ 1,78,560

(B) ₹ 1,50,000

(C) ₹ 1,00,000

(D) ₹ 1,33,920

130. Mr. P whose basic salary is ₹ 15,750 p.m. is provided a motor car by his company of 1800cc to be uses for *partly for official purpose and partly for private purpose.* Other details of car are as follows:

Cost of car to the company	6,00,000
Expenses of running of car	20,000
Expenses on maintenance	10,000
Drivers salary	3,000 p.m.

The company depreciates the car @ 15% p.a. on WDV basis. The company recovered ₹ 1,550 p.m. from the Mr. P towards the use of car.

Taxable value of perquisite of motor car –

(A) Nil

(B) ₹ 1,26,000

(C) ₹ 39,600

(D) ₹ 1,07,400

131. Rohit, an Indian citizen is an officer of Government of India. On 1.9.2018 he was transferred to the Indian Embassy at Germany. On 1.11.2018 he was again called back to India for urgent official work. On 1.2.2019 he was again sent back to Germany. His basic salary per month is 16,000. Dearness allowance 50% of salary when in India. He has been provided rent free house in Delhi while in India and at Berlin while in Germany. Rent of house at Delhi and Germany is ₹ 1,000 & ₹ 20,000 respectively as per Government rule. He is also provided car of 2000 CC both at Delhi and Berlin and car is used by official as well as private purpose. He get entertainment allowance of ₹ 4,000 p.m. while in Germany. The Government of India reimbursed ₹ 80,000 for his medical treatment while he was in Germany. Gross salary of Rohit for AY 2019-2020 is –

(A) ₹ 5,84,000
(B) ₹ 2,83,200
(C) ₹ 5,79,000
(D) ₹ 1,92,000

132. Rama is employed by KLC Ltd. on basic salary of ₹ 25,000 p.m. DA is 60% of basic (out of which 40% is included for retirement benefit). Her employer contributes 16% of salary to URPF and Rama also makes similar contribution. Deduction available Rama under Section 80C is –

(A) ₹ 59,520
(B) ₹ 44,640
(C) ₹ 76,800
(D) Nil

133. Mr. W is working as medical officer in PQR Ltd. He is specified employee as his monetary payments are above ₹ 50,000. The company also gives him motor car of 1.6 litre engine capacity which is used by Mr. W partly for official purpose and partly for private purpose. The expenses on car are incurred by Mr. W which is ₹ 15,000 for the PY 2018-2019. However, driver's salary ₹ 750 p.m. is paid by the company. The said car was purchased by the company in April 2015 for ₹ 5,60,000. The company recovers ₹ 1,000 from Mr. W towards use of car facility. Taxable value of perquisite of motor car –

(A) ₹ 56,762
(B) ₹ 32,400
(C) ₹ 18,000
(D) ₹ 21,600

134. Rinkal is a Government employee working as manager in PWD department. Her basic salary is ₹ 40,000 p.m. She gets DA 50% of basic salary out of which 40% is included for retirement benefit. She also gets entertainment allowance of ₹ 5,000 p.m. Her taxable salary for the AY 2019-2020 is –

(A) ₹ 7,35,000
(B) ₹ 6,31,000

(C) ₹ 7,20,000

(D) ₹ 7,70,000

135. Y is employed in public company and received ₹ 5,70,000 on Voluntary Retirement Scheme (VRS). His monthly salary at the time of retirement is as follows:

Basic Pay – ₹ 9,500; DA – ₹ 5,700 (50% is included for retirement benefit); HRA – ₹ 2,850; Conveyance Allowance – ₹ 760.

The normal age of retirement in the company is 60 years and Y who was 45 years at the time of retirement had completed 20 years of service. Taxable amount of VRS Compensation –

(A) ₹ 70,000

(B) ₹ 5,70,000

(C) ₹ 5,40,000

(D) Nil

136. Mr. X whose basic salary is ₹ 22,750 per month is provided a motor car by his company of 1800cc by hiring from outside agency to be used for private purpose only. Other details of car are as follows:

Hire charges of the car	3,500 p.m.
Expenses of running of car	15,460
Expenses on maintenance	12,540
Drivers salary	2,000 p.m.

The company depreciates the car @ 15% p.a. on WDV basis. The company recovered ₹ 1,500 p.m. from the Mr. X towards the use of car.

Taxable value of perquisite of motor car –

(A) ₹ 39,600

(B) ₹ 94,000

(C) ₹ 32,400

(D) ₹ 76,000

137. Rakesh works as medical officer in PQR Ltd. at Mumbai. He gets basic salary of ₹ 52,500 p.m. He is also entitled to DA 40% of basic (40% of DA is included for retirement benefit). His HRA is fixed 9,750 p.m. He also gets bonus equal to one month basic pay.

During the year he paid rent of ₹ 8,000 p.m. What is the taxable HRA?

(A) ₹ 22,920

(B) ₹ 94,080

(C) ₹ 96,000

(D) Nil

138. ABC Ltd. contributes ₹ 1,75,000 to Approved Superannuation Fund for its employee Mrs. Gita Gupta. Basic Salary and DA of Mrs. Gupta is ₹ 10,00,000 for the year 2018-2019. Taxable emplcyers contribution to Approved Superannuation Fund is –

(A) Nil

(B) ₹ 5,000

(C) ₹ 25,000

(D) ₹ 1,25,000

139. Mr. M is working as supervisor in WGT Ltd. at basic salary of ₹ 50,000 p.m. The company also gives him motor car of 1.8 litre engine capacity which is used by Mr. M partly for official purpose and partly for private purpose. The expenses on car are incurred by Mr. M which is ₹ 12,000 for the PY 2018-2019. However, driver's salary ₹ 850 p.m. is paid by the company. The said car was purchased by the company in April 2016 for ₹ 9,95,000. The company recovers ₹ 1,200 p.m. from Mr. M towards use of car facility. Taxable value of perquisite of motor car –

(A) ₹ 7,200

(B) ₹ 21,600

(C) ₹ 1,13,900

(D) ₹ 18,000

140. W is employed in public company and received ₹ 10,00,000 on Voluntary Retirement Scheme (VRS). His monthly salary at the time of retirement is as follows:

Basic Pay – ₹ 9,500

DA – ₹ 2,850 (100% included for retirement benefit).

The normal age of retirement in the company is 60 years and W who was 45 years at the time of retirement had completed 20 years of service. Taxable amount of VRS Compensation –

(A) ₹ 5,00,000

(B) ₹ 7,41,000

(C) ₹ 10,00,000

(D) ₹ 2,59,000

141. Suraj is employed in XYZ Ltd. at Pune and his last salary for March 2019 was ₹ 15,750 p.m. His DA is fixed at ₹ 2,000 p.m. out of which 30% is included for retirement benefit. He also received commission of ₹ 2,000 p.m. for the turnover achieved by him. During the year he received increment of ₹ 1,570 in basic pay on 1.8.2018. He also gets bonus of 1 month each year which for the year 2018-2019 is 15,750. His HRA is fixed at ₹ 2,500 but the same was increased from 1.9.2018 to ₹ 3,200. For the period April 2018 to Oct 2018 he paid rent of ₹ 1,750. Thereafter he shifted to another house for which he paid rent of ₹ 3,100 for the period Nov 2018 to Jan 2019. From 1st February he started live in his own house. Taxable HRA for the PY 2018-2019 –

(A) ₹ 30,178

(B) ₹ 30,817

(C) ₹ 30,718

(D) Nil

142. Mr. Swapnil Joshi is working as Company Secretary in Reliance Capital Ltd. He has his own car of 2000cc which is used partly for official purpose and partly for private purpose. Total expenses on car for the year 2018-2019 incurred by company are ₹ 40,000. The car driven by Swapnil Joshi himself. Taxable value of perquisite of motor car –

(A) ₹ 40,000

(B) Nil

(C) ₹ 39,600

(D) ₹ 11,200

143. W is employed in public company and received ₹ 28,31,000 on Voluntary Retirement Scheme (VRS). His monthly salary at the time of retirement is as follows:

Basic Pay – ₹ 9,500

DA – ₹ 2,850 (100% included for retirement benefit).

The normal age of retirement in the company is 60 years and W who was 45 years at the time of retirement had completed 20 years of service. Taxable amount of VRS Compensation –

(A) ₹ 23,31,000
(B) ₹ 22,23,000
(C) ₹ 7,41,000
(D) ₹ 28,31,000

144. Richa joined a service in the grade of 10,400 – 400 – 16,000 – 500 – 20,000 on 1.7.2000 and resigned on 15.9.2018. She was entitled to DA @ 50%, which forms part of salary for retirement benefit. Taxable salary of Richa for AY 2019-2020 –

(A) ₹ 1,38,000
(B) ₹ 1,38,750
(C) ₹ 1,40,250
(D) ₹ 1,36,125

145. Interest credited to Approved Superannuation Fund for the employee for the PY is ₹ 10,000. Rate of interest is 10%. Taxable interest is –

(A) ₹ 10,000
(B) ₹ 500
(C) Nil
(D) ₹ 9,500

146. Mr. Rakesh retired from XYZ Ltd. on 15.4.2018. He was entitled to a pension of ₹ 14,000 p.m. At the time of retirement he got 60% of pension commuted and received ₹ 3,00,000 as commuted pension. Mr. Rakesh is not entitled to gratuity. Total amount of pension taxable for the PY 2018-2019 is –

(A) ₹ 50,000
(B) Nil
(C) ₹ 74,600
(D) ₹ 1,11,600

147. Mr. M is an area manager of NSZ Ltd. he gets the following emoluments from his employer:

Basic Salary:

- Up to 31.8.2018 = ₹ 20,000 p.m.
- From 1.9.2018 = ₹ 25,000 p.m.

Employers contribution to RPF = 15% of salary

Children education allowance = ₹ 500 p.m. for two children

Hostel expenditure allowance = ₹ 380 p.m. for two children

Tiffin allowance = ₹ 5,000 (Actual expenses was ₹ 3,700)

Employment tax paid by the employer = ₹ 2,500.

Income taxable under the head salary = ?

(A) ₹ 2,51,850

(B) ₹ 2,89,350

(C) ₹ 2,87,010

(D) ₹ 2,85,850

148. Mr. Mustafa retired from PQR Ltd. on 15.4.2018 from C Ltd. He was entitled to a pension of ₹ 14,000 p.m. At the time of retirement he got 60% of pension commuted and received ₹ 3,00,000 as commuted pension. Mr. Mustafa also received gratuity of ₹ 2,50,000. Total amount of pension taxable for the AY 2019-2020 is ______

(A) Nil

(B) ₹ 1,33,333

(C) ₹ 1,57,733

(D) ₹ 1,57,667

149. N retired from H Ltd. on 31.1.2019 after putting 5 years service and received the following amounts for the year ended 31.3.2019:

Basic Salary = ₹ 10,000 p.m.

DA = ₹ 3,000 p.m.

City Compensatory Allowance = ₹ 2,000 p.m.

Night Duty Allowance = ₹ 1,000 p.m.

Pension = 30% of basic salary from 1.2.2019

Leave encashment = ₹ 75,000 (for 225 days of leave accumulated during 5 years of service @ 45 days leave per year)

Gratuity = ₹ 50,000

Gross salary = ?

(A) ₹ 2,16,000

(B) ₹ 2,41,000

(C) ₹ 2,10,000

(D) ₹ 2,06,000

150. Mr. Rajan retired from Sayadri Chemical Ltd. on 1.2.2019 after completing a service of 24 years and 4 months. His salary at the time of retirement is ₹ 10,000 p.m. He was entitled to DA 120% of basic pay (40% of which is included for retirement benefit). His last increment was on 1.7.2018 for ₹ 1,000. He received gratuity of ₹ 2,40,000 on his retirement. He is not covered under the Payment of Gratuity Act. Taxable Gratuity = ?

(A) ₹ 35,077

(B) ₹ 67,728

(C) Nil

(D) ₹ 77,040

ANSWERS:

1.	(D)	**2.**	(C)	**3.**	(D)	**4.**	(C)	**5.**	(B)	**6.**	(A)	**7.**	(D)
8.	(A)	**9.**	(B)	**10.**	(C)	**11.**	(D)	**12.**	(B)	**13.**	(C)	**14.**	(D)
15.	(D)	**16.**	(D)	**17.**	(D)	**18.**	(D)	**19.**	(D)	**20.**	(C)	**21.**	(A)
22.	(B)	**23.**	(C)	**24.**	(D)	**25.**	(D)	**26.**	(C)	**27.**	(C)	**28.**	(A)
29.	(D)	**30.**	(B)	**31.**	(C)	**32.**	(D)	**33.**	(D)	**34.**	(D)	**35.**	(D)
36.	(D)	**37.**	(D)	**38.**	(C)	**39.**	(C)	**40.**	(C)	**41.**	(D)	**42.**	(A)
43.	(B)	**44.**	(C)	**45.**	(D)	**46.**	(D)	**47.**	(C)	**48.**	(D)	**49.**	(B)
50.	(D)	**51.**	(B)	**52.**	(C)	**53.**	(C)	**54.**	(D)	**55.**	(A)	**56.**	(C)
57.	(A)	**58.**	(C)	**59.**	(C)	**60.**	(B)	**61.**	(C)	**62.**	(B)	**63.**	(A)
64.	(B)	**65.**	(D)	**66.**	(A)	**67.**	(A)	**68.**	(B)	**69.**	(D)	**70.**	(C)
71.	(B)	**72.**	(B)	**73.**	(B)	**74.**	(A)	**75.**	(C)	**76.**	(A)	**77.**	(B)
78.	(C)	**79.**	(B)	**80.**	(C)	**81.**	(C)	**82.**	(D)	**83.**	(B)	**84.**	(C)
85.	(D)	**86.**	(B)	**87.**	(C)	**88.**	(C)	**89.**	(C)	**90.**	(A)	**91.**	(B)

92.	(C)	**93.**	(D)	**94.**	(A)	**95.**	(D)	**96.**	(C)	**97.**	(A)	**98.**	(C)
99.	(D)	**100.**	(A)	**101.**	(D)	**102.**	(A)	**103.**	(C)	**104.**	(A)	**105.**	(C)
106.	(A)	**107.**	(D)	**108.**	(C)	**109.**	(D)	**110.**	(D)	**111.**	(C)	**112.**	(A)
113.	(C)	**114.**	(B)	**115.**	(D)	**116.**	(C)	**117.**	(A)	**118.**	(B)	**119.**	(C)
120.	(D)	**121.**	(A)	**122.**	(B)	**123.**	(A)	**124.**	(B)	**125.**	(B)	**126.**	(A)
127.	(C)	**128.**	(A)	**129.**	(B)	**130.**	(C)	**131.**	(B)	**132.**	(D)	**133.**	(C)
134.	(A)	**135.**	(A)	**136.**	(D)	**137.**	(B)	**138.**	(C)	**139.**	(B)	**140.**	(A)
141.	(B)	**142.**	(D)	**143.**	(D)	**144.**	(A)	**145.**	(C)	**146.**	(C)	**147.**	(A)
148.	(C)	**149.**	(A)	**150.**	(B)								

PAST EXAMINATION MCQs

1. Dec 2014: Bimal is employed in a factory at a salary of ₹ 2,400 per month. He also gets dearness allowance @ ₹ 600 per month and bonus @ ₹ 200 per month. He retired on 31st December, 2018 and received ₹ 75,000 as gratuity under the Payment of Gratuity Act, 1972 after serving 31 years and 4 months in that factory. The amount of gratuity exempt under the Income Tax Act, 1961 will be ________

(A) ₹ 75,000

(B) ₹ 53,654

(C) ₹ 21,346

(D) ₹ 20,00,000

2. Dec 2014: Akash is entitled to get a pension of ₹ 6,000 per month from a private company. He gets 60% of the pension commuted and receives ₹ 3,60,000. He also receives ₹ 2,00,000 as gratuity from the same employer. The taxable portion of commuted value of pension will be —

(A) ₹ 1,60,000

(B) Nil

(C) ₹ 3,60,000

(D) ₹ 60,000

3. Dec 2014: Anjan joins a service in the grade of ₹ 15,600–39,100 plus grade pay of ₹ 6,000 on 1.8.2018. He also gets dearness allowance

@ 107% of salary. His tax liability for AY 2019-2020 will be —

(A) ₹ 920

(B) ₹ 5,940

(C) Nil

(D) ₹ 11,090

4. Dec 2014: Chandan, a handicapped employee receives ₹ 3,000 p.m. as transport allowance from his employer. His actual expenditure on transport is ₹ 2,000 p.m. The amount of transport allowance taxable under the head income from salaries will be —

(A) ₹ 18,000

(B) Nil

(C) ₹ 6,000

(D) ₹ 8,000

5. Dec 2014: Joy Ltd. transfers a Honda City car to its employee Happy after using it for 4 years and 10 months, for ₹ 2,10,000. Cost of the car is ₹ 10,00,000. The value of taxable perquisite in the hands of Happy is —

(A) ₹ 1,17,680

(B) ₹ 1,99,600

(C) Nil

(D) ₹ 7,90,000

6. Dec 2014: Ramesh, an employee of Gauri & Co. of Delhi, received the following payments during the previous year ended 31st March, 2018:

Basic salary: ₹ 2,40,000 and dearness allowance - 40% of basic salary (40% forming part of salary). Rent-free unfurnished accommodation provided by employer for which rent paid by employer being ₹ 50,000. The value of taxable perquisite in the hands of Ramesh will be —

(A) ₹ 41,760

(B) ₹ 50,000

(C) ₹ 36,000

(D) ₹ 52,500

7. Dec 2014: Children education allowance received by an employee from his employer is ₹ 80 per month per child for 3 children. Taxable education allowance will be —

(A) ₹ 960

(B) ₹ 480

(C) Nil

(D) ₹ 1,200

8. June 2015: Which of the following is not correct about the approved superannuation fund?

(A) Employees' contribution qualifies for deduction under section 80C

(B) Any amount contributed by the employer is exempt from tax

(C) Interest on accumulated balance is exempt from income-tax

(D) Under some circumstances, payments from the fund are chargeable to income-tax

9. June 2015: Ashraf is an employee of Moon Public School. His daughter, Zara, is studying in the said school at concessional fees of ₹ 600 p.m. (Actual fee: ₹ 4,000 p.m.) The amount taxable in the hands of Ashraf will be —

(A) ₹ 48,000

(B) ₹ 7,200

(C) Nil

(D) ₹ 40,800

10. June 2015: Ashok took an interest-free loan of ₹ 15,000 from B Ltd. (the employer). Assuming that the market rate of interest on similar loan is 10%, the taxable value of the perquisite in the hands of Ashok will be —

(A) ₹ 150

(B) ₹ 1,500

(C) Nil

(D) None of the above

11. June 2015: During the previous year 2018-2019, Barun received a watch worth ₹ 20,000 from his employer. The taxable value of the watch will be —

(A) ₹ 20,000

(B) ₹ 15,000

(C) Nil

(D) None of the above

12. Dec 2015: Kapil gets salary of ₹ 12,000 p.m. and is provided with rent-free unfurnished accommodation at Pune (population 31 lakh). House is owned by employer, fair rental value of which is ₹ 1,400 p.m. House was provided with effect from 1st July, 2018. Value of the perquisite of rent-free accommodation will be —

(A) ₹ 21,600

(B) ₹ 10,800

(C) ₹ 16,200

(D) ₹ 12,600

13. Dec 2015: Anil is employed in a company with annual salary of ₹ 8,60,000 (computed). The company paid income-tax of ₹ 37,000 on his non-monetary perquisites. He paid ₹ 1,20,000 to recognised provident fund during the year 2018-2019. His total income would be —

(A) ₹ 7,77,000

(B) ₹ 7,40,000

(C) ₹ 7,97,000

(D) ₹ 7,60,000

14. Dec 2015: Rohan retires from private service on 30th April, 2018 and his pension has been fixed at ₹ 1,500 p.m. He gets 1/2 of his pension commuted during January, 2019 and receives ₹ 75,000. He also gets ₹ 60,000 as gratuity. The total pension taxable including commuted value will be —

(A) ₹ 16,500

(B) ₹ 41,500

(C) ₹ 39,250

(D) ₹ 14,250

15. Dec 2015: Govt. of India paid salary of ₹ 5 lakh and allowances and perquisites valued at ₹ 2.20 lakh to a person who is citizen of India for the services rendered by him outside India for 5 months during the previous year. His total income chargeable to tax would be —

(A) ₹ 6,80,000

(B) ₹ 4,60,000

(C) ₹ 5,70,000

(D) Nil

16. Dec 2015: Pankaj joins service on 1st April, 2014 in the grade of 15,000-1,000-18,000-2,000-26,000. He shall be paying tax for the year ended on 31st March, 2019 on the total salary of —

(A) ₹ 2,16,000

(B) ₹ 2,40,000

(C) ₹ 2,28,000

(D) ₹ 1,80,000

17. June 2016: An employee of a company, who was entitled for a gratuity of ₹ 8,00,000, also received ₹ 12,00,000 by commuting 40% of his pension. The taxable amount of commuted pension is —

(A) ₹ 2,00,000

(B) ₹ 4,00,000

(C) ₹ 12,00,000

(D) ₹ 22,00,000

18. June 2016: Ravi is receiving ₹ 10,000 as medical allowance from his employer. Out of this, he spends ₹ 5,000 on his own medical treatment, ₹ 2,000 on the medical treatment of his dependent wife and another ₹ 3,000 for the medical treatment of his major son who is not a dependent on him. The amount of medical allowance taxable in his hand is —

(A) ₹ 10,000

(B) ₹ 5,000

(C) ₹ 3,000

(D) Nil

19. June 2016: Ms. Janhvi is provided with an interest loan by her employer for the purchase of a house. The value of the perquisite shall be –

(A) Simple interest computed at the rate charged by the Central Government to its employees on 1st April of the previous year

(B) Simple interest computed at the rate charged by State Bank of India on 1st April of the previous year

(C) Simple interest computed at the rate charged by National Housing Bank on 1st April of the previous year

(D) Simple interest computed at the rate determined by the employer on 1st April of the previous year

20. June 2016: Murali is employed in Megha Ltd., Delhi. He is paid house rent allowance of ₹ 9,000 per month in financial year 2018-2019 his salary for the purpose of computation or house rent allowance relief may be taken as ₹ 20,000 per month. Murali pays actual rent of ₹ 10,000 per month. How much of the house rent allowance is tax-free -

(A) ₹ 1,08,000

(B) ₹ 1,20,000

(C) ₹ 96,000

(D) ₹ 60,000

21. June 2016: Satish is employed as chief engineer in Gama Ltd., Chennai w.e.f. 1st April, 2018 for a consolidated salary of ₹ 60,000 per month. He is provided with rent-free unfurnished accommodation owned by the employer from 1st July, 2018 onwards. The value of taxable perquisite is —

(A) ₹ 1,08,000

(B) ₹ 81,000

(C) ₹ 72,000

(D) ₹ 54,000

22. June 2016: Mrs. Meena retired from service with Sky Ltd. on 31st January, 2019. She received the following amounts from unrecognized provident fund:

(*i*) Own contribution ₹ 1,50,000

(*ii*) Interest on own contribution ₹ 21,000

(*iii*) Employer's contribution ₹ 1,10,000

(*iv*) Interest on employer's contribution ₹ 15,000

How much of the receipt is chargeable to tax as income from salary -

(A) ₹ 21,000

(B) ₹ 15,000

(C) ₹ 1,25,000

(D) ₹ 1,71,000

23. Dec 2016: A company acquired a motor car for ₹ 8 lakh on 30th June, 2017. It sold the said motor car to its employee, Jayant, for ₹ 6 lakh on 10th June, 2018. The company claimed depreciation @ 15% for the year ended 31st March, 2018. The perquisite value in the hands of Jayant on sale of motor car would be –

(A) ₹ 80,000

(B) Nil

(C) ₹ 2,00,000

(D) ₹ 1,40,000

24. Dec 2016: Pawan, employed in Magic Ltd., was eligible for transport allowance of ₹ 2,000 per month to meet his travel expenses from residence to office. He actually incurred ₹ 1,200 per month towards travel. The amount of travel allowance chargeable to tax as perquisite would be –

(A) ₹ 24,000

(B) ₹ 14,000

(C) ₹ 4,800

(D) Nil

25. Dec 2016: An employee of a public limited company received ₹ 3,00,000 as encashment of leave salary at the time of retirement. He has 18 months leave to his credit at the time of retirement and his average salary for last 10 months is ₹ 24,000. The taxable amount if leave encashment would be –

(A) ₹ 2,40,000

(B) ₹ 3,00,000

(C) ₹ 60,000

(D) Nil

26. Dec 2016: Allowances and perquisites allowed to an employee for services rendered outside India are tax free in case of –

(A) All types of employees

(B) Government employees only

(C) Non-government employees only

(D) None of the above

27. Dec 2016: Company has provided laptop worth ₹ 50,000 to his employee for official as well as personal purposes. The taxable amount of perquisites will be –

(A) ₹ 5,000

(B) ₹ 25,000

(C) ₹ 10,000

(D) Nil

28. June 2017: Mr. Ashwin retired on 31.10.2017 after rendering 35 years of service in PLN & Co. Ltd. He received gratuity of ₹ 18 lakhs. He is governed by Payment of Gratuity Act, 1972. The monetary limit eligible for exemption is:

(A) ₹ 20 lakhs

(B) ₹ 10 lakhs

(C) ₹ 3,50,000

(D) Nil

29. June 2017: Mr. A is employed in ABS Transports as cabin driver. He is paid ₹ 15,000 every month in the whole of previous year 2018-2019 as allowance for meeting his personal expenditure in the course of running the goods vehicle. Mr. A does not receive any other amount by way of daily allowance. The amount of allowance eligible for exemption is:

(A) ₹ 1,80,000

(B) ₹ 1,20,000

(C) ₹ 1,26,000

(D) Nil

30. June 2017: Mr. Arjun employed in KL (P) Ltd. at Mumbai was provided rent-free accommodation by the employer who owned such accommodation. The salary income of Mr. Arjun for the purpose of computing the perquisite value is ₹ 8 lakhs. The perquisite value of rent-free accommodation in the hands of Mr. Arjun is:

(A) 10% of salary i.e. ₹ 80,000

(B) 7.5% of salary i.e. ₹ 60,000

(C) Nil

(D) 15% of salary i.e. ₹ 1,20,000

31. June 2017: Mr. Gupta is given a motor car with chauffeur by the employer which is used for both official and personal purpose. The entire running expenses of the car amounting to ₹ 64,800 was met by the employer in the previous year 2018-2019. The cubic capacity of the engine of the motor car exceeds 1.6 litres. The perquisite value of motor car taxable in the hands of Mr. Gupta is:

(A) ₹ 19,200

(B) ₹ 39,600

(C) ₹ 28,800

(D) ₹ 64,800

32. June 2017: Ashwin Co. Ltd. contributed 15% of the salary of the employee Virat towards recognized provident fund. The amount liable to tax as perquisite in the hands of Virat would be .... of contribution.

(A) 5%

(B) 3%

(C) Nil

(D) Any sum exceeding ₹ 1,50,000

33. June 2017: During the previous year, the employee was reimbursed ₹ 24,000 as medical expenses incurred by him which includes ₹ 7,000 spent in Government hospital. The taxable perquisite in this case shall be:

(A) ₹ 2,000

(B) Nil

(C) ₹ 17,000

(D) ₹ 24,000

34. June 2017: The employee is provided with furniture costing ₹ 1,50,000 along with house w.e.f. 1.7.2018. The value of the furniture to be included in the valuation of unfurnished house shall be:

(A) ₹ 11,250

(B) ₹ 15,000

(C) ₹ 22,500

(D) ₹ 16,875

35. June 2017: Interest credited to statutory provident fund shall be:

(A) Fully exempt

(B) Exempt up to 8.5% p.a.

(C) Fully taxable

(D) Exempt up to 9.5%

36. Dec 2017: Mr. Vijay employed in ABC Ltd. opted for voluntary retirement and received ₹ 22 lakhs by way of gratuity. The Payment of Gratuity Act, 1972 is applicable in his case. The monetary limit for exemption under Section 10(10) is:

(A) ₹ 3,50,000

(B) ₹ 5,00,000

(C) ₹ 20,00,000

(D) ₹ 3,00,000

37. Dec 2017: The maximum amount eligible for exemption in respect of encashment of earned leave on retirement is:

(A) ₹ 3,00,000

(B) ₹ 10,00,000

(C) ₹ 50,000

(D) ₹ 5,00,000

38. Dec 2017: Mr. Murthy is employed in, ABC Management Institute, Pune. He is eligible for ₹ 24,000 as allowance for the year towards academic and research work. The amount of academic and research allowance chargeable to tax is:

(A) ₹ 10,000

(B) ₹ 24,000

(C) Nil

(D) ₹ 9,000

39. Dec 2017: Mr. Amit employed in X Co. Ltd., Salem received ₹ 10,000 per month as house rent allowance in the year 2018-2019. His total salary is ₹ 4 lakhs consisting of Basic Pay + DA. He paid rent of ₹ 8,000 per month. How much of HRA is exempt from tax?

(A) ₹ 40,000

(B) ₹ 56,000

(C) ₹ 1,20,000

(D) ₹ 1,60,000

40. Dec 2017: Mr. Balan is employed in SS Ltd at Madurai. He is provided with a rent free accommodation owned by the employer. The percentage of salary to be adopted for the purpose of valuation of perquisite would be:

(A) 15%

(B) 10%

(C) 7.5%

(D) 20%

41. Dec 2017: Ravi employed in Cotton India Ltd. as accounts manager. The employer paid ₹ 1,60,000 as contribution to approved superannuation fund to benefit the employee Ravi. The amount of such contribution liable to tax as perquisite in the hands of Mr. Ravi is:

(A) Nil

(B) ₹ 10,000

(C) ₹ 1,60,000

(D) ₹ 60,000

42. Dec 2017: Mr. Bobby employed in PQR Ltd. was permitted to admit his only son in the school run by the employer. No fee was charged on such education provided to the son of Mr. Bobby. The cost of such education for other children is ₹ 1,800 per month.

The perquisite value of free education in the hands of Mr. Bobby would be:

(A) ₹ 21,600

(B) ₹ 12,000

(C) ₹ 36,000

(D) ₹ 9,600

43. Dec 2017: When interest on employee's own contribution from unrecognized provident fund is received, it is:

(A) taxable as income from other sources

(B) taxable as income from salary

(C) exempt from tax

(D) taxable if the interest exceeds ₹ 10,000

ANSWERS:

1.	(B)	**2.**	(A)	**3.**	(A)	**4.**	(B)	**5.**	(B)	**6.**	(A)	**7.**	(A)
8.	(B)	**9.**	(D)	**10.**	(C)	**11.**	(B)	**12.**	(C)	**13.**	(B)	**14.**	(C)
15.	(B)	**16.**	(B)	**17.**	(A)	**18.**	(A)	**19.**	(B)	**20.**	(C)	**21.**	(B)
22.	(C)	**23.**	(C)	**24.**	(C)	**25.**	(C)	**26.**	(B)	**27.**	(D)	**28.**	(A)
29.	(B)	**30.**	(D)	**31.**	(B)	**32.**	(B)	**33.**	(C)	**34.**	(A)	**35.**	(A)
36.	(C)	**37.**	(A)	**38.**	(B)	**39.**	(B)	**40.**	(B)	**41.**	(B)	**42.**	(A)
43.	(A)												

HINTS FOR PRACTICAL MCQs

115. In (1) there is employer and employee relationship whereas in (2), (3) & (4) there is no employer and employee relationship; hence option (D) is correct.

116. Medical facility provided to its employees by the hospitals is fully exempt.

117. 1.7.2017 to 30.6.2018 = 25,000 p.m.

1.7.2018 to 30.6.2019 = 26,000 p.m.

However, we need salary for the period 1.4.2018 to 31.3.2019

1.4.2018 to 30.6.2018 = (25,000 × 3) =		75,000
1.7.2018 to 31.3.2019 = (26,000 × 9) =		2,34,000
		3,09,000

118.

	Raghav	Ruchira
Cost of education per month	1,200	900
Amount recovered	-	-
	1,200	900

The perquisite in respect of education facility is exempt if it value is up to ₹ 1,000 otherwise it is fully taxable.

So, taxable perquisite = 1,200 × 12 = 14,400

119. 1,10,000 × 10% × 9/12 = 8,250 – 4,500 = 3,750

120. Tax paid by employer is treated as income of employee. For depositing in PPF deduction u/s 80C is available. Hence, Total income = 3,00,000 + 3,090 – 1,00,000 = 2,03,090

121. Leave travel concession is exempt two times in block of four years. It is exempt for assessee and his family. Wife and children (two) are covered in family for this purpose. In given problem, assessee has three children. Multiple birth after one child, multiple children is regarded as one child and hence it is fully exempt.

122.

Amount received as retrenchment compensation	10,00,000
(-) Exempt u/s 10(10B) $\left[25{,}000 \times \frac{15}{26} \times 30\right]$	(4,32,692)
Taxable retrenchment compensation	5,67,308

Completed year of service will be rounded up to next in case of more than 6 months of service in relevant year.

Salary includes DA for this purpose. In absence of information average salary of last 3 months is taken 25,000.

123. The salary becomes due on the first day of next month. Hence, salary of Jan becomes taxable in the month of Feb. So, we have take salary for the March 2018 to Feb. 2019.

(40,000 × 4) + (50,000 × 8) = 5,60,000

124. Employer's contribution in excess of 12% is taxable. Salary = (10,000 + 3,000) × 12 × 3% = 4,680.

125. When car is used only for private purpose then it immaterial whether it is below 1.6 litre or above 1.6 litre engine capacity. Valuation in both case is same i.e. Valuation in such case will be = 10% cost of car + Running & maintenance expenses met by employer + Drivers wages – amount recovered from the employee. 60,000 + 18,800 + 22,000 + 24,000 – 19,200 = 1,05,600.

126. As per Section 10 (17), in case Indian citizen who is government employee and working outside India all allowance and perquisites are exempt. Thus, only basic salary is taxable. 1,40,000 × 12 = 16,80,000.

127. Mr. Z's basic salary per month is 48,755. Thus, his annual salary is above ₹ 50,000 and hence he is specified employee. Car perquisite is taxable only for specified employee. If car is 1.6 litre engine capacity or below 1.6 litre engine capacity and is partly used for official purpose and partly for private purpose and expenses are met by employer, then valuation will be 1,800 p.m. and 900 p.m. for driver, if given. Amount recovered from employee is immaterial in this case and cannot be deducted. Thus, Car perquisite = (1,800 + 900) × 12 = 32,400.

129. Employees contribution fully qualifies for deduction u/s 80C even if it is above 12% of salary but to limit specified in Section 80C i.e. up to ₹ 1,50,000.

Salary = 9,00,000 + 2,16,000 = 11,16,000

Employees contribution = 11,16,000 × 16% = 1,78,560 (but will be restricted to ₹ 1,50,000)

130. Mr. P's basic salary per month is 15,750. Thus, his annual salary is above ₹ 50,000 and hence he is specified employee. Car perquisite is taxable only for specified employee. If car is above 1.6 litre engine capacity and is partly used for official purpose and partly for private purpose and expenses are met by employer, then valuation will be 2,400 p.m. and 900 p.m. for driver, if given. Amount recovered from employee is immaterial in this case and cannot be deducted. Thus, Car perquisite = (2,400 + 900) × 12 = 39,600.

131. As per **Section 10 (17)**, in case Indian citizen who is government employee and working outside India all allowance and perquisites are exempt.

Total period of work in India = 8 months

Total period of work outside India = 4 months

Basic salary	(16,000 × 12)	1,92,000
DA in Delhi	(16,000 × 8 × 50%)	64,000
DA in Germany	Exempt u/s 10(17)	-
RFA in Delhi	(1,000 × 8)	8,000
RFA in at Berlin	Exempt u/s 10(17)	-
Car facility at Delhi	(2,400 × 8)	19,200
Car facility at Berlin in Germany	Exempt u/s 10(17)	-
Entertainment allowance received in Germany	Exempt u/s 10(17)	-
Medical reimbursement in Germany	Exempt u/s 10(17)	-
Gross salary		2,83,200

132. Deduction u/s 80C is not available in case of URPF.

133. (600 + 900) × 12 = 18,000

134.

Basic salary	(40,000 × 12)	4,80,000
DA	(4,80,000×50%)	2,40,000
Entertainment allowance	(5,000 × 12)	60,000
Gross salary		7,80,000
(-) Deduction for Entertainment allowance		(5,000)
(-) Standard Deduction		(40,000)
		7,35,000

Entertainment allowance is to be deducted only in case of government employee to the extent of minimum of following three:

(1) Amount Received

(2) 20% of basic.

(3) ₹ 5,000

135. As per **Rule 2BA** of the Income Tax Rules, 1961 deduction in case of compensation received on VRS is available only if the amount received as VRS does not exceed the –

(*a*) Last Salary × 3 months × Completed year of service

(*b*) Last Salary × Balance of months service left before retirement

In other words, if the compensation received on VRS exceeds both the above amounts, exemption is not available. In all other cases exemption is available to the extent of lower of following two –

(1) Amount received as VRS compensation

(2) Amount specified i.e. ₹ 5,00,000

Last Salary × 3 months × Completed year of service	(12,350 × 3 × 20)	7,41,000
Last Salary × Balance of months service left before retirement	(12,350 × 15 × 12)	22,23,000

As, Amount received on VRS compensation i.e. ₹ 5,70,000 does not exceed both the above amount exemption will be available to the extent of lower of following two –

(1) Amount received as VRS compensation i.e. ₹ 5,70,000

(2) Amount specified i.e. ₹ 5,00,000

Taxable amount = 5,70,000 – 5,00,000 = 70,000

136. 42,000 + 15,460 + 12,540 + 24,000 – 18,000 = 76,000

137.

HRA Received (9,750 × 12)	1,17,000
(-) Exempt	(22,920)
Taxable HRA	94,080

Minimum of following three is exempt:

(1) Amount received		1,17,000
(2) Rent paid – 10% of salary	(96,000 – 73,080)	22,920
(3) 50% of salary		3,65,400

Salary for the purpose of HRA = 6,30,000 + 1,00,800 = 7,30,800

138. Employers contribution to Approved Superannuation Fund is exempt up to ₹ 1,50,000. Taxable Amount = 1,75,000 – 1,50,000 = 25,000.

139. (900 + 900) × 12 = 21,600

140. Students are advised solve at their own end using the hint of 135.

141.

HRA Received	(2,500 × 5) + (3,200 × 7)	34,900
(-) Exempt	(288 + 3,795)	(4,083)
Taxable HRA		30,817

Month	Basic	DA	Commission	HRA	Rent
April	14,180	600	2,000	2,500	1,750
May	14,180	600	2,000	2,500	1,750
June	14,180	600	2,000	2,500	1,750
July	14,180	600	2,000	2,500	1,750
Aug	15,750	600	2,000	2,500	1,750
Sep	15,750	600	2,000	3,200	1,750
Oct	15,750	600	2,000	3,200	1,750
Nov	15,750	600	2,000	3,200	3,100
Dec	15,750	600	2,000	3,200	3,100
Jan	15,750	600	2,000	3,200	3,100
Feb	15,750	600	2,000	3,200	-
March	15,750	600	2,000	3,200	-

Calculation of exempted HRA

	April to July	Aug	Sep to Oct	Nov to Jan	Feb to March
HRA Received	10,000	2,500	6,400	9,600	No exemption since no rent is paid for this period
Rent paid – 10% of salary	7,000 – 6,712 = 288	1,750 – 1,835 = 0	3,500 – 3,670 = 0	9,300 – 5,505 = 3,795	
40% of salary	26,848	7,340	14,680	22,020	

142. 40,000 – (2,400 × 12) = 11,200

143. Students are advised solve at their own end using the hint of 135.

145. Unlike RPF, interest in case of URPF is not taxable each year.

146.

Uncommuted pension	(5,600 × 11.5)		64,400
Commuted pension received		3,00,0000	
(-) Exempt	$\left[\frac{1}{2} \times \frac{3,00,000}{60\%}\right]$	(2,50,000)	50,000
(-) Standard Deduction			(40,000)
			74,400

147.

Basic salary	(20,000 × 5) + (25,000 × 7)		2,75,000
Employers contribution in excess of 12% of salary	(2,75,000 × 3%)		8,250
Children education allowance received	(500 × 12)	6,000	
(-) Exempt	(100 × 2 × 12)	(2,400)	3,600
Hostel expenditure allowance received	(380 × 12)	4,560	
(-) Exempt	(190 × 2 × 12)	(4,560)	Nil
Tiffin allowance	Full taxable		5 000
Employment tax paid by the employer			2.500
Gross salary			2,94.350
(-) Deduction for employment tax			(2,500)
(-) Standard deduction			(40,000)
Net taxable salary			2,51,850

148.

Uncommuted pension	(5,600 × 11.5)		64.400
Commuted pension received		3,00,0000	
(-) Exempt	$\left[\frac{1}{3} \times \frac{3,00,000}{60\%}\right]$	(1,66,667)	1,33,333
(-) Standard deduction			(40,000)
Taxable income under the head salary			1,57,733

149.

Basic salary	(10,000 × 10)		1,00,000
DA	(3,000 × 10)		30,000
City compensatory allowance	(2,000 × 10)		20,000
Night duty allowance	(1,000 × 10)		10,000
Pension	(10,000 × 30% × 2)		6,000
Leave encashment received		75,000	
(-) Exempt u/s 10(10AA)		(50,000)	25,000
Gratuity received		50,000	
(-) Exempt u/s 10(10)(*iii*)		(25,000)	25,000
Gross salary			2,16,000

Minimum of following four is exempt as leave encashment:

(1) Amount received	75,000
(2) Average salary of last 10 months	1,00,000
(3) Cash equivalent on unavailed leaves on the basis of 30 days (150/30) × 10,000	50,000
(4) Amount specified	3,00,000

Salary for this purpose = Basic + DA (forming part of retirement benefit)

= 1,00,000 + Nil

= 1,00,000

Leave entitled (45 days × 5 years)	225 days
(-) Leave availed	-
Leave unavailed	225 days

Leave entitled on 30 days basis (30 days × 5 years)	150 days
(-) Leave availed	-
Leave unavailed	150 days

Minimum of following three is exempt gratuity:

(1) Amount received	50,000
(2) $\left[\text{Average Salary} \times \frac{1}{2} \times \text{Completed year of service}\right]\left[10{,}000 \times \frac{1}{2} \times 5\right]$	25,000
(3) Amount specified	10,00,000

In absence of specific information employee has to be treated as not covered under the Payment of Gratuity Act, 1972.

150.

Gratuity Received	2,40,000
(-) Exempt u/s 10(10)(*iii*)	(1,72,272)
Taxable Gratuity	67,728

Minimum of following three is exempt gratuity:

(1) Amount received	2,40,000
(2) $\left[\text{Average Salary} \times \frac{1}{2} \times \text{Completed year of service}\right]\left[14{,}356 \times \frac{1}{2} \times 24\right]$	1,72,272
(3) Amount specified	10,00,000

Salary for last 10 months = Basic + DA (forming part of retirement benefit)

$$= (9{,}000 \times 3) + (10{,}000 \times 7) + 46{,}560$$
$$= 1{,}43{,}560$$

$$\text{Average Salary} = \frac{1{,}43{,}560}{10} = 14{,}356$$

HINTS FOR PAST EXAMINATION MCQs

1. *Minimum of following three is exempt as gratuity:*

(1) Amount received	75,000
(2) $\left[\text{Last Salary} \times \frac{15}{26} \times \text{Completed year of service}\right]\left[3{,}000 \times \frac{15}{26} \times 31\right]$	53,654
(3) Amount specified	20,00,000

Salary = Basic + DA (all, as he is covered under Payment of Gratuity Act, 1972)

Salary = 2,400 + 600 = 3,000

2.

Commuted pension received		3,60,0000
(-) Exempt	$\left[\frac{1}{3} \times \frac{3,60,000}{60\%}\right]$	(2,00,000)
		1,60,000

3.

Basic Salary [(15,600 + 6,000) × 8]	1,72,800
DA (1,72,800 × 107%)	1,84,896
Standard deduction	(40,000)
Total income	3,17,696
Tax on total income	3,385
(-) Rebate u/s 87A	(2,500)
	885
(+) Education cess @ 4%	35
	920

4. In case of handicapped employee transport allowance is exempt up to ₹ 3,200. Hence entire allowance is exempt. Actual expenditure incurred does not have any significance.

5.

Cost of Honda City car	10,00,000
(-) Dep for 1st year @ 20% on WDV	(2,00,000)
	8,00,000
(-) Dep for 2nd year @ 20% on WDV	(1,60,000)
	6,40,000
(-) Dep for 3rd year @ 20% on WDV	(1,28,000)
	5,12,000
(-) Dep for 4th year @ 20% on WDV	(1,02,400)
	4,09,600
(-) Amount recovered	(2,10,000)
	1,99,600

6. 15% of salary or actual hire charges, whichever is less.

- 15% of salary ₹ 41,760
- Actual hire charges ₹ 50,000.

7. Children education allowance is amount received per month per child or ₹ 100 whichever is less that too only for two child. Thus, for one child it is taxable 80 × 12 = 960.

9. (4,000 – 600) × 12 = 40,800.

10. Loan up to ₹ 20,000 is exempt. No interest on it is taxable.

11. Gift in excess of ₹ 5,000 is taxable.

12. 12,000 × 9 × 15% = 16,200

13. Section 10(10CC) provides exemption in respect of tax paid by employer on the non-monetary perquisite. Hence such tax paid shall not form part of salary. Hence, total income = 8,60,000 – 1,20,000 = 7,40,000

14.

Uncommuted pension	(1,500 × 8) + (750 × 3)		14,250
Commuted pension received		75,000	
(-) Exempt	$\left[\frac{1}{3} \times \frac{75,000}{50\%}\right]$	(50,000)	25,000
			39,250

15. As per **Section 10(17)**, in case Indian citizen who is government employee and working outside India all allowance and perquisites are exempt. Hence, as per data given in problem, only basic salary is taxable. He will also get standard deduction of ₹ 40,000.

16.

1.4.2014 to 31.3.2015 15,000 p.m.

1.4.2015 to 31.3.2016 16,000 p.m.

1.4.2016 to 31.3.2017 17,000 p.m.

1.4.2017 to 31.3.2018 18,000 p.m.

1.4.2018 to 31.3.2019 20,000 p.m.

17.

Commuted pension received	12,00,0000
(-) Exempt $\left[\frac{1}{3} \times \frac{12,00,000}{40\%}\right]$	(10,00,000)
Taxable commuted pension	2,00,000

18.

Medical allowance is fully taxable.

20.

Minimum of following three is exempt as HRA:

(1) HRA received	2,40,000
(2) Rent paid less 10% of salary (1,20,000 – 24,000)	96,000
(3) 50% of salary	1,20,000

21. 60,000 × 9 × 15% = 81,000

23.

Cost on 30.6.2017	8,00,000
(-) Depreciation 1.7.2017 to 30.6.2018 *[Since car is sold on 10.6.2018 i.e. before completion of year; no depreciation can be deducted]*	-
(-) Amount recovered from employee	(6,00,000)
Taxable perquisite	2,00,000

24. (2,000 – 1,600) × 12 = 4,800

25.

Leave encashment received	3,00,000
(-) Exempt u/s 10(10AA)	(2,40,000)
Taxable leave encashment	60,000

Minimum of following four is exempt as leave encashment:

(1) Amount received	3,00,000
(2) Average salary of last 10 months	2,40,000
(3) Cash equivalent on unavailed leaves on the basis of 30 days	*No data available*
(4) Amount specified	3,00,000

Since for clause (3) no data available, minimum figure can be taken ₹ 2,40,000.

29. For a person employed in transport organization minimum of following two is exempt:

(1) 70% of the allowance (15,000 × 12 × 70%) ₹ 1,26,000

(2) ₹ 10,000 p.m. (10,000 × 12) ₹ 1,20,000

31. (2,400 + 900) × 12 = 39,600

34. 1,50,000 × 10% × 9/12 = 11,250

39.

HRA Received	(10,000 × 12)	1,20,000
(-) Exempt		(56,000)
Taxable HRA		64,000

Calculation of exempted HRA:

HRA Received	1,20,000
Rent paid – 10% of salary [96,000 – 40,000]	**56,000**
40% of salary	1,60,000

40. Population of Madurai as per 2012 census is between 10 to 15 lakh; hence percentage of salary to be adopted for the purpose of valuation of perquisite would be 10%.

42. Cost of education for other children is ₹ 1,800 per month *i.e.* above prescribed sum of ₹ 1,000; hence fully taxable. 1,800 × 12 = 21,600.

CHAPTER 4

INCOME FROM HOUSE PROPERTY

MCQs ON THEORY

1. Which of the following Section of the Income Tax Act, 1961 charge tax on income from house property?

(A) Section 20

(B) Section 21

(C) Section 22

(D) Section 20A

2. Which of the following statement is true in relation taxability of composite rent?

I. As per Section 56(2)(iii), if letting of property is inseparable from letting of other assets then entire income is taxable as 'income from house property'.

II. If the main intention of the house property is to exploit the immovable property by way of complex commercial activities, then composite rent will be taxable under the head 'income from house property'.

Select the correct answer from the options given below -

(A) Statement I is correct while statement II is incorrect

(B) Statement II is correct while statement I is incorrect

(C) Statement I and II both are correct

(D) Statement I and II both are incorrect

3. Which of the following is required to be considered while calculating 'expected rent'?

(1) Notional rent

(2) Municipal value

(3) Standard rent

(4) Period of vacancy

(5) Fair rent

Select the correct answer from the options given below -

(A) (1), (3) & (4)

(B) (2), (4) & (5)

(C) (5), (2) & (3)

(D) (4), (5) & (2)

4. Which of the following can be treated as self occupied property?

1. Property let out but the assessee to this employer and employer allot such property to employee as a rent free accommodation.
2. House property which cannot be occupied by the owner by reason of the fact that owing to employment or business carried on at any other place, he has to reside at that other place in a building not belonging to him.

Select the correct answer from the options given below -

(A) 1 only

(B) 2 only

(C) Both 1 and 2

(D) Neither 1 nor 2

5. If assessee own two house and both are self occupied then -

(A) Both house are exempt

(B) Both houses are deemed to be let out and house having higher house property income is liable to tax.

(C) Both houses are deemed to be let out and house having lower house property income is liable to tax.

(D) At the option of assessee one house can be treated as self occupied whether such house has higher income as compared to other house or not

6. Deduction from 'Net Annual Value' is available under -

(A) Section 23

(B) Section 24

(C) Section 25A

(D) Section 25AB

7. Standard deduction of ______ is allowed while calculating income under the head house property.

(A) 30% of GAV

(B) 25% of NAV

(C) 30% of NAV

(D) 25% of GAV

8. If the property is let out throughout the year, deduction of interest from NAV is -

(A) Maximum ₹ 2,00,000 or ₹ 30,000 as case may be depending upon some conditions

(B) Interest actually paid during the year to the bank

(C) Interest of any amount due whether paid or not to the bank

(D) None of the above is correct

9. Deduction of pre-construction interest is allowed in ______ equal instalments.

(A) 4

(B) 5

(C) 6

(D) 3

10. Which of the following statement is correct?

(*a*) Service fee and other charges in respect of borrowed money treated as 'interest' and hence allowed to be deducted from NAV while calculating income from house property.

(*b*) Interest on unpaid interest is allowed to be deducted from NAV while calculating income from house property.

(*c*) Unrealized rent when received is liable to tax after deduction of 30% of such amount.

Select the correct answer from the options given below -

(A) (a) and (c)

(B) (b) and (c)

(C) (a) and (b)

(D) (a) only

11. In case of house property which is let out but remained vacant for some period during the year, Gross Annual Value (GAV) will be -

(A) AR, if AR > PER

(B) PER, if AR < PER

(C) ER, if AR < PER

(D) (A) or (C)

12. If the property remain vacant for the whole year then -

(A) Annual value of such property shall be equal to 'expected rent'.

(B) Annual value of such property shall be equal to 'municipal value'.

(C) Annual value of such property shall be equal to 'expected rent' or 'municipal value' whichever is less subject to 'standard rent'.

(D) Annual value of such property shall be NIL.

13. Unrealized rent received subsequently is liable to tax under ______ of the Income Tax Act, 1961.

(A) Section 24A

(B) Section 24B

(C) Section 25A

(D) Section 25AB

14. Which of the following statement(s) is/are false in relation to property owned by co-owners?

(I) Where share of each co-owner in property is not definite and ascertainable then such person shall be assessed as 'body of individuals' or 'Firm' at the option of assessing officer.

(II) In case of self-occupied property, annual value of each co-owner shall not be NIL and deemed to be let out and taxed accordingly.

Select the correct answer from the options given below -

(A) Both (I) & (II)

(B) (II)

(C) (I)

(D) Neither (I) nor (II)

15. Identify which of the following statement(s) is/are true (✓) and which are false (×)?

(*a*) If a person has two house properties then annual value of both properties shall be NIL.

(*b*) Municipal tax is allowed to be deducted from net annual value.

(*c*) Gross annual value of the property can exceed standard rent in certain circumstances.

(*d*) Maximum deduction for property which is partly let out and partly self occupied during the year is ₹ 2,00,000.

Select the correct answer from the options given below -

	(*a*)	(*b*)	(*c*)	(*d*)
(A)	×	✓	×	✓
(B)	✓	×	✓	×
(C)	✓	✓	✓	✓
(D)	×	×	×	×

16. Unrealized rent is to be deducted from _____

(A) Income from house property

(B) Net Annual Value

(C) Gross Annual Value

(D) None of the above

17. Which of the following can have negative annual value?

1. Let out property
2. One self occupied property
3. Deemed let out property

4. One property which could not be occupied due employment elsewhere
5. Property which is partly let out and partly self occupied.

Select the correct answer from the options given below -

(A) 5, 3, 1
(B) 2, 4, 1
(C) 2 & 5
(D) All of the above

18. As per Section 25A of the Income Tax Act, 1961, if unrealized rent is received subsequently -

(A) Entire sum is liable to tax without any deduction
(B) Sum so received is liable to tax after deduction of 30% of the amount received.
(C) Will be added in gross annual value to arrive at net annual value.
(D) None of the above

19. In which of the following cases transferor deemed to be owner of the house property?

(*i*) Transfer of house to minor married daughter
(*ii*) Transfer of house to spouse in agreement to live apart.
(*iii*) Transfer of house on lease for 20 years. However, lease is to be renewed every year.

Select the correct answer from the options given below -

(A) (i), (ii) and (ii)
(B) (i) and (ii)
(C) (iii) only
(D) (i) only

20. Which of the following house property is not liable to be taxed under the head income from house property?

(1) Farm house
(2) House property owned by Trade Union

(3) House property owned by Political Party

(4) Property used for carrying profession of Company Secretary.

Select the correct answer from the options given below -

(A) (1) & (4) only

(B) (2) & (3) only

(C) (3), (1) & (2)

(D) (1), (2), (3) & (4)

21. Arrear of rent received is liable to taxed as income from house property as per _____ of the Income Tax Act, 1961.

(A) Section 25BA

(B) Section 25BB

(C) Section 25A

(D) Section 25AAA

22. In case of property which is deemed to be let out, which of the following deduction are allowed u/s 24 of the Income Tax Act, 1961?

(I) Collection charges

(II) Insurance premium

(III) Ground rent

(IV) Annual charge

(V) Interest on money borrowed

(VI) Vacancy allowance

(VII) Standard deduction @ 30%

Select the correct answer from the options given below -

(A) (IV), (V) & (VII)

(B) (V) & (VII)

(C) (II), (IV), (V) & (VII)

(D) (I), (III), (IV), (V) & (VII)

23. After allowing deduction u/s 24 of the Income Tax Act, 1961, which of the following type of property may have loss under the head house property?

(1) One property which could not be occupied due employment elsewhere

(2) Let out property

(3) Deemed let out property

(4) One self occupied property

(5) Property which is partly let out and partly self occupied

Select the correct answer from the options given below -

(A) (5), (3), (1)

(B) (1), (2), (4)

(C) (3), (4), (2), (1)

(D) (5), (3), (1), (4), (2)

24. In which of the following case house property located outside India is taxable?

(*a*) If the owner is Ordinary Resident and rent is received outside India.

(*b*) If the owner is Not-ordinary Resident and rent is received outside India.

(*c*) If the owner is Non Resident and rent is received in India.

Select the correct answer from the options given below -

(A) (a) & (b)

(B) (b) & (c)

(C) (a) & (c)

(D) Any of the above

25. Which of the following condition is required to be fulfilled for deduction of interest paid on money borrowed outside India?

(1) Money is borrowed for construction of self occupied house.

(2) Tax is deducted at source on such interest

(3) There is regular payment of loan installment by the assessee

Select the correct answer from the options given below -

(A) (1) & (3)

(B) (2) only

(C) (3) & (2)

(D) (1), (2) & (3)

26. Which of the following is taxable under the head 'income from house property'?

(1) Rent from vacant land

(2) Rent received by sub-letting of property

(3) Notional rent own shop

(4) Rent received outside India by Ordinary Resident for a property located outside India.

Select the correct answer from the options given below.

(A) (2), (3) & (4)

(B) (4) only

(C) (1) & (4)

(D) None of the above

27. Match the following:

(1) Property used for own business	(I) Income from other sources
(2) Income from sub-letting of house	(II) Income under the head PGBP
(3) Standard deduction	(III) 50%
(4) Letting of property incidental to main business	(IV) Depreciation can be claimed
	(V) 30%

Select the correct answer from the options given below -

	(1)	**(2)**	**(3)**	**(4)**
(A)	(IV)	(II)	(V)	(I)
(B)	(II)	(I)	(III)	(IV)
(C)	(IV)	(I)	(V)	(II)
(D)	(IV)	(II)	(III)	(I)

PRACTICAL MCQs

28. Mr. Suresh owns a big house property which is divided in 4 parts equally. Part I (25%) is self occupied, PART II (25%) is used by him for his profession, Part III (25%) is let out to Mandar for running grocery shop and Part IV let to Mustafa for residential purpose. In relation to these facts which of the following statement is correct.

(A) Out of the total property 75% portion of the property is taxable under the head 'income from house property'.

(B) Out of the total property 25% portion of the property is taxable under the head 'income from house property'.

(C) Out of the total property 50% portion of the property is taxable under the head 'income from house property'.

(D) Out of the total property 100% portion of the property is taxable under the head 'income from house property'.

29. Raja owns a house property which has been let out to Rani on a monthly rent of ₹ 8,500. Rani left the house after 10 months and the house remained vacant for next 2 months. Other details of the house for the *whole year* are as follows:

Fair rent = 1,08,000

Standard rent = 99,000

Municipal value = 1,00,000

Municipal taxes paid by Raja is ₹ 12,500 which includes ₹ 2,500 for last year.

Compute the Net Annual value of the house.

(A) ₹ 72,500

(B) ₹ 70,000

(C) ₹ 86,500

(D) ₹ 75,000

30. Ravi started construction of house on 1.11.2017. He raised loan of ₹ 10,00,000 at 12% on the same date. He took further loan on 1.10.2018 for ₹ 12,00,000 at same rate of interest. What is the interest allowable u/s 24 of the Income Tax Act, 1961 if construction was completed by 31.3.2019?

(A) ₹ 2,02,000

(B) ₹ 1,92,000

(C) ₹ 2,42,000

(D) ₹ 2,00,000

31. Sultan owned house at Satara which was occupied by him for the purpose of his residence. He was transferred to Pune in June 2018 and thereafter he let out the property with effect from 1.7.2018 on monthly rent of 6,000. Corporation tax was ₹ 12,000 out of which he paid 50% before 31.3.2019. Interest on money borrowed is ₹ 40,000. What is the income of Sultan from house property?

(A) Income ₹ 6,200

(B) Loss ₹ 6,400

(C) Income ₹ 16,200

(D) Loss ₹ 5,400

32. Nalini submits following details in respect house which is self occupied:

Municipal value per annum	2,30,000
Fair rent per annum	3,50,000
Standard rent per annum	3,30,000
Municipal taxes (outstanding)	8%
Interest (outstanding)	1,10,000

What is Nalini's income/loss under the head house property?

(A) Loss ₹ 1,28,400

(B) Income ₹ 2,01,600

(C) Loss ₹ 1,06,400

(D) Loss ₹ 1,10,000

33. From the following details calculate the income/loss from house property:

Expected rent for year	1,05,000
Annual rent	90,000
Unrealized rent	7,500
Period of vacancy	3 months

Municipal taxes paid by tenant	4,450
Municipal taxes paid by owner	3,000
Interest on money borrowed	13,560

(A) Income ₹ 57,840

(B) Income ₹ 39,465

(C) Income ₹ 42,090

(D) Loss ₹ 8,640

34. Ramesh owns house at Mumbai which has two units. Unit I is self occupied and Unit II is rented for ₹ 16,000 p.m. The rented unit remained vacant for 2 months. Other details are of the house are as follows:

Standard rent	3,24,000
Municipal valuation	3,80,000
Fair rent	3,70,000
Municipal tax	15%
Interest on borrowed capital	3,000 p.m.

What is Ramesh total income from house property?

(A) 68,025

(B) 74,050

(C) 56,050

(D) 50,425

35. Karan owns a house in Delhi. The house has two identical units. First unit is self occupied by the Karan while other is rented at ₹ 12,000 p.m. the rented unit remained vacant for 3 months. The standard rent, municipal value and fair rent was ₹ 2,20,000, 2,44,000 & 2,35,000 p.a. respectively for the entire house. Karan paid municipal taxes which was 12% of municipal value. Interest on borrowed capital was ₹ 2,000 p.m. Compute income from house property.

(A) 53,352

(B) 41,352

(C) 50,452

(D) 42,652

36. Madhuri, resident individual owns a house in USA. She receives rent of $ 2,000 per month. She paid municipal taxes $ 1,500. What is income of Madhuri under the head house property?

Assume $ 1 = ₹ 45.

(A) ₹ 10,12,500

(B) ₹ 7,05,500

(C) ₹ 6,87,500

(D) ₹ 7,08,750

37. Gayatri owns a two storied house in Mumbai. Ground floor is used for her residence and first floor is let out at a monthly rent of ₹ 10,000. Standard rent for each floor is ₹ 11,000 per month. Municipal taxes paid for the house amounts to ₹ 7,500. Gayatri had constructed house by taking loan from bank on 20.6.2015. She paid loan ₹ 54,000 including interest of ₹ 24,000. Compute income of Gayatri from house property.

(A) 65,775

(B) 55,475

(C) 69,375

(D) 57,375

38. Mr. Z took loan from bank for ₹ 12,75,000 @ 8% on 1st July 2014. Construction of house was completed in May 2017. Entire loan is still outstanding. Calculate preconstruction interest to be deducted for the PY 2018-2019.

(A) 56,100

(B) 61,200

(C) 58,400

(D) 62,200

39. Sita and Gita are co-owner of house which has municipal value ₹ 1,60,000 and fair rent of the house is ₹ 1,50,000. Standard rent is ₹ 1,70,000. Rent received for the house during the year is ₹ 1,80,000. Interest on bank loan taken for construction of house property is ₹ 25,000 out of which ₹ 21,000 has been paid. Interest on unpaid interest is ₹ 450. A fresh loan was taken to repay earlier loan and interest on this loan is ₹ 5,000. Tenant paid the municipal taxes

₹ 5,100. How much income from house property will be taxable in the hands of Gita?

(A) ₹ 46,000

(B) ₹ 48,000

(C) ₹ 47,775

(D) ₹ 45,450

40. Mr. Z is a Practicing Company Secretary. He owns a house in Pune. Half portion of the house is let out for residential purpose on monthly rent of ₹ 8,000. However, this portion remained vacant for 3 months. ¼ portion is used by Mr. Z for his profession while remaining ¼ portion is used for his own residence. Other expenses were: Municipal taxes - ₹ 10,000; Repairs - ₹ 5,000, Interest on loan for renovation of house - ₹ 40,000; Fire insurance premium - ₹ 4,000.

What is the income from house property?

(A) ₹ 26,900

(B) ₹ 16,900

(C) ₹ 22,900

(D) ₹ 23,400

ANSWERS:

1.	(C)	**2.**	(D)	**3.**	(C)	**4.**	(D)	**5.**	(D)	**6.**	(B)	**7.**	(C)
8.	(C)	**9.**	(B)	**10.**	(A)	**11.**	(D)	**12.**	(D)	**13.**	(C)	**14.**	(A)
15.	(D)	**16.**	(C)	**17.**	(A)	**18.**	(B)	**19.**	(C)	**20.**	(D)	**21.**	(C)
22.	(B)	**23.**	(D)	**24.**	(C)	**25.**	(B)	**26.**	(B)	**27.**	(C)	**28.**	(A)
29.	(A)	**30.**	(D)	**31.**	(A)	**32.**	(D)	**33.**	(A)	**34.**	(C)	**35.**	(B)
36.	(D)	**37.**	(D)	**38.**	(A)	**39.**	(B)	**40.**	(B)				

HINTS FOR PRACTICAL MCQs

28. Part of the house used for business or profession is not taxable and other parts of the house are liable to be taxed including self-occupied portion.

29.

ER 99,000	PER 82,500
AR 85,000	

$$PER = 99{,}000 \times \frac{10}{12} = 82{,}500$$

In case of property which is let but remains vacant GAV will be

AR, if AR > PER and

ER, if AR < PER

Thus, GAV for given case = 85,000

NAV = 85,000 - 12,500 = 72,500.

30. Interest on first loan (1.4.2018 to 31.3.2019) 10,00,000 × 12% = 1,20,000

Interest on second loan (1.10.2018 to 31.3.2019) 12,00,000 × 12% × 6/12 = 72,000

Construction of house was completed by 31.3.2019. Thus, interest for the year 2017 - 2018 will be pre-construction interest. Such pre-construction interest is allowed in 5 equal instalments.

1.11.2017 to 31.3.2018 (10,00,000 × 12% × 5/12) = 50,000

50,000 × 1/5 = 10,000

Total interest for year 2018-2019 = 1,20,000 + 72,000 + 10,000 = 2,02,000.

Since, property is self occupied interest of ₹ 2,02,000 will be restricted to ₹ 2,00,000.

31. This property is partly let out and partly self occupied. In this case GAV will be ER or AR whichever is more.

ER = 72,000 (6,000 × 12) *[Calculated on the basis of actual rent]*

AR = 54,000 (6,000 × 9)

Thus, GAV = 72,000

NAV = 72,000 - 6,000 = 66,000

Income from house property = 66,000 - 19,800 (30% of NAV) - 40,000 (interest) = 6,200.

32. Nalini's house is self occupied property. In this case NAV will be ZERO.

Income from house property = 0 - 1,10,000 = - 1,10,000. Interest is deductible on due basis.

33.

ER 1,05,000	PER 78,750
AR 60,000	

$PER = 1,05,000 \times \frac{9}{12} = 78,750;$

$AR = [90,000 \times 9/12] - 7,500 = 60,000$

In case of property which is let out but remains vacant GAV will be

AR, if AR > PER and

ER, if AR < PER

Thus, GAV for given case = 1,05,000

NAV = 1,05,000 - 3,000 = 1,02,000.

Income from house property = 1,02,000 - 30,600 - 13,560 = 57,840

34. Unit I: In case of self occupied property NAV is Nil.

Income from house property = 0 - 18,000 = - 18,000.

Unit II:

ER 1,62,000	PER 1,35,000
AR 1,60,000	

$PER = 1,62,000 \times \frac{10}{12} = 1,35,000$

In case of property which is let out but remains vacant GAV will be -

AR, if AR > PER and

ER, if AR < PER

Thus, GAV for given case = 1,60,000

NAV = 1,60,000 - 28,500 = 1,31,500.

Income from house property = 1,31,500 - 39,450 - 18,000 - 18,000 = 56,050

35. Unit I: In case of self occupied property NAV is Nil.

Income from house property = 0 - 12,000 = - 12,000.

Unit II:

ER 1,10,000	PER 82,500
AR 1,08,000	

$PER = 1,10,000 \times \frac{9}{12} = 82,500$

In case of property which is let out but remains vacant GAV will be -

AR, if AR > PER and

ER, if AR < PER

Thus, GAV for given case = 1,08,000

NAV = 1,08,000 - 14,640 = 93,360.

Income from house property = 93,360 - 28,008 - 12,000 - 12,000 = 41,352.

37. Floor 1: NAV = 1,20,000 - 3,750 = 1,16,250

1,16,250 - 34,875 - 12,000 = 69,375

Ground Floor: 0 - 12,000 = - 12,000

Income from house property = 69,375 - 12,000 = 57,375

38.

Interest payable for the various years:

2014 - 2015	(12,75,000 × 8% × 9/12)	76,500
2015 - 2016	(12,75,000 × 8%)	1,02,000
2016 - 2017	(12,75,000 × 8%)	1,02,000
2017 - 2018	(12,75,000 × 8%)	1,02,000
2018 - 2019	(12,75,000 × 8%)	1,02,000

Since, construction of house is completed in May 2017 i.e. in year 2017-2018, interest payable up to year 2016-2017 will be pre-construction interest and 1/5th of 2,80,500 i.e. 56,100 will be allowed from PY 2017-2018 to 2021-2022 in 5 equal instalments.

39. GAV = 1,80,000;

Income from house property = 1,80,000 - 54,000 - 25,000 - 5,000 = 96,000

Gita's share = 96,000 × ½ = 48,000.

40. Let out portion (50%): *(If fair rent is not given it is calculated on the basis of actual rent)*

ER	96,000	PER	72,000
AR	72,000		

$$PER = 96,000 \times \frac{9}{12} = 72,000$$

In case of property which is let out but remains vacant GAV will be -

AR, if AR > PER and

ER, if AR ≤ PER

Thus, GAV for given case = 72,000

NAV = 72,000 - 5,000 = 67,000

Income from let out portion = 67,000 - 20,100 - 20,000 = 26,900

Portion of house used for profession (25%): Not liable to tax under the head income from house property.

Self occupied portion (25%): NAV = 0

Loss from self occupied portion = 0 - 10,000 = - 10,000

Income from house property = 26,900 - 10,000 = 16,900.

PAST EXAMINATION MCQs

1. Dec 2014: Sajal is the owner of a house property covered under the Rent Control Act. Municipal value ₹ 30,000, actual rent ₹ 25,000, fair rent ₹ 36,000 and standard rent is ₹ 28,000. The gross annual value of the house property will be —

(A) ₹ 30,000

(B) ₹ 25,000

(C) ₹ 36,000

(D) ₹ 28,000

2. Dec 2014: Composite rent of let-out house property is taxable as—

(A) Profits and gains from business or Profession

(B) Income from other sources

(C) Income from house property

(D) Either (A) or (B) above depending upon certain conditions

3. Dec 2014: Suresh owns two house properties. First property was used half for running his business and the other half was let-out at ₹ 4,000 p.m. The second property was wholly used as a residence by Suresh. Municipal values of the two properties were the same at ₹ 72,000 each p.a. and local taxes @ 10%. Suresh's income from house property for the PY 2018-2019 will be —

(A) ₹ 33,600

(B) ₹ 31,080

(C) ₹ 28,560

(D) ₹ 62,160

4. June 2015: Rohit owns a house property in Delhi which he wants to give on rent. He seeks your help to determine the reasonable expected rent when monthly municipal value is ₹ 20,000, fair rent ₹ 25,000 and standard rent ₹ 22,000. The reasonable expected rent will be computed with reference to following amount p.m. —

(A) ₹ 22,000
(B) ₹ 20,000
(C) ₹ 25,000
(D) None of the above

5. Dec 2015: When a house property is let-out throughout the year for a monthly rent of ₹ 22,000 and municipal tax paid for current year is ₹ 24,000 and for the earlier year paid now is ₹ 16,000, the income from house property would be —

(A) ₹ 1,68,000
(B) ₹ 1,56,800
(C) ₹ 1,84,800
(D) ₹ 2,24,000

6. Dec 2015: When share of each co-owner in a house property is not definite, the income from such property shall be —

(A) Taxed equally
(B) Exempt from tax
(C) Taxed as association of persons
(D) Taxed as body of individuals

7. Dec 2015: Ramesh let-out his house on 1.4.2018 on rent of ₹ 15,000 p.m. The fair rent and the municipal value of house are ₹ 13,500 p.m. and ₹ 16,000 p.m. respectively. Municipal taxes paid for the year were ₹ 12,000. Income from house property for the AY 2019-2020 will be —

(A) ₹ 1,26,000
(B) ₹ 1,76,000
(C) ₹ 1,05,000
(D) None of the above

8. June 2016: Ms. Padmaja let out a property for ₹ 20,000 per month during the year 2018-2019. The municipal tax on the let-out property was enhanced retrospectively. Hence, she paid ₹ 60,000 as municipal tax which included arrears of municipal tax of ₹ 45,000. Her income from house property is —

(A) ₹ 80,000

(B) ₹ 1,57,500

(C) ₹ 1,26,000

(D) ₹ 36,500

9. June 2016: The construction of a house was completed on 31st January, 2019. The owner of the house took a loan of ₹ 20,00,000 @ 6% p.a. on 1st May 2018 In this case the deduction allowable for the previous year 2018-2019 towards interest on borrowings is —

(A) ₹ 22,000

(B) ₹ 24,000

(C) ₹ 1,10,000

(D) None of the above

10. Dec 2016: The municipal value of a property is ₹ 2,10,000. Fair rent is ₹ 1,90,000 standard rent is ₹ 1,80,000 and the actual rent is ₹ 2,40,000. The gross annual value of the property would be -

(A) ₹ 1,80,000

(B) ₹ 1,90,000

(C) ₹ 2,40,000

(D) ₹ 2,10,000

11. June 2017: Mr. Ahmed acquired a property in April, 2018 for self-residential use. The loan interest payable to State Bank of India for the financial year 2018-2019 amounts to ₹ 2,10,000. The amount eligible for deduction under section 24 is:

(A) ₹ 30,000

(B) ₹ 2,00,000

(C) ₹ 2,10,000

(D) ₹ 1,50,000

12. June 2017: A borrowed ₹ 5,00,000 @ 12% p.a. on 1.4.2014 for construction of house property which was completed on 15.3.2018. The amount is still unpaid. The deduction of interest for previous year 2018-2019 shall be:

(A) ₹ 60,000

(B) ₹ 96,000

(C) ₹ 1,80,000

(D) ₹ 2,40,000

13. Dec 2017: When a house property is let out for a monthly rent of ₹ 25,000 during the financial year 2018-2019 and maintenance expenses by way of salary to sweeper and watchman is ₹ 6,000 per month, the income from house property would be:

(A) ₹ 2,28,000

(B) ₹ 2,10,000

(C) ₹ 3,00,000

(D) ₹ 2,50,000

14. Dec 2017: Mr. Bala transferred his let out residential property to his wife by way of gift settlement. During the financial year 2018-2019, she earned rental income of ₹ 30,000 per month. She made fixed deposit in a bank out of such rental income and earned interest income during the year of ₹ 21,000. The total amount of income liable for clubbing in the hands of Mr. Bala for the assessment year 2018-2019 is:

(A) Nil

(B) ₹ 21,000

(C) ₹ 2,52,000

(D) ₹ 2,73,000

ANSWERS:

1.	(D)	**2.**	(D)	**3.**	(B)	**4.**	(A)	**5.**	(B)	**6.**	(C)	**7.**	(A)
8.	(C)	**9.**	(C)	**10.**	(C)	**11.**	(B)	**12.**	(B)	**13.**	(B)	**14.**	(A)

HINTS FOR PAST EXAMINATION MCQs

3. House I: Part I used for business and hence not liable to tax.

Part II: GAV = 4,000 × 12 = 48,000; NAV = 48,000 - 3,600 = 44,400

Income = 44,400 - 13,320 = 31,080

House II: Self occupied.

NAV = 0

5. 22,000 × 12 - 24,000 - 16,000 - 67,200 = 1,56,800

7. 16,000 × 12 - 12,000 - 54,000 = 1,26,000

8.

Gross annual value (20,000 × 12)	2,40,000
(-) Municipal tax	(60,000)
Net annual value	1,80,000
(-) Standard deduction @ 30%	(54,000)
Income from house property	1,26,000

9. Construction of house is completed on 31.1.2019. Thus, deduction for interest on loan is allowed from PY 2018-2019. Deduction for interest = 20,00,000 × 6% × 11/12 = 1,10,000.

12.

Interest payable for the various years:

2014-2015	(5,00,000 × 12%)	60,000
2015-2016	(5,00,000 × 12%)	60,000
2016-2017	(5,00,000 × 12%)	60,000
2017-2018	(5,00,000 × 12%)	60,000
2018-2019	(5,00,000 × 12%)	60,000

Since, construction of house is completed on 15.3.2018 i.e. in year 2017-2018, interest payable up to year 2016-2017 will be pre-construction interest and 1/5th of 1,80,000 i.e. 36,000 will be allowed from PY 2017-2018 to 2021-2022 in five equal instalments.

Total deduction for PY 2018-2019 = 60,000 + 36,000 = 96,000

13.

Gross Annual Value (25,000 × 12)	3,00,000
(-) Municipal Taxes	-
Net Annual Value	3,00,000
(-) Standard Deduction @ 30%	(90,000)
Income from house property	2,10,000

14. If an individual transfers any house property to his or her spouse otherwise than for adequate consideration he shall be deemed to be owner. Hence rental income is taxable in the hands of Mr. Bala and clubbing provisions are not applicable.

Interest income of ₹ 21,000 will be taxable in the hands of Mrs. Bala and again clubbing provisions are not attracted.

CHAPTER 5

INCOME FROM BUSINESS OR PROFESSION

MCQs ON THEORY

1. Which of the following is liable to be taxed under the head PGBP?

(1) Any compensation received by any person for managing the whole or substantially the whole of the affairs of an Indian company

(2) Fees received by directors from the company for attending board or general meeting

(3) Profits on sale of a licence granted under the Imports (Control) Order, 1955.

(4) Any interest, salary, bonus, commission or remuneration due to, or received by, a partner of a firm to the extent it is not deductible u/s 40(*b*).

Select the correct answer from the options given below -

(A) (1) & (4)

(B) (2) & (3)

(C) (1), (2) & (3)

(D) (4), (1) & (3)

2. Which of the following will be *added* to the *Net Profit* while calculating income under the head PGBP?

(I) Expenses debited to Profit & Loss A/c but not allowed

(II) Income not credited to Profit & Loss A/c but taxable under PGBP

Select the correct answer from the options given below -

(A) (I) only

(B) Both (I) and (II)

(C) (II) only

(D) Neither (I) nor (II)

3. Which of the following statement(s) is true (✓) and which is false (×)?

(P) Profit and gains of illegal business are not taxable as business income.

(Q) If the business never started or has ceased with no intention to be resumed, then letting income will be taxable as income for other sources.

(R) The loss from speculation business can be carried forward for 8 years.

(S) Only revenue loss is allowed to be deducted from business income.

Select the correct answer from the options given below -

	(P)	**(Q)**	**(R)**	**(S)**
(A)	✓	×	✓	×
(B)	✓	×	×	✓
(C)	×	✓	×	✓
(D)	×	✓	✓	×

4. Which of the following Section of the Income Tax Act, 1961 deals with method of computing business income?

(A) Section 143

(B) Section 144

(C) Section 145

(D) Section 146

5. Which of the following method of accounting is allowed for computing business income?

(A) Accrual system of accounting

(B) Cash system of accounting

(C) Either (A) or (B)

(D) Hybrid system of accounting

6. Which of the following statement is incorrect?

(A) Return of loss is not required to be submitted to carry forward unabsorbed depreciation.

(B) Unabsorbed depreciation shall be given priority of set-off over brought unabsorbed losses.

(C) Unabsorbed depreciation can be carried forward for indefinite period.

(D) Unabsorbed depreciation can be carried forward from last year can be set-off against any head of income except salary.

7. Method of accounting to be followed for inventory valuation is dealt by _____ of the Income Tax Act, 1961.

(A) Section 245A

(B) Section 45A

(C) Section 145A

(D) Section 146A

8. Provisions relating to Investment allowance are contained in ______ of the Income Tax Act, 1961.

(A) Section 32AE

(B) Section 32AB

(C) Section 32AD

(D) Section 32AA

9. Match the following in relation to valuation of closing stock:

List I	*List II*
(P) Regular stock of business	1. Market price on the last day of the previous year
(Q) Capital asset converted on stock in trade	2. Cost or NRV whichever is less
(R) Stock acquired by inheritance or gift	3. Market price on the date of conversion
(S) Stock withdrawn from business	4. Price at which it was recorded in books

	P	**Q**	**R**	**S**
(A)	3	2	4	1
(B)	2	3	4	1
(C)	3	2	1	4
(D)	2	3	1	4

10. Which of the following category of assessee can claim deduction of investment allowance?

(A) Individual

(B) Partnership Firm

(C) Company

(D) Any of the above

11. Which of the following is speculative transaction?

(A) Transaction in which a contract for the purchase or sale of any commodity is periodically or ultimately settled otherwise than by the actual delivery or transfer of the commodity.

(B) Transaction in respect of trading of in derivative in a recognized stock exchange

(C) Both (A) and (B)

(D) Neither (A) nor (B)

12. Which of the following statement(s) is/are true?

(1) Even notional loss relating to business is allowed to be deducted in some cases.

(2) Only revenue loss is deductible and not capital loss.

(3) Burden of proof to prove admissibility of expenditure lies on department.

(4) Any expenditure incurred before commencement of business is allowed immediately in year in which business is actually commenced.

Select the correct answer from the options given below -

(A) (2) only

(B) (3) & (4) only

(C) (2) & (4) only

(D) (4) only

13. Provisions relating to Investment allowance for investment in new plant and machinery located in notified backward area are contained in ______ of the Income Tax Act, 1961.

(A) Section 32AC

(B) Section 32AD

(C) Section 32AE

(D) Section 32BB

14. Who will be allowed depreciation in case the assessee has acquired building on lease basis?

(A) Lessor as he is the real owner

(B) Lessee treating as deemed owner

(C) Partly to lessor and partly to lessee

(D) Lessor or lessee at the option of assessing officer

15. Deduction in respect of investment allowance is available only when investment tin new asset is ______

(A) 25 Crore or more

(B) 10 Crore or more

(C) 30 Crore or more

(D) 20 Crore or more

16. Where any building, plant partly used for business or profession and partly for other purpose then ______

(A) the deduction shall be restricted to 50% of total amount eligible for deduction

(B) the deduction shall be restricted to fair propionate part thereof.

(C) the deduction shall be restricted to amount as agreed by the assessing officer

(D) no deduction is available under the provisions of the Income Tax Act, 1961.

17. Deduction in respect of Notified Skill Development Project is available u/s ______

(A) 35DCC

(B) 35CDC

(C) 35CCD

(D) 35ADD

18. Which of the following section deals with the provisions relating to "depreciation"?

(A) Section 31

(B) Section 32

(C) Section 33

(D) Section 34

19. Deduction in respect of amortization of certain Preliminary Expenses as provided in Section 35D is available to -

(A) Any company

(B) Any company and any resident person other than company

(C) Indian company and any resident person other than company

(D) Company, Firm including LLP

20. Which of the following statement(s) is/are true?

(A) Depreciation is allowed to owner of the asset

(B) Depreciation is allowed in respect of fractional ownership.

(C) Depreciation is allowed co-owner also.

(D) All of the above

21. Deduction in respect of investment allowance u/s 32AD is available @ ______ of the actual cost of new asset acquired and installed during previous year.

(A) 10%

(B) 15%

(C) 20%

(D) 25%

22. In which of the following case 100% depreciation is allowed?

(A) If asset is held by assess more than 180 days and put to use less than 180 days

(B) If asset is held by assess more than 180 days and put to use more than 180 days

(C) If asset is held by assess more than 300 days and put to use more than 180 days

(D) If asset is held by assess more than 260 days and put to use more than 180 days

23. The amount eligible for deduction u/s 33AB in respect of Tea, Coffee & Rubber Development A/c shall be -

(A) Amount deposited in NABARD A/c/Special Deposit A/c or 40% profit of such business whichever is less.

(B) 50% profit of such business

(C) Amount deposited in Tea, Coffee & Rubber Development Reserve A/c or 30% profit of such business whichever is less.

(D) Sum equal to 20% profit of such business before making any deduction under Section 33AB.

24. Intangible assets are depreciated at the rate of ______

(A) 15%

(B) 30%

(C) 25%

(D) 100%

25. If deduction in respect of investment allowance is claimed in earlier year and said asset is sold within _____ of acquisition then deduction claimed earlier is treated as income in year of sale.

(A) 3 years

(B) 2 years

(C) 10 years

(D) 5 years

26. Rate of depreciation chargeable on "Residential building" for the AY 2019-2020 is —

(A) 5%

(B) 10%

(C) 15%

(D) 30%

27. Maximum deduction u/s 33ABA relating to Site Restoration Fund shall be -

(A) A sum equal to amount deposited in special account or 20% profits of such business

(B) 40% profits of such business

(C) A sum equal to amount deposited in Deposit A/c or 25% profits of such business

(D) Sum equal to 20% profit of such business before making any deduction under Section 33ABA.

28. Which of the following is added while calculating 'Actual Cost' of asset as per Section 43(1) of the Income Tax Act, 1961?

(*i*) Cost attributable to bring asset to its present location and condition.

(*ii*) Amount of GST in respect of which GST Credit has been allowed under GST Law.

(*iii*) Interest on capital borrowed on a period before asset put to use.

(*iv*) Decrease in cost due to exchange fluctuations.

Select the correct answer from the options given below -

(A) (ii) & (iii)

(B) (i) & (iv)

(C) (iv) & (ii)

(D) (iii) & (i)

29. For which of the following revenue expenditure on scientific research incurred within 3 years immediately preceding commencement of business 100% deduction is available?

(1) Purchase of material

(2) Basic salary & allowance

(3) Expenditure for providing perquisites

Select the correct answer from the options given below -

(A) (1) only

(B) (1) and (2) only

(C) (2) and (3) only

(D) None of the above

30. Rate of depreciation chargeable on "ships and vessels" for the AY 2019-2020 is —

(A) 20%

(B) 15%

(C) 10%

(D) 5%

31. As per Section 35 (1) (ii) of the Income Tax Act, 1961, in respect of expenditure on scientific research, the deductions shall be allowed an amount equal to ________ times of any sum paid to a research association which has as its object the undertaking of scientific research or to a university, college or other institution to be used for scientific research.

(A) 100%

(B) 125%

(C) 175%

(D) 150%

32. When scientific asset used for business after it ceases to be used for scientific business; WDV is taken at ________

(A) Actual cost less depreciation allowed

(B) Actual cost as reduced by depreciation allowed u/s 35A (i) (d)

(C) Actual cost as determined by assessing officer with previous approval of Joint Commissioner

(D) Actual cost as reduced by depreciation allowed u/s 35(1)(iv)

33. As per Section 35(1)(iia) of the Income Tax Act, 1961, in respect of expenditure on scientific research, the deductions shall be allowed an amount equal to ______ of any sum paid to a company to be used by it for scientific research.

(A) 100%

(B) 150%

(C) 175%

(D) 125%

34. Rate of depreciation chargeable on "motor car" for the AY 2019-2020 is —

(A) 5%

(B) 20%

(C) 15%

(D) 40%

35. Who is/are eligible to claim deduction on Notified Skill Development Project u/s 35CCD?

(a) Individual

(b) Firm

(c) LLP

(d) Company

(e) Co-operative society

Select the correct answer from the options given below -

(A) (c) and (d)

(B) (e) only

(C) (a), (b), (c) and (d)

(D) (d) only

36. Where an eligible assessee incurs any expenditure on preliminary expenses he shall be allowed a deduction of an amount equal to ________ beginning with the previous year in which the business commences, or the previous year in which the extension of the undertaking is completed or the new unit commences production or operation.

(A) 1/4th of such expenditure for each of the 4 successive previous years

(B) 1/5th of such expenditure for each of the 5 successive previous years

(C) 1/3rd of such expenditure for each of the 3 successive previous years

(D) 1/10th of such expenditure for each of the 10 successive previous years

37. Rate of depreciation chargeable on "Motor buses used in business of running on hire" for the AY 2019-2020 is —

(A) 10%

(B) 15%

(C) 20%

(D) 30%

38. Deduction in respect of amortization of expenditure in case of amalgamation/demerger as provided in Section 35DD is available to the extent of ______ starting with the previous year in which amalgamation or demerger takes place.

(A) 1/4th of such expenditure is deductible for each of the 4 successive previous years

(B) 1/5th of such expenditure is deductible for each of the 5 successive previous years

(C) 1/3rd of such expenditure is deductible for each of the 3 successive previous years

(D) 1/10th of such expenditure is deductible for each of the 10 successive previous years

39. *Statement I:*

If asset is acquired by way of gift or inheritance then Actual Cost in the hands of assessee is taken at ZREO as assessee has not incurred any actual expenses.

Statement II:

If previously used motor car is brought to use in business actual cost of the motor car is taken at cost to assessee as reduced by an amount of depreciation at the rate in force on the respective year before motor car is put to use.

Select the correct answer from the options given below -

(A) Statement I is true but Statement II is false

(B) Statement II is true but Statement I is false

(C) Both Statement I and Statement II are true

(D) Both Statement I and Statement II are false

40. Deduction in respect of capital expenditure incurred on scientific research is available _____

(A) To the extent of amount of expenditure incurred

(B) To the extent of amount of expenditure incurred (excluding expenditure on land) and certified by prescribed authority.

(C) 150%

(D) (A) or (C)

41. How much deduction can be claimed by companies on Notified Skill Development Project u/s 35CCD?

(A) 150% of prescribed expenditure including expenditure on land and building

(B) 125% of prescribed expenditure excluding expenditure on land and building

(C) 150% of prescribed expenditure excluding expenditure on land and building

(D) 125% of prescribed expenditure including expenditure on land and building

42. Rate of depreciation chargeable on "Life saving medical equipment" is —

(A) 20%

(B) 40%

(C) 15%

(D) 60%

43. In case of individual assessee deduction in respect of preliminary expense as provided in Section 35D is available to the extent of -

(A) 5% of cost of project or 5% of capital employed whichever is less

(B) 10% of cost of project or 10% of capital employed whichever is less

(C) 5% of cost of project

(D) 10% of capital employed

44. *Assertion (A):*

In case asset first time acquired by the assessee Actual Cost to assessee has to be taken as reduced by the portion of cost met directly or indirectly by any person or authority

Reason (R):

In some cases Actual Cost is taken at notional figures e.g. when asset transferred to other is reacquired again lower of the following is taken actual cost:

- WDV at the time of transfer
- Price paid for reacquiring

Select the correct answer from the options given below -

(A) A is true but R is false

(B) A is false but R is true

(C) Both A and R are true but R is not correct explanation of A

(D) Both A and R are true and R is correct explanation of A.

45. Where the assessee pays any sum to a National Laboratory or a University or an Indian Institute of Technology or a specified person with a specific direction that the said sum shall be used for scientific research undertaken under a programme approved in this behalf by the prescribed authority, then there shall be allowed a deduction of a sum equal ______ of the sum so paid.

(A) 125%

(B) 175%

(C) 150%

(D) 200%

46. Match the following identifying 'Actual Cost' for asset as per *Explanation* to Section 43(1) of the Income Tax Act, 1961:

(P) Assets acquired by way gift or inheritance	1. Cost to resulting company shall be cost to demerged company
(Q) Previously used building brought to use in business	2. Cost to amalgamated company shall be cost to amalgamating company

(R) Demerger

(S) Capital asset transferred in amalgamation

3. Actual cost, as reduced by an amount of depreciation at the rate in force on the respective year.

4. Actual cost to previous owner as reduced by the amount of depreciation allowed to him.

	(P)	(Q)	(R)	(S)
(A)	3	4	1	2
(B)	4	3	2	1
(C)	3	4	2	1
(D)	4	3	1	2

47. As per Section 35ABB of the Income Tax Act, 1961, where any capital expenditure is incurred for obtaining licence to operate telecommunication services then -

(A) 100% of such expenditure is allowed in year in which such expenditure has been incurred.

(B) no deduction shall be allowed

(C) there shall be allowed deduction during the period for which the license shall remain effective

(D) 10% of such expenditure is allowed in each commencing from the year in which such expenditure has been incurred.

48. Rate of depreciation chargeable on Books (annual publication) is —

(A) 80%

(B) 40%

(C) 60%

(D) 30%

49. Which of the following assessee can claim deduction in respect of amortization of expenditure incurred under Voluntary Retirement Scheme u/s 35DDA?

(A) Resident individual

(B) Any Company

(C) Any person

(D) Any firm

50. On which of the following assets additional depreciation u/s 32(1)(iia) is available -

(I) New machinery

(II) New Ship

(III) New Aircraft

(IV) New office appliances

(V) New road transport vehicle

Select the correct answer from the options given below -

(A) (I) only

(B) (I), (II) & (III) only

(C) (I), (III), (IV) & (V) only

(D) None of the above

51. Deduction for expenditure on prospecting, etc. for certain minerals as provided in Section 35E is allowed for each of _____ successive previous years starting from the year in which the commercial production starts.

(A) 10

(B) 5

(C) 4

(D) 20

52. Match the following:

(P) Bonus or commission paid to an employee	1. No deduction
(Q) Provision for bad and doubtful debt	2. 100% deduction
(R) Revenue expenditure by a company for promoting family planning	3. Deduction is subject to the provisions of Section 43B
(S) Expenditure on issue of bonus shares	4. 1/5th of expenditure in 5 successive year
	5. Revenue in nature, hence deductible

Select the correct answer from the options given below:

	(P)	(Q)	(R)	(S)
(A)	3	1	4	5
(B)	3	1	2	5
(C)	5	1	4	3
(D)	2	4	3	1

53. An undertaking located in notified backward area of Andhra, can claim additional depreciation @ _____ on new plant and machinery.

(A) 20%

(B) 10% if asset put to use less than 30 days

(C) 35%

(D) 30%

54. Deduction of bad debt is allowed -

(A) Business wise

(B) Assessee wise

(C) Both (A) and (B)

(D) Neither (A) nor (B)

55. In case of Indian scheduled bank deduction for provision for bad debt is available not exceeding ______ of its total income.

(A) 8.5%

(B) 5%

(C) 10%

(D) 2.5%

56. If new plant is purchased in current year and put use less than 180 days then ______

(A) Additional depreciation @ 10% is available and remaining 10% cannot be claimed in next year as additional depreciation is available in year of purchase only.

(B) Additional depreciation @ 10% is available and remaining 10% can be claimed in next year.

(C) Additional depreciation @ 20% is available whether asset is used 180 days more or not.

(D) None of the above

57. "Heavy goods vehicle" means any goods carriage, the gross vehicle weight of which exceeds -

(A) 10,000 kilograms

(B) 12,000 kilograms

(C) 15,000 kilograms

(D) 7,500 kilograms

58. Which of the following expenditure is/are deductible under the PGBP?

(1) CSR Expenditure

(2) Advertisement expenditure in magazine published by political party

Select the correct answer from the options given below -

(A) (2) only

(B) Both (1) and (2)

(C) (1) only

(D) Neither (1) nor (2)

59. As per Section 35AD, deduction is available to a hospital with at least ________ for patient if its operations are commenced on or after 1-4-2011.

(A) one hundred beds

(B) two hundred beds

(C) three hundred beds

(D) five hundred beds

60. If an assessee incurs an expenditure, which is allowable and claimed as deduction and the payment or aggregate of payments made to a person in a day in respect of such expenditure, otherwise than by an account payee cheque drawn on a bank or account payee bank draft exceeds ________ then, no deduction shall be allowed in respect of such expenditure and in the case of payment made for plying, hiring or leasing goods carriages, the aforesaid limit shall be ________

(A) ₹ 10,000; ₹ 35,000
(B) ₹ 30,000; ₹ 40,000
(C) ₹ 20,000; ₹ 35,000
(D) ₹ 50,000; ₹ 75,000

61. As per Section 35AD, deduction is available to a hotel of .... as classified by Central Government, if its operations are commenced on or after the 1.4.2011.

(A) three star or above category
(B) five star or above category
(C) two star or above category
(D) four star or above category

62. Which of the following expenditure is/are allowed under the head PGBP?

(I) Expenditure on issue of shares
(II) Expenditure on issue of bonus shares

Select the correct answer from the options given below -

(A) Both (I) and (II)
(B) (I) only
(C) Neither (I) nor (II)
(D) (II) only

63. Match the following:

In case a block is transferred in succession of business or profession, WDV shall be ___

(P) WDV in the hands of successor	1. WDV in the hands of demerged company
(Q) WDV in the hands of amalgamated company	2. WDV in the hands holding company
(R) WDV of asset transferred to resulting company	3. WDV in the hands of amalgamating company
(S) WDV in the hands of subsidiary company	4. WDV in the hands of amalgamated company
	5. WDV in the hands of predecessor.

	(P)	(Q)	(R)	(S)
(A)	5	4	1	2
(B)	5	3	2	1
(C)	3	5	2	1
(D)	5	3	1	2

64. As per Section 43B if the sum relates to any previous year for which payment has been made on or before the due date of furnishing the Return of Income of that year then deduction is allowed in the ______

(A) previous year to which it relates

(B) next previous year

(C) next assessment year

(D) none of the above

65. Under Section 35AD deduction is available to specified businesses. From the list given below identify which are specified businesses -

(I) Housing projects

(II) Fertilizer plants

(III) Bee keeping

(IV) Slurry pipe line

Select the correct answer from the options given below -

(A) (I) and (IV)

(B) (II) and (III)

(C) (IV), (I) and (II)

(D) (III), (IV), (I) and (II)

66. A company has WDV of block of asset on 1.4.2018 ₹ 30,00,000. Rate of depreciation is 15%. Assets falling in block are purchased during the year for ₹ 10,00,000. Entire block sold for ₹ 17,60,000. What are the tax consequences?

Select the correct answer from the options given below -

(A) No depreciation is admissible as block cease to exist and there is STCG ₹ 22,40,000

(B) Depreciation admissible ₹ 3,36,000 and block will continue at WDV of ₹ 19,04,000 after claiming depreciation.

(C) Depreciation admissible ₹ 3,36,000 and as block cease to exist.

(D) No depreciation is admissible as block cease to exist and there is STCL ₹ 22,40,000

67. If any asset is transferred which is not capital asset and sale price is less than stamp duty value then ________

(A) Difference between stamp value and actual sale price shall be deemed to be income chargeable under the head PGBP

(B) Difference between market price and actual sale price shall be deemed to be income chargeable under the head PGBP

(C) Difference between stamp value and actual sale price shall be deemed to be income chargeable under the head Capital Gain.

(D) There is no such provision under the Income Tax Act, 1961.

68. As per Section 35AD, for production of fertilizer in India in a new plant or in a newly installed capacity in an existing plant, if its operations are commenced on or after 1.4.2011, ______ of the capital expenditure (not being any expenditure incurred on the acquisition of any land or goodwill or financial instrument) incurred, wholly and exclusively, for the purposes of any specified business carried on by the assessee shall be allowed as deduction during the previous year in which such-expenditure is incurred.

(A) 150%

(B) 125%

(C) 100%

(D) 175%

69. Which of the following payment is subject to provisions of Section 43B?

(A) Employees contribution to any provident fund

(B) Any payment to the Indian Railway for use of Railway assets

(C) Insurance premium

(D) All of the above

70. Deduction for expenditure by way of payment to associations and institutions for carrying out Rural Development Programmes is available u/s ______

(A) 35CC

(B) 35CCB

(C) 35CCA

(D) 35CCC

71. Special provisions relating to consequential changes in rate of exchange of currency are given in ______ of the Income Tax Act, 1961.

(A) Section 42A

(B) Section 44A

(C) Section 43A

(D) Section 45A

72. The profits and gains of any business of insurance, including any such business carried on by a mutual insurance company or by co-operative society, shall be computed in accordance with rules contained in ______ to the Income Tax Act, 1961.

(A) First Schedule

(B) Second Schedule

(C) Third Schedule

(D) Fourth Schedule

73. The profits and gains derived from life insurance business, included in the total income of an assessee, shall be taxable at the rate of ______

(A) 12.5%

(B) 12%

(C) 10%

(D) 14.42%

74. If licence to operate telecommunication services is sold or transferred and sale proceeds (only capital sum) exceeds the expenditure remaining un-allowed ______

(A) Deduction is allowed in the year of transfer to the extent expenditure remaining un-allowed less sale proceeds.

(B) No deduction shall be allowed u/s 35ABB in previous year of transfer or for any subsequent previous year.

(C) Deduction is not allowed even on the part of the licence held by the assessee

(D) Both (B) and (C)

75. _________ of the Income Tax Act, 1961 deals with the provisions relating to maintenance of books of account by certain persons carrying on business or profession.

(A) Section 44AB

(B) Section 44AAA

(C) Section 44AA

(D) Section 44AAB

76. Deduction for expenditure incurred on notified Agricultural Extension Project is available u/s ______ to the extent of ____ of prescribed expenditure.

(A) 35CCB; 100%

(B) 35CCC; 150%

(C) 35CE; 100%

(D) 35CD; 150%

77. As per Section 44AA, maintenance of books of account is compulsory for specified professions if ______

(A) gross receipts exceeds ₹ 1,50,000 in all of the 3 immediately preceding previous years

(B) profession is newly setup and the gross receipts are likely to exceed ₹ 1,50,000 during current previous year

(C) Both (A) and (B)

(D) gross receipts exceeds ₹ 10,00,000 in all of the 3 immediately preceding previous years

78. Person carrying on specified profession is required to keep books of account including carbon copies or counterfoils of bills or receipts issued by him exceeding ______

(A) ₹ 50
(B) ₹ 25
(C) ₹ 100
(D) ₹ 500

79. Person carrying on specified profession is required to keep books of account including original bills issued to him and receipts in respect of expenditure incurred by him. In absence of bills, and where the payment does not exceed ________, payment vouchers.

(A) ₹ 50
(B) ₹ 25
(C) ₹ 100
(D) ₹ 500

80. An Individual or HUF carrying on any business is required to keep books of account if ______

(A) sales/turnover/gross receipts thereof exceeds ₹ 25,00,000 in any of the three previous years immediately preceding the previous year
(B) gross receipts exceeds ₹ 1,50,000 in all of the three immediately preceding previous years
(C) his income from business exceeds ₹ 2,50,000
(D) (A) or (C)

81. In case of person carrying on any specified profession tax audit is compulsory if ________

(A) his gross income exceeds ₹ 25 lakhs in any previous year
(B) his gross receipts exceeds ₹ 50 lakhs in any previous year
(C) Either (A) or (B)
(D) Neither (A) nor (B)

82. Special provision for computing profits and gains of business on presumptive basis are made in ______

(A) Section 44AD
(B) Section 44AB
(C) Section 44AE
(D) Section 44AF

83. As per Section 44AD, income on presumptive basis *(in respect of the amount of total turnover or gross receipts which is received by an account payee cheque or an account payee bank draft or use of electronic clearing system through a bank account)* is calculated at -

(A) 8% of the total turnover or gross profit

(B) 6% of the total turnover or gross receipts

(C) 7.5% of the total turnover or gross receipts

(D) 10% of the total turnover or gross receipts

84. Which of the following type of assessee can opt scheme u/s 44AD?

(1) Individual

(2) LLP

(3) Hindu undivided family

(4) Partnership firm

(5) Company

Select the correct answer from the options given below -

(A) (1) only

(B) (3) and (1) only

(C) (1), (3) and (4) only

(D) (5), (1), (4), (3), (2)

85. Which of the following type of assessee cannot opt scheme u/s 44AD?

(A) a person carrying on specified profession as referred to Section 44AA

(B) a person carrying on business of plying, hiring or leasing goods carriages referred to in Section 44AE

(C) both (A) and (B)

(D) neither (A) nor (B)

86. Special provision for computing profits and gains of business of plying, hiring or leasing goods carriages are made in _____ of the Income Tax Act, 1961.

(A) Section 44AE

(B) Section 44AF

(C) Section 44BB

(D) Section 44EE

87. To opt for special provision for computing profits and gains of business of plying, hiring or leasing goods carriages as provided in Section 44AE, the assessee shall not own more than ______ at any time during the previous year

(A) 10 goods carriages

(B) 20 goods carriages

(C) 15 goods carriages

(D) 5 goods carriages

PRACTICAL MCQs

88. Raja purchased house property on 1.12.2016 for ₹ 10,00,000 and the same was self occupied as residence. On 1.12.2018, the said house was brought into use for his Company Secretary profession. Rate of depreciation at the time of purchase of house was 15%. Rate of depreciation for AY 2019-2020 is 10%. Compute the WDV of assets on 31.3.2019.

(A) ₹ 7,69,500

(B) ₹ 7,86,250

(C) ₹ 8,10,000

(D) ₹ 7,22,500

89. AB Ltd. has disclosed net profit of ₹ 12.50 lakhs. It has debited ₹ 60,000 (paid in cash) as advertisement to sister concern of a director, fair value of which is ₹ 52,000. Taxable income of AB Ltd. = ?

(A) ₹ 13,10,000

(B) ₹ 12,58,000

(C) ₹ 12,50,000

(D) ₹ 13,02,000

90. A company purchased machinery on 1.4.2015 for ₹ 2,00,000. It acquired new machinery on 10.12.2018 for ₹ 2,00,000 and sold some of the machinery for ₹ 3,90,000. What are the tax consequences? *(ignore additional depreciation)*

(A) There is STCL of ₹ 67,175 and block continues at zero value.

(B) Depreciation of ₹ 1,500 can be claimed u/s 32.

(C) There is STCL of ₹ 45,500 and block continues at zero value.

(D) There is STCG of ₹ 67,175 and block continues at zero value.

91. Net profit of retail trader is ₹ 50,000. It was found that some stock omitted to be included in both opening and closing stock, the value of which are ₹ 9,000 and ₹ 18,000 respectively. Business income = ?

(A) ₹ 41,000

(B) ₹ 77,000

(C) ₹ 23,000

(D) ₹ 59,000

92. Rani purchased car on 9.10.2014 for ₹ 6,50,000 and the same was used for personal purpose. On 1.12.2018, the said car was brought into use for business. Market value of car on 1.12.2018 was ₹ 3,00,000. Compute the WDV of car on 31.3.2019.

(A) ₹ 5,85,000

(B) ₹ 2,77,500

(C) ₹ 5,52,500

(D) ₹ 6,01,250

93. Select the correct option from the date given below:

WDV on 1.4.2018	₹ 4,50,000
Purchase of asset and put to use on 1.10.2018	₹ 3,40,000
Purchase of asset and put to use on 5.10.2018	₹ 1,70,000
Some assets sold	₹ 4,18,000
Rate of depreciation	15%

(Ignore additional depreciation)

(A) Depreciation eligible for PY 2018-2019 ₹ 81,300 and WDV on 31.3.2019 ₹ 4,60,700.

(B) Short term capital loss ₹ 5,42,000 and WDV on 31.3.2019 will be Nil.

(C) Depreciation eligible for PY 2018-2019 ₹ 68,550 and WDV on 31.3.2019 ₹ 4,73,450.

(D) Short term capital gain ₹ 5,42,000 and WDV on 31.3.2019 will be Nil.

94. A retail trader has reported sales of ₹ 12,11,500 and net profit of ₹ 1,30,900. Total turnover or gross receipts is received by an account payee cheque/an account payee bank draft/use of electronic clearing system through a bank account. If he opts for presumptive income scheme u/s 44AD, his income under the head PGBP will be -

(A) ₹ 72,690

(B) ₹ 96,920

(C) ₹ 90,862.50

(D) ₹ 1,21,150

95. N Ltd. started its business by purchasing new plant and machinery on 1.4.2018 for ₹ 100 Crore. The plant and machinery put use on the same date. It can claim deduction for normal depreciation and additional depreciation.

WDV of the plant on 31.3.2019 -

(A) ₹ 50 Crore

(B) ₹ 40 Crore

(C) ₹ 65 Crore

(D) ₹ 70 Crore

96. Select the correct option from the date given below:

WDV on 1.4.2018	₹ 4,50,000
Purchase of asset and put to use on 1.10.2018	₹ 3,40,000
Purchase of asset and put to use on 5.10.2018	₹ 1,70,000
Some assets sold	₹ 6,50,000
Rate of depreciation	15%

(Ignore additional depreciation)

(A) Depreciation eligible for PY 2018-2019 ₹ 46,500 and WDV on 31.3.2019 ₹ 2,63,500.

(B) Short term capital loss ₹ 3,10,000 and WDV on 31.3.2019 will be Nil.

(C) Depreciation eligible for PY 2018-2019 ₹ 33,750 and WDV on 31.3.2019 ₹ 2,76,250.

(D) Short term capital gain ₹ 3,10,000 and WDV on 31.3.2019 will be Nil.

97. Ram furnishes following information for the PY 2018-2019.

Income from plying of vehicles	2,10,400
(He owns 5 goods vehicles, the gross weight of which does not exceeds 12,000 kg)	
Income from retail trade of garments	1,40,000
Sale turnover garments	21,70,000
Brought forward depreciation for AY 2017-2018.	1,00,000

Compute the business income of Ram.

(A) ₹ 2,50,400

(B) ₹ 3,50,400

(C) ₹ 6,23,600

(D) ₹ 3,84,000

98. The business income of X Ltd. before claiming deduction on account of following expenditure on family planning is ₹ 6,00,000.

Revenue expenditure = ₹ 7,00,000

Capital expenditure = ₹ 10,00,000

What are the tax implications? Select the correct answer from the options given below:

(A) Unabsorbed family planning expenditure ₹ 3,00,000

(B) Income chargeable under the head PGBP will be ZERO.

(C) Loss under the head PGBP = ₹ 3,00,000

(D) (A) and (B)

99. Select the correct option from the date given below:

WDV on 1.4.2018	₹ 4,50,000
Purchase of asset and put to use on 1.10.2018	₹ 3,40,000
Purchase of asset and put to use on 5.10.2018	₹ 1,70,000
All assets are sold at	₹ 8,33,000
Rate of depreciation	15%

(Ignore additional depreciation)

(A) Depreciation eligible for PY 2018-2019 ₹ 19,050 and WDV on 31.3.2019 ₹ 1,07,950.

(B) Short term capital loss ₹ 1,27,000 and WDV on 31.3.2019 will be Nil.

(C) Depreciation eligible for PY 2018-2019 ₹ 9,525 and WDV on 31.3.2018 ₹ 1,17,475.

(D) Short term capital gain ₹ 1,27,000 and WDV on 31.3.2019 will be Nil.

100. On 1.4.2017 WDV of machine was ₹ 3,50,000 in the books of N Ltd. It sold machine for ₹ 5,00,000 to S Ltd. and S Ltd. leased back this machine to N Ltd. The market value of machine on date of sale was ₹ 4,00,000. The cost to S Ltd. for charging depreciation = ?

(A) ₹ 4,00,000

(B) ₹ 5,00,000

(C) ₹ 3,50,000

(D) Any of the above which is acceptable to the assessing officer

101. Zahir had 4 goods vehicles *(the gross weight of which does not exceeds 12,000 kg)* as on 1.4.2018. He acquired 7 goods vehicles on 27.6.2018 and sold 2 goods vehicles on 31.5.2018. Assuming that he opts for presumptive taxation as per Section 44AE compute his income chargeable to tax?

(A) ₹ 9,90,000

(B) ₹ 8,10,000

(C) ₹ 7,35,000

(D) ₹ 9,00,000

102. Rahul is a Practicing Company Secretary (FCS). His gross receipts and income under the head PGBP for the PY 2018 - 2019 are ₹ 9,18,340 & ₹ 5,40,122 respectively. What are the obligations of Rahul? Select the correct answer from the option given below -

(A) Rahul is compulsorily required to maintain books of accounts u/s 44AA.

(B) Rahul has to get his accounts audited u/s 44AB.

(C) Both (A) and (B)

(D) Neither (A) nor (B)

103. Dr. Patwardhan purchased car for ₹ 2,20,000 on 5.10.2018. 3/4th of the car is used for business purpose. Expenses incurred on car were ₹ 6,000. How much deduction Dr. Patwardhan can claim for depreciation and car expenses while calculating income from profession?

(A) ₹ 24,750 for depreciation and ₹ 4,500 for car expenses.

(B) ₹ 12,375 for depreciation and ₹ 2,250 for car expenses.

(C) ₹ 12,375 for depreciation and ₹ 4,500 for car expenses.

(D) ₹ 24,750 for depreciation and ₹ 6,000 for car expenses.

ANSWERS:

1.	(D)	**2.**	(B)	**3.**	(C)	**4.**	(C)	**5.**	(C)	**6.**	(B)	**7.**	(C)
8.	(C)	**9.**	(D)	**10.**	(C)	**11.**	(A)	**12.**	(A)	**13.**	(B)	**14.**	(B)
15.	(A)	**16.**	(B)	**17.**	(C)	**18.**	(B)	**19.**	(C)	**20.**	(D)	**21.**	(B)
22.	(B)	**23.**	(A)	**24.**	(C)	**25.**	(D)	**26.**	(A)	**27.**	(A)	**28.**	(D)
29.	(B)	**30.**	(A)	**31.**	(D)	**32.**	(D)	**33.**	(A)	**34.**	(C)	**35.**	(D)
36.	(B)	**37.**	(D)	**38.**	(B)	**39.**	(D)	**40.**	(A)	**41.**	(C)	**42.**	(B)
43.	(C)	**44.**	(D)	**45.**	(C)	**46.**	(D)	**47.**	(C)	**48.**	(B)	**49.**	(C)
50.	(A)	**51.**	(A)	**52.**	(B)	**53.**	(C)	**54.**	(A)	**55.**	(A)	**56.**	(B)
57.	(B)	**58.**	(D)	**59.**	(A)	**60.**	(A)	**61.**	(C)	**62.**	(D)	**63.**	(D)
64.	(A)	**65.**	(D)	**66.**	(D)	**67.**	(A)	**68.**	(C)	**69.**	(B)	**70.**	(C)
71.	(C)	**72.**	(A)	**73.**	(A)	**74.**	(D)	**75.**	(C)	**76.**	(B)	**77.**	(C)
78.	(B)	**79.**	(A)	**80.**	(D)	**81.**	(A)	**82.**	(A)	**83.**	(B)	**84.**	(C)
85.	(C)	**86.**	(A)	**87.**	(A)	**88.**	(A)	**89.**	(A)	**90.**	(D)	**91.**	(D)
92.	(D)	**93.**	(C)	**94.**	(A)	**95.**	(C)	**96.**	(C)	**97.**	(A)	**98.**	(D)
99.	(B)	**100.**	(C)	**101.**	(C)	**102.**	(A)	**103.**	(C)				

PAST EXAMINATION MCQs

1. Dec 2014: Where the assessee does not himself carry on scientific research but makes contributions to an approved university, college or institution, to be used for scientific research related or unrelated to the business of assessee, then the amount of deduction from income of business shall be allowed on such contribution to the extent of —

(A) 125%

(B) 150%

(C) 100%

(D) 200%

2. Dec 2014: In the case of companies, capital expenditure incurred for the purpose of promoting family planning amongst the employees would be deductible to the extent —

(A) Equal to 1/5th in each year for 5 years

(B) Equal to 1/6th in each year for 6 years

(C) Equal to 1/4th in each year for 4 years

(D) Equal to 1/10th in each year for 10 years

3. Dec 2014: A person carrying on profession will also have to get his accounts audited before the specified date, if gross receipts from the profession for a previous year or years relevant to assessment year exceed —

(A) ₹ 50 Lakh

(B) ₹ 10 Lakh

(C) ₹ 1 Crore

(D) ₹ 25 Lakh

4. Dec 2014: Rate of depreciation chargeable on temporary wooden structure for the AY 2018-2019 is —

(A) 25%

(B) 10%

(C) 40%

(D) 50%

5. Dec 2014: Anuj owns 6 goods carriage vehicles (weight of vehicles does not exceed 12,000 kg) out of which 2 goods vehicle are acquired by him on 15th January, 2019. His taxable income u/s 44AE will be —

(A) ₹ 4,05,000

(B) ₹ 3,24,000

(C) ₹ 2,46,000

(D) ₹ 3,60,000

6. June 2015: 'Notional Profit' from speculative business is —

(A) Taxable under the head 'income from profits and gains of business and profession'

(B) Taxable under the head 'income from other sources'

(C) Taxable either as income from other sources or as income from profits and gains of business and profession

(D) Not taxable

7. June 2015: A person carrying specified profession will have to maintain books of account prescribed by Rule 6F of the Income Tax Rules, 1962, if gross receipts are more than ₹ 1,50,000 for —

(A) All preceding 5 years

(B) Any of the preceding 5 years

(C) All preceding 3 years

(D) Any of the preceding 3 years

8. June 2015: If a block of assets ceases to exist on the last day of the previous year, depreciation admissible for the block of assets will be —

(A) Nil

(B) 50% of the value of the block of assets on the first day of the previous year

(C) The total value of the block of assets on the first day of the previous year

(D) 50% of the value of the block of assets on the last day of the previous year

9. June 2015: U/s 40A (3) which of the following payment for an expenditure incurred would not be admissible as deduction from business income —

(A) ₹ 15,000 paid in cash to a transporter

(B) ₹ 5,000 paid in cash to a dealer in the morning and ₹ 5,000 paid in cash to the same dealer in the evening

(C) ₹ 40,000 sent through NEFT to the bank account of the dealer for goods purchased

(D) ₹ 19,000 paid through bearer cheque to the dealer for goods purchased.

10. June 2015: Sameer sold goods worth ₹ 50,000 at credit on 1st April, 2017. However, he has written off ₹ 10,000 of it as bad debts and claimed deduction for the same during the year 2017-2018. On 4th April, 2018, the defaulting debtor made payment of ₹ 45,000. The taxable amount of bad debts recovered for the year 2018-2019 would be —

(A) ₹ 5,000

(B) ₹ 50,000

(C) ₹ 45,000

(D) ₹ 10,000

11. June 2015: Under the Income Tax Act, 1961, which of the following outlays incurred by Sun Ltd. during the previous year ended 31st March, 2019 will not be admissible as deduction while computing its business income —

(A) Contribution to a political party in cash

(B) Interest on loan taken for payment of income-tax

(C) Capital expenditure on advertisement

(D) All of the above

12. June 2015: Which of the following business commenced during August, 2016 will not be eligible for deduction u/s 35AD —

(A) Setting-up and operating a cold chain facility

(B) A production unit of fertilizer in India

(C) Operating of a 1 star hotel in a village

(D) Building a hospital of 200 beds.

13. June 2015: Provisions of Section 44AD for computation of presumptive income are not applicable to —

(A) Limited liability partnership

(B) Partnership firm

(C) Resident Hindu Undivided Family

(D) Resident individual

14. June 2015: Vaibhav, deriving business income, owns a car whose WDV as on 1st April, 2018 was ₹ 3,00,000. This is the only asset in the block of assets with rate of 15%. It is estimated that one-third of the total usage of the car is for personal use in both years. The WDV of the block of assets as on 31st March, 2019 would be —

(A) ₹ 2,16,750

(B) ₹ 2,43,000

(C) ₹ 2,55,000

(D) None of the above

15. Dec 2015: A charitable trust acquired two air-conditioners for ₹ 1,40,000 on 10th June, 2018. It claimed the acquisition as application of income. The amount it can claim by way of depreciation for the said air-conditioners for the AY 2019-2020 is —

(A) ₹ 21,000

(B) ₹ 1,40,000

(C) ₹ 35,000

(D) Nil

16. Dec 2015: Sunil acquired a building for ₹ 15 lakh in June, 2016 in addition to cost of land beneath the building of ₹ 3 lakh. It was used for personal purposes until he commenced business in June, 2018 and since then it was used for business purposes. The amount of depreciation eligible in his case for the AY 2019-2020 would be —

(A) ₹ 1,50,000

(B) ₹ 75,000

(C) ₹ 37,500

(D) ₹ 1,21,500

17. Dec 2015: X Ltd. paid ₹ 10 lakh to an approved college to be used for scientific research unrelated to its business. Amount eligible for deduction u/s 35(1)(ii) is —

(A) ₹ 5 lakh

(B) ₹ 17.5 lakh

(C) ₹ 15.00 lakh

(D) Nil

18. Dec 2015: Saraswath Ltd. made provision of ₹ 12 lakh for bonus payable for the year ended 31st March, 2018. It paid ₹ 7 lakh on 31st July, 2018; ₹ 3 lakh on 30th September, 2018; and ₹ 2 lakh on 15th December, 2018. The amount eligible for deduction u/s 43B would be —

(A) ₹ 10 lakh

(B) ₹ 12 lakh

(C) ₹ 7 lakh

(D) ₹ 3 lakh

19. Dec 2015: The maximum penalty leviable for failure to get accounts audited or to furnish report u/s 44AB is —

(A) ₹ 75,000

(B) ₹ 1,00,000

(C) ₹ 1,50,000

(D) ₹ 3,00,000

20. Dec 2015: When a cash payment of ₹ 15,000 is made on 10th May, 2018 towards purchase of raw material effected in the earlier year, *i.e.*, on 5th June 2017, the amount liable for disallowance u/s 40A (3A) would be —

(A) Nil

(B) 100% of payment

(C) 20% of such payment

(D) 30% of such payment

21. Dec 2015: When a person carries on the business of carrying goods for hire for the whole year with 5 self-owned and 3 leasehold goods vehicles *(gross vehicle weight of which does not exceeds 12,000 kg)*, the presumptive income chargeable to tax u/s 44AE would be —

(A) ₹ 4,80,000

(B) ₹ 7,20,000

(C) ₹ 3,96,000

(D) ₹ 3,36,000

22. Dec 2015: X, Manager of XYZ Ltd. since 2005 was terminated by the company on 1st August, 2018 by paying a compensation of ₹ 200 lakh. Such compensation is —

(A) Chargeable under the Wealth-tax Act, 1957

(B) Not chargeable under the Income-tax Act, 1961

(C) Chargeable u/s 17(3)(i)(D)

(D) Chargeable u/s 28(ii)(a)

23. June 2016: Ramson Industries acquired a factory building for self use in November, 2018. The value of land underneath the building was ₹ 5 lakh and value of building was ₹ 10 lakh. The amount of eligible depreciation allowable for assessment year 2019-2020 is -

(A) ₹ 1,50,000

(B) ₹ 25,000

(C) ₹ 1,00,000

(D) ₹ 50,000

24. June 2016: Chola Ltd., engaged in manufacture acquired machineries for ₹ 27 Crore in April, 2018 All the machines were used within 45 days of acquisition. The deduction under Section 32AD for the AY 2019-2020 will be -

(A) ₹ 4,05,00,000

(B) ₹ 4,50,00,000

(C) ₹ 8,55,00,000

(D) ₹ 8,40,00,000

25. June 2016: Where an asset used for scientific research for more than three years is sold without having been used for other purposes, then the sale proceeds to the extent of the cost of the asset already allowed as deduction under section 35 in the past shall be treated as —

(A) Business income
(B) Long-term capital gain
(C) Short-term capital gain
(D) Exempted income

26. June 2016: Where an assessee doing business expenditure in respect of which payments made to a person in a day exceeds ₹ 10,000 should be paid through account payee cheque or demand draft to claim deduction for such expenditure. This restriction does not apply to —

(A) Payments made to RBI
(B) Payments made to cultivators
(C) Payment of terminal benefits to employees not exceeding ₹ 50,000
(D) All of the above

27. June 2016: Appu Ltd. contributed ₹ 8,70,000 towards provident fund account of its employees. It actually remitted ₹ 5,00,000 up to 31st March and ₹ 2,50,000 up to the due date for filing the return specified in Section 139(1). The amount liable to tax in its assessment would be —

(A) ₹ 3,70,000
(B) ₹ 1,20,000
(C) Nil
(D) ₹ 8,70,000

28. June 2016: Under the head 'profits and gains of business or profession', the method of accounting that should be followed by an assessee is —

(A) Cash system only
(B) Mercantile system only
(C) Hybrid system only
(D) Cash system or mercantile system only

29. June 2017: Madhu Ltd. owns machinery (rate of depreciation is 15%) the written down value of which as on 1st April, 2018 ₹ 30,00,000. Due to fire, entire assets in the block were destroyed and the insurer paid ₹ 25,00,000. The eligible depreciation in respect of this machinery is —

(A) ₹ 4,50,000

(B) ₹ 75,000

(C) ₹ 5,00,000

(D) Nil

30. June 2017: Ashwin has speculation business loss brought forward of the assessment years 2013-2014 ₹ 1,00,000; 2014-2015 ₹ 70,000 and 2015-2016 ₹ 60,000. He has income from the same speculation business for the assessment year 2019-2020 ₹ 5,40,000. His total income chargeable to tax for assessment year 2019-2020 would be -

(A) ₹ 3,10,000

(B) ₹ 4,10,000

(C) ₹ 4,80,000

(D) ₹ 4,40,000

31. June 2017: DP & Co. is a partnership firm with 3 partners. The capital of each partner was ₹ 2 lakh. The partnership deed authorized interest on capital @ 15% and working partner salary to each partner @ ₹ 10,000 per month for all the partners. The total sales amounted to ₹ 70 lakh. The total income of the firm under Section 44AD would be —

(A) ₹ 5,60,000

(B) ₹ 4,32,000

(C) ₹ 1,28,000

(D) ₹ 3,50,000

32. Dec 2017: Ekta (P) Ltd., engaged in manufacturing activity, acquired new plant and machinery for ₹ 100 lakh for its manufacturing unit located in Bihar. The acquisition and use was from 1st June, 2018. The assessee is eligible for additional depreciation of -

(A) ₹ 30 lakh

(B) ₹ 20 lakh

(C) ₹ 35 lakh

(D) ₹ 10 lakh

33. Dec 2017: A Company incurred capital expenditure on scientific research viz., (i) land ₹ 5 lakh (ii) building ₹ 10 lakh (iii) equipments ₹ 7 lakh. The amount of expenditure eligible for deduction under Section 35 would be -

(A) ₹ 22 lakh

(B) ₹ 17 lakh

(C) ₹ 15 lakh

(D) ₹ 5 lakh

34. Dec 2016: Which of the following is not deductible while calculating taxable income from business -

(A) Sales Tax

(B) Income-tax

(C) Customs duty

(D) Local taxes

35. Dec 2016: Swan (Pvt.) Ltd. acquired machinery for ₹ 5,75,000 which included GST of ₹ 75,000 eligible for input tax credit. It borrowed ₹ 3,00,000 from a bank for purchase of the said machine. Interest on the bank loan up to the date of usage of machine was ascertained as ₹ 5,000. The machine was put to use from 15th September, 2018. Assume the rate of depreciation at 15%. The eligible amount of depreciation will be -

(A) ₹ 90,000

(B) ₹ 78,750

(C) ₹ 86,250

(D) ₹ 75,000

36. Dec 2016: As per Section 35DDA, total expenditure in a voluntary retirement scheme is deductible in —

(A) 5 equal instalments

(B) 10 equal instalments

(C) 5 equal instalments

(D) The same year

37. Dec 2016: Any capital expenditure incurred on acquiring telecom licence is deductible in —

(A) 5 equal instalments

(B) 10 equal instalments

(C) 15 equal instalments

(D) Equally over the period of the license

38. Dec 2016: Varun Ltd. paid fees for technical services of ₹ 6 lakh has and omitted to deduct tax at source and such omission continued till the 'due date' for filing the return of income specified in Section 139(1). The amount of expenditure available for disallowance would be -

(A) ₹ 1,80,000

(B) ₹ 6,00,000

(C) ₹ 1,20,000

(D) Nil

39. June 2017: Dr. Sen has surgical equipments whose WDV as on 1.4.2018 was ₹ 4,10,000. He acquired some more equipments in December 2018 for ₹ 3,50000. He sold equipment in March 2019 for ₹ 2,00,000 whose original cost was ₹ 1,70,000. The written down value of the block for the purpose of computing depreciation for the assessment year 2019-2020 is:

(A) ₹ 5,90,000

(B) ₹ 5,60,000

(C) ₹ 7,30,000

(D) ₹ 4,30,000

40. June 2017: Rosy Ltd. engaged in manufacture of bio-medicines in August, 2018 converted one equipment which was used for scientific research purposes previously, for regular business use. The original cost of the plant is ₹ 15 lakhs which was acquired in April, 2017. The company had claimed deduction at 200% under section 35(2AB) in the assessment year 2018-2019. The plant used for scientific research would be included in the block of assets now at a value of:

(A) Nil

(B) ₹ 15,00,000

(C) ₹ 30,00,000

(D) ₹ 12,75,000

41. June 2017: Which of the following is a 'specified business' eligible for deduction under section 35AD?

(A) Operating warehousing facility for storage of agriculture produce

(B) Operating leather manufacturing unit

(C) Operating unit for manufacture of tooth paste

(D) Units operating in Jammu & Kashmir

42. June 2017: Malick & Co. engaged in trading activity could not recover ₹ 5 lakhs from a customer. It claimed the entire amount as bad debt by writing off in the books of account. The aggregate sale made during the year to the party amounts to ₹ 30 lakhs. The amount eligible for deduction by way of bad debt is:

(A) Nil

(B) ₹ 3 lakhs

(C) ₹ 5 lakhs

(D) ₹ 60,000

43. June 2017: Andhra Traders a partnership firm paid ₹ 80,000 as contract charges to AKP & Co. (firm). No tax was deducted at source for the above said payment The amount liable for disallowance under section 40A(ia) for the assessment year 2019-2020 is:

(A) Nil

(B) ₹ 80,000

(C) ₹ 40,000

(D) ₹ 24,000

44. June 2017: Ravi & Co. paid ₹ 40,000 by cash to Mr. Balu a supplier on 5.9.2018. The cash payment was made on the day on which the bank was on strike. The amount of expenditure liable for disallowance under section 40A(3) is:

(A) ₹ 40,000

(B) ₹ 12,000

(C) ₹ 20,000

(D) Nil

45. June 2017: Where the payment of an expenditure claimed as deduction by any assessee carrying on business or profession other than who is in transport business exceeds ₹ 10,000, it should be paid by:

(A) Crossed cheque/draft

(B) Account payee cheque/account payee draft

(C) Account payee cheque

(D) Any mode other than cash

46. June 2017: Raju succeeded to the business of his father Ramu consequent to demise of Ramu on 1.2.2019. Raju recovered ₹ 30,000 due from a customer which was written off by late Ramu as bad debt and allowed in the assessment year 2015-2016. The amount recovered is:

(A) Exempt from tax

(B) Fully taxable as business income

(C) ₹ 15,000 being 50% taxable as business income

(D) To be set off against current year bad debts

47. June 2017: Mr. Siraj engaged in retail trade reports a turnover of ₹ 43 lakhs for the previous year 2018-2019. He deposited ₹ 30,000 in his PPF account held with SBI. *Turnover or gross receipts represents amount received by an account payee cheque or an account payee bank draft or use of electronic clearing system through a bank account during the previous year or before the due date specified in Section 139(1).* His total income for the assessment year 2019-2020 by applying section 44AD provision is:

(A) ₹ 3,14,000

(B) ₹ 3,44,000

(C) ₹ 2,28,000

(D) ₹ 4,00,000

48. Dec 2017: DPM Ltd. constructed staff quarters and let out the same during the financial year 2018-2019. Its rent received ₹ 7,50,000 by way of rent from employees during the year. The rental receipt is taxable as:

(A) Income from house property

(B) Income from business

(C) Perquisite in the hands of employees

(D) Income from 'other sources'

49. Dec 2017: Vikram Mfg. Co. Ltd. located in a backward area in the State of Andhra Pradesh acquired some machinery for ₹ 20 lakhs on 10.8.2018. It was put to use from 1.9.2018. The applicable rate of depreciation is 15%. How much would be the eligible additional depreciation for the assessment year 2019-2020 in respect of the said machinery?

(A) ₹ 3,00,000

(B) ₹ 4,00,000

(C) ₹ 7,00,000

(D) ₹ 20,00,000

50. Dec 2017: When ABC Ltd. incurred ₹ 10 lakhs in FY 2018-2019 as capital expenditure for the purpose of family planning amongst the employees, the expenditure allowable for the assessment year 2019-2020 would be:

(A) Nil

(B) ₹ 2,00,000

(C) ₹ 10,00,000

(D) ₹ 5,00,000

51. Dec 2017: Alpha & Co is a proprietary concern owned by Vimala. The total turnover for the Year 2018-2019 is ₹ 52 lakhs which includes proceeds realized through banking channel ₹ 12 lakhs. The presumptive income under Section 44AD would be:

(A) ₹ 4,16,000

(B) ₹ 2,60,000

(C) ₹ 3,92,000

(D) ₹ 5,20,000

52. Dec 2017: Dr. Ravi practicing medicine has gross receipt of ₹ 18,40,000 for the financial year 2018-2019. His presumptive income under Section 44ADA would be:

(A) ₹ 1,47,200 @ 8%

(B) ₹ 92,000 @ 5%

(C) ₹ 9,20,000 @ 50%

(D) ₹ 4,60,000 @ 25%

53. Dec 2017: Rahim had 5 goods carriage vehicles on 1.4.2018. He acquired and used 3 vehicles from 1.9.2018. What is the presumptive income under Section 44AE?

(A) ₹ 8,10,000

(B) ₹ 3,64,500

(C) ₹ 2,02,500

(D) ₹ 6,07,500

54. Dec 2017: Books of account of an individual is liable for tax audit under section 44AB on mandatory basis, if the annual turnover exceeds:

(A) ₹ 40 lakhs

(B) ₹ 60 lakhs

(C) ₹ 100 lakhs

(D) ₹ 200 lakhs

55. Dec 2017: Ranga & Co. had as on 1.4.2018 plant and machinery whose written down value was ₹ 12,00,000. It acquired 2 plants on 3.11.2018 for ₹ 6 lakhs. The applicable depreciation rate is 15%. The eligible depreciation *including additional depreciation* for the AY 2019-2020 would be:

(A) ₹ 2,70,000

(B) ₹ 2,55,000

(C) ₹ 2,85,000

(D) ₹ 2,25,000

ANSWERS:

1.	(B)	**2.**	(A)	**3.**	(D)	**4.**	(C)	**5.**	(A)	**6.**	(D)	**7.**	(C)
8.	(A)	**9.**	(B)	**10.**	(A)	**11.**	(D)	**12.**	(C)	**13.**	(A)	**14.**	(B)
15.	(D)	**16.**	(D)	**17.**	(C)	**18.**	(A)	**19.**	(C)	**20.**	(B)	**21.**	(B)
22.	(D)	**23.**	(D)	**24.**	(A)	**25.**	(A)	**26.**	(D)	**27.**	(B)	**28.**	(D)
29.	(D)	**30.**	(C)	**31.**	(A)	**32.**	(C)	**33.**	(B)	**34.**	(B)	**35.**	(D)
36.	(B)	**37.**	(D)	**38.**	(A)	**39.**	(B)	**40.**	(A)	**41.**	(A)	**42.**	(C)
43.	(D)	**44.**	(D)	**45.**	(B)	**46.**	(A)	**47.**	(C)	**48.**	(B)	**49.**	(C)
50.	(B)	**51.**	(C)	**52.**	(C)	**53.**	(D)	**54.**	(C)	**55.**	(C)		

HINTS FOR PRACTICAL MCQs

88. As per **Explanation 5 to Section 43(1)**, the rate of depreciation to be applied is the rate in force in the year in which 'building' is brought into business use i.e. 10%.

Cost on 1.12.2016	10,00,000
(-) Depreciation for PY 2016-2017 @ 5% (use less than 180 days)	(50,000)
WDV on 31.3.2017	9,50,000
(-) Depreciation for PY 2017-2018 @ 10%	(95,000)
WDV on 31.3.2018	8,55,000
(-) Depreciation for PY 2018-2019 @ 10%	(85,500)
WDV on 31.3.2019	7,69,500

89.

Net profit	12,50,000
(+) Disallowance u/s 40A(2)	8,000
(+) Disallowance u/s 40A(3)	52,000
Taxable income	13,10,000

90.

Cost on 1.4.2015	2,00,000
(-) Depreciation for PY 2015-2016 @ 15%	(30,000)

WDV on 1.4.2018	1,22,875
(+) Additions during the year	

WDV on 31.3.2016	1,70,000
(-) Depreciation for PY 2016-2017 @ 15%	(25,500)
WDV on 31.3.2017	1,44,500
(-) Depreciation for PY 2017-2018 @ 15%	(21,675)
WDV on 31.3.2018	1,22,875

- Put to use less than 180 days	2,00,000
- Put to use more than 180 days	-
(-) Sold during the year	(3,90,000)
STCG	(67,125)

91.

Net profit	50,000
(-) Opening stock not recorded	(9,000)
(+) Closing stock not recorded	18,000
Business income	59,000

92.

Explanation 5 to Section 43(1) is applicable to 'building' only and not to car.

Cost on the date of conversion 1.12.2018 (actual cost)	6,50,000
(-) Depreciation for PY 2018-2019 @ 7.5% (use less than 180 days)	(48,750)
WDV on 31.3.2019	6,01,250

93.

WDV on 1.4.2018	4,50,000
(+) Additions during the year	
- Put to use less than 180 days	1,70,000
- Put to use more than 180 days	3,40,000
(-) Sold during the year	(4,18,000)
	5,42,000
Depreciation for PY 2018-2019	(68,550)
WDV on 31.3.2019	4,73,450

Depreciation for PY 2018-2019	
- On assets put to use less than 180 days	12,750
- On assets put to use more than 180 days	55,800
Total depreciation	68,550

94. 12,11,500 × 6% = 72,690

95.

Particulars	₹ in Crore
WDV on 1.4.2018	100
Depreciation for PY 2018-2019	(15)
Additional depreciation for PY 2018-2019	(20)
WDV on 31.3.2019	65

96.

WDV on 1.4.2018	4,50,000
(+) Additions during the year	
- Put to use less than 180 days	1,70,000
- Put to use more than 180 days	3,40,000
(-) Sold during the year	(6,50,000)
	3,10,000
Depreciation for PY 2018-2019	(33,750)
WDV on 31.3.2019	2,76,250

Depreciation for PY 2018-2019	
- On assets put to use less than 180 days	12,750
- On assets put to use more than 180 days	21,000
Total depreciation	33,750

97.

Income as per Section 44AE (5 × 7,500 × 12)	4,50,000
Income as per Section 44AD (21,70,000 × 8%)	1,73,600
Income as per presumptive taxation (A)	6,23,600

Income from plying of vehicles	2,10,400
Income from retail trade of garments	1,40,000
Brought forward depreciation for AY 2018-2019	(1,00,000)
Income as per books of account (B)	2,50,400

Total income as income from books of account is less than presumptive taxation. Hence Mr. Ram will claim income as per books of account.

98.

Income before claiming deduction expenditure on family planning	6,00,000
(-) Revenue expenditure (₹ 7,00,000 but restricted to ₹ 6,00,000)	(6,00,000)
	0
(-) Capital expenditure (1/5th of 10,00,000 but restricted to Zero)	0
Income chargeable under the head PGBP	0

Unabsorbed family planning expenditure	
- Revenue	1,00,000
- Capital	2,00,000
	3,00,000

99.

WDV on 1.4.2018	4,50,000
(+) Additions during the year	
- Put to use less than 180 days	1,70,000
- Put to use more than 180 days	3,40,000
(-) Sold during the year	(8,33,000)
STCL *(As all assets are sold)*	1,27,000

101.

Month	Calculation	Amount
April	(4 × 7,500)	30,000
May	(4 × 7,500)	30,000
June	(9 × 7,500)	67,500
July	(9 × 7,500)	67,500
Aug	(9 × 7,500)	67,500
Sep	(9 × 7,500)	67,500
Oct	(9 × 7,500)	67,500
Nov	(9 × 7,500)	67,500
Dec	(9 × 7,500)	67,500

Month	Calculation	Amount
Jan	(9 × 7,500)	67,500
Feb	(9 × 7,500)	67,500
March	(9 × 7,500)	67,500
		7,35,000

102.

Month	Calculation	Amount
April	(10 × 7,500)	75,000
May **	(11 × 7,500)	82,500
June	(10 × 7,500)	75,000
July	(10 × 7,500)	75,000
Aug	(10 × 7,500)	75,000
Sep	(10 × 7,500)	75,000
Oct	(10 × 7,500)	75,000
Nov	(10 × 7,500)	75,000
Dec	(10 × 7,500)	75,000
Jan	(10 × 7,500)	75,000
Feb	(10 × 7,500)	75,000
March	(10 × 7,500)	75,000
		9,07,500

** On 2nd May, Shekhar sold one vehicle and on 6th May he purchased one more vehicle. Part of the month is treated as full of the month. Hence, for calculation purpose vehicle sold as well as purchased will be considered. However, he does not own 10 vehicles on any day in May, hence eligible for presumptive taxation u/s 44AE.

105.

Depreciation on car @ 7.5% as put to use less than 180 days (2,20,000 × 7.5% × 3/4)	12,375
Car expenses (6,000 × 3/4)	4,500

HINTS FOR PAST EXAMINATION MCQs

5. (4 × 12 × 7,500) + (2 × 3 × 7,500) = 4,05,000

14.

WDV on 1.4.2017	3,00,000
(-) Depreciation for PY 2017-2018 (3,00,000 × 15% × 2/3)	(30,000)

WDV on 31.3.2018	2,70,000
(-) Depreciation for PY 2018-2019 (2,66,250 × 15% × 2/3)	(27,000)
WDV on 31.3.2019	2,43,000

16. Depreciation is available on building only not on land. ₹ 15 lakh does not include the cost of land. Read the MCQ carefully.

Cost on 1.6.2016	15,00,000
(-) Depreciation for PY 2016-2017	(1,50,000)
WDV on 31.3.2017	13,50,000
(-) Depreciation for PY 2017-2018	(1,35,000)
WDV on 31.3.2018	12,15,000

Depreciation for PY 2018-2019 = 12,15,000 × 10% = 1,21,500

21. 8 × 7,500 × 12 = 7,20,000

23. 10,00,000 × 10% × ½ = 50,000. Depreciation is not available on land. On building half depreciation is eligible as asset put to use is less than 180 days.

24. 27,00,00,000 × 15% = 4,05,00,000

29. Amount received from insurance company is more than WDV hence excess amount of ₹ 5,00,000 (30,00,000 - 25,00,000) will be STCG and liable to tax under the head 'Capital Gain'. Since, all assets are destroyed WDV for charging depreciation will be zero.

30. 5,40,000 - 60,000 = 4,80,000. Speculation business loss can be carried forward and set-off only for 4 years.

31.

Deemed income	(70,00,000 × 8%)	5,60,000
~~(-) Interest up to 12%~~	~~(2,00,000 × 3 × 12%)~~	~~(72,000)~~
~~(-) Salary~~	~~(10,000 × 3 × 12)~~	~~(3,60,000)~~
		5,60,000

~~*Where eligible assessee is firm, salary and interest paid to partners shall be deducted from the deemed income subject to conditions and limits of Section 40 (b).*~~ *[This provision is deleted]*

33.

Capital expenditure on scientific research	
- Land (not eligible)	-
- Building	10 lakh
- Equipments	7 lakh
	17 lakh

35. 5,75,000 - 75,000 × 15% = 75,000

39.

WDV of equipment on at the beginning	4,10,000
(+) Addition during year	3,50,000
(-) Sold during year	(2,00,000)
WDV for charging depreciation	5,60,000

43. 80,000 × 30% = 24,000

47.

Deemed income u/s 44AD (43,00,000 × 6%)	2,58,000
(-) Deduction u/s 80C	(30,000)
Total income	2,28,000

49. 20,00,000 × 35% = 7,00,000.

50. 10,00,000 × 1/5 = 2,00,000.

51. (12,00,000 × 6%) + (40,00,000 × 8%) = 3,92,000.

53. (5 × 7,500 × 12) + (3 × 7,500 × 7) = 6,07,500.

55.

Regular depreciation:	
- On asset put to use more than 180 days (12,00,000 × 15%)	1,80,000
- On asset put to use less than 180 days (6,00,000 × 7.5%)	45,000
Additional depreciation on new assets:	
- On asset put to use less than 180 days (6,00,000 × 10%)	60,000
Total depreciation	2,85,000

CHAPTER 6

INCOME FROM CAPITAL GAINS

MCQs ON THEORY

1. Which of the following is/are essential conditions for taxing capital gains?

(I) Capital gain should not be exempt u/s 54

(II) Capital asset transferred must be rural agricultural land

(III) Capital gain should not be exempt u/s 54GB.

(IV) Capital asset is owned by the assessee.

Select the correct answer from the options given below –

(A) (II) and (IV)

(B) (I), (II) and (IV)

(C) (III), (I) and (IV)

(D) (I) and (IV)

2. Capital asset –

(A) means property of any kind

(B) does not include personal effects

(C) includes jewellery whether used for personal purpose or not

(D) all of the above

3. Cost inflation index for the PY 2018–2019 is –

(A) 270

(B) 271

(C) 280

(D) 273

4. Identify correct statement from the following:

(A) In case of sale of depreciable asset there is always short term capital gain even if period of holding is more than 36 months.

(B) In case of Zero Coupon Bond if period of holding is more than 36 months then only gain on sale is treated as long term capital gain.

(C) Both (A) and (B)

(D) Neither (A) nor (B)

5. Reference to valuation officer can be made if fair market value of the asset exceeds the value of asset as claimed by assessee by –

(A) ₹ 25,000 or 15% of value claimed by assessee

(B) ₹ 50,000 or 20% of value claimed by assessee

(C) ₹ 20,000 or 10% of value claimed by assessee

(D) ₹ 1,00,000 or 25% of value claimed by assessee

6. Where the capital asset became the property of the assessee under modes specified in Section 49(1) –

(A) The cost of acquisition has to be taken Nil.

(B) Fair market value on the date of transfer has to be taken as cost of acquisition

(C) The cost of acquisition has to be taken cost for which the previous owner of the property acquired it, as increased by the cost of any improvement incurred or borne by the previous owner or the assessee.

(D) Any of the (B) and (C) at the option of assessee

7. Which of the following are capital assets?

1. Tenancy right
2. Personal effects
3. Motor car used for personal use
4. Loose diamonds

Select the correct answer from the options given below –

(A) 1, 2 & 3

(B) 4 only

(C) 1 & 4 only

(D) 1, 3 & 4

8. When capital asset is transferred in business as stock in trade, then business profit = ?

(A) Sale price (-) FMV of stock on the date of conversion

(B) Sale price (-) Cost of acquisition

(C) Sale price (-) indexed cost of acquisition

(D) (B) or (C)

9. Which of the following is 'Capital Asset' with the meaning of Section 2(14) of the Income Tax Act, 1961?

(1) Building held as stock-in-trade

(2) Furniture

(3) 6.5% Gold Bonds, 1977

(4) Archaeological collections

Select the correct answer from the options given below –

(A) (3) & (2)

(B) (2) & (4)

(C) (1), (2) & (4)

(D) (4), (3) & (1)

10. Which of the following is liable to capital gain tax?

(a) Urban agricultural land

(b) Rural agricultural land

Select the correct answer from the options given below –

(A) (a) only

(B) (b) only

(C) Both (a) and (b)

(D) Neither (a) nor (b)

11. Which of the following statement(s) is/are false?

(*i*) Silver utensils used by assessee in his kitchen or dining room are capital asset and liable to capital gain tax (*ii*) Cost of acquisition of bonus shares has to be taken to be Nil whether bonus was made before 1.4.1981 or not.

(*iii*) Distribution of assets on partition of HUF amount to 'transfer' and liable to capital gain tax

Select the correct answer from the options given below –

(A) (i) only

(B) (i) and (ii) only

(C) (i), (ii) and (iii)

(D) None of the above

12. When there is transfer of a capital asset by a partner to a firm, by way of capital contribution for the purpose of computation of taxable capital gain, full value of consideration shall be –

(A) Fair market value of the asset on the date of such transfer

(B) Amount recorded in the books of account of the partner as capital contribution

(C) Market value of asset on the date of transfer

(D) Amount recorded in the books of account of the firm as the value of the capital asset

13. Short term capital asset means any asset held by the assessee for ______

(A) Held by the assessee for less than 36 months

(B) Held by the assessee for less than 24 months for unlisted shares

(C) An immovable property being land and building held for less than 24 months.

(D) All of the above

14. Match the following:

List I	*List II*
(P) Transfer of capital asset by demerged company to resulting company	1. No indexation is allowed
(Q) Transaction not regarded as transfer	2. Section 47

(R) Debentures
(S) Property acquired through mode specified in Section 49(1)

3. Cost to previous owner
4. Liable to capital gain
5. Exempt

Select the correct answer from the options given below –

	(P)	(Q)	(R)	(S)
(A)	5	2	1	3
(B)	4	1	5	3
(C)	5	2	1	3
(D)	5	2	3	1

15. In case of compulsorily acquisition of capital asset under any law –

(A) Enhanced compensation is fully taxable

(B) Capital loss on initial compensation can be set-off from enhanced compensation

(C) 50% of enhanced compensation is taxable and remaining 50% shall be exempt.

(D) None of the above

16. If unlisted shares are sold after 24 months but before 36 months then it is ______

(A) Short term capital gain

(B) Long term capital gain

(C) Not a capital gain at all

(D) Short term capital gain but currently exempt

17. Exemption u/s 54 is available to the extent of –

(A) Amount invested in new asset

(B) Amount invested in new asset which is proportionate to net sale consideration

(C) To the extent amount actually invested in new residential property

(D) All of the above

18. If a company distribute capital asset at the time of liquidation then capital gain arising out of such transaction is –

(A) taxable in the hands of company

(B) taxable in the hands of shareholder

(C) taxable in the hands of liquidator

(D) neither taxable in the hands of company or shareholder or liquidator

19. If non-resident sales capital asset and capital gain is calculated in foreign currency then such capital is required to be converted in Indian currency at –

(A) Telegraphic transfer selling rate

(B) Telegraphic transfer buying rate

(C) Telegraphic transfer average rate

(D) Rate notified by CBDT

20. Transfer of capital assets by holding company to subsidiary company and vice versa shall not be regarded as transfer and hence not liable to tax if –

(A) Holding company owns 75% shares of subsidiary company

(B) Holding company owns 90% shares of subsidiary company

(C) Holding company owns 100% shares of subsidiary company

(D) Holding company owns 51% shares of subsidiary company

21. The option to opt for FMV as on 1.4.2001 is available ________

(A) For all capital assets

(B) For all capital assets other than depreciable assets

(C) For all capital assets other than depreciable assets and goodwill, tenancy rights, loom hours and route permits.

(D) None of the above

22. Exemption u/s 54 on capital gain arising from transfer of residential property is available to –

(A) Individual

(B) HUF

(C) Firm

(D) (A) and (B)

23. If convertible debentures are converted in shares the cost of acquisition of such shares shall be –

(A) Cost of acquisition of debentures

(B) Market value of debenture on the date of conversion

(C) Market value of shares on the date of conversion

(D) Market value of debentures on the date of sale of such shares.

24. Exemption u/s 54 on capital gain arising from transfer of residential property is available if such residential property is –

(A) Long term capital asset (LTCA)

(B) Short term capital asset (STCA)

(C) Either (A) or (B)

(D) Both (A) and (B)

25. If goodwill, tenancy rights, loom hours and route permits is acquired before 1.4.2001, the cost of acquisition of such asset shall be –

(A) Actual cost of acquisition

(B) FMV as on 1.4.2001

(C) Actual cost of acquisition or FMV as on 1.4.2001 whichever is beneficial to assessee

(D) Nil

26. Exemption u/s 54 is available on sale of residential property, the income of which is chargeable under the head

(A) Income from business or profession

(B) Income from house property

(C) Income from capital gain

(D) (A) and (B)

27. To which of the following benefit of indexation is not available?

P. Bonds

Q. Debentures

R. Slump sale

S. Global depository receipts

Select the correct answer from the options given below –

(A) P & S

(B) Q & R

(C) P, Q & S

(D) P, Q, R & S

28. The interest received on enhanced compensation shall be taxable in the previous year in which it is received, as income under the head __________ to the extent of _____ of such interest.

(A) 'Capital gain'; 50%

(B) 'Income from other sources'; 25%

(C) 'Income from other sources'; 50%

(D) 'Capital gain'; 25%

29. Where any person receives any money or other assets under an insurance from an insurer on account of damage or destruction of any capital asset –

(A) then, any profits or gains arising from receipt of such money or other assets shall be taxable as capital gains

(B) then, any profits or gains arising from receipt of such money or other assets shall not be taxable as capital gains as there is not 'transfer' of capital asset

(C) then, any profits or gains arising from receipt of such money or other assets shall be taxable as capital gains only if it is long term capital asset

(D) then, any profits or gains arising from receipt of such money or other assets shall be not be taxable as capital gains as currently such capital gains are exempted

30. Lock in period specified for exemption u/s 54 is _______

(A) 2 years

(B) 3 years

(C) 5 years

(D) 4 years

31. Exemption u/s 54B is available on sale of _____ capital asset being land which, in the 2 years immediately preceding the date on which the transfer took place, was being used by the HUF or individual or his parents for agricultural purposes.

(A) short term

(B) long term

(C) short term or long term

(D) (A) but not (B)

32. If bonus shares are allotted on or after 1.4.2001, the cost of acquisition such bonus shares shall be –

(A) FMV as on 1.4.2001

(B) Market value on the date of allotment of bonus shares

(C) Nil

(D) Market value of original shares on the basis of which bonus shares has been allotted

33. For availing exemption u/s 54B, the assessee shall purchase any other land for using agricultural purposes –

(A) within a period of 2 years after the date of transfer

(B) within a period of 1 year before or 2 years after the date of transfer

(C) within a period of 2 year before or 2 years after the date of transfer

(D) within a period of 2 year before or 3 years after the date of transfer

34. While calculating short term capital gain exemption is available _____

(A) Under sections 54B, 54D, 54G & 54GA

(B) Under sections 54, 54B, 54D, 54EC, 54F, 54G, 54GA & 54GB

(C) Under sections 54, 54D, 54EC, 54GA & 54GB

(D) Under sections 54, 54B, 54D, 54F, 54G, 54GA & 54GB

35. Exemption u/s 54D is available to –

(A) Individual

(B) Firm

(C) Company

(D) Any of the above

36. While calculating long term capital gain exemption is available ______

(A) u/ss 54, 54D, 54EC, 54GA & 54GB

(B) u/ss 54, 54D, 54EC, 54F & 54GB

(C) u/ss 54, 54B, 54D, 54EC, 54F, 54G, 54GA & 54GB

(D) u/ss 54B, 54D, 54G & 54GA

37. For claiming exemption u/s 54D in respect of capital gain on compulsory acquisition of land and buildings, the assessee, within a period of ______, shall purchase any other land or building or any right in any other land or building or constructed any other building for the purposes of shifting or re-establishing the said undertaking or setting up another industrial undertaking.

(A) 4 years

(B) 2 years

(C) 3 years

(D) 5 years

38. Cost of improvement includes –

(A) Expenditure chargeable under the head 'house property' or 'PGBP' in making additions to the asset.

(B) Any expenditure made by previous owner in additions to the capital asset

(C) Any expenditure whether the efficiency of asset is increased or not

(D) All of the above

39. Exemption u/s 54B for short term or long term capital gain is available if assessee purchases ______

(A) any urban agricultural land

(B) any rural agricultural land

(C) purchases any other land for being used for agricultural purposes

(D) any long term capital asset

40. When Sweat Equity Shares are allotted to employee and subsequently such shares are sold by the employee then ______

(A) Actual cost incurred by the employee for acquiring such shares

(B) There is no capital gain tax as already at the time of allotment of sweat equity shares difference between price paid by employee and fair market value of shares on the date of allotment is taxed as perquisite under the head 'income from salary'

(C) Cost of acquisition shall be fair market value which has been taken into account while computing the value of perquisite for such sweat equity shares

(D) None of the above

41. Exemption u/s 54EC for investment in bonds of NHAI or REC if capital gain on sale of capital asset is ______

(1) Short term capital asset

(2) Long term capital asset

Select the correct answer from the options given below –

(A) (1) only

(B) (2) only

(C) Both (1) and (2)

(D) Neither (1) nor (2)

42. For claiming exemption u/s 54G, the assessee shall acquire the new asset within ______

(A) One year before or 3 year from the date of transfer

(B) 2 year after the date of transfer

(C) One year before or 2 year after the date of transfer

(D) 3 year after the date of transfer

43. Which of the following is/are eligible for exemption u/s 54G on transfer or shifting of industrial undertaking from urban area?

1. Long term capital gain on building
2. Short term capital gain on plant
3. Short term capital gain on furniture

4. Short term capital gain on land
5. Expenses incurred on shifting industrial undertaking

Select the correct answer from the options given below –

(A) 1, 2 & 5
(B) 2, 3 & 4
(C) 1, 2, 4 & 5
(D) Except 3 & 5 all other

44. Exemption u/s 54EC is available for investment in bonds of –

(i) National Highways Authority of India (NHAI)
(ii) Industrial Development Bank of India (IDBI)
(iii) Rural Electrification Corporation (REC)
(iv) National Thermal Power Corporation of India (NTPC)

Select the correct answer from the options given below –

(A) (i) & (ii)
(B) (iii) & (iv)
(C) (ii) & (iii)
(D) (i) & (iii)

45. Exemption for investment in new residential house as provided in Section 54F is available for –

(A) Long term capital asset being residential house
(B) Short term or long term capital asset being residential house
(C) Any long-term capital asset
(D) Any long-term capital asset, not being a residential house.

46. Where any person receives any money or other assets under an insurance from an insurer on account of damage or destruction of any capital asset then while calculating capital gain –

(A) Full value of consideration shall be market value of such asset on the date of damage or destruction of capital asset has to be taken
(B) Full value of consideration shall be fair market value of assets on the date of such receipt of compensation has to be taken

(C) Full value of consideration shall be book value of assets on the date of damage or destruction of capital asset has to be taken

(D) Full value of consideration need not to be taken as such gain is taxable as capital gain

47. Which of the following sentence is correct for exemption as provided in Section 54F?

(A) If the cost of the new house is not less than the net consideration in respect of the original asset, the whole of such capital gain shall be exempt.

(B) If the cost of the new house is less than the net consideration in respect of the original asset, then

$$\text{Amount of exemption} = \text{Capital gain} \times \frac{\text{Cost of the new asset}}{\text{Net sale consideration}}$$

(C) LTCG or Cost of new asset whichever is less.

(D) (A) or (B)

48. In which case it was held that indexation benefit in respect of gifted asset apply from the year in which the asset was first acquired by the previous owner?

(A) *Devi Prasad* vs. *CIT*

(B) *CIT* vs. *Mahindra Ltd.*

(C) *CIT* vs. *Manjula J Shah*

(D) *Narayanmurthy* vs. *CIT*

49. Exemption u/s 54EC is available to the extent of –

(A) Actual amount invested in bonds of NHAI or REC without any limit

(B) Actual amount invested subject to maximum ₹ 50 lakhs per financial year or the capital gain whichever is less.

(C) Actual amount invested subject to maximum ₹ 50 lakhs.

(D) Actual amount invested subject to maximum ₹ 25 lakhs per financial year or the capital gain whichever is less.

50. If the right shares are purchased by a person in whose favour right was renounced, then cost of acquisition for him shall be –

(A) Fair market value on the date of renouncement in favour of such person

(B) Fair market value on the date of announcement of right shares by the company

(C) Aggregate of purchase price paid to a company and amount paid by him for renouncement in his favour.

(D) Fair value as determined by the Assessing Officer in consultation with valuation officer.

51. Exemption for investment in new residential house as provided in Section 54F is available if the assessee ______

(A) Purchases house 1 year before the transfer took place

(B) Purchases house 2 years after the date on which the transfer took place

(C) Constructs house within a period of 3 years after the date on which the transfer took place

(D) All of the above

52. Section 54GB of the Income Tax Act, 1961 deals with –

(A) Extension of time for acquiring new asset or depositing amount of capital gain

(B) Exemption of capital gain on transfer of residential property invested in equity shares of eligible company

(C) Capital gains on transfer of shares of an Indian company by non-residents

(D) Transfer of industrial undertaking from SEZ to Domestic Tariff Area

53. After depositing the amount under capital gain scheme, the assessee dies, in such case the amount lying in the capital gain account scheme ________

(A) Shall be exempt in the hands of legal heirs

(B) Shall be utilized by legal heirs for specified purpose

(C) Shall be taxable in the hands of legal heirs

(D) None of the above

54. As per Section 111A, there is special rate of tax on STCG on sale of listed shares –

(A) @ 15%

(B) @ 17.304%

(C) @ 10%

(D) @ 11.54%

55. Long term capital gain on sale listed equity shares on which securities transaction has been paid –

(A) is liable to tax u/s 112A

(B) is liable to capital gain tax @ 7.5%

(C) is liable to tax @ 10% with benefit of indexation

(D) is taxable @ 15%

56. Which of the following statement is true?

(1) Capital gain arises from the transfer of any capital asset.

(2) Conversion of debenture into share shall not be regarded as transfer for the purpose of capital gain

(3) There is no capital gain on the transfer of goodwill of a business which is self generated

(4) Benefit of indexation is allowable in the case of capital asset being capital indexed bond issued by government if there is long term capital gain

Select the correct answer from the options given below –

(A) (1) & (3)

(B) (2) & (4)

(C) (1) & (4)

(D) (2) & (3)

ANSWERS:

1.	(C)	**2.**	(D)	**3.**	(C)	**4.**	(A)	**5.**	(A)	**6.**	(C)	**7.**	(C)
8.	(A)	**9.**	(B)	**10.**	(B)	**11.**	(C)	**12.**	(D)	**13.**	(D)	**14.**	(A)
15.	(A)	**16.**	(B)	**17.**	(C)	**18.**	(A)	**19.**	(B)	**20.**	(C)	**21.**	(C)

22.	(D)	**23.**	(A)	**24.**	(A)	**25.**	(A)	**26.**	(B)	**27.**	(D)	**28.**	(C)
29.	(A)	**30.**	(B)	**31.**	(C)	**32.**	(C)	**33.**	(A)	**34.**	(A)	**35.**	(D)
36.	(C)	**37.**	(C)	**38.**	(B)	**39.**	(C)	**40.**	(C)	**41.**	(B)	**42.**	(A)
43.	(C)	**44.**	(D)	**45.**	(D)	**46.**	(B)	**47.**	(D)	**48.**	(C)	**49.**	(B)
50.	(C)	**51.**	(D)	**52.**	(B)	**53.**	(C)	**54.**	(A)	**55.**	(A)	**56.**	(B)

PAST EXAMINATION MCQs

1. Dec 2014: Capital asset excludes all except —

(A) Stock-in-trade

(B) Personal effects

(C) Jewellery

(D) Rural agricultural land in India

2. Dec 2014: On 15th November, 2018, Mohan sold 1 kg of gold, the sale consideration of which was ₹ 1,14,000. He had acquired the gold on 11th December, 2000 for ₹ 64,000. Fair market value of 1 kg gold on 1st April, 2001 was ₹ 62,000. The amount of capital gains chargeable to tax for the AY 2019-2020 shall be —

(A) 17,200

(B) 50,000

(C) (65,200) loss

(D) (70,080) loss

3. Dec 2014: Cost of acquisition in case of bonus shares allotted before 1.4.2001 will be —

(A) Face value on the date of allotment

(B) Nil

(C) Market value as on 1.4.2001

(D) Current market value

4. June 2015: Which of the following is not a requisite for charging income-tax on capital gains?

(A) The transfer must have been effected in the relevant assessment year

(B) There must be a gain arising on transfer of capital asset

(C) Capital gains should not be exempt u/s 54

(D) Capital gains should not be exempt u/s 54EC

5. June 2015: In order to enjoy exemption u/s 54EC, the resultant long-term capital gains should be invested in specified bonds within a period of ________ from the date of transfer.

(A) 36 Months

(B) 4 Months

(C) 6 Months

(D) 12 Months

6. June 2015: Sarath has received a sum of ₹ 3,40,000 as interest on enhanced compensation for compulsory acquisition of land by State Government in May, 2018. Of this, only ₹ 12,000 pertains to the current year and the rest pertains to earlier years. The amount chargeable to tax for the AY 2019-2020 would be —

(A) ₹ 12,000

(B) ₹ 6,000

(C) ₹ 3,40,000

(D) ₹ 1,70,000

7. June 2015: In terms of Section 2(42A), unlisted securities are treated as long-term capital asset, if they are held for a period of more than —

(A) 24 Months

(B) 36 Months

(C) 12 Months

(D) 48 Months

8. June 2015: For claiming exemption u/s 54G, an assessee has to invest the resultant capital gains within a specified period. Which of the following is not eligible for such investment?

(A) Furniture

(B) Land

(C) Building

(D) Plant or machinery

9. June 2015: Long-term capital gains on zero coupon bonds are chargeable to tax —

(A) @ 20% computed after indexation of such bonds

(B) @ 10% computed without indexation of such bonds

(C) Higher of (A) or (B)

(D) Lower of (A) or (B)

10. June 2015: Section 50C makes special provision for determining the full value of consideration in cases of transfer of —

(A) Plant and machinery

(B) Land or building

(C) All movable property other than plant & machinery and computers

(D) Computers

11. June 2015: U/s 115E, the tax rate applicable for any income from investment or income from long-term capital gains of an asset other than a specified asset, for a non-resident as envisaged by Section 115C, is—

(A) 5%

(B) 20%

(C) 15%

(D) 10%

12. Dec 2015: A residential house is sold for ₹ 90 lakh and the long-term capital gains computed are ₹ 50 lakh. The assessee bought two residential houses for ₹ 30 lakh and ₹ 20 lakh respectively. The amount eligible for exemption u/s 54 would be —

(A) ₹ 50 lakh

(B) ₹ 20 lakh

(C) ₹ 30 lakh

(D) Nil

13. Dec 2015: When shares of a listed company held for more than 36 months are transferred privately for ₹ 8 lakh, with original cost of acquisition of ₹ 1 lakh whose indexed cost of acquisition is ₹ 2 lakh, the income-tax payable would be —

(A) ₹ 1,44,200

(B) ₹ 72,800

(C) ₹ 1,23,600

(D) ₹ 61,800

14. Dec 2015: Aman entered into an agreement with Brij for sale of a building for ₹ 20 lakh in June, 2018. Aman received advance of ₹ 2 lakh. Subsequently, the agreement was cancelled and Aman forfeited the advance money. The advance money is —

(A) To be reduced from the cost of acquisition

(B) To be reduced from indexed cost of acquisition

(C) Taxable as capital gains

(D) Taxable as income under the head 'Income from other sources'.

15. Dec 2015: Ramesh received ₹ 7 lakh by way of enhanced compensation in March, 2019. A further sum of ₹ 2 lakh decreed by the Court is due but not received till 31st March, 2019. The amount of income chargeable to tax for the AY 2019-2020 would be —

(A) ₹ 3,50,000

(B) ₹ 7,00,000

(C) ₹ 9,00,000

(D) ₹ 4,50,000

16. Dec 2015: Ramji Charitable Trust had sold a capital asset costing ₹ 70,000 on 13th June, 2018 for ₹ 1,50,000. It purchased new assets on 1st July, 2018 for ₹ 1,20,000. The amount taxable as capital gains for Ramji Charitable Trust after exemption u/s 11(1A) in AY 2019-2020 is —

(A) ₹ 80,000

(B) Nil, because of charitable trust

(C) ₹ 30,000

(D) ₹ 40,000

17. June 2016: Ms. Smita inherited a vacant site land consequent to the demise of her father on 10th June, 2011. The land was acquired by her father on 10th April, 1991 for ₹ 40,000. The fair market value of the land on 1st April, 2001 was ₹ 60,000 and on the date of inheritance, i.e., 10th June, 2011 was ₹ 2,00,000. The cost of acquisition for Ms. Smita is —

(A) ₹ 10,000

(B) Nil

(C) ₹ 60,000

(D) ₹ 2,00,000

18. June 2016: Under which section, the assessee has to reinvest the entire net consideration to claim full exemption for the long-term capital gains earned during a previous year —

(A) Section 54EC

(B) Section 54F

(C) Section 54GA

(D) Section 54D

19. June 2016: Short-term capital gains arising from the transfer of equity shares in a company or units of an equity oriented fund or units of a business trust charged with security transaction tax are subject to income-tax at the rate of —

(A) 10%

(B) 15%

(C) 20%

(D) Normal rate

20. June 2016: A foreign institutional investor (FII) has total income which includes short-term capital gains-on sale of listed shares of ₹ 30 lakh. The rate of tax for charging such income to tax is —

(A) 10%

(B) 30%

(C) 15%

(D) 40%

21. June 2016: Manoj acquired 1,000 equity shares of ₹ 10 each in a listed company for ₹ 35,000 on 1st July, 2012. The company issued 1,000 rights shares in April, 2014 at ₹ 15 per share. The company issued 2,000 bonus shares in June, 2018. The market price was ₹ 50 per share before bonus issue and ₹ 25 after such issue. The cost of acquisition of bonus shares would be —

(A) Nil

(B) ₹ 20,000

(C) ₹ 50,000

(D) ₹ 1,00,000

22. Dec 2016: Cost of acquisition of securities held with depositories is to be computed by –

(A) Average cost method

(B) First in first out

(C) Last in first out

(D) Weighted average cost method

23. Dec 2016: Long-term capital gains on sale of a long-term capital asset in October, 2018 is ₹ 105 lakh. The assessee invested ₹ 50 lakh in REC bonds in March, 2019 and ₹ 55 lakh in MIAI bonds in May, 2019. The amount of exemption eligible under Section 54EC is –

(A) Nil

(B) ₹ 50 lakh

(C) ₹ 55 lakh

(D) ₹ 105 lakh

24. Dec 2016: Rajat purchased a car for his personal use for ₹ 5,00,000 in April 2018 and sold the same for ₹ 5,50,000 in July 2018. The taxable capital gains would be –

(A) Nil

(B) ₹ 5,50,000

(C) ₹ 50,000

(D) ₹ 4,00,000

25. June 2017: Mrs. Lakshmi purchased shares of ABB Ltd. for ₹ 5 lakhs on 3rd April, 2016. The shares were sold on 5th June, 2018 for ₹ 7 lakhs. She paid STT of ₹ 700 and brokerage of ₹ 500. Capital gain chargeable to tax:

(A) Nil, as it is exempt u/s 10(38)

(B) @ 10% u/s 112A without benefit of indexation

(C) @ 20% u/s 112 without benefit of indexation

(D) @ 10% u/s 112A with benefit of indexation

26. June 2017: Ms. Netra acquired 1,000 equity shares of MMC Ltd. (unlisted company) for ₹ 4 lakhs in April, 2007. She received bonus shares on 1:1 basis in April, 2017 from the company. She sold bonus shares in January, 2019 for ₹ 8 lakhs. The capital gain chargeable to tax in the hands of Ms. Netra for the assessment year 2019-2020 is:

(A) ₹ 8 lakhs

(B) Nil, since the entire gain is exempt from tax

(C) ₹ 2 lakhs

(D) ₹ 80,000

27. June 2017: Mr. Madan sold a vacant land for ₹ 120 lakhs on 10.10.2018. The indexed cost of acquisition amounts to ₹ 18 lakhs. He deposited ₹ 50 lakhs in REC bonds in January 2019 and another ₹ 50 lakhs in March, 2019. The amount of capital gain liable to tax after deduction under section 54EC is:

(A) ₹ 2 lakhs

(B) ₹ 52 lakhs

(C) ₹ 102 lakhs

(D) ₹ 18 lakhs

28. Dec 2017: Which of the following is not a capital asset for Mr. Rao who is employed in a public sector bank?

(A) Urban land

(B) Agricultural land within 2 km from local limits of municipality

(C) Deposit certificate issued under Gold Monetization Scheme, 2015

(D) Jewellery

29. Dec 2017: On 1.6.2018 Kamlesh transferred his vacant land to Rajesh for ₹ 12 lakhs. The land was acquired on 1.9.2015 for ₹ 3 lakh. The indexed cost of acquisition of the said land is ₹ 3,70,909. The taxable capital gain would be:

(A) long term capital gain ₹ 8,29,091

(B) short-term capital gain ₹ 9 lakhs

(C) long-term capital gain ₹ 9 lakhs

(D) short term capital gain ₹ 8.70 lakhs

30. Dec 2017: Dr. Sam sold a vacant land to Mr. Roy for ₹ 36 lakhs. For stamp-duty purpose, the value of land was ₹ 41 lakhs. The indexed cost of acquisition of land was computed at ₹ 20 lakhs. The taxable long-term capital gain would be:

(A) ₹ 21 lakhs

(B) ₹ 16 lakhs

(C) ₹ 5 lakhs

(D) ₹ 20 lakhs

ANSWERS:

1.	(C)	**2.**	(C)	**3.**	(C)	**4.**	(A)	**5.**	(C)	**6.**	(D)	**7.**	(A)
8.	(A)	**9.**	(D)	**10.**	(B)	**11.**	(B)	**12.**	(C)	**13.**	(B)	**14.**	(D)
15.	(B)	**16.**	(C)	**17.**	(C)	**18.**	(B)	**19.**	(B)	**20.**	(C)	**21.**	(A)
22.	(B)	**23.**	(B)	**24.**	(A)	**25.**	(B)	**26.**	(A)	**27.**	(B)	**28.**	(C)
29.	(B)	**30.**	(A)										

HINTS FOR PAST EXAMINATION MCQs:

2.

Full value of consideration		1,14,000
(-) Indexed cost of acquisition	$\left[64{,}000 \times \frac{280}{100}\right]$	(1,79,200)
LTCL		(65,200)

6. 50% interest on enhanced compensation is exempt and balance 50% is taxable under the head 'Income from other sources'.

13.

Full value of consideration	8,00,000
(-) Cost of acquisition	(1,00,000)
	7,00,000

Full value of consideration	8,00,000
(-) Indexed cost of acquisition	(2,00,000)
	6,00,000

10% of 7,00,000 = 70,000

20% of 6,00,000 = 1,20,000

70,000 + 2,800 (Education cess @ 4%) = 72,800

16.

Full value of consideration		1,50,000
(-) Cost of acquisition		(70,000)
Capital gain		80,000
(-) Exemption: Lower of the following two –		
- Capital gain	80,000	
- (Cost of new asset – Cost of asset transferred) [1,20,000 – 70,000]	50,000	
		(50,000)
		30,000

17. In case gift and inheritance cost to previous owner has to taken into consideration for the purpose of computation of capital gain. In case of asset acquired before 1.4.2001, the option to take actual cost or FMV on 1.4.2001 is available. Hence, cost to Ms. Smita will be ₹ 60,000.

24. Capital asset, as defined by Section 2(14) of Income Tax Act, 1961, does not include items held for personal use such as furniture, air-conditioners, refrigerators, motor cars etc. Therefore, a car used for personal purpose (depreciation is not charged), is not a capital asset. When it is sold, no capital gains, either short-term or long-term can arise. The profit cannot be brought to income tax.

26. Bonus shares are short term asset and gain on sale of such shares is taxable as shown below:

Sales price	8,00,000
(-) Cost of acquisition	-
Short term capital gain	8,00,000

27.

Sale price	1,20,00,000
(-) Indexed cost of acquisition	(18,00,000)
LTCG	1,02,00,000
(-) Exemption u/s 54EC	(50,00,000)
Taxable LTCG	52,00,000

29. Since period of holding is less than 36 months, there will be short term capital gain. 12,00,000 – 3,00,000 = 9,00,000.

CHAPTER 7

INCOME FROM OTHER SOURCES

MCQs ON THEORY

1. Which of the following is/are essential condition(s) for taxability of any income under the head 'income from other sources'?

(1) There must be an income

(2) Income is exempt under the provisions of Income Tax Act, 1961

(3) Income is not chargeable to tax under any other heads

Select the correct answer from the options given below –

(A) (1) only

(B) (3) only

(C) (1) & (3) only

(D) (1), (2) & (3)

2. Standard deduction shall be allowed for family pension received by the legal heirs after the death of the employee to the extent lower of the following –

(A) 1/3rd of such pension or ₹ 15,000

(B) 1/2 of such pension or ₹ 15,000

(C) 1/3rd of such pension or ₹ 20,000

(D) 1/2 of such pension or ₹ 20,000

3. Which of the following incomes are normally included under the head 'income from other sources'?

(a) Income from sub-letting of a house property

(b) Gifts received by individual from employer

(c) Examiner ship fees received by a teacher from University

(d) Agricultural income from agricultural land situated outside India

Select the correct answer from the options given below –

(A) (a) & (d) only

(B) (b), (c) & (d)

(C) (d), (c) & (a)

(D) (c) & (d) only

4. Any distribution by a company of accumulated profits whether capitalized or not, if such distribution entails the release by the company to its shareholders of all or any part of the assets of the company is deemed dividend as per ________

(A) Section 2(22)(a)

(B) Section 2(20)(a)

(C) Section 2(22a)

(D) Section 2(a)(22)

5. Ex-gratia payment made to the widow or other legal heirs of an employee, who dies while still in active service, will not be taxable as income under the Income-tax Act, 1961, if it is paid by ________

(A) Central Government

(B) Local Authority

(C) Public Sector Units

(D) Any of the above

6. Dividend u/s 2(22)(*a*) to 2(22)(*d*) shall be _____

(A) liable to tax @ 15% on the gross amount of dividends + 12% Surcharge + 4% EC i.e. 20.5552941% in hands of company

(B) exempt in the hands of shareholders

(C) Both (A) and (B)

(D) Either (A) or (B)

7. Lump sum payment made gratuitously or by way of compensation or otherwise to the ________ of an employee who dies while in active service is not taxable as income under the Income Tax Act, 1961.

(A) widow

(B) other legal heirs

(C) widow or other legal heirs

(D) widow or other legal heirs or relatives or next best friend

8. Which of the following is/are exempted income and hence cannot be taxed under the head 'income from other sources'?

P. Interest on 6% National Plan Paper

Q. 9% Tax-free Government loan of Uttar Pradesh

R. Interest on National Saving Certificate

S. Dividend from UTI

Select the correct answer from the options given below –

(A) P, Q & S

(B) Q & P

(C) Q & S

(D) P & S

9. Dividend received from a foreign company shall be ______

(A) taxable

(B) exempt

(C) taxable in the hands of foreign company

(D) exempt in the hands of shareholder

10. Which of the following expense is/are not allowed while calculating 'income under the head other sources'?

(I) Interest paid outside India on which TDS is deducted

(II) Excessive expenditure or unreasonable payments to certain specified persons as provided in Section 40A(2)

(III) Income-tax

(IV) Expenditure incurred by the assessee for the activity of owning and maintaining race horses

Select the correct answer from the options given below –

(A) (I) & (III)

(B) (II) & (IV)

(C) (III) & (II)

(D) (IV), (II) & (III)

11. In which of the following case(s) deemed dividend is/are taxable in relation to bonus issue u/s 2(22)(*a*)?

(A) Issue of bonus shares to equity shareholder

(B) Sale of bonus shares by equity shareholder to third person

(C) Redemption of bonus equity shares by the company

(D) All of the above

12. Interest on Post Office Saving Bank Account shall be exempt from tax to the extent of ______ in case of an individual account.

(A) ₹ 2,500

(B) ₹ 3,500

(C) ₹ 5,000

(D) ₹ 7,500

13. Which of the following is deemed dividend within the meaning of Section 2(22) of the Income Tax Act, 1961?

(A) Distribution by a company of deposit certificates to its shareholders

(B) Issuance of bonus shares to its preference shareholders

(C) Both (A) and (B)

(D) Neither (A) nor (B)

14. Income in form of interest on securities is subject to TDS u/s 193 @ 10% if it exceeds –

(A) ₹ 2,500

(B) ₹ 3,000

(C) ₹ 5,000

(D) ₹ 10,000

15. Winnings from lotteries, crossword puzzles, races including horse races, card games and other games of any sort or from gambling or betting of any form or nature whatsoever are taxable at the rate of –

(A) 30%

(B) 15%

(C) 20%

(D) 45%

16. Which of the following is/are exempted income and hence cannot be taxed under the head 'Income from other sources'?

P. Gifts received by individual of ₹ 49,000

Q. Agricultural income in India

R. Interest on bonds of notified public sector companies

S. Preference dividend of Indian companies

Select the correct answer from the options given below –

(A) Q & S

(B) Q, R & S

(C) P, Q, R & S

(D) S & P

17. Income in form of winnings from lotteries etc. is subject to TDS u/s 194B if it exceeds –

(A) ₹ 10,000

(B) ₹ 5,000

(C) ₹ 8,000

(D) ₹ 20,000

18. Which if the following amounts to deemed dividend u/s 2(22)(*e*) of the Income Tax Act, 1961?

(A) Any payment by private company by way of advance to the extent of accumulated capitalized profits to equity shareholder who is beneficial holding is less than 10% of the voting power

(B) Any distribution to its shareholders by a company on the reduction of its capital, to the extent to which the company possesses accumulated profits, whether capitalized or not.

(C) Both (A) and (B)

(D) Neither (A) nor (B)

19. Income from horse races is subject to TDS u/s 194BB if it exceeds –

(A) ₹ 5,000
(B) ₹ 2,500
(C) ₹ 7,500
(D) ₹ 10,000

20. Interest on Post Office Saving Bank Account shall be exempt from tax to the extent of _____ in case of joint account.

(A) ₹ 10,500
(B) ₹ 7,000
(C) ₹ 15,000
(D) ₹ 20,000

21. Winnings from races other than horse races are –

(A) subject to TDS @ 10%
(B) subject to TDS @ 5%
(C) not subject to TDS
(D) exempt from tax

22. Which of the following is liable to tax under Section 56(2)(viib) as 'income from other sources'?

(A) Issue of shares by private company at premium which exceeds fair market value of the shares and fair market value is more than face value
(B) Issue of shares by private company at discount which exceeds fair market value of the shares and fair market value is less than face value
(C) Issue of shares by private company at discount which exceeds fair market value of the shares and fair market value and issue price both are less than face value
(D) Both (A) and (B)

23. Income by way of interest received on compensation or enhanced compensation is taxable under the head ________ and a deduction of a sum equal to _______ of such interest income shall be allowed

(A) 'income from other sources'; 25%

(B) 'capital gain'; 50%

(C) 'income from other sources'; 50%

(D) 'capital gain'; 25%

24. Any sum of money received as an advance or otherwise in the course of negotiations for transfer of a capital asset, if such sum is forfeited and the negotiations do not result in transfer of such capital asset then such advance money forfeited is taxable under the head ______

(A) 'capital gain'

(B) 'income from house property'

(C) 'income from other sources'

(D) Any of the above

25. As per Section 56(2)(*vii*), where an individual or HUF receives, in any previous year, from any person or persons any sum of money, without consideration, the aggregate value of which exceeds ______ is taxable under the head 'income from other sources'.

(A) ₹ 25,000

(B) ₹ 1,00,000

(C) ₹ 50,000

(D) ₹ 5,00,000

26. Which of the following gift is/are taxable in the hands of individual under the head 'income from other sources'?

1. Cash gift received on the occasion of second marriage of the individual after first divorce
2. Cash gift received from relative on birthday

Select the correct answer from the options given below –

(A) 1 only

(B) 2 only

(C) Both 1 and 2

(D) Neither 1 nor 2

27. If a person buys securities ______ before the record date and sales it within ______ after the record date, then loss on sale of securities to the extent of dividend income shall be ignored.

(A) 3 months; 3 months
(B) 3 months; 9 months
(C) 9 months; 3 months
(D) 3 months; 6 months

28. Where an individual or HUF receives, in any previous year, from any person or persons any property, other than immovable property without consideration, the aggregate fair market value of which exceeds ₹ 50,000 then taxable amount is –

(A) Aggregate fair market value (-) ₹ 50,000
(B) Whole of the aggregate fair market value of movable property
(C) Aggregate fair market value of such property (-) Consideration
(D) Stamp duty value (-) ₹ 50,000

29. Which of the following property is covered under Section 56(2)(*vii*) of the Income Tax Act, 1961?

(I) Shares
(II) Furniture
(III) Jewellery
(IV) Motor car

Select the correct answer from the options given below –

(A) (I) and (II)
(B) (III) and (IV)
(C) (I) and (III)
(D) (II) and (III)

30. Income under the head 'income from other sources' is taxable on –

(A) Due basis
(B) Receipt basis
(C) Hybrid accounting basis
(D) The basis of method of accounting regularly followed by the assessee

31. Dividend received from domestic company is –

(A) Fully taxable in the hands of shareholder

(B) Fully taxable but deduction is available under Chapter VI-A.

(C) Fully exempt in the hands of shareholder except where the aggregate amount of dividend exceeds ₹ 10,00,000, where such excess is chargeable to tax @ 10% as provided in Section 115BBDA.

(D) Fully exempt in the hands of shareholder except where the aggregate amount of dividend exceeds ₹ 5,00,000, where such excess is chargeable to tax @ 20% as provided in Section 115BBDA.

32. Which of the following property is covered (✓) and which is not covered (✕) under Section 56(2)(*vii*) of the Income Tax Act, 1961?

I. Painting

II. Archaeological collection

III. Drawings

IV. Sculpture

Select the correct answer from the options given below –

	I	**II**	**III**	**IV**
(A)	✓	✕	✓	✕
(B)	✕	✓	✕	✓
(C)	✕	✕	✕	✕
(D)	✓	✓	✓	✓

33. Loan given to shareholder by closely held company to its shareholder having 12% voting power is –

(A) Deemed dividend and taxable in the hands of shareholder

(B) Deemed dividend but taxable in the hands of company @ 20.5552941%

(C) Deemed dividend to the extent of accumulated profits and taxable in the hands of shareholder

(D) deemed dividend and not taxable in the hands of shareholder; the company will pay tax @ 34.944%

34. Winning from lotteries, crossword puzzles, horse race are casual income and hence –

(A) Fully taxable

(B) Fully exempt

(C) Exempt up to ₹ 5,000

(D) Exempt up to ₹ 2,500

35. Winning from lotteries, crossword puzzles, horse race are taxable at –

(A) Normal slab rate of income tax

(B) 20% plus education cess 3%

(C) 30% plus surcharge if applicable plus education cess 3%

(D) 40% plus surcharge if applicable plus education cess 3%

36. Which of the following statement is/are false?

(a) Deemed dividend u/s 2(22)(e) is taxable to the extent of accumulated profit excluding capitalized profits

(b) Interest on securities is always taxable under the head 'income from other sources'.

(c) Dividend declared by UTI is exempt up to ₹ 10,000.

Select the correct answer from the options given below –

(A) (a) only

(B) (b) only

(C) (a), (b) and (c)

(D) (b) and (c) only

37. Dividend includes any ______ which entails the release of Company's ______

(A) Collection; liabilities

(B) Distribution; liabilities

(C) Collection; assets

(D) Distribution; assets

38. An income which is not fall under any first four head of income ______

(A) Shall always be exempted income

(B) Is taxable under the head 'income from other sources'

(C) Is taxable under the head 'income from other sources' if not otherwise exempt

(D) Is taxable under the head 'income from other sources' only if it is covered by Section 56.

PRACTICAL MCQs

39. Anil let house to Sunil at monthly rent of ₹ 12,000 which Sunil sub-let to the Mohan at monthly rent of ₹ 15,000. Sunil's income –

(A) ₹ 1,80,000 taxable under the head 'Income from house property'.

(B) ₹ 1,80,000 taxable under the head 'Income from other sources'.

(C) ₹ 36,000 taxable under the head 'Income from house property'.

(D) ₹ 36,000 taxable under the head 'Income from other sources'.

40. XYZ (Pvt.) Ltd. issued 12,375 shares of ₹ 100 each at ₹ 135 per share. Fair value of shares is ₹ 120 per share. How much income is taxable under the head "income from other sources"?

(A) ₹ 20 per share

(B) ₹ 4,33,125

(C) ₹ 1,85,625

(D) ₹ 16,70,625

41. Anil entered into agreement to sale his house with Mahesh on 1.4.2018 and received advance of ₹ 3,75,000. However, Mahesh made default and Anil forfeited advance money. What are the tax implications?

(A) Advance money forfeited will be reduced from cost of acquisition while calculating income chargeable to tax under the head 'Capital gain'.

(B) Advance money forfeited is not chargeable to tax under any head of income.

(C) Advance money forfeited will be taxable under the head 'Income from other sources'.

(D) Advance money forfeited will be taxable under the head 'Income from house property'.

42. M (Pvt.) Ltd. distributed asset of ₹ 10,000 each to its five shareholders. Accumulated profit of the company on that date was ₹ 1,00,000.

(A) ₹ 10,000 is taxable in the hands of each shareholder as deemed dividend u/s 2(22)(a).

(B) ₹ 50,000 is deemed dividend u/s 2(22)(a) and not taxable in the hands of shareholders

(C) ₹ 50,000 is deemed dividend u/s 2(22)(a) and taxable in the hands of company.

(D) (B) and (C)

43. PQR (Pvt.) Ltd. issued 1,00,000 shares of ₹ 100 each at ₹ 120 per share. Fair value of shares is ₹ 130 per share. Which of the following is correct tax implication of this transaction?

(A) The provisions of Section 56(2)(viib) is not attracted at all.

(B) The provisions of Section 56(2)(viib) is attracted and ₹ 10 per share i.e. ₹ 10,00,000 is taxable under the head 'income from other sources'.

(C) The provisions of Section 56(2)(viib) is attracted since shares are issue at premium. However, no sum is chargeable to tax under the head 'income from other sources' as issue price is less than fair market value.

(D) The provisions of Section 56(2)(viib) is not attracted at all and no sum is chargeable to tax under the head 'income from other sources'.

44. K (Pvt.) Ltd. holds 26% shares in L (Pvt.) Ltd. (foreign company). During the year 2017-2018 K (Pvt.) Ltd. received dividend of ₹ 5,00,000 from L (Pvt.) Ltd. How much tax is payable on such dividend by K (Pvt.) Ltd.? Assume total income does not exceed ₹ 10 crore.

(A) 5,00,000 × 22.35764% = 1,11,788

(B) Nil

(C) 5,00,000 × 16.692% = 83,460

(D) 5,00,000 × 16.995% = 84,975

45. Ravan hold 19% shares in HTP (P) Ltd. During the PY 2018-2019 HTP (P) Ltd. gives loan of ₹ 88,000 to Ravan. Accumulated profit of HTP (P) Ltd. on the date of above transaction is ₹ 60,000 which includes capitalized profit of ₹ 28,000. What are the tax implications?

(A) ₹ 88,000 is taxable as deemed dividend u/s 2(22)(e) in the hands of Ravan.

(B) ₹ 60,000 is taxable as deemed dividend u/s 2(22)(e) in the hands of HTP (P) Ltd.

(C) ₹ 32,000 is taxable as deemed dividend u/s 2(22)(e) in the hands of Ravan.

(D) ₹ 32,000 is taxable as deemed dividend u/s 2(22)(e) in the hands of HTP (P) Ltd. and the company is liable to pay tax @ 34.944% on the amount of deemed dividend.

46. K (Pvt.) Ltd. distributed asset of ₹ 10,000 each to its five shareholders. Accumulated profit of the company on that date was ₹ 35,000 including capitalized profit ₹ 15,000. Deemed dividend taxable in the hands of company = ?

(A) ₹ 50,000

(B) ₹ 35,000

(C) ₹ 25,000

(D) ₹ 20,000

47. Rakhi won lottery and received ₹ 14,000 from the lottery company. How much amount will be included as income while calculating total income of Rakhi?

(A) ₹ 14,000

(B) ₹ 20,000

(C) ₹ 17,500

(D) ₹ 15,555

48. Sunita receives gift of ₹ 51,000 from her friend Babita on her birthday. Sunita spend ₹ 1,000 on the birthday. Amount taxable as per Section 56(2)(*vii*) = ?

(A) ₹ 50,000

(B) Nil

(C) ₹ 51,000

(D) ₹ 49,000

49. XYZ (Pvt.) Ltd. issued 12,375 shares of ₹ 100 each at ₹ 98 per share. Fair value of shares is ₹ 90 per share. How much income is taxable under the head "income from other sources"?

(A) ₹ 99,000

(B) ₹ 2,22,750

(C) Nil

(D) ₹ 24,750

50. Arun receives gift of immovable property on his birthday from his friend Varun. Stamp duty value of immovable property is ₹ 75,000. However, market value of the property on the date of gift is ₹ 90,000. Amount taxable per Section 56(2)(*vii*) = ?

(A) ₹ 40,000

(B) ₹ 90,000

(C) ₹ 75,000

(D) ₹ 25,000

51. Nikita won lottery and received ₹ 6,300 from the lottery company. How much amount will be included as income while calculating total income of Nikita?

(A) ₹ 6,300

(B) ₹ 9,000

(C) ₹ 7,875

(D) ₹ 7,000

52. Maya gifts kitchen appliances of ₹ 51,000 to her friend Mrs. Malini Gupta on her birthday. Amount taxable per Section 56(2)(*vii*) = ?

(A) ₹ 1,000

(B) ₹ 51,000

(C) ₹ 50,000

(D) Nil

53. XYZ (Pvt.) Ltd. issued 12,375 shares of ₹ 100 each at ₹ 115 per share. Fair value of shares is ₹ 90 per share. How much income is taxable under the head "income from other sources"?

(A) ₹ 1,23,750

(B) ₹ 1,85,625

(C) Nil

(D) ₹ 3,09,375

54. Mr. A receives gift of ₹ 30,000 from B and ₹ 21,000 from C on his passing CS Final Exam. Amount taxable per Section 56(2)(*vii*) –

(A) ₹ 1,000

(B) ₹ 21,000

(C) ₹ 50,000

(D) ₹ 51,000

55. Mrs. Rameshwari receives following gifts during the PY 2017-2018.

(1) ₹ 90,000 on her marriage out of ₹ 70,000 is received from relatives.

(2) ₹ 18,000 from cousin of her mother

(3) A cell phone of ₹ 21,000 from her employer.

(4) ₹ 25,000 from elder brother of her grandfather

(5) ₹ 2,000 from her friend.

Amount taxable per Section 56(2)(*vii*) = ?

(A) ₹ 65,000

(B) ₹ 86,000

(C) Nil

(D) ₹ 45,000

56. Mrs. Gita receives following gifts during the PY 2018-2019 on her wedding anniversary.

(*i*) Cash gift of ₹ 51,000 on her 25th birthday.

(*ii*) Diamond necklace of ₹ 2,00,000 from her sister living in London.

Amount taxable per Section 56(2)(*vii*) = ?

(A) ₹ 51,000

(B) ₹ 2,51,000

(C) ₹ 2,01,000

(D) Nil

57. Mrs. Amruta receives cash gift of ₹ 1,02,000 from her friend on occasion of marriage of her son. How much amount will be included in total income of Mrs. Amruta as "income from other sources"?

(A) ₹ 52,000

(B) ₹ 50,000

(C) Nil

(D) ₹ 1,02,000

58. Ruchira received ₹ 70,000 as wining amount from horse race? How much amount will be included as income while calculating total income of Ruchira?

(A) ₹ 70,000

(B) ₹ 1,00,000

(C) ₹ 80,750

(D) ₹ 1,30,000

59. Ram received two plot of land as gift from Shyam and Mohan having stamp value of ₹ 4,00,000 and ₹ 50,000 respectively. How much will be taxable under the head 'income from other sources'?

(A) ₹ 4,00,000

(B) ₹ 4,50,000

(C) ₹ 3,50,000

(D) Nil

60. Gupta received gift of Sculpture and jewellery worth ₹ 45,000 and ₹ 30,000 from Sharma and Varma? How much will be taxable under the head 'Income from other sources'?

(A) ₹ 25,000

(B) ₹ 30,000

(C) ₹ 75,000

(D) Nil

61. Sanjay received ₹ 5,00,000 towards interest on enhanced compensation on 15.11.2018. Out of this interest ₹ 1,90,000 relates to financial year 2017-2018. Sanjay incurred ₹ 40,000 legal expenses to receive interest on enhanced compensation. How much interest on enhanced compensation would be chargeable to tax for AY 2019-2020?

(A) ₹ 3,10,000

(B) ₹ 2,30,000

(C) ₹ 2,10,000

(D) ₹ 2,50,000

62. Tanushri received ₹ 3,000 as winning amount from horse race? How much amount will be included as income while calculating total income of Tanushri?

(A) ₹ 3,000

(B) ₹ 4,286

(C) ₹ 3,750

(D) ₹ 4,444

63. LMN (Pvt.) Ltd. distributed asset of ₹ 1,00,000 to its shareholders. Accumulated profit of the company is ₹ 80,000 out of which capitalized profit is ₹ 60,000. How much dividend distribution tax is payable by the company for deemed dividend u/s 2(22)(*a*)?

(A) ₹ 20,000

(B) ₹ 16,444

(C) ₹ 4,072

(D) ₹ 20,358

64. Rajat purchased units of UTI for ₹ 12,36,800 on 1.4.2018. He received dividend of ₹ 1,60,000 on units on 1.5.2018. He sold these units on 30.10.2018 for ₹ 9,60,000. His income under the head capital gain is ₹ 8,00,000. Compute total income of Rajat for AY 2019-2020.

(A) ₹ 8,00,000

(B) ₹ 6,83,200

(C) ₹ 9,60,000

(D) ₹ 7,60,000

65. From the following detail calculate the income of Mangesh under the head 'income from other sources'?

Winning from lotteries (Net)	33,936
Royalty on book	9,000
Interest on debenture of unlisted company (Net)	3,600
Interest on post office saving bank account	500
Interest on government securities	2,200
Interest on monthly income scheme of Post Office	33,000

Mangesh paid ₹ 1,000 for typing the manuscript of book written by him.

(A) ₹ 62,680

(B) ₹ 81,236

(C) ₹ 95,680

(D) ₹ 96,180

ANSWERS:

1.	(C)	2.	(A)	3.	(C)	4.	(A)	5.	(D)	6.	(C)	7.	(C)
8.	(D)	9.	(A)	10.	(C)	11.	(C)	12.	(B)	13.	(C)	14.	(C)
15.	(A)	16.	(C)	17.	(A)	18.	(B)	19.	(D)	20.	(B)	21.	(C)
22.	(D)	23.	(C)	24.	(C)	25.	(C)	26.	(D)	27.	(A)	28.	(B)
29.	(C)	30.	(D)	31.	(C)	32.	(D)	33.	(D)	34.	(A)	35.	(C)
36.	(D)	37.	(D)	38.	(C)	39.	(D)	40.	(C)	41.	(C)	42.	(D)
43.	(C)	44.	(C)	45.	(D)	46.	(B)	47.	(B)	48.	(C)	49.	(C)
50.	(C)	51.	(A)	52.	(D)	53.	(D)	54.	(D)	55.	(C)	56.	(A)
57.	(D)	58.	(B)	59.	(A)	60.	(C)	61.	(D)	62.	(A)	63.	(B)
64.	(B)	65.	(C)										

PAST EXAMINATION MCQs

1. Dec 2014: Which of the following is not included in taxable income —

(A) Income from smuggling activity

(B) Casual income

(C) Gifts of personal nature subject to a maximum of ₹ 50,000 received in cash

(D) Income received in kind

2. Dec 2014: The amount deductible from family pension is up to—

(A) ₹ 15,000 or 1/3rd of family pension whichever is less

(B) ₹ 15,000 or 1/2 of family pension whichever is less

(C) ₹ 10,000 or 1/3rd of family pension whichever is less

(D) No deduction

3. Dec 2014: Sameer received the following income during PY 2018-2019: Director's fees ₹ 5,000, income from agricultural land in Pakistan ₹ 15,000, rent from let-out of land in Jaipur ₹ 20,000, interest on deposit with HDFC Bank ₹ 1,000 and dividend from Indian company ₹ 5,000. His income from other sources is —

(A) ₹ 41,000

(B) ₹ 46,000

(C) ₹ 31,000

(D) ₹ 26,000

4. Dec 2014: Akshay received a gift of ₹ 35,000 each on 22nd May, 2018 from his three friends. The amount chargeable to tax in this case would be —

(A) ₹ 50,000

(B) ₹ 1,05,000

(C) Nil

(D) ₹ 55,000

5. June 2015: Which of the following income will be taxable as income from other sources?

(A) Purchase of house from husband for inadequate consideration

(B) Purchase of painting from registered dealer at invoice value less than fair market value

(C) Cash gift from a non-resident friend on marriage anniversary

(D) All of the above

6. June 2015: Hemant holds 100 shares of Gold Ltd., a domestic company. He has been paid dividend of ₹ 10,000 during the year 2017-2018. Dividend distribution tax payable u/s 115-O will be —

(A) ₹ 1,765, payable by Gold Ltd.

(B) ₹ 1,765, payable by Hemant

(C) ₹ 1,545, payable by Gold Ltd.

(D) ₹ 1,000, payable by Hemant.

7. June 2015: John, engaged in fertiliser trade, received rent by sub-letting a building. This will be taxable under the head —

(A) Income from house property

(B) Income from capital gains

(C) Income from profits and gains of business and profession

(D) Income from other sources

8. Dec 2015: A private limited company engaged in manufacturing activity had general reserve of ₹ 20 lakh. It granted a loan of ₹ 5 lakh to a director who held 13% shareholding *cum* voting rights in the company. The said loan was re-paid by him before the end of the year. The amount of deemed dividend arising out of the above transaction is —

(A) ₹ 2,60,000

(B) ₹ 2,40,000

(C) ₹ 5,00,000

(D) Nil

9. Dec 2015: Rajiv (aged 28 years) received cash gift of ₹ 2 lakh on the occasion of his marriage. It includes gift from non-relative of ₹ 80,000. His income by way of lottery winnings is ₹ 3 lakh. His net income tax liability (ignoring TDS) would be —

(A) ₹ 93,600

(B) ₹ 22,660

(C) ₹ 12,360

(D) ₹ 25,750

10. Dec 2015: Ms. Sitara is in receipt of family pension of ₹ 15,000 p.m. during 2018-2019. Income chargeable to tax for AY 2019-2020 of Ms. Sitara is —

(A) ₹ 1,80,000

(B) ₹ 1,20,000

(C) ₹ 1,65,000

(D) Nil

11. Dec 2015: Where a foreign institutional investor received income in respect of securities other than income by way of dividend referred to in Section 115-O or received in respect of securities other than units referred to in section 115AB, such income is taxable @ —

(A) 15%

(B) 10%

(C) 20%

(D) 30%

12. June 2016: Rishabh received the following gifts during the previous year:

(*i*) ₹ 50,000 from his employer

(*ii*) ₹ 1,00,000 from mother's sister

(*iii*) ₹ 10,000 from his friend on the occasion of his marriage

(*iv*) ₹ 60,000 in the form of scholarship from a registered charitable trust

The amount of taxable gift under the head 'income from other sources' is —

(A) Nil

(B) ₹ 50,000

(C) ₹ 1,50,000

(D) ₹ 2,10,000

13. June 2016: Comfort (Pvt.) Ltd. issued 10,000 equity shares to Pawan at ₹ 18 per share when the fair market value of each share was determined at ₹ 11 per share. The tax implication of the transaction is —

(A) ₹ 70,000 taxable as income for Comfort (Pvt.) Ltd.

(B) ₹ 20,000 taxable as income for Pawan

(C) ₹ 10,000 taxable as income for Pawan

(D) Nil

14. June 2016: While making payment of winnings from horse race, tax will be deducted at source, if the payment exceeds —

(A) ₹ 5,000

(B) ₹ 10,000

(C) ₹ 25,000

(D) ₹ 50,000

15. Dec 2016: A member of Parliament received ₹ 1,50,000 per month as salary and ₹ 4,50,000 as daily allowances during PY 2017-2018. The taxable amount will be —

(A) Salary ₹ 18,00,000

(B) Income from profession ₹ 22,50,000

(C) Income from other sources ₹ 18,00,000

(D) Nil

16. Dec 2016: A lady received gifts worth ₹ 1,00,000 from her relatives as defined under the Income Tax Act, 1961 and ₹ 60,000 from her office colleagues on her marriage anniversary. The taxable amount of gifts would be –

(A) ₹ 1,60,000

(B) ₹ 60,000

(C) ₹ 10,000

(D) ₹ 1,10,000

17. Dec 2016: Amit received ₹ 70,000 being winnings from lottery after deduction of tax at source. His gross winnings from lottery to be included in the total income is —

(A) Nil

(B) ₹ 1,00,000

(C) ₹ 70,000

(D) ₹ 30,000

18. June 2017: Mr. Ram received cash gift of ₹ 51,000 from his friends on the occasion of his 50th birthday. None of the friends are relative. The amount liable to tax in the hands of Mr. Ram would be:

(A) Nil

(B) ₹ 1,000

(C) ₹ 51,000

(D) ₹ 46,000 after deducting causal income of ₹ 5,000

19. June 2017: Agni (P) Ltd. issued equity shares of ₹ 10 each at ₹ 40 per share. The fair market value of the share on the date of issue was ascertained as ₹ 25 per share. The company issued 1,00,000 equity shares. The amount liable to tax in the hands of the company would be:

(A) ₹ 15,00,000

(B) ₹ 30,00,000

(C) Nil

(D) ₹ 40,00,000

20. June 2017: R has taken a house on rent and sublets the same to G. Income from such house property shall be taxable under the head:

(A) income from house property

(B) income from other sources

(C) income from house property or income from other sources as decided by R

(D) none of the above

21. June 2017: Ms. Mala received family pension of ₹ 15,000 per month during the previous year 2018-2019. Also, she was employed in a private firm where she got a monthly consolidated salary of ₹ 20,000 per month. Her total income chargeable to tax is:

(A) ₹ 4,20,000

(B) ₹ 2,40,000

(C) ₹ 3,60,000

(D) ₹ 4,05,000

22. June 2017: Libra P. Ltd. engaged in trading activity had accumulated profits of ₹ 15,00,000 as on 1.4.2018, Mr. Gautam having 30% of the equity shares and voting rights in the company received ₹ 5 lakhs as loan on 1.6.2018 from the company. The loan was repaid by him on 30.11.2017. The amount liable to tax in the hands of Mr. Gautam as deemed dividend is:

(A) ₹ 4,50,000

(B) ₹ 15,00,000

(C) ₹ 5,00,000

(D) ₹ 1,50,000

23. June 2017: Rakesh acquired a motor car for ₹ 3,00,000 from his friend (non-relative) when the fair market value of the motor car was ₹ 5,00,000. The amount liable to tax in the hands of Rakesh from the transaction is:

(A) ₹ 3,00,000

(B) ₹ 2,00,000

(C) ₹ 1,50,000

(D) Nil

24. June 2017: Where a firm or closely held company received from any person any property being shares of closely held company without consideration:

(A) the whole of the fair market value of the shares shall be taxable

(B) the whole of the FMV shall be taxable if it exceeds ₹ 50,000

(C) the whole of FMV shall be exempt

(D) the whole of the cost of such shares shall be exempt

25. June 2017: Mr. Ravi solved a crossword puzzle and received ₹ 84,000 after deduction of tax at source. His income from crossword puzzle chargeable to tax would be:

(A) ₹ 84,000

(B) Nil

(C) ₹ 72,000

(D) ₹ 1,20,000

26. Dec 2017: Ram received ₹ 80,000 by way of gift from friends upon retirement from service in a private company. The amount of gift chargeable to income-tax would be:

(A) Nil

(B) ₹ 30,000

(C) ₹ 70,000

(D) ₹ 80,000

27. Dec 2017: Ms. Laxmi received ₹ 60,000 by way of family pension from State Government. The amount of family pension eligible for exemption under section 10(19) is:

(A) ₹ 60,000

(B) ₹ 40,000

(C) ₹ 20,000

(D) ₹ 15,000

28. Dec 2017: Ms. Anshu received dividend of ₹ 80,000 for her equity shareholding in MNO Ltd. (a listed company). She paid interest of ₹ 12,500 for the amounts borrowed for investment in those shares. The taxable dividend income would be:

(A) ₹ 80,000

(B) Nil

(C) ₹ 67,500

(D) ₹ 92,500

29. Dec 2017: Lokesh (age 62) received following gifts on the occasion of his birthday:

(*i*) Cash gift from elder brother ₹ 30,000;

(*ii*) Gold chain from younger sister market value on the date of gift ₹ 38,000;

(*iii*) Cash gifts from friends (non-relatives) ₹ 45,000;

(*iv*) Purchased shares from younger brother for ₹ 1 lakh when the market value of the shares was ₹ 1,35,000.

Amount of income chargeable to tax in respect to the above transactions would be:

(A) ₹ 1,48,000

(B) ₹ 1,18,000

(C) ₹ 80,000

(D) Nil

30. Dec 2017: Suresh (age 65) won a prize on lottery ticket on 30.9.2018. The prize amount was ₹ 5,50,000. He had bought lottery tickets for ₹ 75,000 during the year. Assuming that he had no other income chargeable to tax for the year, his income tax liability (including cess @ 4%) would be:

(A) ₹ 1,71,600

(B) ₹ 30,900

(C) ₹ 36,050

(D) ₹ 10,300

ANSWERS:

1.	(C)	**2.**	(A)	**3.**	(A)	**4.**	(B)	**5.**	(C)	**6.**	(**)	**7.**	(D)
8.	(C)	**9.**	(A)	**10.**	(C)	**11.**	(C)	**12.**	(A)	**13.**	(A)	**14.**	(B)
15.	(C)	**16.**	(B)	**17.**	(B)	**18.**	(C)	**19.**	(A)	**20.**	(B)	**21.**	(D)
22.	(C)	**23.**	(D)	**24.**	(B)	**25.**	(D)	**26.**	(D)	**27.**	(D)	**28.**	(B)
29.	(D)	**30.**	(A)										

** ***Note:*** *None of the given option is correct.*

HINTS FOR PRACTICAL MCQs

39. Income from sub-let is taxable under the head 'income from other sources'.

1,80,000 – 1,44,000 = 36,000.

40. *For taxability under Section 56(2)(viib) 'issue price' should be more than both 'face value' and 'FMV' and if this condition is satisfied then difference between 'issue price' and 'FMV' shall be income.*

(135 – 120) × 12,375 = 1,85,625

45. Capitalized profit is excluded while calculating deemed dividend u/s 2(22)(*e*).

47. $\frac{14,000}{70\%} = 20,000$

51. Income in form of winnings from lotteries, crossword puzzles, card games or other games of any sort is subject to TDS u/s 194B if it exceeds ₹ 10,000.

52. "Kitchen appliances" is not property for the purpose of Section 56(2)(*vii*).

53. (115 – 90) × 12,375 = 3,09,375

55.

₹ 90,000 on her marriage out of ₹ 70,000 is received from relatives. (Not taxable)	-
₹ 18,000 from cousin of her mother	18,000
A cell phone of ₹ 21,000 from her employer (taxable under the head salary)	-
₹ 25,000 from elder brother of her grandfather	25,000
₹ 2,000 from her friend.	2,000
	45,000

Since, aggregate value of gift is less than 50,000; nothing will be taxable u/s 56(2)(*vii*).

56. Diamond necklace is received from sister i.e. relative hence not taxable only cash gift will be taxable.

57. Cash gift for self marriage is not taxable and not for son's marriage.

58. $\frac{7,000}{70\%} = 10,000$

Income in form of winnings from lotteries, crossword puzzles, card games or other games of any sort is subject to TDS u/s 194B if it exceeds ₹ 10,000 and income from horse races is subject to TDS u/s 194BB if it exceeds ₹ 5,000.

59. In case of gift of immovable property not aggregation is allowed. Individual stamp value of property should go above ₹ 50,000 then only it is taxable.

61. Interest on enhanced compensation is taxable in year of receipt whether it pertains current year or last year after 50% deduction.

62. No grossing up as amount is less than ₹ 5,000.

63. 80,000 × 20.5552941% = 16,286.

64.

Income from units of UTI (Exempt)		Nil
STCL on sale of units (12,36,800 – 9,60,000)	2,76,800	
(-) Loss to be ignored due dividend stripping provisions	(1,60,000)	1,16,800
Other income under the head capital gain		8,00,000
		6,83,200

If a person buys securities 3 months before the record date and sales it within 3 months after the record date, then loss on sale of securities to the extent of dividend income shall be ignored.

Similarly, if a person buys units 3 months before the record date and sales it within 9 months after the record date, then loss on sale of units to the extent of dividend income shall be ignored. **[Section 94(7)]**

65.

Winning from lotteries (33,936/70%)	48,480
Royalty on book (9,000 – 1,000)	8,000
Interest on debenture of unlisted company (3,600/90%)	4,000
Interest on post office saving bank account (exempt up to ₹ 3,500)	-
Interest on government securities	2,200
Interest on monthly income scheme of Post Office	33,000
	95,680

PAST EXAMINATION MCQs HINTS

12. Taxability of gift under the head income from other sources:

Type of gift	Taxable Amount	Reason
Gift from employer	Nil	Taxable under 'Salary' not under the head 'income from other sources'
Gift from mother sister	Nil	Gift from relative is exempt.
Gift on occasion of marriage	Nil	Gift on occasion of marriage is exempt.
Scholarship gift	Nil	Exempt
Total	Nil	

13. 'Issue price' should be more than both 'face value' and 'FMV' and if this condition is satisfied then difference between 'issue price' and 'FMV' shall be income.

$(18 - 11) \times 10{,}000 = 70{,}000$

17. Gross winnings $= \dfrac{70{,}000}{70\%} = 1{,}00{,}000$

19. $(40 - 25) \times 1{,}00{,}000 = 15{,}00{,}000.$

21.

Salary income (20,000 × 12)		2,40,000
Family pension received (15,000 × 12)	1,80,000	
(-) Exempt (1/3rd of such pension or ₹ 15,000 whichever is less)	(15,000)	1,65,000
Total income		4,05,000

23. For the purpose of Section 56(2)(*vii*), 'Motor Car' is not included in definition of 'Property' and hence is no tax liability is attracted even if it is purchased for amount less than fair market value.

25. $\dfrac{84{,}000}{70\%} = 1{,}20{,}000$

27.

Family pension received		60,000
(-) Exemption: Lower of the following two		
- 1/3rd of the family pension received	20,000	

- Amount specified	15,000	**(15,000)**
Taxable amount		45,000

29.

Particulars	Reason	₹
Cash gift from elder brother	Gift from relative is exempt	–
Gold chain from younger sister market value on the date of gift	Gift from relative is exempt	–
Cash gifts from friends (non-relatives)	Cash gift up to ₹ 50,000 exempt.	–
Purchased shares from younger brother	In case of purchase of movable property from relative difference in purchase price and market value (*inadequate consideration*) is less than ₹ 50,000 then it is exempt.	–
		Nil

30. 5,50,000 × 31.2% = 1,71,600.

CHAPTER 8
CLUBBING OF INCOMES

MCQs ON THEORY

1. Provisions relating to "clubbing of transfer of income without transfer of asset" are contained in _____ of the Income Tax Act, 1961.

(A) Section 59

(B) Section 60

(C) Section 61

(D) Section 62

2. Which of the following statement(s) is/are correct?

(1) Every income of minor is included in income of that parent whose income before inclusion of income of minor is greater.

(2) Income on clubbed income is also clubbed.

(3) As per clubbing provisions only income has to be clubbed but loss has to be ignored.

Select the correct the answer from the options given below –

(A) (2) only

(B) (3) only

(C) (1) & (2) only

(D) None of the above

3. Which of the following statement is/are true (✓) and which is/are false (×)?

(*i*) If there is revocable transfer but such transfer is not revocable during the life of transferee then income from transferred asset is treated as income of transferee.

(*ii*) If husband transfers house to his wife without adequate consideration then income from such house is treated as income of wife as per Section 27.

(*iii*) If house is transferred to minor married daughter then income from such asset is included in the hands of parents.

(*iv*) Exemption of ₹ 1,500 in respect of child is available whether income of child is clubbed or not in the hands of parents.

Select the correct answer from the options given below –

	(*i*)	**(*ii*)**	**(*iii*)**	**(*iv*)**
(A)	✓	×	✓	×
(B)	×	×	×	×
(C)	✓	×	×	×
(D)	×	✓	×	✓

4. Income of minor married daughter –

(A) be clubbed in the hands her husband.

(B) not to be clubbed and taxable in her hand

(C) be clubbed in the hands that parent whose total income excluding the income of the minor married daughter is greater.

(D) None of the above

5. In which of the following case(s) the income will be treated as income of transferor?

(I) Transfer by way of trust which is revocable during the lifetime of the beneficiary

(II) Transfer which is revocable during the lifetime of the transferee.

Select the correct answer from the options given below –

(A) (I) only

(B) (II) only

(C) (I) and (II)

(D) Neither (I) nor (II)

6. If income is clubbed as per Section 64, then it is clubbed ______

(A) Under the head 'income from salary'

(B) Under the head 'income from other sources'

(C) Under relevant head to which it belongs

(D) None of the above

7. X is owner of house on which he receives rent of ₹ 8,000. He confers right to receive rent on such house to his wife without transfer of house. Rental income in this is taxable in the hands of –

(A) Husband

(B) Wife

(C) Partly husband partly wife

(D) None of the above

8. As per Section 60 of the Income Tax Act, 1961, if there is transfer of income without transfer of asset then income from such transferred asset is treated as income of _____

(A) Transferor

(B) Transferee

(C) Transferor if transfer is revocable

(D) Transferee if transfer is irrevocable

9. Which of the following revocable transfer?

(i) If transfer agreement contains any provision for the re-transfer of the whole or any part of the income or assets to the transferor

(ii) If transfer agreement does not give, in any way to the transferor, a right to re-assume power over the whole or any part of the income or the assets

Select the correct answer from the options given below –

(A) Both (i) and (ii)

(B) (ii) only

(C) Neither (i) nor (ii)

(D) (i) only

10. Which of the following statement is correct?

(A) If salary of wife is always included as income of husband if both wife and husband works in same establishment.

(B) Remuneration of wife is included as income of husband if salary of husband is more than wife and both works in same establishment.

(C) Any remuneration derived by a spouse from a concern in which the other spouse has a substantial interest, shall be clubbed in the hands of the spouse who has a substantial interest in that concern.

(D) All of the above

11. An individual shall be deemed to have substantial interest in a concern –

(A) In a case of company, if individual holds 10% or more equity shares in company.

(B) In a case of company, if individual along with his wife holds 15% or more equity shares in company.

(C) In a case of company, if individual holds 15% or more equity shares in company along with his relative.

(D) In a case of company, if individual holds 20% or more equity shares in company along with his relative.

12. If an individual transfers any asset to his/her spouse, the income from such asset shall be included in the total income of the ______

(A) transferor

(B) transferee

(C) beneficiary

(D) any one of the above

13. In which of the following case income from asset will be treated as income of transferor?

(A) Income from asset transferred by husband to wife before marriage.

(B) Income from asset transferred by husband to wife after marriage for adequate consideration.

(C) Income from asset transferred by husband after dissolution of marriage for inadequate consideration.

(D) None of the above

14. Relative for the purpose of Section 64(1)(*ii*) means –

(A) Husband, wife and brother of the individual.

(B) Husband, wife and sister of the individual.

(C) Husband, wife, brother, sister, brother and sister of wife

(D) Husband, wife, brother, sister or any lineal ascendant/descendant of the individual.

15. If individual transfers house to spouse without consideration, then –

(A) Income from such house is treated as income of individual u/s 64.

(B) Income from such house is treated as income of individual u/s 22.

(C) Income from such house is treated as income of individual u/s 64(3).

(D) Income from such house is treated as income of individual u/s 27.

16. As per Section 64(1)(*vi*) clubbing provisions are applicable when asset is transferred without adequate consideration to –

(A) Son in law

(B) Son's wife

(C) Major son

(D) Major daughter

17. Exemption of ______ is available u/s 10(32) to the parent in respect of minor's income clubbed with the parent.

(A) ₹ 1,500 for all child

(B) ₹ 500 per child

(C) ₹ 4,500 for all child

(D) ₹ 1,500 per child

18. Which of the following income of minor child can be clubbed in the hands of parents?

(I) Income of a minor child suffering from disability specified in Section 80U like physically disabled, totally blind, etc.

(II) Income of minor child on account of any manual work done by him.

(III) Income of minor child on account of any activity not involving application of his skills, talent or specialized knowledge and experience.

Select the correct answer from the options given below –

(A) (II) only

(B) (I) only

(C) (III) only

(D) None of the above

19. Ankur transferred a house to Padma on 1.4.2015. Padma married to Gopal who is son of Ankur on 1.4.2018. Income from house property will be taxable in the hands of –

(A) Ankur

(B) Padma

(C) Gopal

(D) Any of the above at the option of Assessing Officer.

20. Which of the following statement is/are false?

1. Agricultural income of minor son has to be clubbed in the hands of parents for determining the rate of income tax applicable to the income of parents.
2. Interest received by minor child on compulsory acquisition of land will be taxable in the hands of parents.

Select the correct answer from the options given below –

(A) 2 only

(B) 1 only

(C) Both 1 and 2

(D) Neither 1 nor 2

PRACTICAL MCQs

21. Ram transfers 10% Debentures of ₹ 10,00,000 to his wife without consideration. His wife earns ₹ 1,00,000 as interest on such debentures. She deposit ₹ 1,00,000 received on account of interest and earns ₹ 10,000 as interest on such deposit. How the above income will be taxed?

(A) ₹ 1,10,000 will be taxed in the hands of wife.

(B) ₹ 1,10,000 will be taxed in the hands of husband.

(C) ₹ 1,00,000 will be taxed in the hands of wife and ₹ 10,000 will be taxed in the hands of husband.

(D) ₹ 1,00,000 will be taxed in the hands of husband and ₹ 10,000 will be taxed in the hands of wife.

22. Mosin, a fashion designer having lucrative business pays salary of ₹ 20,000 p.m. to his wife who is model. What are the tax implications?

(A) Mosin can claim deduction of ₹ 2,40,000 as business expenditure while calculating his income under the head profits and gains of business and profession and salary received by wife will be clubbed in his hand as per Section 64(1)(ii).

(B) Mosin cannot claim deduction of ₹ 2,40,000 as business expenditure while calculating his income under the head profits and gains of business and profession and salary received by wife will be taxable in the hands of wife only.

(C) Mosin can claim deduction of ₹ 2,40,000 as business expenditure while calculating his income under the head profits and gains of business and profession and salary received by wife will be taxable in the hands of wife only.

(D) None of the above

23. Mrs. X started business on 1.4.2017 by investing ₹ 2,25,000. Her husband gifted ₹ 1,50,000 on 10.5.2017 which Mrs. X invested in business on the same date. She earns profits of ₹ 1,12,500 and ₹ 2,92,500 for PY 2017-2018 and 2018-2019 respectively. How much income will be clubbed in the hands of Mr. X for AY 2019-2020?

(A) ₹ 90,000

(B) ₹ 1,17,000

(C) ₹ 2,92,500

(D) ₹ 1,50,000

24. Mrs. Varsha Jadhav received the following amounts during PY 2018-2019:

Gross salary	4,50,000
Family pension @ 1,125 p.m.	13,500
Income of minor child	6,000
Balance in PF received after death of her husband	75,000
Gratuity received after the death of her husband	60,000

Calculate taxable income of Mrs. Varsha Jadhav.

(A) ₹ 5,23,500

(B) ₹ 4,63,500

(C) ₹ 4,53,000

(D) ₹ 5,22,000

25. Total income of Mr. G and Mrs. G for the PY 2018-2019 is ₹ 3,60,000 and ₹ 2,70,000 respectively. Their child is mentally retarded and has income of ₹ 1,80,000. What is the treatment of income of child?

(A) Income of child will be clubbed in the hands of father i.e. Mr. G.

(B) Income of child will be clubbed in the hands of mother i.e. Mrs. G.

(C) Income of child cannot be clubbed in the hands of father or mother.

(D) Income of minor child who is mentally retarded is totally exempt.

26. Mr. Gupta has four children – 2 daughters and 2 sons. Annual incomes of daughters were ₹ 9,000 & ₹ 4,500 and of sons were ₹ 6,200 & ₹ 4,300 respectively. One daughter having income of ₹ 4,500 is suffering from disability specified in Section 80U. How much income of children will be clubbed in the hands of Mr. Gupta?

(A) ₹ 19,500

(B) ₹ 18,000

(C) ₹ 15,000

(D) ₹ 14,500

27. From the following details calculate the total income of Mr. X and Mrs. X.

Total income of Mr. X and Mrs. X before considering following income is ₹ 7,80,000 and 4,60,000 respectively.

Income of minor son from bank deposits	30,000
Income of minor daughter from special talent	64,000
Interest on bank deposit of minor daughter out of sum deposited from special talent	6,000
Gift received by minor daughter from friend of Mrs. X	5,000

(A) ₹ 8,08,500 & ₹ 4,60,000

(B) ₹ 8,16,000 & ₹ 4,60,000

(C) ₹ 7,80,000 & ₹ 4,93,000

(D) ₹ 4,60,000 & ₹ 8,13,000

28. Rahul gifted ₹ 5,00,000 to his wife and the said gifted money was invested by Rahul's wife in partnership firm. Wife receives ₹ 1,05,000 as her share of profit from such firm. How much amount has to be clubbed in the hands of Rahul?

(A) ₹ 1,05,000

(B) ₹ 1,05,000 after giving effect to deduction u/s 40(b)

(C) Nil, as share of profit of firm is exempt.

(D) None of the above

29. Mr. X is employed in PQR Ltd. at monthly salary of ₹ 25,000 and is holding 25% shares of the company. His wife is employed in same company having salary of ₹ 10,000 p.m. Other income of Mr. X and Mrs. X is respectively ₹ 30,000 and ₹ 1,00,800. They have twin daughter and their income is ₹ 2,000 p.a. They have one son whose income is ₹ 1,200 p.a. Compute the total income of Mr. X & Mrs. X.

(A) ₹ 4,20,000 & ₹ 2,20,800

(B) ₹ 4,53,200 & ₹ 2,20,800

(C) ₹ 4,30,000 & ₹ 1,00,800

(D) ₹ 4,50,000 & ₹ 1,00,800

30. Raj gifted ₹ 20,00,000 to her wife on 1.4.2013 which she invested as capital in partnership firm. She received interest every year and her capital balance on 1.4.2018 was ₹ 30,00,000. During the year

2018-2019 she earned interest of ₹ 2,50,000 on her capital. The income to be clubbed in the hands of Raj shall be –

(A) Nil

(B) ₹ 2,50,000

(C) ₹ 1,66,667

(D) ₹ 1,33,333

31. Pavan transfers his self acquired property to HUF. The HUF earns interest of ₹ 52,500 every year on 1.4.2018 HUF is partitioned and property is divided as under:

Pavan	1/5 share
Pavan's minor son	1/5 share
Pavan's major son	1/5 share
Mrs. Pavan	1/5 share
Pavan's brother	1/5 share

Calculate the total income of Pavan?

(A) ₹ 30,000

(B) ₹ 31,500

(C) ₹ 52,500

(D) ₹ 40,500

32. Ram transfers 1,000 debentures of ₹ 100 each carrying 10% interest to Raman on the condition that he will get 3% interest during his life time. Which of the following shows correct taxable implication for this transaction?

(A) Interest income of ₹ 7,000 will be taxable in the hands of Raman and ₹ 3,000 interest will be taxable in the hands of Ram as it is revocable transaction for ₹ 3,000 interest income only.

(B) Interest income of ₹ 10,000 will be taxable in the hands of Raman as it is not revocable transfer.

(C) Interest income of ₹ 10,000 will be taxable in the hands of Ram as it is revocable transfer.

(D) Interest income of ₹ 3,000 will be taxable in the hands of Raman and ₹ 7,000 interest will be taxable in the hands of Ram.

33. X gifts ₹ 5,00,000 to his wife Mrs. X and Mrs. X gifts the same money to her son's wife. If son's wife receives ₹ 50,000 income then in whose hand the ₹ 50,000 will be taxable?

(A) Mr. X

(B) Mrs. X

(C) Son's wife

(D) Son of X

34. Y transferred agricultural land to Z with a condition that 60% of income from land should be handed over to him. Z earned ₹ 1,00,000 from such agricultural land. What are the tax implications?

(A) ₹ 1,00,000 is taxable in the hands of Z

(B) ₹ 1,00,000 is taxable in the hands of Y as it is revocable transfer

(C) ₹ 60,000 is taxable in the hands of Y and ₹ 40,000 is taxable in the hands of Z.

(D) Nothing is taxable Y or Z.

35. Mrs. K receives salary of ₹ 1,20,000 and taxable allowance of ₹ 45,000 from M Ltd. in which her father in law holds 25% equity shares. Income from salary of Mrs. K is taxable in the hands of –

(A) Mr. K

(B) Father in law of Mrs. K

(C) Mrs. K

(D) 25% salary income will be clubbed in the hands of father in law of Mrs. K and remaining 75% is taxable in the hands of Mrs. K.

36. In HUF there are three members Mr. B (Karta), Mrs. B and a minor child. Karta set apart ₹ 2,00,000 out of family funds for maintenance of his wife. Mrs. B deposit the money in bank. Which of the following statement is correct?

(A) Income on deposit will be clubbed with income of HUF.

(B) Income on deposit will be clubbed in the hands of Mrs B in his personal capacity.

(C) Income cannot be clubbed either with income of HUF or in personal capacity of Mr. B and same is taxable in the hands of Mrs. B.

(D) None of the above

Answers:

1.	(B)	**2.**	(D)	**3.**	(C)	**4.**	(C)	**5.**	(C)	**6.**	(C)	**7.**	(A)
8.	(A)	**9.**	(D)	**10.**	(C)	**11.**	(D)	**12.**	(A)	**13.**	(D)	**14.**	(D)
15.	(D)	**16.**	(B)	**17.**	(D)	**18.**	(C)	**19.**	(B)	**20.**	(D)	**21.**	(D)
22.	(C)	**23.**	(A)	**24.**	(B)	**25.**	(C)	**26.**	(C)	**27.**	(A)	**28.**	(C)
29.	(D)	**30.**	(C)	**31.**	(A)	**32.**	(C)	**33.**	(A)	**34.**	(D)	**35.**	(C)
36.	(C)												

PAST EXAMINATION MCQs

1. June 2015: Shyam transferred 2,000 shares of X Ltd. to Ms. Babita without any consideration. Later, Shyam and Ms. Babita got married to each other. The dividend income from the shares transferred would be —

(A) Taxable in the hands of Shyam both before and after marriage

(B) Taxable in the hands of Shyam before marriage but not after marriage

(C) Taxable in the hands of Shyam after marriage but not before marriage

(D) Never taxable in the hands of Shyam

2. Dec 2015: Rohit (a Chartered Accountant) is working as Accounts Officer in Raj (P) Ltd. on a salary of ₹ 20,000 p.m. He got married to Ms. Pooja who holds 25% shares of this company. What will be the impact of salary paid to Rohit by the company in the hands of Ms. Pooja —

(A) 100% salary to be clubbed

(B) 50% salary to be clubbed

(C) No amount be clubbed

(D) 25% salary be clubbed

3. June 2017: Mr. Shiva gifted a let-out building which fetches rental income of ₹ 10,500 per month to his son's wife on 1.11.2017. The municipal tax of ₹ 6,000 on the property was paid on 10.1.2019. The total income from all other sources (computed) amounts to ₹ 2,60,000 except income from above said property. His total income chargeable to tax is:

(A) ₹ 3,11,450

(B) ₹ 3,44,000

(C) ₹ 3,80,000

(D) ₹ 3,33,500

4. Dec 2017: Baby Meena (age 12) a child artist acted in feature films and earned ₹ 3,50,000. The total income of her father is ₹ 5,20,000 and mother is ₹ 4,80,000. The minor's income would be:

(A) Chargeable to tax in the hands of father

(B) Chargeable to tax in the hands of mother

(C) Chargeable to tax in her own hands

(D) Fully exempt from tax

ANSWERS:

1.	(D)	2.	(C)	3.	(B)	4.	(C)

HINTS FOR PRACTICAL MCQs

21. Income on clubbed income cannot be clubbed. Hence only ₹ 1,00,000 can be clubbed in the hands of Ram and ₹ 10,000 will be taxable in the hands of Mrs. Ram.

22. Salary paid by Mosin to her wife is business expenditure and such salary cannot be clubbed in the hands of Mosin as modelling is profession and such income cannot be clubbed as per Section 64(1)(*ii*).

23. Capital on 1.4.2018 = 2,25,000 + 1,50,000 + 1,12,500 = 4,87,500.

$$\text{Income to be clubbed for PY 2018-2019} = 2{,}92{,}500 \times \frac{1{,}50{,}000}{4{,}87{,}500}$$

= 90,000

24.

Gross salary		4,50,000
Family pension	13,500	
(-) 1/3rd or ₹ 15,000 whichever is less is exempt	(4,500)	9,000
Income of minor child	6,000	
(-) Exempt	(1,500)	4,500
Balance in PF received after death of her husband (Not taxable)		-
Gratuity received after the death of her husband (Not taxable)		-
		4,63,500

25. Any income of minor child suffering from disability specified in Section 80U cannot be clubbed in the hands of parents.

26.

First daughter	9,000	
(-) Exempt	(1,500)	7,500
Second daughter *(not taxable as child suffering from disabilities specified in Section 80U)*		-
First son	6,200	
(-) Exempt	(1,500)	4,700
Second son	4,300	
(-) Exempt	(1,500)	2,800
		15,000

27.

	Mr. X	Mrs. X
Gross income	7,80,000	4,60,000
Income of minor son *(Clubbed in the hands of Mr. X)*	30,000	
(-) Exempt	(1,500)	
	8,08,500	4,60,000

Note: Income of minor daughter from special talent cannot be clubbed in the hand of either parent. Similarly, interest on bank deposit of minor daughter out of sum deposited from special talent cannot be clubbed.

Gift received by minor daughter from friend of Mrs. X is exempt as amount is less than 50,000.

28. Share of profit from partnership firm is exempt and hence cannot be clubbed.

29. Mr. X = (25,000 × 12) + (10,000 × 12) wife salary clubbed + 30,000 = 4,50,000

Mrs. X = 1,00,800

Income of twin daughter is 2,000 i.e. per daughter ₹ 1,000. Exemption per child is ₹ 1,500 hence after exemption nothing is taxable in the hands of Mr. X. Similarly income of son is ₹ 1,200 i.e. below ₹ 1,500 hence nothing to be clubbed for son also.

30. Interest on capital invested is not exempt. Hence, proportionate amount has to be clubbed.

Income to be clubbed for PY 2018-2019 = $2{,}50{,}000 \times \frac{20{,}00{,}000}{30{,}00{,}000}$

= 1,66,667.

31.

Pavan	1/5 share	10,500
Pavan's minor son	1/5 share	10,500
(-) Exemption		(1,500)
Pavan's major son	1/5 share	-
Mrs. Pavan	1/5 share	10,500
Pavan's brother	1/5 share	-
		30,000

34. Income from agricultural land is exempt.

36. Money is transferred by HUF and not by Mr. B in his personal capacity and hence clubbing provision is not applicable.

HINTS FOR PAST EXAMINATION MCQs

3. Income of house property up to 1st Nov will be taxable in the hands of Mr. Shiva. He had transferred asset on 1st Nov to his son's wife without consideration. Hence, income after 1st Nov will also clubbed in the hands of Mr. Shiva. Thus, practically whole year income from house property is taxable in the hands of Mr. Shiva.

Rent receivable (10,500 × 12)	1,26,000
(-) Municipal tax	(6,000)
Gross annual value	1,20,000
(-) Standard deduction @ 30%	(36,000)
Income from house property	84,000
Income from other sources	2,60,000
Total income of Mr. Shiva	3,44,000

CHAPTER 9

AGGREGATION OF INCOME AND SET-OFF OR CARRY FORWARD OF LOSSES

MCQs ON THEORY

1. Loss from speculation business can be set-off against profits of -

(A) Any business

(B) Any business other than speculation business

(C) Any other speculation business

(D) Income from other sources

2. STCL of particular year can be set-off against ______ of that year.

(A) STCG

(B) LTCG

(C) (A) or (B)

(D) Neither (A) nor (B)

3. Match the following:

1. Unexplained expenditure	(*i*) Section 68
2. Amount borrowed or repaid on hundi	(*ii*) Section 69A
3. Unexplained cash credit	(*iii*) Section 69B
4. Unexplained money	(*iv*) Section 69C
	(*v*) Section 69
	(*vi*) Section 69D

Select the correct answer from the following options -

	1	2	3	4
(A)	*(iv)*	*(vi)*	*(ii)*	*(i)*
(B)	*(vi)*	*(iv)*	*(i)*	*(ii)*
(C)	*(iv)*	*(vi)*	*(i)*	*(ii)*
(D)	*(iii)*	*(v)*	*(i)*	*(ii)*

4. Loss under the head other sources from activity of owning and maintaining race horses ....

(A) Cannot be set-off from income under any other head

(B) Can be carried forward if return is filed in time

(C) Can be carried forward for 4 more years

(D) All of the above

5. Loss from lottery, card games, gambling, betting, etc. -

(A) Can be carried forward to next year

(B) Can be set-off against any other income of same nature

(C) Cannot be set-off against any income

(D) None of the above

6. As per Section 72A of the Income Tax Act, 1961, which of the following can be carried forward for 8 years by the Amalgamated Company?

(I) Business loss

(II) Unabsorbed depreciation

(III) Speculation business loss

Select the correct answer from the following options -

(A) (I) only

(B) (I), (II) only

(C) (I) & (III) only

(D) (II) only

7. Loss under the head capital gains cannot be set-off -

(1) against income under the head "salaries"

(2) against income under the head "house property"

Select the correct answer from the following options -

(A) (1) only

(B) (2) only

(C) Both (1) and (2)

(D) None of the above

8. Section 72A of the Income Tax Act, 1961 is applicable to -

1. Company owning an industrial undertaking
2. Company owning a ship
3. Public Sector Company
4. Companies engaged in the business of operation of aircraft

Select the correct answer from the following options -

(A) 1 and 4 only

(B) 1 and 2 only

(C) 2, 3 and 4 only

(D) 1, 2, 3 and 4

9. Loss under the head house property -

(A) Cannot be set-off against income under the head "salaries"

(B) Cannot be set-off against income under the head "capital gain"

(C) Can be carried forward only if return is filed in time

(D) Can be carried forward even if return is not filed

10. Which of the following is/are correct condition(s) to be fulfilled by 'amalgamating company' u/s 72A so that amalgamated company can carry forward the losses and unabsorbed depreciation of the amalgamating company?

(1) The amalgamating company has held continuously 50% of assets for last 2 years prior to the date of amalgamation.

(2) The amalgamating company has loss or depreciation for last 3 years.

Select the correct answer from the following options -

(A) (1) only

(B) Both (1) and (2)

(C) (2) only

(D) Neither (1) nor (2)

11. Long term capital loss of particular year can be set-off against _____ of that year.

(A) Short term capital loss

(B) Long term capital loss

(C) (A) or (B)

(D) Neither (A) nor (B)

12. As per Section 72A(4), in the case of a demerger, the accumulated loss and unabsorbed depreciation (other than speculation business loss) of the demerged company shall be treated as accumulated loss and unabsorbed depreciation of the resulting company if it is directly relatable to the undertakings transferred to the resulting company. Loss can be carried forward and set off _____

(A) For further 4 years

(B) Only for next 8 previous years

(C) Only for the remaining period out of 8 years

(D) Against profits of next financial year

13. As per Section 68 of the Income Tax Act, 1961, where any sum is found _____ in the books of an assessee maintained for any previous year, and the assessee offers no explanation about the nature and source thereof or the explanation offered by him is not, in the opinion of the Assessing Officer, satisfactory, the sum so credited may be charged to income-tax as the income of the assessee of that previous year.

(A) Debited

(B) Recorded

(C) Credited

(D) Deleted

14. As per Section 72A(6), in case of business organization i.e. firm is succeeded by company, then loss of firm is deemed to be loss of the successor company. However, such conversion of firm into company should be as per conditions laid down in ________

(A) Section 47(xiib)

(B) Section 47(xiii)

(C) Section 47(xiv)

(D) Section 47(xiii)

15. Loss under the head PGBP can be carried forward for _____

(A) 10 years

(B) Infinite years

(C) 8 years

(D) even if return is not filed in time

16. As per Section 69, unexplained investment are taxable if -

(A) investments are not recorded in the books of account

(B) assessee offers no explanation about the nature and source of the investments

(C) explanation offered by him is not, in the opinion of the Assessing Officer, satisfactory

(D) all of the above

17. Provisions in respect of Section 79 is not applicable for _____

(A) Losses

(B) Depreciation

(C) Speculation business loss

(D) All of the above

18. Which of the following is taxable under Section 69A of the Income Tax Act, 1961?

I. Money

II. Diamond

III. Costly furniture

Select the correct answer from the following options -

(A) I only

(B) II only

(C) III only

(D) All of the above

19. Loss from specified business referred to in Section 35AD can be carried forward for ____

(A) 4 years

(B) 8 years

(C) 10 years

(D) Indefinitely

20. Loss from one house property can be set-off against -

(A) income from any other house property

(B) income from speculation business

(C) income under the head salary

(D) any of the above

21. Loss from specified business referred to in Section 35AD can be carried forward and set-off against -

(*a*) income of specified business

(*b*) income of any other business

Select the correct answer from the following options -

(A) (a) only

(B) (b) only

(C) Both (a) and (b)

(D) Neither (a) nor (b)

22. Loss from speculation business can be set off against -

(A) income from other sources

(B) profits of any other speculation business

(C) income from house property

(D) any of the above

23. Which of the following is/are correct condition(s) to be fulfilled by 'amalgamated company' u/s 72A so that it can carry forward the losses and unabsorbed depreciation of the amalgamating company?

(a) The amalgamated company continues the business of the amalgamating company for period of 3 years from the date of amalgamation.

(b) The amalgamated company holds continuously for 3 years 50% of fixed assets of the amalgamating company acquired in a scheme of amalgamation.

Select the correct answer from the following options -

(A) (a) only

(B) (b) only

(C) Both (a) and (b)

(D) Neither (a) nor (b)

24. Loss from derivative trading in shares carried on in a recognized stock exchange

I. is a loss from speculation business

II. can be set-off from income of any other speculation business

III. can be set-off from income of any other non-speculative business

IV. can be carried forward for 8 years

Select the correct answer from the following options -

(A) I only

(B) I and II only

(C) III and IV only

(D) II, III and IV only

25. Losses from general business can be set-off against -

(A) Income from any other house property

(B) Income from speculation business

(C) Both (A) and (B)

(D) Neither (A) nor (B)

26. Loss from trading in commodity derivatives through a recognized stock exchange -

1. is a loss from speculative business
2. can be carried forward for 4 years only

Select the correct answer from the following options -

(A) Neither 1 nor 2

(B) Both 1 and 2

(C) 1 only

(D) 2 only

27. Any loss computed in respect of any specified business referred u/s 35AD can be set-off against -

(A) Profits of any other business

(B) Profits from speculation business

(C) Income under the head salary

(D) None.of the above

28. Match the following:

List I	List II
1. Loss under the head house property	(*i*) Carried forward for 8 years
2. Loss from speculation business	(*ii*) Carried forward for infinite years
3. Loss from specified business	(*iii*) Carried forward for 4 years
4. Loss from lotteries, cross-word puzzles card games	(*iv*) Cannot be carried forward

Select the correct answer from the following options -

	1	2	3	4
(A)	(*i*)	(*iii*)	(*iv*)	(*ii*)
(B)	(*iii*)	(*i*)	(*ii*)	(*iv*)
(C)	(*i*)	(*iii*)	(*ii*)	(*iv*)
(D)	(*iii*)	(*iv*)	(*i*)	(*ii*)

29. Long term capital loss from sale of listed equity shares referred to in Section 10(38) can be set-off against -

(1) Short term capital gain on sale of listed equity shares

(2) Long term capital gain on sale of building

(3) Long term capital gain on sale of listed equity shares

Select the correct answer from the following options -

(A) (1) only

(B) (3) only

(C) (2) and (3) only

(D) None of the above

30. *Statement I:*

Unabsorbed depreciation can be carried forward for more than 8 years

Statement II:

Where any person carrying on any business has been succeeded by another person by inheritance, the losses can be carried forward and set off by the successor.

Select the correct answer from the following options -

(A) Statement I is true but Statement II is false

(B) Statement II is true but Statement I is false

(C) Statement I and II both are false

(D) Statement I and II both are true

PRACTICAL MCQs

31. Chandan borrowed on hundi a sum of ₹ 15,000 by way of bearer cheque 11.10.2018 and repaid the same with interest amounting to ₹ 20,000 by account payee cheque on 12.11.2018. How much amount is chargeable to tax as per Section 69D of the Income Tax Act, 1961?

(A) ₹ 20,000

(B) ₹ 5,000

(C) ₹ 15,000

(D) ₹ 35,000

32. From the following details calculate the total income of Rajat:

Income from house property	42,000
Loss from textile business	40,000
b/f loss of textile business of PY 2014-2015	95,000

Bad recovered during the year (earlier allowed to be deducted)	35,000
b/f loss of chemical business of PY 2015-2016	50,000
Share of profit in a firm	16,000
Profits from leather business	1,00,000

(A) ₹ 42,000

(B) ₹ 1,35,000

(C) Nil

(D) Loss ₹ 8,000

33. Rahul submits the following information:

Short term capital gain on sale of gold	35,000
Long term capital loss on sale of building	10,000
Contribution to LIC towards premium	10,000

Total income of Rahul = ?

(A) ₹ 35,000

(B) ₹ 15,000

(C) ₹ 25,000

(D) Nil

34. ABC Ltd. was amalgamated with XYZ Ltd. on 1.4.2018. ABC Ltd. has following balances as on 1.4.2018:

Speculative loss	4 lakhs
Unabsorbed depreciation	18 lakhs
Unabsorbed capital expenditure on family planning	2 lakhs
Business loss	120 lakhs

Total income of XYZ Ltd. for PY 2018-2019 was ₹ 147.5 lakhs. Calculate total income of XYZ Ltd.

(A) ₹ 7.5 lakhs

(B) ₹ 3.5 lakhs

(C) ₹ 4.5 lakhs

(D) ₹ 27.5 lakhs

35. N & Co. has four partners - A, B, C & D having equal profit sharing ratio. There position of losses and unabsorbed depreciation as on 31.3.2018 is as follows:

PY		₹
2015-2016	Business loss	1,20,000
2016-2017	Business loss	1,90,000
2016-2017	unabsorbed depreciation	1,20,000

D retires on 31.3.2017. Income of firm for PY 2018-2019 is ₹ 4,00,000 before giving effect to above. Total income of the firm chargeable to tax = ?

(A) Nil

(B) Loss ₹ 30,000

(C) ₹ 47,500

(D) Data given is not sufficient

36. From the following details calculate the gross total income of Sundar:

Loss from house property	67,500
Income from business	3,30,000
Income from speculation business	22,500
LTCG on sale of building	1,95,000
STCL on sale of gold	40,500
Loss under the head "other sources" (normal)	18,000

Tax payable by Sundar for PY 2018-2019 = ?

(A) ₹ 22,710

(B) ₹ 19,490

(C) ₹ 19,680

(D) ₹ 24,770

37. NSZ (Pvt.) Ltd. gives the following information:

PY	2016-2017	2017-2018	2018-2019
Business income/(loss)	(6,00,000)	(10,00,000)	20,00,000
Unabsorbed depreciation	1,60,000	3,20,000	-
Shareholding as on last date of PY	A - 35%	A - 35%	A - 35%
	B - 20%	B - 20%	G - 20%
	C - 15%	E - 15%	E - 15%
	D - 30%	F - 30%	F - 30%

Total income of NSZ (Pvt.) Ltd. for 2018-2019 = ?

(A) Nil

(B) Loss ₹ 80,000

(C) ₹ 5,20,000

(D) ₹ 6,80,000

38. Rohit discontinued his proprietary business in PY 2018-2019 for which he had unabsorbed depreciation of ₹ 1,50,000. He has only income in current year is income from other sources. In relation to these facts select the correct option given below -

(A) Rohit cannot set-off the unabsorbed depreciation of ₹ 1,50,000 of last year against the current year income from other sources.

(B) Rohit will have to carry forward the unabsorbed depreciation of ₹ 1,50,000 to next PY 2018-2019.

(C) Both (A) and (B)

(D) Rohit can set-off the unabsorbed depreciation of ₹ 1,50,000 of last year against the current year income from other sources as it will from part of the current depreciation.

39. Ravi submits following details for PY 2018-2019:

Loss from house property	(8,000)
STCL on sale of unlisted shares	(95,000)
LTCG on sale of building	1,65,000
Interest on government securities	3,00,000
Unabsorbed depreciation of PY 2016-2017.	40,000

Tax payable by Ravi for PY 2018-2019 = ?

(A) Nil

(B) ₹ 5,360

(C) ₹ 7,620

(D) ₹ 4,530

40. From the following details calculate total income -

Income from salary	1,14,000
Loss from house property	7,500
Speculation business profit	12,000
Normal business profit	51,000
Current depreciation	19,500
b/f business loss	13,500
Short term capital gain	48,000
Long term capital gain	15,600
Long term capital loss	37,500

(A) ₹ 1,74,500

(B) ₹ 1,80,500

(C) ₹ 1,62,600

(D) ₹ 1,84,500

41. A, B, C are equal partners in a firm. The firms loss for the year ended 31.3.2018 is ₹ 1,56,000. On 31.3.2018 C retired and D joined the firm as equal partner. The firm made a profit of ₹ 1,68,000 for the year ended 31.3.2019. Share of each partner in the firm income for the year 2018-2019 -

	A	B	D
(A)	10,667	10,667	10,666
(B)	21,333	21,333	21,334
(C)	4,000	4,000	56,000
(D)	30,000	30,000	4,000

42. From the following details calculate the total income:

	Situation I	*Situation II*
Long term capital gain/(loss)	3,80,000	(7,00,000)
Short term capital gain/(loss)	(1,20,000)	2,80,000
Business income/(loss)	(1,80,000)	5,80,000

Select the correct answer from the following options:

	Situation I	*Situation II*
(A)	2,60,000	5,80,000
(B)	3,80,000	8,60,000
(C)	80,000	8,60,000
(D)	80,000	1,60,000

43. During the previous year an assessee has incurred business loss in his business of ₹ 2,40,000. His income from house property for the same previous year was ₹ 2,20,000. The assessee can carry forward -

(A) Business loss of ₹ 2,24,000 and claim full exemption for other income.

(B) Business loss of ₹ 20,000 and his total income will be nil.

(C) Any of the above at the choice of assessee.

(D) None of the above

44. From the following details calculate the tax payable by D Ltd. which annual turnover for past few years is above ₹ 60 Crore:

	₹
Business loss	50,00,000
Income from house property	45,00,000
Income other sources	1,00,000
Short term capital gain	3,00,000
Long term capital gain	10,00,000

(A) ₹ 2,80,800

(B) ₹ 1,87,200

(C) ₹ 2,15,100

(D) ₹ 1,92,800

45. From the following details calculate the total income of assessee:

- Salary received as a partner from firm ₹ 7,50,000.
- Loss on sale of shares listed in BSE ₹ 3,00,000 on which STT was paid. Shares were held for 16 months.
- Long term capital gain on sale of land ₹ 5,00,000.
- Gift received from friend in party ₹ 51,000.
- Dividend received from listed companies ₹ 55,000.
- Brought forward business loss of last year ₹ 12,50,000. *Return was filed in time.*

(A) ₹ 5,51,000

(B) ₹ 13,01,000

(C) ₹ 8,51,000

(D) ₹ 9,06,000

46. Loss from house property in excess of ₹ ______ is not allowed to be set-off against any other income.

(A) 1,50,000

(B) 2,00,000

(C) 5,00,000

(D) There is no such provision in Income Tax Law.

ANSWERS:

1.	(C)	**2.**	(C)	**3.**	(C)	**4.**	(D)	**5.**	(C)	**6.**	(B)	**7.**	(C)
8.	(D)	**9.**	(D)	**10.**	(C)	**11.**	(B)	**12.**	(C)	**13.**	(C)	**14.**	(B)
15.	(C)	**16.**	(D)	**17.**	(B)	**18.**	(D)	**19.**	(D)	**20.**	(D)	**21.**	(A)
22.	(B)	**23.**	(D)	**24.**	(D)	**25.**	(C)	**26.**	(B)	**27.**	(D)	**28.**	(C)
29.	(D)	**30.**	(D)	**31.**	(C)	**32.**	(A)	**33.**	(C)	**34.**	(A)	**35.**	(C)
36.	(C)	**37.**	(C)	**38.**	(D)	**39.**	(D)	**40.**	(D)	**41.**	(C)	**42.**	(C)
43.	(B)	**44.**	(B)	**45.**	(A)	**46.**	(B)						

PAST EXAMINATION MCQs:

1. June 2015: If an individual, having a sales turnover of ₹ 60 lakh files his return of income for the AY 2019-2020 after the due date, showing unabsorbed business loss of ₹ 23,000 and unabsorbed depreciation of ₹ 45,000, he can carry forward to the subsequent assessment years —

(A) Both unabsorbed business loss of ₹ 23,000 and unabsorbed depreciation of ₹ 45,000

(B) Only unabsorbed business loss of ₹ 23,000

(C) Only unabsorbed depreciation of ₹ 45,000

(D) Neither unabsorbed business loss of ₹ 23,000 nor unabsorbed depreciation of ₹ 45,000.

2. June 2015: Loss from the activity of owning and maintaining race horses could be set-off —

(A) Against income under any of the five heads of income

(B) Only against income under the head 'income from other sources'

(C) Only against income under the head 'profits and gains of business or profession'

(D) Only against income from same activity.

3. Dec 2015: If a person is eligible to claim:

(1) Unabsorbed depreciation

(2) Current scientific research expenditure

(3) Current depreciation

(4) Brought forward business loss

The order of priority to set-off would be —

(A) (4), (3), (2) & (1)

(B) (2), (3), (4) & (1)

(C) (3), (4), (1) & (2)

(D) (1), (2), (3) & (4)

4. Dec 2015: A partnership firm with 4 equal partners brought forward depreciation of ₹ 3 lakh and business loss of ₹ 3 lakh relating to AY 2018-2019. On 1st April, 2018, two partners retired.

The amount that assessee-firm can set-off against its income for the AY 2019-2020 would be —

(A) Unabsorbed depreciation of ₹ 3 lakh plus brought forward business loss of ₹ 3 lakh

(B) Unabsorbed depreciation 'nil' plus brought forward business loss ₹ 3 lakh

(C) Unabsorbed depreciation ₹ 3 lakh plus brought forward business loss 'nil'.

(D) Unabsorbed depreciation ₹ 3 lakh plus brought forward business loss of ₹ 1.50 lakh.

5. June 2016: Which of the following losses available after inter source set-off, cannot be set-off from incomes in other heads in the same assessment year —

(A) Speculation losses

(B) Loss from specified business

(C) Loss under the head capital gains

(D) All of the above

6. June 2016: To carry forward and set-off losses, a loss return must be filed by the assessee within the stipulated time and gets the loss determined by the Assessing Officer. However, this condition is not applicable to —

(A) Loss from house property

(B) Loss from speculation

(C) Loss from discontinued business

(D) Loss from capital assets

7. June 2016: Biren discontinued wholesale trade in medicines from 1st July 2015. He recovered ₹ 1,50,000 in October 2018 being a bad debt which was written-off and allowed in assessment year 2016-2017. He has eligible brought forward business loss of wholesale trade in medicines of ₹ 1,70,000. The consequence of bad debt recovery is that —

(A) It is chargeable to tax

(B) It is eligible for set-off against brought forward business loss

(C) The brought forward business loss is taxable now

(D) 50% of the amount recovered now is taxable

8. Dec 2016: Unabsorbed loss from house property can be carried forward for —

(A) 4 years

(B) 8 years

(C) Indefinite period

(D) Cannot be carried forward

9. Dec 2016: Loss from speculation business is eligible for carry forward for a period of —

(A) 4 Years

(B) 6 Years

(C) 8 Years

(D) 12 Years

10. Dec 2016: No loss can be set off against -

(A) Income from salaries

(B) Income from house property

(C) Income from capital gains

(D) Winnings from lotteries

11. Dec 2016: The amount of depreciation not absorbed in the same year can be carried forward -

(A) For a period of 4 years

(B) For a period of 8 years

(C) For a period of 6 years

(D) Indefinitely

12. Dec. 2016: Loss from speculation business can be set off against -

(A) Income from salaries

(B) Income from house property

(C) Income from speculation business only

(D) Any head of income

13. June 2017: Mr. Shahu has loss from house property of ₹ 1,10,000 (computed) for the assessment year 2019-2020. He can carry forward such loss for subsequent .... assessment years.

(A) 4

(B) Nil

(C) 8

(D) Indefinite

14. June 2017: Mr. Hussey for the previous year has -

(*i*) Business loss of ₹ 1,30,000;

(*ii*) Income from salary ₹ 2,40,000; and

(*iii*) Speculation gain of ₹ 1,10,000.

His total income for income tax assessment is:

(A) ₹ 3,50,000

(B) ₹ 2,20,000

(C) ₹ 2,40,000

(D) ₹ 1,10,000

15. June 2017: Mathur Storage (P) Ltd. engaged in chain cold storage has brought forward business loss of ₹ 12 lakhs relating to assessment year 2018-2019. During the previous year 2018-2019, its income from the said business is ₹ 9 lakhs. It also has profit from trade in food grains of ₹ 6 lakhs. The total income of the company for the assessment year 2019-2020 is:

(A) ₹ 15 lakhs

(B) ₹ 6 lakhs

(C) ₹ 9 lakhs

(D) ₹ 3 lakhs

16. June 2017: A Co. Ltd. has business loss and unabsorbed depreciation of ₹ 10 Crore. B Co. Ltd is profit making company. B Co. Ltd. wanted to acquire A Co. Ltd. with the benefit of set off of brought forward loss and unabsorbed depreciation. The legally permissible method is:

(A) Reverse merger

(B) Outright purchase

(C) Slump sale of A Co. Ltd.

(D) Converting A Co. Ltd. into subsidiary of B. Co. Ltd.

17. Dec 2017: When an assessee has loss from house property, it is eligible for carry forward for the subsequent .... assessment years.

(A) 2

(B) 4

(C) 6

(D) 8

18. Dec 2017: Mr. Siddharth is employed in a company. His income under various heads are

(*i*) Salary ₹ 5,60,000;

(*ii*) Loss from let out properly ₹ 65,000;

(*iii*) Loss from business ₹ 1,10,000 and

(*iv*) Loss under the head other sources ₹ 30,000.

His total income after set off of losses would be:

(A) ₹ 3,55,000

(B) ₹ 4,65,000

(C) ₹ 4,20,000

(D) ₹ 5,30,000

19. Dec 2017: A company has the following:

(*i*) Current scientific research expenditure;

(*ii*) Current depreciation;

(*iii*) Unabsorbed depreciation;

(*iv*) Brought forward business loss.

The order sequence of set off is:

(A) (i), (ii), (iii), (iv)

(B) (iv), (iii), (i), (ii)

(C) (i), (ii), (iv), (iii)

(D) (iv), (ii), (i), (iii)

20. Dec 2017: Rohan engaged in multifarious activities reports the following:

(i) Loss from business ₹ 80,000;

(ii) Loss from house property ₹ 1,20,000;

(iii) Long term capital loss ₹ 70,000;

He filed his return beyond the 'due date' specified in Section 139(1). Which of the above losses cannot be carried forward to subsequent assessment year?

(A) Loss from business

(B) Loss from house property

(C) Long term capital loss

(D) None of the above

21. Dec 2017: Speculation loss can be carried forward for .... subsequent assessment years.

(A) 8

(B) Nil

(C) 4

(D) 6

ANSWERS:

1.	(C)	**2.**	(D)	**3.**	(B)	**4.**	(D)	**5.**	(D)	**6.**	(A)	**7.**	(B)
8.	(B)	**9.**	(A)	**10.**	(D)	**11.**	(D)	**12.**	(C)	**13.**	(C)	**14.**	(C)
15.	(B)	**16.**	(B)	**17.**	(D)	**18.**	(B)	**19.**	(C)	**20.**	(**)	**21.**	(C)

** *MCQs are wrongly drafted. For further clarification please see the hints.*

HINTS FOR IMPORTANT PRACTICAL MCQs:

31. Borrowing on hundi a sum of by way of bearer cheque of ₹ 15,000 will be taxable only not repayment as repayment was made in account payee cheque.

32.

Income from house property		42,000
Profits from leather business	1,00,000	

Bad recovered during the year	35,000	
Loss from textile business	(40,000)	
b/f loss of textile business of PY 2014-2015	(95,000)	Nil
		42,000

Share of profit in a firm is exempt.

b/f loss of chemical business of PY 2015-2016 ₹ 50,000 will be carried forward.

33. Long term capital loss cannot be set-off against short term capital gain.

Income = 35,000 (STCG) - 10,000 (80C deduction) = 25,000

34. Speculation business loss cannot be carried forward by Amalgamated Company. **[Section 72A]**

Total income of XYZ Ltd. = 147.5 - 18 - 2 - 120 = 7.5 lakhs.

35. Loss proportionate to profit sharing ratio of retiring partner cannot be carried forward by the firm. This provision is not applicable for unabsorbed depreciation. Thus, out of total loss of ₹ 3,10,000 loss of ₹ 77,500 cannot be carried forward by the firm.

Total income = 4,00,000 - 2,32,500 - 1,20,000 = 47,500.

36.

Income from business		3,30,000
Income from speculation business		22,500
LTCG on sale of building	1,95,000	
(-) Loss from house property	(67,500)	
(-) Loss under the head "other sources" (normal)	(18,000)	
(-) STCL on sale of gold	(40,500)	69,000
Total income		4,21,500

Calculation of tax:

On first	2,50,000	-	Nil
On next	1,02,500	@ 5%	5,125
On LTCG	69,000	@ 20%	13,800
	4,21,500		18,925

(+) Education cess @ 4%	757
	19,682
Rounded up to	19,680

37. In case of closely held company (i.e. private and unlisted company), loss can be set-off if 51% shareholder are same for the year in which loss is to be set-off and year in which loss is actually incurred. **[Section 79]**

This provision is not applicable for unabsorbed depreciation.

Total income of NSZ (Pvt.) Ltd. = 20,00,000 - 10,00,000 - 3,20,000 - 1,60,000 = 5,20,000

39. Set-off losses and unabsorbed depreciation against LTCG.. Calculate total income. Calculate tax and don't forget to give rebate u/s 87A.

41. Loss proportionate to profit sharing ration of retiring partner cannot be carried forward by the firm. Thus, out of loss of ₹ 1,56,000 loss of ₹ 52,000 cannot be carried forward.

Total income of firm = 1,68,000 - 1,04,000 = 64,000

Share of each partner:

A :	(56,000 - 52,000)	4,000
B :	(56,000 - 52,000)	4,000
D :		56,000
		64,000

44. Alternative I:

Business loss of ₹ 50,00,000 will be set-off as follows:

- ₹ 45,00,000 against house property
- ₹ 1,00,000 against income from other sources
- ₹ 3,00,000 against STCG
- ₹ 1,00,000 against LTCG.

Thus, net LTCG taxable = 10,00,000 - 1,00,000 = 9,00,000

Tax (9,00,000 × 20%)	1,80,000
(+) EC @ 4%	7,200
	1,87,200

Alternative II:

If business loss of ₹ 50,00,000 set-off as follows:

- ₹ 10,00,000 against LTCG
- ₹ 40,00,000 against house property

Tax (9,00,000 × 30%)	2,70,000
(+) EC @ 4%	10,800
	2,80,800

Thus, Alternative I is better as tax liability is minimum.

45.

Salary received as a partner from firm (business income)	7,50,000	
Brought forward business loss of last year	7,50,000	Nil
Long term capital gain on sale of land		5,00,000
Dividend received from listed companies		Exempt
Gift received from friend in party		51,000
		5,51,000

Brought forward business loss of last year to be carried forward = 12,50,000 - 7,50,000 = 5,00,000

HINTS FOR PAST EXAMINATION MCQs:

14.

Income from speculation business	1,10,000	
(-) Business loss (₹ 1,30,000 but restricted to ₹ 1,10,000)	(1,10,000)	Nil
Income from salary		2,40,000
Total income		2,40,000

Loss under the head PGBP cannot be set-off against income under the head salary.

15. "Cold chain facilities" is specified business u/s 35AD. Any loss computed in respect of any specified business referred u/s 35AD can be set-off only against profits of any specified business carried on by the assessee.

Income from specified business u/s 35AD	9,00,000	
(-) Brought forward business loss specified business u/s 35AD		
(₹ 12,00,000 but restricted to ₹ 9,00,000)	(9,00,000)	Nil
Income from food grain business		6,00,000
Total income		6,00,000

18. Loss from business cannot be set-off against income from salary.

20. *Question is not correctly drafted.*

If return is not filed in time then losses cannot be carried forward to next year except loss from house property. Thus, loss from house property can be carried forward to next year even is return is not filed in time.

The question requires "which of the losses cannot be carried forward to subsequent assessment year?" Question need to be correct as follows:

"Which of the loss can be carried forward to subsequent assessment year?"

If question is corrected as above then Option (B) will be correct.

CHAPTER 10

DEDUCTIONS FROM TOTAL INCOME

MCQs ON THEORY

1. In computing the total income the deductions specified in _______ are allowed.

(A) Sections 80A to 80U

(B) Sections 80C to 80V

(C) Sections 80CC to 80HH

(D) Sections 80C to 80U

2. If expenditure is incurred on the medical treatment of prescribed disease then assessee can claim deduction u/s _______ of the Income Tax Act, 1961.

(A) Section 80DD

(B) Section 80DDA

(C) Section 80DDB

(D) Section 80DBB

3. The aggregate amount of deductions under Chapter VI-A _____

(A) shall not exceed the total income of the assessee

(B) Can exceed the gross total income of the assessee if allowed by Assessing Officer

(C) Are limited to ₹ 5,00,000 or gross total income whichever is less.

(D) Shall not exceed the gross total income of the assessee

4. Senior citizen means an individual resident in India who is of the age of ______ or more at any time during the relevant previous year.

(A) 67 years

(B) 75 years

(C) 60 years

(D) 90 years

5. From which type of income deduction under Chapter VI-A is/are not allowed?

(1) LTCG referred u/s 112

(2) Income from specified business referred u/s 35AD

(3) STCG referred u/s 111A

(4) Incomes referred to in Section 115A

Select the correct answer from the options given below –

(A) (1) and (2) only

(B) (3) and (1) only

(C) (1), (2), (3) and (4)

(D) (4), (1) and (3) only

6. Maximum possible deduction u/s 80QQB is –

(A) ₹ 2,00,000

(B) ₹ 5,00,000

(C) ₹ 3,00,000

(D) ₹ 7,50,000

7. Who is eligible to claim deduction u/s 80C?

(A) An Individual

(B) HUF

(C) Resident Individual or HUF

(D) Resident Individual or HUF as well non-resident Individual or HUF

8. If assessee's father is senior citizen and assessee incurs expenses on medical treatment of prescribed disease on his father then assessee can claim deduction u/s 80DDB up to –

(A) Amount of expenses actually incurred or ₹ 1,00,000 whichever is less

(B) ₹ 75,000 irrespective of expenditure incurred.

(C) Amount of expenses actually incurred or ₹ 1,25,000 whichever is less

(D) ₹ 1,25,000 irrespective of expenditure incurred.

9. Deduction in respect of interest on loan taken for residential property u/s 80EE is available to –

(A) Individual

(B) HUF

(C) Individual and HUF

(D) Any assessee

10. Maximum possible deduction u/s 80C is –

(A) ₹ 1,00,000

(B) ₹ 1,25,000

(C) ₹ 1,50,000

(D) ₹ 2,00,000

11. Which of the following assessee is/are eligible to claim deduction u/s 80G of the Income Tax Act, 1961?

1. Resident Individual
2. Firm
3. Private Company
4. Non-resident individual
5. Co-operative society
6. LLP
7. Foreign company

Select the correct answer from the options given below –

(A) (1), (2), (3) & (6)

(B) (2), (4), (1), (3) & (5)

(C) (7), (2), (4), (6), (1), (3) & (5)

(D) (1) & (4) only

12. Deduction u/s 80C is available for –

(A) Payment of premium on insurance policy up to 10% of the actual sum assured shall not qualify for deduction for the policies issued on or after 1.4.2012.

(B) Payment of premium on insurance policy up to 20% of the actual sum assured shall not qualify for deduction for the policies issued on or before 1.4.2012.

(C) Payment of premium on insurance policy up to 15% of the actual sum assured shall not qualify for deduction for the policies issued on or after 1.4.2013.

(D) Any of the above

13. Deduction in respect of employment of new workmen is available u/s ________

(A) 80JJA

(B) 80JBB

(C) 80JJAA

(D) 80JJBB

14. To avail deduction u/s 80C for depositing sum in PPF, the amount can be deposited in the name of –

(I) Individual

(II) Dependant parents

(III) Spouse

(IV) Dependent child

(V) Independent child

Select the correct answer from the options given below –

(A) (IV), (I) and (III) only

(B) (II), (IV), (II) & (I) only

(C) (V), (I), (III) & (IV) only

(D) (I), (II) and (IV) only

15. Deduction u/s 80DDB is available for medical expenditure in respect of prescribed diseases. For the purpose of deduction which of the following persons are covered for individual assessee?

(1) Spouse

(2) Independent sister

(3) Dependent children

(4) Parents of individual

(5) Dependent brothers

(6) Independent children

Select the correct answer from the options given below –

(A) (1), (6), (3), (4) & (2)

(B) (3), (1), (4) & (5) only

(C) (1), (4) & (3) only

(D) (3), (1), (4) & (5)

16. Deduction in respect of royalty income is available u/s 80QQB to –

(A) Any individual being an author of text books

(B) Resident as well as non-resident individual being an author of any book other than text books

(C) Resident as well as non-resident individual being an author of any text books

(D) Resident individual being an author of any book other than text books

17. Which of the following payment to annuity plan is/are eligible for deduction u/s 80C?

1. Jeevan Dhara
2. Jeevan Sangam
3. Jeevan Akshay

Select the correct answer from the options given below –

(A) 1 only

(B) 2 and 1 only

(C) 1 and 3 only

(D) 3 only

18. *Statement I:*

No deduction shall be allowed under section 80G in respect of any donation unless such donation is of a sum of money.

Statement II:

No deduction shall be allowed under Section 80G in respect of donation of any sum exceeding ₹ 2,000 unless such sum is paid by any mode other than cash.

(A) Statement I is incorrect but Statement II is correct.

(B) Statement II is incorrect but Statement I is correct.

(C) Statement I and Statement II both are correct.

(D) Statement I and Statement II both are incorrect.

19. Deduction under Section 80E is available for –

(A) Principal amount of loan

(B) Interest amount

(C) Both (A) and (B)

(D) None of the above

20. In whose name subscription made in Sukanya Samriddhi Account Scheme is/are eligible for deduction u/s 80C?

(a) Individual

(b) Any girl child of the individual

(c) Any girl child for whom such individual is the legal guardian

Select the correct answer from the options given below –

(A) (b) only

(B) (c) and (b) only

(C) (a), (b) and (c)

(D) (a) only

21. If an assessee is engaged in business of collecting and processing of biodegradable waste then how much deduction he can claim u/s 80JJA?

(A) 100% of profits and gains for a period of 5 consecutive years beginning from the year in which the business commences.

(B) 50% of profits and gains for a period of 5 consecutive years beginning from the year in which the business commences.

(C) 100% of profits and gains for a period of 5 consecutive years beginning from the year in which the business commences and 50% of profits and gains for next 5 years.

(D) 50% of profits and gains for a period of 5 consecutive years beginning from the year in which the business commences and 25% of profits and gains for next 5 years.

22. Deduction in respect of patent is available u/s _____

(A) Section 80TTA

(B) Section 80RRA

(C) Section 80RRB

(D) Section 80RRT

23. Which of the following is/are eligible for deduction u/s 80C of the Income Tax Act, 1961?

(*i*) Subscription to units of UTI

(*ii*) Subscription to deposit scheme of vehicle finance company

(*iii*) Subscription to units of mutual fund notified u/s 10 (23D)

(*iv*) Term deposit for a fixed period of 5 years or more with a co-operative bank

Select the correct answer from the options given below –

(A) (i), (ii) and (iii)

(B) (iv) and (ii)

(C) (iii) and (i)

(D) (i), (iii) and (iv)

24. Which of the following is/are not eligible to get deduction for contributions to political parties?

I. Individual

II. Company

III. Local authority

IV. LLP

V. Co-operative society

VI. Artificial juridical person

Select the correct answer from the options given below –

(A) I & IV only

(B) V, II, III & VI only

(C) III & VI only

(D) IV, II & V only

25. Deduction for interest on deposits in savings accounts u/s 80TTA is available to ______

1. Individual
2. HUF
3. Firm

Select the correct answer from the options given below –

(A) 1 but not 2 & 3

(B) 1 and 2 but not 3

(C) 1, 2 and 3

(D) Only 2

26. Deduction in respect of contribution to certain pension funds as provided in Section 80CCC of the Income Tax Act, 1961 is available to –

(A) Resident individual

(B) Resident individual & HUF

(C) Individual whether resident or non-resident

(D) Individual & HUF whether resident or non-resident

27. Maximum deduction available u/s 80CCC is –

(A) ₹ 1,00,000

(B) ₹ 1,25,000

(C) ₹ 1,50,000

(D) ₹ 2,00,000

28. The deduction u/s 80E shall be allowed in ______

(A) 8 years

(B) 5 years

(C) 10 years

(D) 4 years

29. Deduction in respect of contribution to Pension Scheme of Central Government as provided in Section 80CCD is available to –

(A) An individual employed by the Central Government on or after the 1.1.2004

(B) An individual employed by the Central Government on or after the 1.1.2004 or, being an individual employed by any other employer

(C) An individual employed by the Central Government on or after the 1.1.2004 or, being an individual employed by any other employer or any other individual assessee

(D) Any of the above

30. On which of the following payment as per Section 80G, 100% deduction is available without qualifying limit?

(a) National Children's Fund

(b) Prime Minister's Drought Relief Fund

(c) Clean Ganga Fund

(d) Donations to Government for the purpose of promoting family planning

(e) National Sports Fund

(f) Swachh Bharat Kosh

Select the correct answer from the options given below –

(A) (a), (b), (d), (e) and (f)

(B) (c), (e) and (f)

(C) (b), (d) & (a)

(D) (a), (c), (e) and (f)

31. For the purpose of deduction u/s 80CCD, 'Salary' includes –

1. Basic pay
2. Dearness allowance (always included)
3. Dearness allowance if the terms of employment so provide
4. Taxable allowances
5. Taxable perquisites

Select the correct answer from the options given below –

(A) 1, 2 and 4

(B) 1, 3 and 4

(C) 3, 5 and 1

(D) 1 and 3

32. If assessee taken loan for higher education pursuing his higher education or higher education of his relative then he can claim the deduction u/s 80E. Relative in relation to an individual means –

I. Spouse

II. Children

III. Student for whom the individual is the legal guardian

Select the correct answer from the options given below –

(A) I only

(B) I and II only

(C) I, II, and III

(D) None of the above

33. Co-operative society having income from interest on securities or from house property chargeable u/s 22 can get deduction u/s 80P if its gross total income does not exceed ____

(A) ₹ 20,000

(B) ₹ 50,000

(C) ₹ 1,00,000

(D) ₹ 60,000

34. The maximum amount of deduction u/ss 80C and 80CCC and u/s 80CCD(1) (i.e. employee's contribution or an individual assessee's contribution to pension scheme of Central Government), is restricted to ______

(A) ₹ 1,50,000

(B) ₹ 4,50,000

(C) ₹ 2,00,000

(D) ₹ 5,00,000

35. Deduction is allowed u/s 80JJAA ______ of additional employee cost to new persons employed by assessee in such factory in the previous year. The deduction is allowed for ______ including the assessment year relevant to previous year in which such employment is provided.

(A) 20%; two assessment years

(B) 30%; three assessment years

(C) 30%; five assessment years

(D) 20%; four assessment years

36. Deduction for interest u/s 80TTA is available on ________

(I) Savings deposits account

(II) Time deposits

(III) Debenture interest received in saving account

Select the correct answer from the options given below–

(A) (I) only

(B) (I) and (II)

(C) (I), (II) and (III)

(D) None of the above is correct

37. Deduction in respect of investment made under an equity savings scheme as provided in Section 80CCG is available to –

(A) Individual

(B) Resident individual

(C) Individual and HUF

(D) Any assessee

38. To avail deduction for incomes of Offshore Banking Units, the report of Chartered Accountant has to be submitted in ______

(A) Form No. 10FCC

(B) Form No. 10CCF

(C) Form No. 10CF

(D) Form No. 10FFC

39. Deduction u/s 80CCG shall be allowed for ________ from the previous year in which the listed equity shares or listed units of equity oriented fund were first acquired.

(A) 2 consecutive AY

(B) 5 consecutive AY

(C) 3 consecutive AY

(D) 4 consecutive AY

40. Who is eligible to deduction u/s 80U?

(A) Resident individual

(B) Any individual

(C) Any resident person

(D) Except company all other assessees.

41. Maximum possible deduction u/s 80D if none of the eligible person is senior citizen and mediclaim premium if paid for both family and parents is –

(A) ₹ 25,000

(B) ₹ 50,000

(C) ₹ 30,000

(D) ₹ 60,000

42. As per Section 80G, 50% deduction shall be allowed subject to the qualifying amount, if donations are made to –

(a) Corporation for promoting interests of minority community

(b) Organizations of political nature

(c) Organization created for promotion of religious activities

Select the correct answer from the options given below –

(A) (a) and (b) but not (c)

(B) (c) and (a) but not (b)

(C) (a) only and not (b) & (c)

(D) (c) only and not (b) & (a)

43. Deduction in respect of treatment of a dependant disabled person u/s 80DD is available to –

(A) Resident individual

(B) Individual and HUF

(C) Individual whether resident or non-resident

(D) Resident individual or HUF

44. Which of the following is eligible to get deduction under Section 80LA having an Offshore Banking Unit in a SEZ?

I. A scheduled bank

II. Foreign bank

III. A unit of an International Financial Services Centre

Select the correct answer from the options given below –

(A) I and not II & III

(B) I and II but not III

(C) I and III but not II

(D) I, II and III

45. Deduction u/s 80GGA is available to all assessees except having income under the head ________

(A) House property

(B) Salary

(C) Business and profession

(D) Other sources

46. What is maximum possible deduction u/s 80JJAA?

(A) 25% of additional wages paid to new regular workman employed for more than 300 days.

(B) 50% of additional wages paid to new regular workmen employed for more than 300 days.

(C) 25% of additional employee cost for new workmen employed for more than 240 days.

(D) 30% of additional employee cost for new workmen employed for more than 240 days.

47. Deduction as provided in Section 80C is available to the extent of –

(A) ₹ 1,00,000

(B) ₹ 2,00,000

(C) ₹ 2,50,000

(D) ₹ 1,50,000

48. Which of the following is correct deduction u/s 80LA?

(A) 100% of income for first 10 years

(B) 100% of income for first 5 years and 50% for the next 5 years

(C) 100% of income for first 5 years and 75% for the next 5 years

(D) 50% of income for first 5 years and 25% for the next 5 years

49. Maximum possible deduction u/s 80U for severe disability is –

(A) ₹ 75,000

(B) ₹ 1,00,000

(C) ₹ 1,25,000

(D) ₹ 1,50,000

50. Maximum possible deduction u/s 80DD in respect of treatment of a dependant disabled person for 80% or more of disability is –

(A) ₹ 75,000

(B) ₹ 80,000

(C) ₹ 1,25,000

(D) ₹ 1,50,000

51. Which of the following type of company can claim deduction u/s 80GGB for contributions to political parties?

1. Indian private company
2. Foreign private company
3. Indian public company
4. Foreign public company

Select the correct answer from the options given below –

(A) 3 only

(B) 1, 2 and 3 only

(C) 3 and 1 only

(D) 1, 2, 3 & 4

52. For the purpose of Section 80G, "Qualifying Amount" means –

(A) 10% of adjusted total income

(B) 25% of adjusted gross total income

(C) 10% of adjusted gross total income

(D) 25% of adjusted total income

53. For the purpose of Section 80GG, deduction available shall be restricted to –

(A) 10% of adjusted total income

(B) 25% of adjusted gross total income

(C) 10% of adjusted gross total income

(D) 25% of adjusted total income

54. Maximum possible deduction u/s 80TTA for interest on deposits in savings accounts is –

(A) ₹ 5,000

(B) ₹ 2,500

(C) ₹ 10,000

(D) ₹ 7,500

55. Which of the following amount can be deducted while calculating adjusted gross total income for the purpose of Section 80G?

(*i*) STCG on sale of gold

(*ii*) Incomes included in the gross total income on which no tax is payable

(*iii*) Long term capital gain on sale of listed shares

(*iv*) STCG on sale of listed shares

(*v*) Deduction allowable u/ss 80C to 80U except 80G

(*vi*) Long term capital gain on sale of land

Select the correct answer from the options given below –

(A) (i), (ii), (iv), (v) & (vi)

(B) (iii), (vi), (i) & (v)

(C) (iv), (iii), (vi) and (v)

(D) (vi), (v), (iv) & (ii)

PRACTICAL MCQs

56. Rohit having age of 35 years has Gross Total Income of ₹ 3,70,000 which includes LTCG ₹ 2,00,000 and income from lottery ₹ 10,000. He has deposited ₹ 70,000 in PPF. What is tax liability of Rohit for AY 2019-2020?

(A) ₹ 6,180

(B) ₹ 9,000

(C) ₹ 8,760

(D) ₹ 8,840

57. From the following details calculate the deduction available u/s 80C.

	₹
LIP on policies taken on:	
Self (Policy amount ₹ 5,00,000)	80,000
Wife (Policy amount ₹ 1,80,000)	40,000
Dependant son (Policy amount ₹ 1,00,000)	25,000
Independent daughter (Policy amount ₹ 1,00,000)	20,000
Married daughter (Policy amount ₹ 1,00,000)	25,000
Dependant father (Policy amount ₹ 1,00,000)	40,000
Dependant grandfather (Policy amount ₹ 1,00,000)	40,000

All policies are issued before 1.4.2012.

(A) ₹ 1,76,000

(B) ₹ 1,50,000

(C) ₹ 1,65,000

(D) ₹ 1,45,000

58. Rani is Government employee and her employer deducted ₹ 1,85,000 from her salary for the purpose of securing to her deferred annuity plan. Her salary for the year was ₹ 7,40,000. How much deductions Rani can claim u/s 80C of the Income Tax Act, 1961?

(A) Nil

(B) ₹ 1,50,000

(C) ₹ 1,85,000

(D) ₹ 1,48,000

59. Gross total income Rakshit is ₹ 3,11,500. He has not his own house and he resides in rented house for which he pays rent of ₹ 3,750 per month. Calculate the total income of Rakshit for PY 2018-2019?

(A) ₹ 2,99,000

(B) ₹ 2,97,650

(C) ₹ 2,87,500

(D) ₹ 2,33,625

60. Vishal a Government employee has only salary income and income from other sources, pays ₹ 1,00,000 to research association which has object of undertaking of scientific research.

(A) Vishal can claim deduction of ₹ 1,75,000 u/s 35(1)(ii) being 175% of sum paid

(B) Vishal can claim deduction of ₹ 1,25,000 u/s 35(1)(iia) being 125% of sum paid

(C) Vishal can claim deduction of ₹ 1,00,000 u/s 80GGA.

(D) None of the above is correct

61. From the following details calculate the deduction available u/s 80C to Mr. X?

LIP on self (policy for ₹ 2,50,000 taken on 15.4.2011)	52,000
LIP on spouse (policy for ₹ 1,80,000 taken on 10.5.2013)	18,500
Handicapped minor son [eligible for deduction u/s 80U] (policy for ₹ 4,50,000 taken on 1.6.2015)	72,000

(A) ₹ 1,76,000

(B) ₹ 1,50,000

(C) ₹ 1,28,500

(D) ₹ 1,35,500

62. Gross total income of Sampada is ₹ 5,95,000 which includes STCG u/s 111A ₹ 25,000 and LTCG ₹ 20,000. She has contributed following amounts to various funds:

Swachh Bharat Kosh	20,000
Clean Ganga Fund	10,000
Prime Minister Drought Relief Fund	20,000
State Government for family planning	30,000
Donation to approved charitable institutions	25,000
Contribution to PPF	5,000

Calculate the total income of Sampada for PY 2018-2019.

(A) ₹ 5,07,750

(B) ₹ 5,07,500

(C) ₹ 4,90,000

(D) ₹ 4,98,750

63. Lala works in a company. On 1st January, 2018, he took a loan of ₹ 2,40,000 from his company for the education of his son. During the year 2018-2019, he paid an interest of ₹ 46,000 towards the said loan and repaid principal component of ₹ 10,000. The deduction that he can claim u/s 80E would be —

(A) Nil

(B) ₹ 24,000

(C) ₹ 10,000

(D) ₹ 46,000

64. XYZ Ltd. pays ₹ 1,00,000 as a donation to political party out of which ₹ 40,000 was paid in cash and published advertisement on behalf of political party by incurring ₹ 40,000 in addition to donation stated above.

(A) XYZ Ltd. can claim deduction of ₹ 1,00,000 u/s 80GGC.

(B) XYZ Ltd. can claim deduction of ₹ 60,000 u/s 80GGB.

(C) XYZ Ltd. can claim deduction of ₹ 1,00,000 u/s 80GGB.

(D) XYZ Ltd. can claim deduction of ₹ 60,000 u/s 80GGC.

65. Prathmesh who are required to be audited u/s 44AB, employs following new employees in his business:

(1) On 1.4.2018 – 6 persons as accounting staff on monthly salary of ₹ 21,000.

(2) On 1.6.2018 – 3 persons as technical staff on monthly salary of ₹ 23,500.

(3) On 1.7.2018 – 15 persons as supervisors on monthly salary of ₹ 25,500.

(4) On 1.11.2018 – 20 persons as helpers on monthly salary of ₹ 12,400.

How much deduction Prathmesh can claim u/s 80JJAA for PY 2018-2019?

(A) ₹ 28,40,000

(B) ₹ 22,17,000

(C) ₹ 45,12,000

(D) ₹ 11,36,000

66. During the PY 2018-2019 Suresh incurred ₹ 1,00,000 for the medical treatment of his dependent mother (resident having age 64 years) who is suffering from prescribed disease and disability. He has taken policy for mother and gets reimbursed by insurer by ₹ 10,000 for medical treatment of mother. His employer LMN Ltd. also reimbursed ₹ 20,000 for medical treatment of mother. How much deduction Suresh can claim u/s 80DDB of the Income Tax Act, 1961?

(A) ₹ 60,000

(B) ₹ 40,000

(C) ₹ 1,00,000

(D) ₹ 70,000

67. From the following details of XYZ of co-operative society, calculate the deduction u/s 80P?

Income from house property	35,000
Interest from members on delayed payment of price of goods purchased	10,000
Processing of agricultural produce of its members	60,000
Agency business	56,000
Dividend from other co-operative society	10,000
Income from letting of godowns	50,000

(A) ₹ 50,000

(B) ₹ 2,21,000

(C) ₹ 1,76,000

(D) ₹ 1,80,000

68. Mr. Datey is author of book (other than text book) and he received royalty of ₹ 2,00,000 which is 20% value of book sold. He incurred expenditure of ₹ 20,000 for earning royalty. His other income is ₹ 10,50,000. Compute the deduction available to Mr. Datey u/s 80QQB.

(A) ₹ 1,30,000

(B) ₹ 1,80,000

(C) ₹ 2,00,000

(D) ₹ 1,50,000

69. From the following details calculate the total income:

	₹
Gross total income	5,00,000
Repayment of housing loan for property under construction	1,10,000
Repayment of housing loan from relative for self occupied property	50,000
Contribution to PPF in the name of her mother	70,000

(A) ₹ 4,30,000

(B) ₹ 2,90,000

(C) ₹ 3,00,000

(D) ₹ 3,20,000

70. Mr. Chatur who has invented a new machine in medical field had received royalty of ₹ 4,50,000. He incurred ₹ 50,000 for earning royalty income. His other income is ₹ 50,40,000. How much deduction Mr. Chatur can claim u/s 80RRB?

(A) ₹ 3,50,000

(B) ₹ 4,00,000

(C) ₹ 4,50,000

(D) ₹ 3,00,000

ANSWERS:

1.	(D)	**2.**	(C)	**3.**	(D)	**4.**	(C)	**5.**	(D)	**6.**	(C)	**7.**	(D)
8.	(A)	**9.**	(A)	**10.**	(C)	**11.**	(C)	**12.**	(D)	**13.**	(C)	**14.**	(C)

15.	(D)	**16.**	(D)	**17.**	(C)	**18.**	(B)	**19.**	(B)	**20.**	(C)	**21.**	(A)
22.	(C)	**23.**	(C)	**24.**	(C)	**25.**	(B)	**26.**	(C)	**27.**	(C)	**28.**	(A)
29.	(D)	**30.**	(D)	**31.**	(D)	**32.**	(C)	**33.**	(A)	**34.**	(A)	**35.**	(B)
36.	(A)	**37.**	(B)	**38.**	(B)	**39.**	(C)	**40.**	(A)	**41.**	(B)	**42.**	(C)
43.	(D)	**44.**	(D)	**45.**	(C)	**46.**	(D)	**47.**	(D)	**48.**	(B)	**49.**	(C)
50.	(C)	**51.**	(C)	**52.**	(C)	**53.**	(B)	**54.**	(C)	**55.**	(D)	**56.**	(D)
57.	(B)	**58.**	(D)	**59.**	(B)	**60.**	(C)	**61.**	(D)	**62.**	(A)	**63.**	(D)
64.	(C)	**65.**	(B)	**66.**	(D)	**67.**	(D)	**68.**	(A)	**69.**	(A)	**70.**	(D)

PAST EXAMINATION MCQs

1. Dec 2014: For the year ended 31st March, 2019 Paresh receives a salary of ₹ 2,80,000. Paresh's contribution to employees recognised provident fund account is ₹ 59,000 and matching contribution has been made by employer. Taxable income of Paresh will be —

(A) ₹ 2,06,400

(B) ₹ 3,05,400

(C) ₹ 3,39,000

(D) ₹ 2,80,000

2. Dec 2014: The maximum possible amount of deduction u/s 80DDB for senior citizen is —

(A) ₹ 75,000

(B) ₹ 1,25,000

(C) ₹ 1,00,000

(D) ₹ 60,000

3. Dec 2014: The following is not allowed as deduction u/s 80TTA —

(A) Interest on deposits in a savings account with bank up to ₹ 10,000

(B) Interest on time deposits with bank up to ₹ 10,000

(C) Interest on deposits in a savings account with post office up to ₹ 10,000

(D) Interest on deposits with co-operative society engaged in carrying on the business of banking up to ₹ 10,000

4. Dec 2014: The maximum amount of deduction u/s 80U allowed to a person with 80% or more of one or more disabilities is —

(A) ₹ 40,000

(B) ₹ 60,000

(C) ₹ 50,000

(D) ₹ 1,25,000

5. Dec 2014: An Indian resident patentee is entitled to a deduction u/s 80RRB to the extent of —

(A) 100% of such income

(B) 50% of such income

(C) 100% of such income or ₹ 3,00,000 whichever is less

(D) 50% of such income or ₹ 3,00,000 whichever is more

6. June 2015: Deduction under section 80CCG is available to an eligible resident individual whose gross total income does not exceed —

(A) ₹ 10,00,000

(B) ₹ 12,00,000

(C) ₹ 5,00,000

(D) No such limit

7. June 2015: Sahil works in a technology company. On 1st January, 2018, he took a loan of ₹ 2,40,000 from his company for the education of his daughter. During the year 2018-2019, he paid an interest of ₹ 46,000 towards the said loan and repaid principal component of ₹ 10,000. The deduction that he can claim u/s 80E would be —

(A) Nil

(B) ₹ 24,000

(C) ₹ 46,000

(D) ₹ 10,000

8. June 2015: Under the Income-tax Act, 1961, which of the following can claim deduction for any sum contributed during the previous year to a political party or electoral trust —

(A) Local authority

(B) Individual

(C) Artificial juridical person

(D) None of the above

9. June 2015: Deduction in respect of donations to National Defence Fund is allowed u/s —

(A) 80G

(B) 80CCG

(C) 80C

(D) None of the above

10. June 2015: Raman purchased a residential house property in Ahmedabad on loan for which he paid an interest of ₹ 50,000 during the previous year. He is working in Delhi and getting an HRA of ₹ 4,000 per month. He can claim exemption/deduction for —

(A) Only HRA

(B) Only interest paid

(C) Either interest paid or HRA but not both

(D) Both HRA and interest paid.

11. June 2015: Which of the following cannot claim deduction for the loan taken to purchase a house property?

(A) Karta, in respect of property purchased by HUF

(B) An individual, in respect of property purchased by him

(C) Partner, in respect of property purchased by the firm

(D) Spouse of an individual, in respect of property purchased jointly by the individual and his/her spouse.

12. Dec 2015: Monetary limit for deduction in respect of royalty on patents received by a resident individual is —

(A) ₹ 1,00,000

(B) ₹ 3,00,000

(C) ₹ 5,00,000

(D) Nil

13. Dec 2015: An individual has made investments in the schemes approved u/ss 80C and 80CCD of ₹ 2,50,000 and ₹ 1,00,000 respectively during the year ended 31st March, 2018. Amount that can be claimed by him as deduction out of income in AY 2019-2020 is —

(A) 50% of ₹ 3,50,000

(B) ₹ 1,50,000 u/s 80C and ₹ 1,00,000 u/s 80CCD

(C) ₹ 1,50,000

(D) None of the above

14. Dec 2015: Raghu's father is dependent on him and suffering with 90% disability. Raghu has incurred an amount of ₹ 72,500 in maintaining and medical treatment of his father. The deduction he can claim in his income-tax return for AY 2019-2020 is —

(A) ₹ 72,500

(B) ₹ 50,000

(C) ₹ 1,25,000

(D) None of the above

15. June 2016: Bharat, engaged in business, claimed that he paid ₹ 10,000 per month by cheque as rent for his residence. He does not own any residential building. His total income computed before deduction under section 80GG is ₹ 3,40,000. The amount he can claim as deduction under section 80GG is —

(A) ₹ 60,000

(B) ₹ 86,000

(C) ₹ 1,20,000

(D) ₹ 85,000

16. June 2016: Rajan paid ₹ 25,000 to LIC of India for the maintenance of his disabled son and incurred ₹ 15,000 for the treatment of his handicapped wife who is working in State Bank of India. The deduction allowable to him under Section 80DD is —

(A) ₹ 15,000

(B) ₹ 25,000

(C) ₹ 50,000

(D) ₹ 75,000

17. June 2016: Deduction in respect of interest on savings accounts under Section 80TTA shall be allowed with respect to savings account with —

(A) Bank

(B) Co-operative society

(C) Post office

(D) All of the above

18. June 2016: Deduction under section 80C can be claimed for fixed deposit made in any scheduled bank, if the minimum period of deposit is —

(A) 5 Years

(B) 8 Years

(C) 10 Years

(D) 12 Years

19. June 2016: In case of which of the following co-operative society, the deduction under Section 80P is restricted to ₹ 1,00,000 —

(A) Consumers' co-operative society

(B) Society engaged in collection and disposal of labour

(C) Society engaged in fishing

(D) Society engaged in processing of agricultural produce without the aid of power

20. June 2016: When a person suffers from severe disability, the quantum of deduction allowable under Section 80U is -

(A) ₹ 50,000

(B) ₹ 75,000

(C) ₹ 1,25,000

(D) ₹ 1,00,000

21. Dec 2016: Under Section 80QQB, the maximum deduction in respect of royalty is allowed up to –

(A) ₹ 1,00,000

(B) ₹ 1,50,000

(C) ₹ 2,50,000

(D) ₹ 3,00,000

22. Dec 2016: An amount up to a maximum of ₹ 10,000 is deductible under Section 80TT from the gross total income of –

(A) Individual only

(B) HUF and Individual only

(C) Company only

(D) All assessees

23. Dec 2016: Deduction available u/s 80GG in respect of rent paid cannot be more than –

(A) ₹ 6,000 p.m.

(B) ₹ 5,000 p.m.

(C) ₹ 2,000 p.m.

(D) ₹ 10,000 p.m.

24. June 2017: Raghunath repaid during previous year 2018-2019 education loan of ₹ 60,000 and interest on education loan of ₹ 18,000 taken from Punjab National Bank for his son to pursue MS in Germany. The loan was taken in the financial year 2010-2011 and the payment commenced from financial year 2011-2012. The amount eligible for deduction under section 80E for the assessment year 2019-2020 is:

(A) ₹ 60,000

(B) ₹ 78,000

(C) ₹ 18,000

(D) Nil

25. June 2017: Shravan engaged in business paid monthly rent of ₹ 5,000 by cheque for his residence during the previous year 2018-2019. His adjusted total income is ₹ 3,40,000. The amount eligible for deduction under section 80GG is:

(A) ₹ 86,000

(B) ₹ 60,000

(C) ₹ 24,000

(D) ₹ 85,000

26. June 2017: Deduction under Section 80G on account of donation is allowed to:

(A) A business assessee only

(B) Any assessee

(C) Individual or HUF only

(D) Any resident assessee

27. Dec 2017: Donation to university for research in Social Science is eligible for deduction at:

(A) 100%

(B) 25%

(C) 150%

(D) 175%

28. Dec 2017: Mr. Mithun acquired a house property for ₹ 8 lakhs and paid stamp duty and registration fee of ₹ 80,000. He borrowed housing loan and repaid principal of ₹ 60,000 and interest of ₹ 20,000. The amount eligible for deduction under Section 80C would be:

(A) ₹ 80,000

(B) ₹ 60,000

(C) ₹ 1,00,000

(D) ₹ 1,40,000

29. Dec 2017: Mr. Uday is a resident individual having patent registered on 1.7.2014 under the Patents Act, 1970. He received ₹ 5 lakhs by way of royalty from ABC Ltd. during the financial year 2018-2019. The quantum of royalty eligible for deduction would be:

(A) ₹ 5 lakhs

(B) ₹ 3 lakhs

(C) ₹ 1 lakh

(D) ₹ 2 lakhs

30. Dec 2017: Mr. Veer earns monthly rental income of ₹ 60,000 from a house property. He suffers from severe disability and has obtained certificate from the prescribed medical authority. He has not incurred any expenditure towards treatment of severe disability. His total income chargeable to tax after deduction under Section 80U would be:

(A) ₹ 3,79,000

(B) ₹ 4,29,000

(C) ₹ 5,04,000

(D) ₹ 7,20,000

31. Dec 2017: Mr. Baskar a person with disability referred to in Section 80U is employed in a bank. He paid ₹ 50,000 as premium on life insurance policy taken on himself and whose sum assured is ₹ 4 lakhs. The amount of premium eligible for deduction under Section 80C would be:

(A) ₹ 40,000 (10% of sum assured)

(B) ₹ 50,000

(C) Nil (since it exceeded 10%)

(D) None of the above

32. Dec 2017: Mr. Anand engaged in business wants to deposit in pension fund of Life Insurance Corporation of India. The maximum amount of contribution eligible for deduction from total income is:

(A) ₹ 10,000

(B) ₹ 50,000

(C) ₹ 1,00,000

(D) ₹ 1,50,000

33. Dec 2017: Sudhan Ltd. incorporated in April 2018 commenced commercial production from 1.6.2018. It deployed 100 employees who were employed for 260 days during the year and recruited 50 casual workmen who were employed for 100 days during the financial year 2018-2019. The salary paid to 100 employees was ₹ 25 lakhs and salary paid to casual workmen was ₹ 6 lakhs. The quantum of deduction under section 80JJAA is:

(A) ₹ 7.50 lakhs

(B) ₹ 9.30 lakhs

(C) ₹ 25 lakhs

(D) ₹ 6 lakhs

34. Dec 2017: Mr. Rath borrowed loan of ₹ 10 lakhs for higher education in India in the year 2007-2008. He completed the course study in 2010-2011. He started repayment of the loan from April 2012. He paid interest of ₹ 41,000 and principal of ₹ 1,20,000 during the financial year 2018-2019. The amount eligible for deduction under section 80E would be:

(A) ₹ 1,20,000

(B) ₹ 1,61,000

(C) ₹ 41,000

(D) ₹ 1,00,000 (monetary limit)

35. Dec 2017: Mr. Ganesh gave donation by way of cheque of ₹ 40,000 and by cash ₹ 5,000 to an approved charitable trust having recognition under section 80G. His gross total income for the assessment year 2019-2020 is ₹ 5 lakhs. The quantum of deduction under section 80G would be:

(A) ₹ 45,000

(B) ₹ 5,000

(C) ₹ 40,000

(D) ₹ 20,000

ANSWERS:

1.	(A)	**2.**	(C)	**3.**	(B)	**4.**	(D)	**5.**	(C)	**6.**	(B)	**7.**	(C)
8.	(B)	**9.**	(A)	**10.**	(D)	**11.**	(C)	**12.**	(B)	**13.**	(B)	**14.**	(C)
15.	(A)	**16.**	(D)	**17.**	(D)	**18.**	(A)	**19.**	(A)	**20.**	(C)	**21.**	(D)
22.	(B)	**23.**	(B)	**24.**	(C)	**25.**	(B)	**26.**	(B)	**27.**	(A)	**28.**	(D)
29.	(B)	**30.**	(A)	**31.**	(B)	**32.**	(D)	**33.**	(A)	**34.**	(C)	**35.**	(D)

HINTS FOR PRACTICAL MCQs:

56. Total income of Rohit is ₹ 3,70,000 – 70,000 (deduction for PPF) = 3,00,000 which includes LTCG ₹ 2,00,000 and income from lottery ₹ 10,000. Thus his normal income is ₹ 90,000. Basic exemption for him is ₹ 2,50,000. Which will be taken from normal income ₹ 90,000 and remaining from LTCG i.e. ₹ 1,60,000.

On first	90,000	Nil
On LTCG	1,60,000	Nil
	2,50,000	Nil

On LTCG	40,000	@ 20%	8,000
On lottery	10,000	@ 30%	3,000
	3,00,000		11,000
(-) Rebate u/s 87A			(2,500)
			8,500
(+) Education Cess @ 4%			340
Total tax			8,840

57.

Self (Policy amount ₹ 5,00,000)	80,000	-	80,000
Wife (Policy amount ₹ 1,80,000)	40,000	Restricted to 20% of policy amount	36,000
Dependant son (Policy amount ₹ 1,00,000)	25,000	Restricted to 20% of policy amount	20,000
Independent daughter (Policy amount ₹ 1,00,000)	20,000	-	20,000
Married daughter (Policy amount ₹ 1,00,000)	25,000	Restricted to 20% of policy amount	20,000
Dependant father (Policy amount ₹ 1,00,000)	40,000	Not eligible	-
Dependant grandfather (Policy amount ₹ 1,00,000)	40,000	Not eligible	-
			1,76,000

Maximum deduction u/s 80C is ₹ 1,50,000 hence above amount of ₹ 1,76,000 will be restricted to ₹ 1,50,000.

58. Maximum deduction u/s 80C for deferred annuity plan is 20% of salary subject to overall limit of ₹ 1,50,000.

$7{,}40{,}000 \times 20\% = 1{,}48{,}000$

59.

Gross total income	3,11,500
(-) Deduction u/s 80GG	(13,850)
Total Income	2,97,650

Minimum of following three is deductible u/s 80GG:

(1) Rent paid (-) 10% of Adjusted Total Income	(45,000 – 31,150)	13,850
(2) 25% of Adjusted Total income	(3,11,500 × 25%)	77,875
(3) ₹ 5,000 per month		60,000

60. Vishal can claim deduction of ₹ 1,00,000 u/s 80GGA as his income does not include income from PGBP. Business assessee can claim deduction for this 35 (1) (*ii*) being 175% of sum paid.

61.

	Sum paid	Deduction	
LIP on self (policy for ₹ 2,50,000 taken on 15.4.2011)	52,000	50,000	Restricted to 20% of sum assured
LIP on spouse (policy for ₹ 1,80,000 taken on 10.5.2013)	18,500	18,000	Restricted to 10% of sum assured
Handicapped minor son [eligible for deduction u/s 80U] (policy for ₹ 4,50,000 taken on 1.6.2015)	72,000	67,500	Restricted to 15% of sum assured
		1,35,500	

62.

Gross total income	5,95,000
(-) Deduction u/s 80C (PPF)	(5,000)
(-) Deduction u/s 80G (see note)	(82,250)
Total Income	5,07,750

Deduction u/s 80G:

	Sum paid	Deduction	
100% deduction without qualifying limit			
Swachh Bharat Kosh	20,000	20,000	
Clean Ganga Fund	10,000	10,000	

50% deduction without qualifying limit			
Prime Minister Drought Relief Fund	20,000	10,000	
100% deduction with qualifying limit			
State Government for family planning	30,000	30,000	
50% deduction with qualifying limit			*54,500 – 30,000 = 24,500*
Donation to approved charitable institutions	25,000	12,250	*So, 25,000 restricted to 24,500*
		82,250	*24,500 × 50% = 12,250*

Calculation of adjusted total income:

Gross total income	5,95,000
(-) All the deduction u/ss 80C to 80U except 80G	(5,000)
(-) STCG u/s 111A	(25,000)
(-) LTCG	(20,000)
Adjusted Total Income	5,45,000

Qualifying limit = 10% of 5,45,000 = 54,500

65. *Deduction u/s 80JJAA:*

Accounting staff (21,000 × 6 × 12)	15,12,000
Technical staff (23,500 × 3 × 10)	7,05,000
Supervisors staff (*No deduction as monthly salary exceeds ₹ 25,000*)	-
Helper staff (*No deduction as employed less than 240 days*)	-
Total deduction u/s 80JJAA	22,17,000

66. Deduction u/s 80DDB is available to the extent minimum of following:

(1) Sum paid	₹ 1,00,000
(2) Amount prescribed i.e. ₹ 1,00,000 for senior citizen (1,00,000 – 10,000 – 20,000) (This amount will be reduced by amount reimbursed by insurer & employer)	₹ 70,000

67.

Gross total income (35,000 + 10,000 + 60,000 + 56,000 + 10,000 + 50,000)	2,21,000
(-) Deduction u/s 80P	
- Income from house property (*not deductible as GTI exceeds ₹ 20,000*)	-
- Interest from members on delayed payment of price of goods purchased	(10,000)
- Processing of agricultural produce of its members	(60,000)
- Agency business (*Profit or ₹ 50,000 whichever is less*)	(50,000)
- Dividend from other co-operative society	(10,000)
- Income from letting of godowns	(50,000)
	41,000

68. Royalty received of ₹ 2,00,000

Royalty computed @ 15% (2,00,000/20% × 15%) 1,50,000

Eligible income = 1,50,000 – 20,000 (expenditure) = 1,30,000

Deduction u/s 80QQB: Minimum of following two –

100% of eligible income	1,30,000
Amount specified	3,00,000

69.

Gross total income	5,00,000
(-) Deduction u/s 80C	
- Repayment of housing loan for property under construction (Note 1)	-
- Repayment of housing loan from relative for self occupied property (Note 2)	-

- Contribution to PPF in the name of her mother (Note 2)	-
(-) Deduction u/s 80CCD	(70,000)
Total income	4,30,000

Note 1: *Not eligible for deduction as property is under construction, still it is not taxable under the head house property.*

Note 2: *Loan from relative not eligible for deduction u/s 80C.*

Note 3: *Mother is not specified person as per Section 80C and hence no deduction is available.*

70. Deduction u/s 80RRB is available 100% of royalty income or ₹ 3,00,000 whichever is less. (*Expense not to be deducted like Section 80QQB*)

HINTS FOR PAST EXAMINATION MCQs

1.

Salary	2,80,000
(+) Employer's contribution in excess of 12% [59,000 – (2,80,000 × 12%)]	25,400
(-) Standard deduction	(40,000)
Gross total income	2,65,400
(-) Deduction u/s 80C for employees contribution	(59,000)
Total income	2,06,400

15.

Minimum of following three is exempt u/s 80GG:

(1) Rent paid *less* 10% of Adjusted total income (1,20,000 – 34,000)	86,000
(2) 25% of Adjusted total income (3,40,000 × 25%)	85,000
(3) ₹ 5,000 p.m.	60,000

24. Deduction u/s 80E is allowed for 8 year from the year in which first interest is paid. Deduction is allowed only for interest and not for principal. Thus, total deduction allowed is ₹ 18,000.

25. Minimum of following three is deductible u/s 80GG:

(1) Rent paid (-) 10% of Adjusted Total Income	(1,20,000–34,000)	86,000
(2) 25% of Adjusted Total Income	(3,40,000 × 25%)	85,000
(3) ₹ 5,000 per month		60,000

28. Stamp duty, registration fee and repayment of principal is eligible for deduction u/s 80C.

80,000 + 60,000 = 1,40,000.

29. As per Section 80RRB, 100% of royalty income or ₹ 3,00,000 whichever is less is exempt.

30.

Net annual value (60,000 × 12)	7,20,000
(-) Standard deduction @ 30%	(2,16,000)
Income from house property/Total income	5,04,000
(-) Deduction u/s 80U	(1,25,000)
Total income	3,79,000

31. Premium on insurance policy in excess of 15% of the actual sum assured shall not qualify for deduction in respect of policies issued *on or after* 1.4.2013, where the policy, is for insurance on life of any person, who is —

(*i*) a person with disability or a person with severe disability as referred to in Section 80U, or

(*ii*) suffering from disease or ailment as specified in the rules made u/s 80DDB.

33. 25,00,000 × 30% = 7,50,000.

35. No deduction shall be allowed under section 80G in respect of donation of any sum exceeding ₹ **2,000** unless such sum is paid by any mode other than cash.

Thus, eligible amount of donation is ₹ 40,000. (50% deduction with qualifying limit)

Gross total income (Assumed adjusted total income) = 5,00,000.

Qualifying limit = 5,00,000 × 10% = 50,000.

Qualifying limit is covering full amount of eligible donation. Thus, deduction will be 40,000 × 50% = 20,000.

CHAPTER **11**

AGRICULTURAL INCOME & EXEMPTED INCOMES

MCQs ON THEORY

1. Which of the following statement is/are true?

(1) Any sum received from Sukanya Samriddhi Account is exempt.

(2) Unspent balance of scholarship received by student is taxable.

(3) Salary received by Member of Parliament is exempt.

(4) Any income to trade union under the head capital gain is exempt.

Select the correct answer from the options given below -

(A) (1) and (3) only

(B) (2) and (4) only

(C) (1) only

(D) (4) and (1) only

2. Income from post office saving bank account is -

(A) Exempt up to ₹ 10,000

(B) Exempt up to ₹ 7,000 for joint holder and ₹ 3,500 for individual

(C) Fully exempt

(D) Exempt up to ₹ 10,000 for joint holder and ₹ 5,000 for individual

3. Which of the following income is agricultural income -

(A) Rent received from agricultural land

(B) Income from dairy farm

(C) Income from poultry farm

(D) Dividend from a company engaged in agriculture

4. Income accruing from agriculture in a foreign country is taxable in the case of an assessee who is -

1. Resident
2. Not-ordinarily resident
3. Non-resident

Select the correct answer from the options given below -

(A) 1 only
(B) 2 only
(C) 1 and 2 only
(D) 3 only

5. Which of the following income is an agriculture income-

(A) Income from brick making
(B) Income from agriculture land situated in Pakistan
(C) Prize from Government on account of higher crop yield
(D) Compensation received from insurance company on account of loss of crop

6. The income of minor child shall be taxable in excess of ________ in the hands of parents.

(A) ₹ 500
(B) ₹ 1,000
(C) ₹ 1,500
(D) ₹ 5,000

7. Which of the following statement is/are true (✓) and which is/are false (X)?

(I) Casual income received by assessee is exempt up to ₹ 5,000.
(II) Prize given to Suhesh by the Government of Madhya Pradesh on account of higher crop yield is an agricultural income.
(III) Voluntary contribution received by electoral trust shall be exempt in all cases.

Select the correct answer from the options given below -

	(I)	(II)	(III)
(A)	✓	×	×
(B)	×	✓	×
(C)	×	×	✓
(D)	×	×	×

8. Under ________ of the Income Tax Act, 1961 various items of income are totally exempt from income-tax. Therefore, these incomes are not included in the total income of an assessee.

(A) Section 10
(B) Section 11
(C) Section 12
(D) Section 13

9. Under the Constitution only ________ are empowered to levy tax on agricultural income.

(A) State Governments
(B) Central Government
(C) Both (A) and (B)
(D) RBI

10. Any income derived from sampling or seedling grown in a nursery ________

(A) shall not be deemed to be agricultural income
(B) shall be liable to taxed like any other income
(C) shall be deemed to be agricultural income
(D) shall be deemed to be agricultural income but 50% if such income is liable to be taxed

11. Which of the following is agricultural income and which is not?

1. Income from growing flowers
2. Salary of a farm manager
3. Remuneration received by partners engaged in agricultural operations
4. Income from brick making

Select the correct answer from the options given below -

	1	2	3	4
(A)	Yes	Yes	No	No
(B)	No	No	Yes	Yes
(C)	Yes	No	Yes	No
(D)	No	Yes	No	Yes

12. *Statement I:*

Partial integration of agricultural income is applicable if agricultural income exceeds ₹ 2,500.

Statement II:

Income from growing jute and cotton is not agricultural income.

Select the correct answer from the options given below -

(A) Statement I is correct while Statement II is incorrect

(B) Statement I is incorrect while Statement II is correct.

(C) Statement I and Statement II both correct

(D) Statement I and Statement II both incorrect

13. As per _______ allowances or perquisites paid or allowed as such outside India by the Central Government to a citizen of India for his services rendered outside India, would be wholly exempt from income-tax.

(A) Section 10(5)

(B) Section 10(6A)

(C) Section 10(7)

(D) Section 10(5A)

14. Any income by way of pension received by an individual who has been awarded ______ are exempt.

(A) Param Vir Chakra

(B) Maha Vir Chakra

(C) Vir Chakra

(D) All of the above

15. Who is liable to pay tax on dividend?

(A) Shareholder

(B) Depository

(C) Merchant Banker

(D) Company

16. *Statement X:*

Interest on Gold Deposit Bonds issued under the notified Gold Deposit Scheme, 1999 is exempt.

Statement Y:

As per Section 10AA units located in SEZ can claim 100% exemption for first 10 years.

Select the correct answer from the options given below -

(A) Statement X is correct while Statement Y is incorrect

(B) Statement X is incorrect while Statement Y is correct.

(C) Statement X and Statement Y both correct

(D) Statement X and Statement Y both incorrect

17. Special provisions relating to incomes of political parties are in _______ of the Income Tax Act, 1961.

(A) Section 12A

(B) Section 13A

(C) Section 14A

(D) Section 15A

18. Which of the following income is exempt and which is taxable?

(*i*) Income under the head capital gain to local authority is _______

(*ii*) Income under the head capital gain to trade union is _______

Select the correct answer from the options given below -

	(*i*)	(*ii*)
(A)	Exempt	Taxable
(B)	Taxable	Taxable
(C)	Taxable	Exempt
(D)	Exempt	Exempt

19. Which of the following statement is true and which is false?

(*a*) Dividend received by domestic company from another domestic company is not exempt.

(*b*) Scholarship received by student is exempt to the extent amount spent by him for his education.

Select the correct answer from the options given below -

(A) (a) is true but (b) is false

(B) (b) is true but (a) is false

(C) Both (a) and (b) are false

(D) Both (a) and (b) are true

20. Income of an assessee engaged in the business of coffee (grown & cured by seller in India) is taxable to the extent of —

(A) 75%

(B) 40%

(C) 60%

(D) 25%

21. Income from growing and manufacturing of rubber is exempt to the extent of —

(A) 65%

(B) 45%

(C) 35%

(D) 75%

PRACTICAL MCQs

22. Bazaar Ltd. exports articles and furnishes following particulars for the current previous year:

	₹
Export sales	72,00,000
Domestic sales	24,00,000
Total Sales	96,00,000
Money brought to India in convertible foreign exchange	60,00,000
Profits from business	19,20,000

Exemption available u/s 10AA = ?

(A) ₹ 19,20,000

(B) ₹ 14,40,000

(C) ₹ 9,60,000

(D) ₹ 12,00,000

23. Sagar gives the following details for computation of total income:

Interest credited to his Non-Resident (External) A/c	3,57,000
Interest on bank fixed deposit	45,000
Interest on saving bank account	4,500

Total income = ?

(A) ₹ 45,000

(B) ₹ 4,06,500

(C) ₹ 45,000

(D) ₹ 4,02,000

24. Z Ltd., a unit located in SEZ gives you following details:

Total receipts = ₹ 64 Lakhs

Export receipts = ₹ 50 Lakhs

Profit = ₹ 7 Lakhs

Out of total export ₹ 5 lakh could not be received on account of death of Foreign Service Recipient. The plant and machinery used in the business had been depreciated @ 20% on SLM basis and depreciation of ₹ 4 Lakh was charged to Profit & Loss A/c. Compute the total income of the company.

(A) ₹ 8,00,000

(B) ₹ 2,37,500

(C) ₹ 2,53,125

(D) ₹ 1,37,500

25. A Limited company gives you following details and request to calculate deduction u/s 10AA.

Particulars	*Unit in DTA*	*Unit in SEZ*
Total sales	2,00,000	4,00,000
Export sales	1,60,000	3,00,000
Profit	20,000	60,000

The company was established 7 years back.

Exemption available u/s 10AA = ?

(A) ₹ 23,000

(B) ₹ 11,500

(C) ₹ 45,000

(D) ₹ 22,500

26. NSZ Ltd. furnishes following information:

Particulars	₹
Profit of Unit X	30,00,000
Profit of Unit Y	20,00,000
Total turnover of Unit X located in SEZ	1,00,00,000
Export turnover of Unit X	50,00,000
Total turnover of Unit Y located in DTA	2,00,00,000

Exemption available u/s 10AA = ?

(A) ₹ 35,00,000

(B) ₹ 15,00,000

(C) ₹ 20,00,000

(D) ₹ 27,66,667

27. A political party registered under Representation of People Act, 1951 submits the following details.

Particulars	₹ in Crores
Income from house property	2.75
Income from other sources	1.35
Income under the head capital gain	5.67

Total income of political party = ?

(A) ₹ 2.75 Crore

(B) ₹ 7.02 Crore

(C) ₹ 5.67 Crore

(D) Nil

28. Raj Ltd. exports articles and furnishes following particulars for the current previous year:

	₹
Total Sales	60,00,000
Export sales	50,00,000
Domestic sales	10,00,000
Money brought to India in convertible foreign exchange	46,00,000
Profits from business	6,00,000

Exemption available u/s 10AA = ?

(A) ₹ 4,60,000

(B) ₹ 5,00,000

(C) ₹ 6,00,000

(D) ₹ 5,50,000

29. Total income of Shekhar, a businessman is ₹ 4,00,000 which includes share of income from HUF ₹ 65,000 and interest on Government securities ₹ 25,000. Tax payable by Shekhar = ?

(A) Nil

(B) ₹ 2,500

(C) ₹ 3,610

(D) ₹ 1,820

30. From the following details calculate the tax payable by Mrs. Laxmi whose age is 52 years.

Particulars	₹
Lottery income (Gross)	7,000
Receipt of accumulated balance in PPF	80,000
Share of income from partnership firm	40,000
Income from house property	3,50,000

(A) ₹ 2,160

(B) Nil
(C) ₹ 2,580
(D) ₹ 5,200

31. Gross total income under the various heads of income of Mr. Raj (Age 37 years) is ₹ 12,15,000 and his agricultural income is ₹ 1,80,000. Compute his tax liability.

(A) ₹ 2,30,880
(B) ₹ 2,32,270
(C) ₹ 2,25,500
(D) ₹ 2,42,380

32. Gross total income of Karina (Age 32 years) is ₹ 6,75,000 which includes STCG u/s 111A ₹ 38,000 and LTCG ₹ 1,02,000. Her agricultural income is ₹ 45,000 which is not included in above gross total income. Compute her tax liability.

(A) ₹ 64,480
(B) ₹ 54,450
(C) ₹ 40,690
(D) ₹ 42,380

Answers:

1.	(C)	**2.**	(B)	**3.**	(A)	**4.**	(A)	**5.**	(D)	**6.**	(C)	**7.**	(D)
8.	(A)	**9.**	(A)	**10.**	(C)	**11.**	(C)	**12.**	(D)	**13.**	(C)	**14.**	(D)
15.	(D)	**16.**	(A)	**17.**	(B)	**18.**	(C)	**19.**	(C)	**20.**	(D)	**21.**	(A)
22.	(D)	**23.**	(A)	**24.**	(B)	**25.**	(D)	**26.**	(B)	**27.**	(D)	**28.**	(A)
29.	(D)	**30.**	(D)	**31.**	(A)	**32.**	(B)						

PAST EXAMINATION MCQs:

1. Dec 2014: Income of an assessee engaged in the business of growing and manufacturing tea in India is taxable to the extent of—

(A) 40% of such income
(B) 60% of such income
(C) 70% of such income
(D) 30% of such income

2. Dec 2014: If non-agricultural income is ₹ 2,52,000 and net agricultural income is ₹ 40,000, the tax liability of an individual assessee will be —

(A) Nil

(B) ₹ 200

(C) ₹ 206

(D) ₹ 4,326

3. Dec 2014: Incomes of two minor children are included in the income of their father. Father is entitled to exemption u/s 10 (32) up to —

(A) ₹ 1,500

(B) ₹ 1,000

(C) ₹ 3,000

(D) ₹ 2,000

4. June 2015: Which of the following additional incomes will not be treated as agricultural income?

(A) Additional income from selling ginned cotton as compared to unginned cotton

(B) Additional income from selling dried-up coffee as compared to raw coffee

(C) Additional income from selling cured tobacco as compared to green tobacco leaves

(D) Additional income from selling dried-up tea leaves as compared to raw tea leaves.

5. Dec 2015: Pawan reports net income of ₹ 5 lakh from the activity of growing and manufacturing rubber. How much of such income is to be treated as non-agricultural income —

(A) ₹ 1,75,000

(B) ₹ 2,00,000

(C) ₹ 1,25,000

(D) Nil

6. Dec 2016: Murali received ₹ 1 lakh from the HUF of which he is a coparcener. The HUF consists of four coparceners including his father who is the Karta of the HUF. The amount paid was by way of debit to the capital account of HUF engaged in textile business. Is the amount of receipt chargeable to tax -

(A) Yes, full amount is taxable

(B) 50%, i.e. ₹ 50,000 is taxable

(C) Nil, i.e. it is exempt from tax

(D) 25%, i.e. ₹ 25,000 is taxable

7. Dec 2016: Tax holiday under Section 10AA in respect of newly established units in SEZ is allowed for a total period of -

(A) 5 Years

(B) 10 Years

(C) 15 Years

(D) 20 Years

8. Dec 2016: Mrs. Rose derives ₹ 5,40,000 by way of income from sale of coffee grown and manufactured in India. The income chargeable to income tax would be -

(A) 50%, i.e. ₹ 2,70,000

(B) 35%, i.e. ₹ 1,35,000

(C) 40%, i.e. ₹ 2,16,000

(D) 60%, i.e. ₹ 3,24,000

9. June 2017: Mr. Robert aged 52 years received monthly pension of ₹ 30,000 during the financial year 2018-2019. His agricultural income in India is ₹ 50,000. His net income-tax liability is:

(A) ₹ 14,420

(B) ₹ 9,270

(C) ₹ 4,120

(D) ₹ 11,330

10. June 2017: Mr. Vinayak derived income from sale of tea manufactured and grown in Coorg, Karnataka. His income for the previous year 2018-2019 from the said activity is ₹ 20 lakhs. The amount exempt from tax by way of agricultural income is:

(A) ₹ 8 lakhs (40%)

(B) ₹ 5 lakhs (25%)

(C) ₹ 12 lakhs (60%)

(D) ₹ 7 lakhs (35%)

11. June 2017: Mr. Sankar received ₹ 50,000 as educational scholarship from Nehru Memorial Trust (a charitable trust). The scholarship is to assist Mr. Sankar for pursuing M.A. (History) at Jawaharlal Nehru University, New Delhi. The amount of scholarship liable to tax is:

(A) ₹ 50,000

(B) ₹ 10,000

(C) ₹ 25,000

(D) Nil

12. June 2017: Mr. Ramesh engaged in the business of growing and manufacturing tea in India received ₹ 2 lakhs from Tea Board towards replacement of tea bushes destroyed by forest fire. The amount received from Tea Beard by Mr. Ramesh is:

(A) Liable to tax

(B) Exempt from tax

(C) 50% is exempt from tax

(D) 25% is exempt from tax

13. Dec 2017: Mr. Menon having tea estate in Munnar (Kerala) earned ₹ 5 lakh by way of growing tea leaves and manufacturing tea. The income chargeable to tax would be:

(A) ₹ 2,00,000

(B) ₹ 1,75,000

(C) ₹ 1,25,000

(D) ₹ 3,00,000

14. Dec 2017: A registered trade union earned income by way of interest on fixed deposit held with State Bank of India of ₹ 5,60,000. The interest income chargeable to tax in the hands of trade union would be:

(A) ₹ 5,60,000

(B) Nil

(C) ₹ 2,60,000

(D) ₹ 3,10,000

15. Dec 2017: Registered political parties have to maintain a record of the contributions and names and addresses of the persons who have made such contribution where each contribution exceeds:

(A) ₹ 1,000

(B) ₹ 5,000

(C) ₹ 10,000

(D) ₹ 20,000

16. Dec 2017: An electoral trust receiving voluntary contributions for the purpose of distributing to political parties registered under Section 29A of the Representation of the People Act, 1951 must distribute .... of such contributions.

(A) 100%

(B) 95%

(C) 75%

(D) 50%

17. Dec 2017: Mr. Sridhar employed in K L Ltd., took voluntary retirement in December 2018 and received ₹ 2,00,000 from National Pension System Trust. The amount so received chargeable to income-tax is:

(A) Nil as 100% is exempt

(B) ₹ 1,20,000 as 40% is exempt

(C) ₹ 1,00,000 as 50% is exempt

(D) ₹ 80,000 as 60% is exempt

ANSWERS:

1.	(A)	**2.**	(A)	**3.**	(C)	**4.**	(**)	**5.**	(A)	**6.**	(C)	**7.**	(C)
8.	(B)	**9.**	(**)	**10.**	(C)	**11.**	(D)	**12.**	(B)	**13.**	(A)	**14.**	(B)
15.	(D)	**16.**	(B)	**17.**	(B)								

** *None of the given answer is correct.*

For further clarification please see the hints.

HINTS FOR PRACTICAL MCQs:

22.

$$\text{Exempted Profit} = \text{Profits} \times \frac{\text{Export Turnover}}{\text{Total Turnover}}$$

$$= 19{,}20{,}000 \times \frac{60{,}00{,}000}{96{,}00{,}000} = 12{,}00{,}000$$

23.

Interest credited to his Non-Resident (External) A/c (exempt)	-
Interest on bank fixed deposit	45,000
Interest on saving bank account	4,500
Gross total income	49,500
(-) Deduction u/s 80TTA	(4,500)
Total income	45,000

24.

Profit	7,00,000
(+) Depreciation on SLM basis	4,00,000
(-) Depreciation u/s 32 @ 15% [4,00,000/20% × 15%]	(3,00,000)
Corrected profits	**8,00,000**
(-) Exemption u/s 10AA	(5,62,500)
Total income	2,37,500

$$\text{Exempted Profit} = \text{Profits} \times \frac{\text{Export Turnover}}{\text{Total Turnover}}$$

$$= 8{,}00{,}000 \times \frac{45{,}00{,}000}{64{,}00{,}000} = 5{,}62{,}500$$

25. $\text{Exempted Profit} = \text{Profits} \times \frac{\text{Export Turnover}}{\text{Total Turnover}}$

$$= 60{,}000 \times \frac{3{,}00{,}000}{4{,}00{,}000} = 45{,}000$$

45,000 × 50% = 22,500 *(SEZ unit can claim exemption of 50% profit after expiry of 5 years for next 5 years)*

26.

$$\text{Exempted Profit} = \text{Profits} \times \frac{\text{Export Turnover}}{\text{Total Turnover}}$$

$$= 30{,}00{,}000 \times \frac{50{,}00{,}000}{1{,}00{,}00{,}000} = 15{,}00{,}000$$

29. Share of income from HUF is exempt.

4,00,000 - 65,000 = 3,35,000

Tax on total income	4,250
(-) Rebate u/s 87A	(2,500)
	1,750
(+) Education cess @ 4%	70
	1,820

30.

Receipt of accumulated balance in PPF and share of income from partnership firm is exempt.

Total income = 3,57,000

Tax on lottery income = 7,000 × 30% = 2,100

Tax on other income = 3,50,000 - 2,50,000 = 1,00,000 × 5% = 5,000

Tax on total income	5,000
(-) Rebate u/s 87A	Nil
	5,000
(+) Education cess @ 4%	200
	5,200

31.

Step 1: Calculate tax on: Agricultural income + Non-agricultural income

1,80,000 + 12,15,000 = 13,95,000

On first	2,50,000		Nil
On next	2,50,000	@ 5%	12,500
On next	5,00,000	@ 20%	1,00,000

On balance	3,95,000	@ 30%	1,18,500
	13,95,000		2,31,000

Step 2: Calculate tax on: Agricultural income + Basic exemption limit

1,80,000 + 2,50,000 = 4,30,000

On first	2,50,000		Nil
On next	1,80,000	@ 5%	9,000
	4,30,000		9,000

Step 3:

Tax as per Step 1	2,31,000
(-) Tax as per Step 2	(9,000)
	2,22,000
(+) Education cess @ 4%	8,880
	2,30,880

32. Step 1: Calculate tax on: Agricultural income + Non-agricultural income

45,000 + 6,75,000 (This includes STCG u/s 111A ₹ 38,000 and LTCG ₹ 1,02,000)= 7,20,000

5,80,000 + 38,000 + 1,02,000 = 7,20,000

On first	2,50,000		Nil
On next	2,50,000	@ 5%	12,500
On next	80,000	@ 20%	16,000
STCG u/s 111A	38,000	@ 15%	5,700
LTCG	1,02,000	@ 20%	20,400
	7,20,000		54,600

Step 2: Calculate tax on: Agricultural income + Basic exemption limit

45,000 + 2,50,000 = 2,95,000

On first	2,50,000		Nil
On next	45,000	@ 5%	2,250
	2,95,000		2,250

Step 3:

Tax as per Step 1	54,600
(-) Tax as per Step 2	(2,250)
	52,350
(+) Education cess @ 4%	2,094
	54,444
Rounded up	54,450

HINTS FOR PAST EXAMINATION MCQs:

9. Pension (30,000 × 12) = 3,60,000

Step 1: Calculate tax on: Agricultural income + Non-agricultural income

50,000 + 3,60,000 = 4,10,000

On first	2,50,000		Nil
On next	1,60,000	@ 5%	8,000
	4,10,000		8,000

Step 2: Calculate tax on: Agricultural income + Basic exemption limit

50,000 + 2,50,000 = 3,00,000

On first	2,50,000		Nil
On next	50,000	@ 5%	2,500
	3,00,000		2,500

Step 3:

Tax as per Step 1	8,000
(-) Tax as per Step 2	(2,500)
	5,500
(-) Rebate u/s 87A	(2,500)
	3,000
(+) Education cess @ 4%	120
	3,120

None of the given option contains the correct answer i.e. 3,120.

12. Exempt. Refer to Section 10(30) of the Income Tax Act, 1961.

13. 5,00,000 × 40% = 2,00,000

14. Any income chargeable under the head 'income from house property' and 'income from other sources' of a registered Trade Union within the meaning of the Indian Trade Unions Act, 1926, formed primarily for the purposes of regulating the relations between workmen and the employers or between the workmen and the workmen is exempt from income-tax and also of a federation of such unions. **[Section 10(24)]**

CHAPTER 12

ASSESSMENT OF INDIVIDUAL HUF, PARTNERSHIP FIRMS, TRUST, AOP, BOI & COMPANIES

MCQs ON THEORY

1. Special provisions for payment of tax by certain persons other than a company are contained in ________

(A) Section 115JB

(B) Section 115JBC

(C) Section 115JJB

(D) Section 115JC

2. A firm shall be assessed as a firm if -

(1) the partnership is evidenced by an instrument i.e. partnership deed

(2) the individual shares of the partners are specified in instrument

Select the correct answer from the options given below -

(A) (1) only

(B) (2) only

(C) Both (1) and (2)

(D) Neither (1) nor (2)

3. In computing the income of an AOP/BOI under the head PGBP which of the following shall be allowed?

(I) Interest to members

(II) Salary, bonus, commission or remuneration to a member

Select the correct answer from the options given below -

(A) (I) only

(B) (II) only
(C) Both (I) and (II)
(D) Neither (I) nor (II)

4. If regular income-tax payable for a previous year is less than the Alternate Minimum Tax (AMT) payable then the adjusted total income shall be deemed to be the total income of that person for such previous year and he shall be liable to pay tax on such income ______ of adjusted total income.

(A) @ 17.5%
(B) @ 20%
(C) @ 18.5%
(D) @ 15.5%

5. In computing the income under the head PGBP of a Firm, interest to partner in excess of ___ simple interest p.a. shall be disallowed.

(A) 10%
(B) 12%
(C) 15%
(D) 7.5%

6. How much surcharge is levied if the total income of company exceeds ₹ 1 Crore but does not exceed ₹ 10 Crore?

(A) 5%
(B) 10%
(C) 7%
(D) 12%

7. A domestic company is liable to pay tax on distributed profits _______ of any net amount declared, distributed or paid by such company by way of dividends whether interim or otherwise [other than dividends referred u/s 2(22)(e)] whether out of current or accumulated profits.

(A) 20.5552941%
(B) 15%
(C) 17.25%
(D) 16.995%

8. The special provisions for payment of tax by certain persons other than a company as contained in Section 115JC shall apply to an individual or HUF or an AOP/BOI or an artificial juridical person, if the adjusted total income exceeds _____

(A) ₹ 20 lakhs

(B) ₹ 10 lakhs

(C) ₹ 5 lakhs

(D) ₹ 50 lakhs

9. As per Section 115BBD, "specified foreign company" means company in which Indian company holds ______ nominal value of equity share capital

(A) Less than 24%

(B) 26% or more

(C) 25%

(D) Less than 20%

10. The principal officer of the domestic company and the company shall be liable to pay the tax on distributed profits to the credit of the Central Government within _____ from the date of declaration of any dividend.

(A) 14 days

(B) 7 days

(C) 30 days

(D) 15 days

11. The credit for tax paid by a person under AMT provisions shall be allowed shall be carried forward and set-off during ______

(A) 15 subsequent assessment years

(B) 10 subsequent assessment years

(C) 12 subsequent assessment years

(D) 20 subsequent assessment years

12. Which of the following section makes "special provision for payment of tax by certain companies" i.e. MAT provision?

(A) Section 115B

(B) Section 115JJB

(C) Section 115BJ

(D) Section 115JB

13. As per MAT provisions, the company has to pay tax _____ of book profit. However, MAT rate for unit located in International Financial Service Centre shall be ______

(A) 12.5%; 8.5%

(B) 17.5%; 5.5%

(C) 18.5%; 9%

(D) 17.5%; 9%

14. Which of the following company comes within the definition of "company in which the public are substantially interested"?

(i) Company which is registered under Section 8 of the Companies Act, 2013

(ii) Company in which 40% of the shares are held by the Government

(iii) Listed public company having less than 5,000 shareholders

Select the correct answer from the options given below -

(A) (i) & (iv) only

(B) (ii) & (iii) only

(C) (iii), (i), & (ii)

(D) (i), (ii), (iii) only

15. Where the principal officer of a domestic company and the company fails to pay the whole or any part of the tax on distributed profits within 14 days as aforesaid he or it shall be liable to pay simple interest at the rate of _______ or part thereof on the amount of such tax for the period beginning on the date immediately after the last date on which such tax was payable and ending with the date on which the tax is actually paid.

(A) 1% p.a.

(B) 4% p.m.

(C) 1% p.m.

(D) 10% p.a.

16. Section 271C provides that, if any person fails to comply with the provisions of Section 115-O, he shall be liable to pay as penalty ______

(A) ₹ 5,00,000 which shall not be less than ₹ 1,00,000 to be imposed by Joint Commissioner

(B) a sum equal to the amount of tax which he has failed to pay

(C) a sum equal to twice the amount of tax which he has failed to pay

(D) ₹ 1,00,000 which shall not be less than ₹ 50,000 to be imposed by Joint Commissioner.

17. If a person fails to pay to the credit of the Central Government the tax payable by him, as required by or under the provisions of section 115-O, he shall be punishable with rigorous imprisonment for a term which shall not be less than ______ but which may extend to ______ and with fine.

(A) 6 months; 5 years

(B) 2 months; 3 years

(C) 3 months; 7 years

(D) 6 months; 10 years

18. How much surcharge is levied if the total income of foreign company exceeds ₹ 10 Crore?

(A) 7%

(B) 10%

(C) 12%

(D) 5%

19. As per Section 178 of the Income Tax Act, 1961, every liquidator or receiver of any asset of company has to give a notice of his appointment within ______ to the Assessing Officer who is entitled to assess the income of the company.

(A) 30 days

(B) 60 days

(C) 90 days

(D) 45 days

20. As per Section 115QA, a domestic company shall in addition to the income-tax chargeable in respect of the total income be liable to pay additional income-tax at the rate of ________ on distributed income i.e. consideration paid by the company for buyback of its own unlisted shares which is in excess of the sum received by the company at the time of issue of such shares.

(A) 15% (plus surcharge @ 12% and education cess @ 4%) i.e. 17.472%

(B) 20% (plus surcharge @ 7% and education cess @ 4%) i.e. 22.256%

(C) 15% (plus surcharge @ 7% and education cess @ 4%) i.e. 16.692%

(D) 20% (plus surcharge @ 12% and education cess @ 4%) i.e. 23.296%

21. Amalgamation in relation to companies means, the merger of one or more companies with another company or the merger of two or more companies to form one company provided -

(A) Shareholders holding at least 3/4th in value of shares of the amalgamating company should become shareholders of the amalgamated company

(B) Shareholders holding at least 2/3rd in value of shares of the amalgamating company should become shareholders of the amalgamated company

(C) Shareholders holding at least 1/3rd in value of shares of the amalgamating company should become shareholders of the amalgamated company

(D) Shareholders holding at least 3/5th in value of shares of the amalgamating company should become shareholders of the amalgamated company

22. As per Section 178 of the Income Tax Act, 1961, the Assessing Officer shall, notify to the liquidator within ______ from the date on which he receives notice of the appointment of the liquidator the amount which, in the opinion of the Assessing Officer, would be sufficient to provide for any tax which is then, or is likely thereafter to become, payable by the company.

(A) 1 month

(B) 3 months
(C) 60 days
(D) 120 days

23. Maximum exemption in case of company assessee is -
(A) ₹ 2,50,000
(B) ₹ 10,00,000
(C) ₹ 5,00,000
(D) Nil

24. MAT provisions are applicable to -
(A) Company
(B) AOP
(C) LLP
(D) All of the above

PRACTICAL MCQs

25. Total income of Manav is ₹ 13,90,000 after claiming deduction u/s 10AA amounting to ₹ 21,60,000. Compute his tax liability applying provisions of Section 115JC.
(A) ₹ 2,36,390
(B) ₹ 6,56,750
(C) ₹ 6,83,020
(D) ₹ 4,29,510

26. Total income of Manav is ₹ 3,45,000 after claiming deduction u/s 10AA amounting to ₹ 15,45,000. Compute his tax liability applying provisions of Section 115JC.
(A) ₹ 8,760
(B) ₹ 3,62,050
(C) ₹ 2,340
(D) ₹ 10,820

27. X, Y & Z are partners sharing profits and losses in the ratio of 5:3:2 as per partnership deed. There book profit is ₹ 14,44,660. Remuneration as per partnership deed is as follows:

X: ₹ 5,00,000; Y: 3,00,000 & Z: 2,00,000. How much deduction firm can claim u/s 40(b) while calculating profits and gains of business and profession?

(A) ₹ 14,44,660

(B) ₹ 10,00,000

(C) ₹ 9,56,796

(D) ₹ 12,00,728

28. Total income of XYZ Ltd. registered under the Companies Act, 2013 is ₹ 56,43,920 which includes LTCG on sale of building ₹ 12,07,830 and STCG on sale of listed shares ₹ 5,03,810. Tax on total income = ?

(A) ₹ 11,79,690

(B) ₹ 14,21,250

(C) ₹ 14,96,822

(D) ₹ 15,56,700

29. Total income of HI-FI Ltd. a domestic company is ₹ 1,02,06,710. After claiming marginal relief of ______, total tax payable by the company is ______

(A) ₹ 2,06,710; ₹ 30,90,000

(B) ₹ 69,644; ₹ 33,34,980

(C) ₹ 76,350; ₹ 32,76,350

(D) ₹ 69,644; ₹ 33,02,910

30. X Ltd. has computed total income of ₹ 9,00,000 as per the provisions of the Income Tax Act, 1961. Its book profit as per Section 115JB is ₹ 16,11,000. Compute the tax payable by X Ltd.

(A) ₹ 2,78,100

(B) ₹ 3,09,960

(C) ₹ 2,98,035

(D) ₹ 2,70,000

31. ZPA Ltd. has computed 'total income' and 'book profit' ₹ 5,00,000 and ₹ 8,00,000 respectively for the PY 2018-2019. It has carried forward credit of ₹ 2,00,000 u/s 115JAA from PY 2017-2018. Compute the tax payable by ZPA Ltd. for PY 2018-2019 and MAT credit to carried forwarded to PY 2019-2020.

(A) ₹ 1,53,920; 1,97,920

(B) ₹ 1,97,940; 1,52,440

(C) ₹ 1,52,440; 2,00,000

(D) ₹ 1,48,520; 1,97,440

32. H Ltd. holds 60% shares in S Ltd. For the PY 2018-2019 S Ltd. declared dividend of ₹ 35,00,000 and paid dividend distribution tax on 16.7.2018. H Ltd. declared interim dividend of ₹ 50,00,000 on 16.10.2018. Compute the dividend distribution tax payable by H Ltd.

(A) ₹ 5,96,104

(B) ₹ 3,05,365

(C) ₹ 6,61,623

(D) ₹ 10,17,882

Answers:

1.	(D)	**2.**	(C)	**3.**	(D)	**4.**	(C)	**5.**	(B)	**6.**	(C)	**7.**	(A)
8.	(A)	**9.**	(B)	**10.**	(A)	**11.**	(B)	**12.**	(D)	**13.**	(C)	**14.**	(C)
15.	(C)	**16.**	(B)	**17.**	(C)	**18.**	(D)	**19.**	(A)	**20.**	(D)	**21.**	(A)
22.	(B)	**23.**	(D)	**24.**	(A)	**25.**	(C)	**26.**	(C)	**27.**	(C)	**28.**	(D)
29.	(B)	**30.**	(B)	**31.**	(A)	**32.**	(A)						

PAST EXAMINATION MCQs:

1. Dec 2014: Profit earned during the year by a partnership firm is ₹ 1,40,000. The maximum amount of remuneration deductible from profit is —

(A) ₹ 1,50,000

(B) ₹ 1,40,000

(C) ₹ 1,26,000

(D) ₹ 50,000

2. Dec 2014: Number of years for which credit of MAT excess paid u/s 115JB can be carried forward is —

(A) 10 Assessment years

(B) 8 Assessment years

(C) 15 Assessment years

(D) 9 Assessment years

3. Dec 2014: According to section 2 (1B), "amalgamation, in relation to companies means, the merger of one or more companies with another company or the merger of two or more companies to form one company" provided all conditions except the following are satisfied:

(A) All assets to be transferred from amalgamating company to the amalgamated company

(B) All liabilities including contingent liabilities to be transferred from amalgamating company to amalgamated company

(C) Shareholders holding at least 3/4th in value of shares of the amalgamating company should become shareholders of the amalgamated company

(D) Shareholders holding at least 9/10th in value of shares of the amalgamating company should become shareholders of the amalgamated company.

4. June 2015: Under the Income Tax Act, 1961, LLP is chargeable to tax @ —

(A) 30% plus cess and SHEC or AMT @ 18.5% plus cess and SHEC

(B) 30% plus cess and SHEC or AMT @ 17.5%

(C) 30% plus cess and SHEC or MAT @ 18.5% plus cess and SHEC

(D) 30% plus cess and SHEC or MAT @ 18.5%.

5. June 2015: Arjun has a salary income of ₹ 4,60,000. He also received an interest of ₹ 18,000 on his fixed deposit (after deducting TDS @ 10%) and ₹ 2,000 on his savings account with SBI. He deposited ₹ 50,000 in PPF account. The net income-tax liability of Arjun is —

(A) ₹ 13,390

(B) ₹ 15,330

(C) ₹ 16,270

(D) None of the above

6. June 2015: Under the Income Tax Act, 1961, interest on capital received by a partner from a partnership firm is chargeable under the head —

(A) Profits and gains of business or profession
(B) Income from other sources
(C) Capital gains
(D) None of the above

7. June 2015: Under the Income Tax Act, 1961, dividend derived from the shares held as stock-in-trade are taxable under the head—

(A) Income from other sources
(B) Income from profits and gains of business or profession
(C) Capital gains
(D) Either capital gains or income from profits and gains of business or profession

8. June 2015: Provisions of Section 115JC are not at all applicable to —

(A) LLPs
(B) Companies
(C) Partnership firms
(D) Individuals

9. June 2015: A non-professional firm M/s Bright has book profits of ₹ 9,36,000. The admissible remuneration to working partners for income-tax purpose shall be —

(A) ₹ 6,51,600
(B) ₹ 6,81,600
(C) ₹ 2,70,000
(D) None of the above

10. June 2015: MAT credit in respect of excess taxes paid u/s 115JB can be carried forward for —

(A) 7 Assessment years
(B) 10 Financial years
(C) 15 Assessment years
(D) 7 Financial years

11. June 2015: During the year 2018-2019, Basu won ₹ 4,00,000 from a motor car rally out of which he deposited ₹ 1,50,000 in his

PPF account. He does not have any other income. Net tax payable by Basu for AY 2019-2020 will be —

(A) ₹ 1,24,800

(B) ₹ 15,450

(C) ₹ 1,23,600

(D) None of the above

12. June 2015: In order to be entitled to concessional rate of tax for dividend received from a foreign company, the Indian company should have the following minimum shareholding in such foreign company —

(A) 10%

(B) 25%

(C) 26%

(D) 51%

13. Dec 2015: The voluntary contributions received by an electoral trust during the year is not included in its income —

(A) When 85% of contribution is distributed in the year

(B) When 95% of contribution is distributed in the year

(C) To the extent of ₹ 10 lakh

(D) To the extent of 50% of contribution or ₹ 100 lakh whichever is less.

14. Dec 2015: Alternate minimum tax u/s 115JC is not applicable to —

(A) Company

(B) Individual

(C) Partnership firm

(D) Association of persons

15. Dec 2015: When an LLP has book profit of ₹ 6 lakh, the maximum amount allowable towards the salary of working partners would be—

(A) ₹ 4,50,000

(B) ₹ 6,00,000

(C) ₹ 3,00,000

(D) Nil

16. Dec 2015: When a partnership firm has total sales of ₹ 90 lakh, the maximum amount deductible as salary of working partners on the basis of presumptive income determined u/s 44AD is —

(A) ₹ 5,22,000

(B) ₹ 3,60,000

(C) ₹ 3,30,000

(D) Nil

17. Dec 2015: A limited company declared ₹ 20 lakh as dividend on its paid-up capital of ₹ 100 lakh. The dividend distribution tax payable by it would be —

(A) ₹ 3 lakh

(B) ₹ 3.351233 lakh

(C) ₹ 4.0715294 lakh

(D) ₹ 6.1547808 lakh

18. Dec 2015: From tax point of view, a limited liability partnership (LLP) is treated as —

(A) Sole trader concern

(B) General partnership firm

(C) Private limited company

(D) Public limited company.

19. June 2016: Dividend distribution tax u/s 115-O shall be deposited within _____ days from the date of declaration/distribution/payment of dividend, whichever is earlier.

(A) 7 Days

(B) 10 Days

(C) 14 Days

(D) 20 Days

20. June 2016: Balu paid ₹ 1,00,000 to Raj for purchase of standing crop (paddy). He harvested the produce *i.e.* paddy by incurring expenditure of ₹ 25,000. He sold the said paddy for ₹ 1,80,000 to a trader. His other income for the year ended 31st March, 2019 was ₹ 4,60,000. The total income of Balu is —

(A) ₹ 6,40,000

(B) ₹ 5,15,000

(C) ₹ 4,85,000

(D) ₹ 5,60,000

21. June 2016: The book profit of a partnership firm is ₹ 1,20,000. The actual remuneration paid to working partners is ₹ 3,54,000. The allowable deduction under Section 40(b) towards remuneration to partners is —

(A) ₹ 1,50,000

(B) ₹ 3,54,000

(C) ₹ 1,08,000

(D) ₹ 1,20,000

22. June 2016: The assessment of Julie (Pvt.) Ltd. under Section 143(3) for the assessment year 2017-2018 was completed on 12th October 2018. The notice of demand was served on 27th October 2018. The assessee has to file appeal before the Commissioner (Appeals) within —

(A) 30 Days

(B) 60 Days

(C) 15 Days

(D) 90 Days

23. June 2016: Mrs. Laxmi, 70 years old, received ₹ 30,000 every month from SBI under reverse mortgage scheme by mortgaging her residential house property. She also received monthly family pension of ₹ 15,000. Her total income for the assessment year 2019-2020 is -

(A) ₹ 5,40,000

(B) ₹ 1,80,000

(C) ₹ 1,65,000

(D) ₹ 3,60,000

24. June 2016: Tax credit in respect of MAT paid as per Section 115JB will be allowed only in the previous year in which the tax payable on the total income at the normal rate is—

(A) More than the tax payable under section 115JB
(B) Less than the tax payable under section 115JB
(C) Equal to the tax payable under section 115JB
(D) All of the above

25. June 2016: A domestic company distributed a dividend of ₹ 30,00,000 to its shareholders. Out of this dividend ₹ 4,00,000 paid to a person on behalf of the New Pension System Trust and ₹ 1,00,000 paid to another corporate shareholder. The company also received a dividend of ₹ 2,00,000 from its subsidiary which paid dividend distribution tax under Section 115-O. In this case, the amount of dividend subject to dividend distribution tax for the domestic company will be —

(A) ₹ 24,00,000
(B) ₹ 27,00,000
(C) ₹ 28,00,000
(D) ₹ 30,00,000

26. June 2016: When a non-domestic company is a member in an AOP and its share of profit is indeterminate, the tax on total income of the AOP is charged at the —

(A) Nominal rate
(B) Maximum marginal rate
(C) Rate applicable to the company
(D) Least of the above three rates

27. June 2016: Salary received by a partner from his partnership firm is considered in his personal assessment as —

(A) Income from salary
(B) Profit from business or profession
(C) Income from other sources
(D) Exempted income

28. Dec 2016: A partnership firm had net profit of ₹ 6,20,000 before deducting interest on capitals to partners @ 15% of ₹ 1,50,000 and working partners salary of ₹ 1,80,000 (as per deed of partnership) total income of firm chargeable to tax with the-

(A) ₹ 1,10,000

(B) ₹ 3,20,000

(C) ₹ 2,90,000

(D) ₹ 1,00,000

29. Dec 2016: An association of persons (AOP) has paid tax at the maximum marginal rate. Yash, a member of AOP received ₹ 1 lakh as his share income. Such income is chargeable to tax in his assessment @ -

(A) 10%

(B) Nil

(C) 20%

(D) 30%

30. Dec 2016: If an LLP claims deduction under Section 35AD, the provisions of Alternate Minimum Tax (AMT) under Section 115JC will apply when the adjusted total income exceeds -

(A) ₹ 10 i.e. no limit

(B) ₹ 10 lakh

(C) ₹ 20 lakh

(D) ₹ 3 Crore

31. Dec 2016: Provisions of Section 115JB are applicable in case of -

(A) Domestic companies only

(B) Foreign companies only

(C) All companies

(D) Closely held companies

32. Dec 2016: Dividend distribution tax u/s 115-O is payable by -

(A) Domestic companies only

(B) Foreign companies only

(C) Both domestic and foreign companies

(D) None of the above

33. Dec 2016: A charitable trust registered u/s 12AA has gross receipts of ₹ 40 lakh, it spent ₹ 28 lakh towards its objects. The total income of the trust chargeable to income-tax would be -

(A) Nil

(B) ₹ 12 lakh

(C) ₹ 6 lakh

(D) ₹ 2 lakh

34. Dec 2016: A registered trade union earned ₹ 1,00,000 by way of interest on bank deposit and ₹ 1,50,000 by way of rent from let out premises. Total income of the Trade union chargeable to tax would be -

(A) ₹ 2,24,000

(B) ₹ 2,80,000

(C) ₹ 2,50,000

(D) Nil

35. Dec 2016: An Indian company having 30% voting power in a foreign company received dividend of ₹ 10 lakh form the foreign company. The dividend so received by the Indian company is-

(A) Exempt

(B) Taxable @ 15%

(C) Taxable at the regular rates

(D) Taxable @ 20%

36. June 2017: Surabi Textiles (firm) incurred business loss of ₹ 4,40,000 for the assessment year 2019-2020 before allowance of working partner salary. The firm paid working partner salary of ₹ 1,20,000 each to three partners. The business income of the firm for the assessment year 2019-2020 after deduction of working partner salary is:

(A) Loss ₹ 5,90,000

(B) Loss ₹ 4,40,000

(C) Loss ₹ 80,000

(D) Loss ₹ 8,00,000

37. June 2017: The provisions of alternate minimum tax under section 115JC are applicable for limited liability partnership when the adjusted total income exceeds:

(A) ₹ 10 lakhs

(B) ₹ 20 lakhs

(C) ₹ 100 lakhs

(D) ₹ 5 lakhs

38. June 2017: Radha Ltd. received dividend of ₹ 100 lakhs from King (P) Ltd. of Singapore in December 2018. The company declared interim dividend of ₹ 200 lakhs in January 2019. The dividend distribution tax payable by Radha Ltd. would be ....

(A) on ₹ 200 lakhs

(B) on ₹ 100 lakhs

(C) Nil since dividend declared is more than dividend received

(D) None of the above

39. June 2017: For computing the Book Profit under section 115JB, which of the following is not added back to the profits?

(A) Income-tax

(B) Provision for Tax

(C) Dividend Distribution Tax u/s 115-O

(D) Securities Transaction Tax

40. June 2017: Which of the following is not a requirement for amalgamation of two companies?

(A) All the assets are transferred from amalgamating company to amalgamated company

(B) More than 50% of the directors of the amalgamating company become directors of the amalgamated company

(C) All liabilities including contingent liabilities are transferred from amalgamating company to amalgamated company

(D) Shareholders having 3/4th in value of shares of the amalgamating company become shareholders of the amalgamated company

41. Dec 2017: Ms. Pinky (age 61) pledged her residential building with State Bank of India and received ₹ 10,000 every month under reverse mortgage scheme during the financial year 2018-2019. The amount liable to income-tax in respect of such receipt would be:

(A) ₹ 1, 20,000 (fully taxable)

(B) ₹ 84,000 (after deducting 30%)

(C) ₹ 60,000 (after deducting 50%)

(D) Nil (as it is exempted from tax)

42. Dec 2017: Murali & Co. a partnership firm consisting of 3 partners is engaged in textile trade. Its net profit before allowing interest on capital and working partner salary to partners was ₹ 9 lakhs. The partnership deed does not provide for interest on capital. It provides for working partner salary at ₹ 25,000 per month for all the 3 partners. The income of the firm after allowance of working partner salary would be:

(A) ₹ 90,000

(B) ₹ 2,70,000

(C) Nil

(D) ₹ 3,60,000

43. Dec 2017: When Mr. X retired from X & Co. a partnership firm on 1.1.2019, he was paid ₹ 5 lakhs for not doing a competing business for the next 5 years. The amount so received chargeable to tax in the hands of Mr. X is:

(A) Nil

(B) ₹ 5,00,000

(C) ₹ 1,00,000

(D) ₹ 2,50,000

44. Dec 2017: The provisions of Alternate Minimum Tax (AMT) will apply only when the adjusted total income computed under section 115JC exceeds:

(A) ₹ 5 lakhs

(B) ₹ 20 lakhs

(C) ₹ 50 lakhs

(D) ₹ 100 lakhs

45. Dec 2017: Mr. Vijay is partner in Tools & Co., a partnership firm in Mumbai. He received ₹ 30,000 as share income from the firm for the year ended 31.3.2019. He also received interest at 12% per annum on the capital invested in the firm and the amount being ₹ 24,000. His income from the firm includible in individual assessment is:

(A) ₹ 54,000
(B) ₹ 24,000
(C) ₹ 30,000
(D) Nil

46. Dec 2017: Mr. Chandan (age 70) received ₹ 30,000 every month during the financial year 2018-2019 on reverse mortgage of his property with State Bank of India. The amount of receipt liable to tax in the hands of Mr. Chandan is:

(A) ₹ 3,60,000
(B) ₹ 2,52,000
(C) ₹ 40,000
(D) Nil

47. Dec 2017: Ray Charitable Trust (registered under section 12AA) has total income of ₹ 20 lakhs. It applied ₹ 10 lakhs towards its objects. How much is chargeable to tax in case the trust does not opt for accumulation of income under section 11(2) of the Act?

(A) ₹ 10 lakhs
(B) ₹ 7 lakhs
(C) ₹ 5 lakhs
(D) ₹ 3 lakhs

ANSWERS:

1.	(C)	**2.**	(C)	**3.**	(D)	**4.**	(A)	**5.**	(D)	**6.**	(A)	**7.**	(**)
8.	(B)	**9.**	(A)	**10.**	(C)	**11.**	(A)	**12.**	(C)	**13.**	(B)	**14.**	(A)
15.	(A)	**16.**	(D)	**17.**	(C)	**18.**	(B)	**19.**	(C)	**20.**	(B)	**21.**	(A)
22	(A)	**23**	(C)	**24**	(A)	**25**	(A)	**26**	(C)	**27**	(B)	**28**	(B)
29	(B)	**30**	(C)	**31**	(C)	**32**	(A)	**33**	(C)	**34**	(D)	**35**	(B)
36	(A)	**37**	(A)	**38**	(A)	**39**	(D)	**40**	(B)	**41**	(D)	**42**	(B)
43	(B)	**44**	(B)	**45**	(B)	**46**	(D)	**47**	(B)				

** *MCQ is wrongly drafted. None of the given option is correct.*

HINTS FOR PRACTICAL MCQs:

25.

Total income	13,90,000
Tax on total income [A]	2,29,500
Adjusted total income (13,90,000 + 21,60,000)	35,50,000
Tax on adjusted total income as per Section 115JC (35,50,000 × 18.5%) [B]	6,56,750
[A] or [B] whichever is more	6,56,750
(+) Education cess @ 4%	26,270
	6,83,020

26. Adjusted total income does not exceed ₹ 20,00,000 hence Section 115JC is not applicable and tax on total income of ₹ 3,45,000 amounting to ₹ 2,340 is payable after rebate u/s 87A.

27. Deduction u/s 40 (b) is as follows:

(1) On first ₹ 3,00,000 @ 90% on balance @ 60% [(3,00,000 × 90%) + (11,44,660 × 60%)] = 9,56,796

(2) Remuneration as per partnership deed = ₹ 10,00,000

Whichever is less.

29. *Step 1: Calculate tax on total income*

Tax on total income (1,02,06,710 × 30%)	30,62,013
(+) Surcharge @ 7%	2,14,341
(A)	32,76,354

Step 2: Calculate tax on total income assuming it is ₹ 1 Crore and add excess income over ₹ 1 Crore

Tax on total income (1,00,00,000 × 30%)	30,00,000
(+) Excess income over ₹ 1 Crore	2,06,710
(B)	32,06,710

Marginal Relief = 32,76,354 - 32,06,710

= 69,644

Tax on total income	32,06,710
(+) Education Cess @ 4%	1,28,268
	33,34,978
Rounded up	33,34,980

30.

Total income	9,00,000
Tax on total income [A]	2,70,000
Book Profit	16,11,000
Tax on Book Profit as per Section 115JB (16,11,000 × 18.5%) [B]	2,98,035
[A] or [B] whichever is more	2,98,035
(+) Education cess @ 4%	11,921
	3,09,956
Rounded up	3,09,960

31.

Tax on total income (5,00,000 × 31.2%)	[A]	1,56,000
Tax on book profit (8,00,000 × 19.24%)	[B]	1,53,920
Difference between [A] & [B]	[C]	2,080
Tax credit b/f from last year	[D]	2,00,000
MAT credit set-off [C] or [D] whichever is less	[E]	2,080
Tax payable (1,56,000 - 2,080)	[F]	1,53,920
MAT credit to c/f to PY 2019 - 2020 (2,00,000 - 2,080)	[G]	1,97,920

32.

Dividend payable by H Ltd.	50,00,000
(-) Dividend received by S Ltd. (35,00,000 × 60%)	(21,00,000)
	29,00,000
Dividend distribution tax (29,00,000 × 20.5552941%)	5,96,104

HINTS FOR PAST EXAMINATION MCQs:

1. 1,40,000 × 90% = 1,26,000

5.

Salary income	4,60,000
Interest on fixed deposit (18,000/0.9) (grossed up)	20,000
Interest on saving bank account	2,000
Gross Total Income	4,82,000
(-) Deduction u/s 80C	(50,000)
(-) Deduction u/s 80TTA	(2,000)
Total Income	4,30,000
Tax on total income	9,000
(+) Education cess @ 4%	360
	9,360

9,270 does not appear in any first three options; hence Option D is correct i.e. none of the above.

9. (3,00,000 × 90%) + (6,36,000 × 60%) = 6,51,600

16. Deduction to firm u/s 40(b) is not available if firm opts for presumptive taxation scheme referred to in Section 44AD.

17. 20 lakh × 20.5552941% = 4.11105882 lakh.

20. Income from harvesting paddy is not agricultural income.

Total income = 1,80,000 - 1,00,000 - 25,000 + 4,60,000 = 5,15,000.

21. As per Section 40(b) deduction allowable to partnership firm on first ₹ 3,00,000 of book profit or in case of loss is 90% of book profit or ₹ 1,50,000, whichever is more. As book profit is only ₹ 1,20,000, the firm can get deduction of ₹ 1,50,000.

23.

Monthly instalment received under reverse mortgage scheme [Exempt u/s 10 (43)]		Nil
Family pension received (15,00 × 12)	1,80,000	
(-) Exempt (1/3rd of income or ₹ 15,000 whichever is less)	(15,000)	1,65,000
Total income		1,65,000

25.

Total dividend payable	30,00,000
(-) Dividend received form subsidiary	(2,00,000
(-) Dividend paid on behalf of the New Pension System Trust **[Section 115-O(1A)]**	(4,00,000)
Net taxable dividend	24,00,000

28.

Net profit	6,20,000
(+) Interest up to 12%	(1,20,000)
Book profit	5,00,000
(-) Deduction u/s 40(b) *[See Note]*	(1,80,000)
Taxable profit	3,20,000

Note:

Deduction u/s 40(b) - lower of the following		
[1]		
- On first 3,00,000; 90% of book profit or ₹ 1,50,000 whichever is more	2,70,000	
- On balance 60% of book profit	1,20,000	3,90,000
[2] Remuneration as per partnership deed		1,80,000

36. *Remuneration to working partners:*

[A]

Book Profits	Allowable Remuneration
On first ₹ 3,00,000 of book profits or in case of a loss.	₹ 1,50,000 or 90% of book profits, whichever is more.
On balance book profits	60% of the book profits.

[B]

Remuneration as per partnership deed.

[A] or [B] whichever is less.

Book Profit	(4,40,000)
(-) Deduction u/s 40(b)	(1,50,000)
Income/(loss) under the head PGBP	(5,90,000)

37. Special provisions for payment of tax by certain persons other than a company [Section 115JC]: Provisions shall be applicable to a person, other than a company, whose regular income-tax payable for a previous year is less than the Alternate Minimum Tax (AMT) payable.

Adjusted total income to be deemed income: If regular income-tax payable for a previous year is less than the alternate minimum tax payable then the adjusted total income shall be deemed to be the total income of that person for such previous year and he shall be liable to pay tax on such income **@ 18.5%** of adjusted total income.

Provisions applicable when adjusted total income exceeds ₹ 20 lakhs: The above provisions shall apply to an individual or HUF or an AOP/BOI or an artificial juridical person, if the adjusted total income exceeds ₹ 20 lakhs.

Thus, above relaxation is not available to LLP. Hence, none of the given option is correct.

38. Dividend received from subsidiary company has to be reduced from dividend distributed by holding company. **[Section 115-O]**

As per facts given in case Radha Ltd. and King (P) Ltd. do not have holding subsidiary relationship and hence Radha Ltd. has to pay corporate dividend tax on 200 lakhs.

42.

Net profit/book profit		9,00,000
(-) Deduction u/s 40(b): Lower of the following two:		
(1) On first ₹ 3,00,000 of book profits or in case of a loss - ₹ 1,50,000 or 90% of book profits, whichever is more. On balance book profits 60% of the book profits. [(3,00,000 × 90%) + (6,00,000 × 60%)]	6,30,000	
(2) Remuneration as per partnership deed (25,000 × 3 × 12)	9,00,000	(6,30,000)
Net business income		2,70,000

45. Share income of a person being a partner of a firm (includes LLP) which is separately assessed as such is exempt from tax.

In computing the income under the head PGBP of a Firm, interest to partner in excess of 12% simple interest p.a. shall be disallowed. In other words interest up to 12% is taxable in the hands of partner in his individual capacity and Interest above 12% is taxable in the hands of the firm.

Hence, only ₹ 24,000 will be taxable in the hands of Vijay.

47.

Total income of charitable trust	20,00,000
(-) Income applied by charitable trust towards its objects	(10,00,000)
(-) Free accumulation u/s 11(1)(a) @ 15%	(3,00,000)
(-) Accumulation u/s 11(2)	-
Income liable to be taxed	7,00,000

CHAPTER 13

TDS, ADVANCE TAX, INTEREST PAYABLE BY/TO ASSESSEES

MCQs ON THEORY

1. Person responsible for paying 'Salaries' has deduct TDS @ rate of -

(A) 10%

(B) 15%

(C) Rate differ for each payee depending upon his salary and other income

(D) 20%

2. If company pays interest on securities to resident individual by an account payee cheque then no TDS will be deducted if amount does not exceed ______

(A) ₹ 5,000

(B) ₹ 10,000

(C) ₹ 7,500

(D) ₹ 15,000

3. Advance tax is payable if assessees estimated tax liability exceed -

(A) 5,000

(B) 10,000

(C) 20,000

(D) 2,50,000

4. What is rate of TDS for premature withdrawal from RPF if PAN number is furnished?

(A) 10%

(B) 10.3%

(C) 35.535%

(D) 30%

5. Which of the following section makes provisions relating to TDS for "Interest other than interest on securities"?

(A) Section 194

(B) Section 194A

(C) Section 194AA

(D) Section 194B

6. If dividend is paid to individual by an account payee cheque and amount does not exceed _____ then no TDS is to be deducted.

(A) ₹ 2,500

(B) ₹ 5,000

(C) ₹ 10,000

(D) ₹ 7,500

7. Person responsible for paying interest on securities has to deduct TDS -

(1) At the time of credit of such income to the account of the payee

(2) At the time of payment of cash

Select correct answer form the options given below -

(A) (1) only

(B) (2) only

(C) (1) or (2) whichever is earlier

(D) (1) or (2) whichever later

8. Match the following:

List I	*List II*
P. Winnings from lottery or crossword puzzle	1. Section 194B
Q. Payments to contractors	2. 1% where the payment is made to an individual
R. Payments to non-resident sportsmen	3. No TDS if amount does not exceed ₹ 15,000

List I	*List II*
S. Insurance commission	4. TDS Rate - 20%
	5. 2% where the payment is to an individual
	6. Section 194BB

Select correct answer from the options given below -

	P	**Q**	**R**	**S**
(A)	1	5	4	3
(B)	6	5	3	4
(C)	1	2	4	3
(D)	3	2	1	5

9. How much TDS has to be deducted by co-operative society if it makes payment for interest (other than on securities)?

(A) 20%

(B) 10%

(C) 2%

(D) 5%

10. What is the rate of TDS for "interest on securities" as specified Section 193?

(A) 5%

(B) 10%

(C) 20%

(D) 30%

11. If interest is payable by banking company, co-operative society, post office other than on securities then it will not deduct TDS if amount does not exceed __________

(A) ₹ 10,000

(B) ₹ 5,000

(C) ₹ 2,500

(D) ₹ 25,000

12. *Statement X:*

No TDS when payment made to goods transport agency owning 10 or less goods carriages and PAN number is furnished u/s 194C of the Income Tax Act, 1961.

Statement Y:

TDS rate for payment in respect of life insurance policy u/s 194DA is 2%.

(A) Statement X is incorrect but Statement II is correct.

(B) Statement X is correct but Statement II is incorrect.

(C) Both Statement X and Statement II are correct.

(D) Both Statement X and Statement II are incorrect.

13. If interest is payable on any security by the Central or State Government, then rate of TDS is -

(A) 10%

(B) 5%

(C) Nil

(D) 20%

14. What is rate of TDS u/s 192A for premature withdrawal from RPF if PAN number is not furnished?

(A) 20.6%

(B) 20%

(C) 35.88%

(D) 30%

15. No tax shall be deducted if winnings from lottery or crossword puzzle does not exceed -

(A) ₹ 5,000

(B) ₹ 2,500

(C) ₹ 7,500

(D) ₹ 10,000

16. No tax shall be deducted if winnings from horse races does not exceed ________

(A) ₹ 5,000

(B) ₹ 7,500

(C) ₹ 2,500

(D) ₹ 10,000

17. Tax shall be deducted ______ if the interest payable on 7.75% Savings (Taxable) Bonds, 2018 exceeds ______ during the financial year.

(A) @ 10%; ₹ 10,000

(B) @ 5%; ₹ 5,000

(C) @ 10%; ₹ 5,000

(D) @ 8%; ₹ 20,000

18. If a company being contractee makes a payment to contractor who is individual, the company has to deduct TDS @ -

(A) 2%

(B) 1%

(C) 10%

(D) 2.6%

19. If a company being contractee makes a payment to contractor, a person other than individual or HUF, the company has to deduct TDS @ -

(A) 2.6%

(B) 10%

(C) 1%

(D) 2%

20. No TDS shall be deducted as per Section 194DA for payment in respect of life insurance policy where the amount does not exceed ______

(A) ₹ 1,00,000

(B) ₹ 5,00,000

(C) ₹ 10,000

(D) ₹ 50,000

21. For payments to non-resident sportsmen or sports associations the rate of TDS as per Section 194E is -

(A) 20%

(B) 2%

(C) 10%

(D) 30%

22. No TDS will be deducted if payment is made to contractor and amount of payment does not exceed ______ or the aggregate of the amounts does not exceed ______

(A) ₹ 30,000; ₹ 75,000

(B) ₹ 25,000; ₹ 70,000

(C) ₹ 30,000; ₹ 1,00,000

(D) ₹ 10,000; ₹ 40,000

23. Person responsible for paying any income by way of commission, remuneration or prize on stocking, distributing, purchasing or selling lottery tickets is not required to deduct TDS if amount does not exceed ______

(A) ₹ 15,000

(B) ₹ 1,000

(C) ₹ 5,000

(D) ₹ 10,000

24. Who is responsible to deduct tax at source for payment of commission or brokerage as per Section 194H?

(A) Individual

(B) HUF

(C) LLP

(D) All of the above

25. What is the rate of TDS for commission or brokerage payable by BSNL or MTNL to their public call office franchisees?

(A) 10%

(B) 20%

(C) 2%

(D) Nil

26. An individual or HUF has to deduct TDS u/s 194-I for payment of rent if -

(A) If amount of rent exceed ₹ 1,80,000 p.m.

(B) If their sales, gross receipts or turnover from the business or profession exceeds the monetary limits specified u/s 44AB i.e. if they are liable to tax audit

(C) If sales, gross receipts or turnover from the business or profession of the receiver of rent exceeds the monetary limits specified u/s 44AB

(D) All of the above

27. What is the rate of TDS for the use of any machinery or plant or equipment as per Section 194-I?

(A) ₹ 2%

(B) ₹ 10%

(C) ₹ 20%

(D) ₹ 5%

28. Who is responsible to deduct tax at source for payment of fees for professional or technical services as per Section 194J?

(A) Every individual or HUF

(B) Individual or HUF if their sales, gross receipts or turnover from the business or profession exceeds the monetary limits specified u/s 44AB

(C) Every person other than Individual or HUF if their sales, gross receipts or turnover from the business or profession does not exceeds the monetary limits specified u/s 44AB

(D) Both (B) and (C)

29. No TDS is to deducted where the amount paid or credited or the aggregate of the amounts credited or paid in respect of professional or technical services does not exceed ______

(A) ₹ 30,000

(B) ₹ 60,000

(C) ₹ 70,000

(D) ₹ 1,00,000

30. Section 194LA provides that where the amount or the aggregate amount of payments to a resident during the financial year on account of any compensation or the enhanced compensation on account of compulsory acquisition of any immovable property other than agricultural land does not exceed ________ no TDS is required to be deducted.

(A) ₹ 2,50,000

(B) ₹ 5,00,000

(C) ₹ 10,00,000

(D) ₹ 2,00,000

31. As per Section 194LC, Indian company or business trust responsible for paying income by way of interest to a non-resident or to a foreign company is required to deduct TDS at the rate of ______ at the time of payment of interest income

(A) 5%

(B) 5% plus surcharge plus EC @ 4%

(C) 10% plus surcharge plus EC @ 4%

(D) 10%

32. Person responsible for paying to Foreign Institutional Investor (FII) or Qualified Foreign Investor (QFI) is required to deduct TDS at the rate of ______ at the time of payment of interest income.

(A) 10% plus surcharge plus EC @ 4%

(B) 20% plus surcharge plus EC @ 4%

(C) 5%

(D) 5% plus surcharge plus EC @ 4%

33. As per Section 201, in case of default of failure to deduct TDS, the person shall be liable to pay simple interest at ______ on amount of such tax for the period from the date on which such tax was deductible/collectible to the date on which such tax is deducted.

(A) 1% p.m. or part thereof

(B) 1% p.a. or part thereof

(C) 1.5% p.m. or part thereof

(D) 1.5% p.a. or part thereof

34. As per Section 201, in case of non-payment of TDS, the person shall be liable to pay simple interest at ______ on amount of such tax for the period from the date on which such tax was deducted to the date on which such tax is actually paid.

(A) 1% p.m. or part thereof

(B) 1.5% p.m. or part thereof

(C) 2% p.m. or part thereof

(D) 2.5% p.m. or part thereof

35. If the PAN is not furnished, then the tax shall be deducted at -

(A) Rate specified in the relevant provision of the Act

(B) Rate in force as per the annual Finance Act

(C) the rate of 20%

(D) highest of the above three

36. What is rate of TCS for Tendu leaves?

(A) 1%

(B) 5%

(C) 2.5%

(D) 1.25%

37. What is rate of TCS for Alcoholic liquor for human consumption?

(A) 5%

(B) 1%

(C) 1.25%

(D) 2.5%

38. What is rate of TCS for Timber obtained under a forest lease?

(A) 2.25%

(B) 1%

(C) 5%

(D) 2.5%

39. Every person who sells motor vehicle of the value exceeding ______ shall collect tax equal to ______ of consideration at the time of receipt of amount.

(A) ₹ 5,00,000; 2%

(B) ₹ 20,00,000; 1%

(C) ₹ 10,00,000; 2%

(D) ₹ 10,00,000; 1%

40. The amount in respect interest payable under the Income Tax Act, 1961 is to be calculated shall be rounded off to the nearest multiple of _______

(A) ₹ 1

(B) ₹ 10

(C) ₹ 100

(D) ₹ 50

41. On 15th June each year an individual has to pay advance tax equal to -

(A) Not less than 45% of advance tax liability, as reduced by the amount, if any, paid in the earlier instalment

(B) Nil

(C) Not less than 15% of advance tax liability

(D) Not less than 30% of advance tax liability

ANSWERS:

1.	(C)	**2.**	(C)	**3.**	(B)	**4.**	(A)	**5.**	(B)	**6.**	(A)	**7.**	(C)
8.	(C)	**9.**	(B)	**10.**	(B)	**11.**	(A)	**12.**	(B)	**13.**	(C)	**14.**	(C)
15.	(D)	**16.**	(D)	**17.**	(A)	**18.**	(B)	**19.**	(D)	**20.**	(A)	**21.**	(A)
22.	(C)	**23.**	(A)	**24.**	(C)	**25.**	(D)	**26.**	(B)	**27.**	(A)	**28.**	(D)
29.	(A)	**30.**	(A)	**31.**	(A)	**32.**	(D)	**33.**	(A)	**34.**	(B)	**35.**	(D)
36.	(B)	**37.**	(B)	**38.**	(D)	**39.**	(D)	**40.**	(C)	**41.**	(C)		

PAST EXAMINATION MCQs

1. Dec 2014: Interest payable by a non-corporate assessee for deferment of advance tax is —

(A) 1.03% p.m.

(B) 15% p.a.

(C) 18% p.a.

(D) 1% p.m.

2. Dec 2014: The maximum amount of rent payment where deduction of tax at source is not required in a financial year is —

(A) ₹ 1,20,000

(B) ₹ 1,80,000

(C) ₹ 2,00,000

(D) None of the above

3. Dec 2014: At what rate, will the tax be deducted at source by a banking company, responsible for paying to a resident any income by way of interest other than interest on securities amounting to more than ₹ 10,000, when the payee does not furnish his PAN to deductor —

(A) 10%

(B) 20%

(C) 30%

(D) 40%

4. Dec 2014: In a contest, Amit wins ₹ 50,000 cash and a motor-cycle worth ₹ 50,000. The amount of tax deducted at source will be —

(A) ₹ 30,000

(B) ₹ 15,000

(C) ₹ 27,000

(D) ₹ 27,810

5. Dec 2014: Calculate advance tax payable by Sumit on or before 15th September, 2018 from the following: Rent from house property ₹ 75,000 per month; municipal taxes paid by him ₹ 60,000 —

(A) ₹ 48,311

(B) ₹ 7,245

(C) ₹ 14,087

(D) ₹ 36,227

6. Dec 2014: An assessee liable to pay advance tax is not liable to pay interest u/s 234B, if advance tax paid by him is not less than —

(A) 90% of advance tax payable by him

(B) 80% of advance tax payable by him

(C) 100% of advance tax payable by him

(D) 70% of advance tax payable by him

7. June 2015: Which of the following assessee is not liable to pay advance tax u/s 207?

(A) A senior citizen having income chargeable under the head 'profits and gains of business or profession'

(B) A senior citizen not having income chargeable under the head 'profits and gains of business or profession'

(C) A super senior citizen having income chargeable under the head 'profits and gains of business or profession'

(D) A resident individual not being senior citizen having income chargeable under the head 'profits and gains of business or profession'.

8. June 2015: Zen Ltd. made a payment of ₹ 11,00,000 to Amar, a resident transport contractor who has intimated his PAN details. The tax to be deducted at source u/s 194C will be —

(A) ₹ 10,000

(B) ₹ 200

(C) Nil

(D) ₹ 11,000

9. June 2015: Interest payable u/s 234C is computed at —

(A) Compound interest @ 1% p.m.

(B) Simple interest @ 1% p.a.

(C) Compound interest @ 1% p.a.

(D) Simple interest @ 1% p.m.

10. June 2015: Interest for default in payment of instalments of advance tax is levied u/s —

(A) 234A

(B) 234B

(C) 234C

(D) 234D

11. June 2015: U/s 208, it is obligatory for an assessee to pay advance tax where the tax payable is —

(A) 10,000 or more

(B) 20,000 or more

(C) 5,000 or more

(D) 8,000 or more

12. June 2015: An HUF, not subject to tax audit in the earlier year, paying fees of ₹ 35,000 to a Practising Company Secretary shall —

(A) Not deduct TDS

(B) Deduct TDS @ 10%

(C) Deduct TDS @ 20%

(D) Deduct TDS @ 10.3%

13. Dec 2015: Laxmi & Co. paid ₹ 6,10,000 as contract payments to Monu Ltd. during the financial year 2018-2019. It did not deduct tax at source u/s 194C. The amount liable for disallowance is —

(A) ₹ 6,10,000

(B) ₹ 3,05,000

(C) ₹ 12,200

(D) ₹ 1,83,000

14. Dec 2015: Steam (P) Ltd. reports total income of ₹ 20 lakh for the year ended 31st March, 2018. The total tax liability payable before 15th September, 2018 by way of advance tax is —

(A) ₹ 92,700

(B) ₹ 1,85,400

(C) ₹ 2,80,800

(D) ₹ 3,09,600

15. Dec 2015: Interest for deferment in payment of advance tax u/s 234C is calculated on the tax liability computed on —

(A) Assessed income

(B) Returned income

(C) Disputed income

(D) Appealed income

16. Dec 2015: The person responsible for paying any income by way of winnings from lottery an amount exceeding ₹ 10,000, shall deduct —

(A) TDS @ 30.9%

(B) No TDS

(C) TDS @ 31.2%

(D) TDS @ 30%

17. Dec 2015: An assessee is required to make payment of interest where he failed to make the payment of demand before the expiry of 30 days from the service of notice of demand @ —

(A) 1% for every month or part thereof till the date of payment

(B) 2% p.m. till the date of payment

(C) 1.5% p.m. till the date of payment

(D) 1.25% for every month or part thereof till the date of payment

18. June 2016: Raghu, aged 62 years, has pension income of ₹ 2,40,000 and rental income (computed) of ₹ 3,60,000 for the financial year 2018-2019. How much amount be must have paid as advance tax in September, 2018?

(A) ₹ 12,000

(B) ₹ 10,000

(C) ₹ 30,000

(D) Nil

19. June 2016: Interest is payable to assessee on refund under the Income Tax Act, 1961 at the rate of —

(A) 5% per annum

(B) 6% per annum

(C) 9% per annum

(D) 12% per annum

20. June 2016: Pradip acquired an urban land from Chitra for ₹ 70 lakh on 10th October 2018. At what rate, tax is deductible at source in respect of such transaction?

(A) 2%

(B) 5%

(C) 1%

(D) 3%

21. June 2016: Deduction of tax from salary as per Section 192 shall be at —

(A) 10% of salary

(B) The average rate of income tax computed, on the basis of rates in force for the financial year in which the payment is made

(C) The maximum marginal rate of 30%

(D) None of the above

22. June 2016: Rohan won a State Government lottery of ₹ 1,00,000 on 11th October 2018. The government should deduct tax on such winning amounting to —

(A) ₹ 30,000

(B) ₹ 33,000

(C) ₹ 33,990

(D) ₹ 30,900

23. Dec 2016: If a payee eligible for commission exceeding ₹ 50,000 does net furnish his PAN to the payer, tax is deductible at source at -

(A) Nil rate

(B) 20%

(C) 10%

(D) 30%

24. Dec 2016: When an assessee has paid advance tax more than the tax due on the returned income and the return is filed before the "due date" specified in Section 139(1), the refund amount is eligible for interest -

(A) @ 12% p.a.

(B) @ 6% p.a.

(C) @ 9% p.a.

(D) @ 8% p.a.

25. Dec 2016: The liability to deduct tax at source on insurance commission will arise when the commission paid or payable to an agent for the year exceeds —

(A) ₹ 5,000

(B) ₹ 10,000

(C) ₹ 15,000

(D) ₹ 20,000

26. Dec 2016: If a person responsible for deduction of tax at source, after deduction, fails to deposit the same into the Government treasury, be will be liable to pay interest @ -

(A) 1% p. m. or part of the month

(B) 1.5% p. m. or part of the month

(C) 2% p. m. or part of the month

(D) 15% p. m. or part of the month

27. Dec 2016: The liability to pay interest u/s 234B would arise when the advance tax plus TDS/TCS to the credit of the assessee is less than -

(A) 75% of the assessed tax

(B) 90% of the assessed tax

(C) 60% of the assessed tax

(D) 100% of the assessed tax

28. Dec 2016: A senior citizen is not liable to pay advance tax if he does not have income from -

(A) Interest on securities

(B) Capital gains

(C) Profits and gains from business or profession

(D) All of the above

29. Dec 2016: When an employee makes premature withdrawal from employees provident fund account, the requirement of the deduction is attracted when the quantum of withdrawal exceeds -

(A) ₹ 10,000

(B) ₹ 30,000

(C) ₹ 50,000

(D) None of the above

30. June 2017: Mr. Nitin after serving Lion Ltd. for 4 years resigned his job to commence a business of his own. His provident fund account consisted of his own contribution ₹ 50,000; employer's contribution ₹ 50,000 and interest of ₹ 20,000 being attributable equally to the said contributions. How much would be the amount deductible at source under section 192A?

(A) ₹ 12,000 being 10% of total withdrawal

(B) ₹ 10,000 being 10% of total contributions

(C) ₹ 6,000 being 10% of employer's contribution and interest thereon

(D) ₹ 2,000 being 10% of interest on the contributions

31. Dec 2017: A Co. Ltd. made payments to B Co. Ltd. towards contracts executed during the financial year 2018-2019. They are

(i) Contract-1 ₹ 15,000 on 15.6.2018

(ii) Contract-2 ₹ 22,000 on 29.9.2018

(iii) Contract-3 ₹ 27,000 on 30.12.2018

(iv) Contract-4 ₹ 29,000 on 13.3.2019

The tax deductible at source would be:

(A) ₹ 1,560 @ 2% on ₹ 78,000

(B) ₹ 1,860 @ 2% on ₹ 93,000

(C) ₹ 780 @ 1% on ₹ 78,000

(D) Nil

32. P & Co. a partnership firm whose turnover was ₹ 42,60,000 in the previous year 2017-2018 and ₹ 1,01,30,000 in the previous year 2018-2019 paid brokerage of ₹ 21,000 to Mr. Ashwin during the financial year 2018-2019. Mr. Ashwin furnished his PAN to the firm. The amount of tax deductible at source on such brokerage payment would be:

(A) ₹ 2,100 @ 10%

(B) ₹ 1,050 @ 5%

(C) Nil

(D) ₹ 4,200 @ 20%

33. Mr. Rajan (a trader in furniture items) acquired a motor car for ₹ 11 lakhs by availing loan from a nationalized bank. The amount was paid by demand draft. The amount of tax collectible at source by the car dealer who sold the car is:

(A) Nil

(B) ₹ 22,000 @ 2%

(C) ₹ 11,000 @ 1%

(D) ₹ 1,10,000 @ 10%

ANSWERS:

1.	(D)	**2.**	(C)	**3.**	(A)	**4.**	(A)	**5.**	(C)	**6.**	(A)	**7.**	(B)
8.	(C)	**9.**	(D)	**10.**	(C)	**11.**	(A)	**12.**	(A)	**13.**	(D)	**14.**	(C)
15.	(A)	**16.**	(D)	**17.**	(B)	**18.**	(D)	**19.**	(B)	**20.**	(C)	**21.**	(B)
22.	(A)	**23.**	(B)	**24.**	(B)	**25.**	(C)	**26.**	(A)	**27.**	(B)	**28.**	(C)
29.	(C)	**30.**	(A)	**31.**	(D)	**32.**	(B)	**33.**	(C)				

HINTS FOR PAST EXAMINATION MCQs:

5.

Rent (55,000 × 12)	9,00,000
(-) Municipal taxes	(60,000)
	8,40,000
(-) Standard deduction @ 30%	(2,52,000)
Income from house property/Total income	5,88,000
Tax on total income	30,100
(+) Education cess @ 4%	1,204
	31,304

Advance tax payable by Sumit on 30th Sep. = 31,304 × 45% = 14,087

13. 6,10,000 × 30% = 1,83,000

14.

Total income	20,00,000
Tax on total income @ 30%	6,00,000
(+) Education cess @ 4%	24,000
	6,24,000

Advance tax payable by Steam (P) Ltd. on 30th Sep. = 6,24,000 × 45% = 2,80,800

18. No advance tax is payable by assessee if his age exceed 60 years and he has no income under the head "PGBP".

CHAPTER 14

RETURN OF INCOME

MCQs ON THEORY

1. Voluntary return has to be filed -

(A) u/s 143(2)

(B) u/s 139(1)

(C) u/s 144

(D) u/s 139(4A)

2. What is the last date of filing return of income for an assessee who is required to furnish audit report u/s 92E in respect of international transactions or specified domestic transaction?

(A) 31st July of the assessment year

(B) 30th September of the assessment year

(C) 30th November of the assessment year

(D) 31st October of the assessment year

3. Which of the following assessee shall mandatorily file their return electronically using digital signature?

(1) Every firm

(2) Individual liable for tax audit u/s 44AB

(3) Every company

Select the correct answer from the options given below -

(A) (3) only

(B) (1) and (3) only

(C) (1), (2) and (3)

(D) (2) and (3) only

4. If any person, having furnished a return u/s 139(1), 139(4) or in pursuance of a notice issued u/s 142(1), discovers any omission or any wrong statement, then, he may furnish a revised return at any time -

(A) before the expiry of one year from the end of the relevant assessment year

(B) before assessing officer issue notice to file return

(C) before the expiry of two year from the end of the relevant previous year

(D) before the end of the relevant assessment year

5. What is the last date of filing return of income for person other than a company to whom tax audit provisions are applicable?

(A) 30th September of the assessment year

(B) 30th November of the assessment year

(C) 31st October of the assessment year

(D) 31st July of the assessment year

6. What is last date for applying PAN for a person whose total income or total income of any other person in respect of which he is assessable exceeded the maximum amount not chargeable to tax?

(A) Before the end of that financial year

(B) Within 120 days when assessable income exceeded the maximum amount not chargeable to tax

(C) One year from the end of relevant assessment year

(D) On or before 31st May of AY for which such income is assessable

7. If individual has income from salary and house property and to whom tax audit provisions are not applicable has to file return of income -

(A) 31st July of the assessment year

(B) 30th September of the assessment year

(C) 31st October of the assessment year

(D) 30th November of the assessment year

8. The defect in return of income has to be rectified within ______ from date of intimation of defect by Assessing Officer.

(A) 30 days

(B) 15 days

(C) 60 days

(D) 45 days

9. Which of the following assessee shall mandatorily file their return electronically using digital signature?

(a) Every person (not being a company or a person filing return in ITR-7) if total income exceeds ₹ 5,00,000

(b) Every person claiming deduction u/ss 80C to 80G

(c) Every person claiming tax relief u/s 90, 90A or 91

Select the correct answer from the options given below -

(A) (a) only

(B) (b) and (c) only

(C) (a) and (c) only

(D) (a), (b) and (c)

10. Who has to sign return of income for company?

I. Managing director

II. Independent director if there is no MD

Select the correct answer from the options given below -

(A) I only

(B) II only

(C) If signing by I is not possible then II

(D) Both I and II

11. Which of following person can become tax return preparers?

1. Advocate
2. Part time officer of co-operative bank
3. Chartered Accountant
4. Officer of Scheduled Bank

Select the correct answer from the options given below -

(A) 1 and 2

(B) 3 and 4

(C) 2 only

(D) 4 only

12. If any person has sustained a loss in any previous year then, such loss can be carried forward and set-off, only if the person furnishes a return of loss in prescribed form on or before the due date specified in _____

(A) Section 139(1)

(B) Section 143(2)

(C) Section 144

(D) Section 135(1)

13. On which of the following transaction/ documents, quoting of PAN is compulsory?

I. Deposit with a bank ₹ 49,995

II. Payment to hotels ₹ 20,001

III. Purchase of any immovable property ₹ 3,00,001

IV. Sale of securities ₹ 50,005

Select the correct answer from the options given below -

(A) II and III

(B) I and IV

(C) II and III

(D) None of the above

14. What is the rate of interest for default in furnishing return of income?

(A) Simple interest of 2% p.m. or part of a month

(B) Compounded interest of 1% p.a.

(C) Simple interest of 1.% p.m. or part of a month

(D) Compounded interest of 1.25% p.m. or part of a month

15. Which of following can be carried forward to next year even if return is not filed in time?

1. Loss from house property
2. Loss from business and profession
3. Loss from other sources
4. Unabsorbed depreciation

Select the correct answer from the options given below -

(A) 1 and 4 only
(B) 2 and 4 only
(C) 1, 3 and 4 only
(D) 2, 3 and 4 only

16. As per Section 234F of the Income Tax Act, where a person required to furnish a return of income u/s 139, fails to do so within the time prescribed time, he shall pay, by way of fee, a sum of — (*a*) _______, if the return is furnished on or before the 31st day of December of the assessment year; (*b*) ______ in any other case.

(A) ₹ 1000; ₹ 5,000
(B) ₹ 5,000; ₹ 10,000
(C) ₹ 10,000; ₹ 20,000
(D) ₹ 10,000; ₹ 5,000

17. Which of the following person can file return through Tax Return Preparer?

(*i*) Private company having income below ₹ 5,00,000
(*ii*) A person carrying business having loss of ₹ 2,50,000 but having turnover ₹ 1.25 Crore

Select the correct answer from the options given below -

(A) (i) only
(B) Both (i) and (ii)
(C) (ii) only
(D) Neither (i) nor (ii)

18. Belated return can filed -

(A) Before the end of relevant assessment year
(B) Before the completion of assessment u/s 144

(C) (A) and (B) whichever is earlier

(D) None of the above is correct

19. As per Section 139(1), an individual whose age is below 60 years shall file return of income if -

(A) His total income exceeds ₹ 2,50,000

(B) His gross total Income exceeds ₹ 2,50,000

(C) His total income exceeds ₹ 5,00,000

(D) His gross total Income exceeds ₹ 5,00,000

20. Who has to sign return of income for LLP?

(A) Designated partner

(B) Principal officer

(C) Chief executive officer

(D) Any of the above

21. What is last date for applying PAN for a person who is carrying on a business or profession and whose total sales/turnover/ gross receipts are likely to exceed ₹ 5,00,000?

(A) On or before 31st May of AY for which such income is assessable

(B) One year from the end of relevant assessment year

(C) Within 120 days when total sales/ turnover/gross receipts are likely to exceed ₹ 5,00,000

(D) Before the end of that financial year

22. Charitable trust and institutions ______

(A) shall file return of income mandatorily in every case whether it has income or loss

(B) shall file return of income if the total income before giving exemptions u/ss 11 & 12 exceeds maximum amount not chargeable to tax

(C) shall file return of income if the total income before giving exemptions u/s 10 exceeds ₹ 5,00,000

(D) shall not required to file return of income

23. As per Section 234F of the Income Tax Act, 1961, where a person required to furnish a return of income u/s 139, fails to do so within the time prescribed time, he shall pay, by way of fee, a sum of,—

(*a*) ...., if the return is furnished on or before the 31st day of December of the assessment year;

(*b*) .... in any other case.

However, if the total income of the person does not exceed ...., the fee payable under this section shall not exceed ....

Select the correct answer from the options given below -

(A) ₹ 10,000; ₹ 20,000; ₹ 5,00,000; ₹ 1,000

(B) ₹ 5,000; ₹ 10,000; ₹ 5,00,000; ₹ 2,000

(C) ₹ 5,000; ₹ 5,000; ₹ 5,00,000; ₹ 2,000

(D) ₹ 5,000; ₹ 10,000; ₹ 5,00,000; ₹ 1,000

24. Which of the following statement is true (✓) and which is false (×)?

(I) Revised return cannot be further revised.

(II) Belated return can be revised provided that it is revised before the end of relevant assessment year.

(III) Unabsorbed depreciation can be carried forward even if return is not filed in time.

Select the correct answer from the options given below -

	(*I*)	(*II*)	(*III*)
(A)	✓	×	✓
(B)	×	×	✓
(C)	×	✓	✓
(D)	✓	✓	×

25. A company, other than a company claiming exemption u/s 11 is required to file return of income in -

(A) Form ITR-6

(B) Form ITR-3

(C) Form ITR-5

(D) Form ITR-2

26. If person fails to file return of income in time for PY 2018-2019, then what is the last date for filing return late?

(A) 31.3.2020

(B) 31.3.2021

(C) 31.7.2020

(D) 31.7.2021

ANSWERS:

1.	(B)	**2.**	(C)	**3.**	(D)	**4.**	(D)	**5.**	(A)	**6.**	(D)	**7.**	(A)
8.	(B)	**9.**	(C)	**10.**	(C)	**11.**	(C)	**12.**	(A)	**13.**	(D)	**14.**	(C)
15.	(A)	**16.**	(B)	**17.**	(D)	**18.**	(C)	**19.**	(B)	**20.**	(A)	**21.**	(D)
22.	(B)	**23.**	(D)	**24.**	(C)	**25.**	(A)	**26.**	(A)				

PAST EXAMINATION MCQs

1. Dec 2014: Regular assessment means assessment made under—

(A) Section 143(3)

(B) Section 144

(C) Both (A) and (B) above

(D) None of the above

2. Dec 2014: It is not mandatory for an assessee to file a return of loss, if it pertains to —

(A) Loss under the head 'profits and gains from business or profession'

(B) Loss from maintenance of race horses

(C) Loss under the head 'capital gains'

(D) Loss under the head 'income from house property'

3. Dec 2014: Any person who has not filed the return within the time allowed under section 139(1), 139(4) or within the time allowed under a notice issued by the Assessing Officer under section 142 (1), may file a belated return u/s 139(4) —

(A) Before the end of relevant assessment year

(B) Before the completion of the assessment

(C) (A) or (B) above, whichever is earlier

(D) (A) or (B) above, whichever is later

4. Dec 2014: In the case of an individual assessee, the return of income must be signed and verified by following, except —

(A) Individual himself

(B) Where he is absent from India, by some person duly authorised by him in this behalf

(C) Where he is mentally incapacitated from attending to his affairs, by his guardian or any other person competent to act on his behalf

(D) Spouse

5. Dec 2014: If the Assessing Officer has reason to believe that any income chargeable to tax has escaped assessment for any assessment year, he may initiate proceedings of —

(A) Re-assessment

(B) Regular assessment

(C) Self assessment

(D) Best judgment assessment

6. June 2015: A partnership firm whose sales turnover is ₹ 90 lakh has derived income from an industrial undertaking entitled to deduction u/s 80-IB. The due date for filing the return of income for the AY 2018-2019 will be —

(A) 31st July, 2019

(B) 30th September, 2019

(C) 31st October, 2019

(D) None of the above

7. Dec 2015: The 'due date' specified u/s 139(1) for filing the return of income in case of companies engaged in international transactions and who have to furnish a report u/s 92E is —

(A) 31st July

(B) 31st August

(C) 30th September

(D) 30th November

8. Dec 2015: A return of income when notified as defective, has to be rectified within —

(A) 30 Days

(B) The financial year

(C) 15 Days

(D) 60 Days

9. Dec 2015: As per Section 234F of the Income Tax Act, 1961, where a person required to furnish a return of income u/s 139, fails to do so within the time prescribed time, he shall pay, by way of fee, a sum of .... if the return is furnished on or before the 31st day of December of the assessment year.

(A) ₹ 1,000

(B) ₹ 10,000

(C) ₹ 5,000

(D) ₹ 2,000

10. Dec 2015: Quoting of PAN is mandatory when a person is entering into following transactions:

(1) Sale of immovable property of ₹ 5 lakh or more

(2) Deposit of ₹ 50,000 or more in Post Office Savings Bank

(3) Deposit of cash aggregating ₹ 40,000 in one day in a bank

(4) Contract of sale and purchase of securities exceeding ₹ 2 lakh

Select the correct answer from the options given below—

(A) (1), (2) and (3)

(B) (1), (2) and (4)

(C) (1), (3) and (4)

(D) (1), (2), (3) and (4)

11. Dec 2015: XYZ Ltd. filed its return of income for the AY 2018-2019 on 1st February, 2019. The return was selected for scrutiny assessment u/s 143(3). The Assessing Officer is required to serve upon the assessee a notice u/s 143(2) up to —

(A) 31st July, 2019

(B) 30th September, 2019

(C) 31st July, 2020

(D) 30th September, 2020

12. Dec 2015: A partnership firm having 9 trucks engaged in the business of plying these trucks on hire is to file its return of income for the AY 2019-2020 on the basis of provisions of Section 44AE. The partnership firm is required to file its return of income in —

(A) Form ITR-4

(B) Form ITR-3

(C) Form ITR-2

(D) Form ITR-4S

13. June 2016: A return filed by Ms. Mala was found to be defective. The Assessing Officer gave notice of the defect to the assessee. The time-limit for rectification of the defect is —

(A) 30 Days

(B) 15 Days

(C) 45 Days

(D) 60 Days

14. June 2016: Chand Ltd. filled its return of income on 7th December 2018 declaring loss of ₹ 3,50,000. Later, it noticed a claim of expenditure omitted in the return filed. The revised return —

(A) Must be filed before 31st March 2020

(B) Cannot be filed

(C) Must be filed before 31st March 2019

(D) Can be filed before completion of the assessment

15. June 2016: Rose Ltd. filed its return of income for the assessment year 2018-2019 on 10th August, 2018. The notice under Section 143(2) for scrutiny assessment should be served on the assessee by —

(A) 31st March, 2019

(B) 31st March, 2020

(C) 10th February, 2019

(D) 30th September, 2019

16. June 2016: Zeet Ltd. engaged in manufacturing of cement also had wind mills to generate power. Entire power generated by it was used by its wholly owned subsidiary Zoom Ltd. The amount received for the said power supply was ₹ 7 Crore. Zeet Ltd. disclosed total income of ₹ 10 Crore for the assessment year 2019-2020. The due date for filing return of income by Zeet Ltd. is —

(A) 31st July 2019

(B) 30th September 2019

(C) 31st October 2019

(D) 30th November 2019

17. June 2016: As per Section 139(1), an individual other than an individual of the age of 60 years or more shall have to file return of income if —

(A) His total income exceeds ₹ 2,50,000

(B) His total income exceeds ₹ 3,00,000

(C) His total income exceeds ₹ 2,00,000

(D) His total income before allowing deduction under Sections 80C to 80U exceeds ₹ 2,50,000

18. June 2016: The due date of filing return of income for assessment year 2019-2020 in case of a working partner of a firm whose accounts are liable to be audited shall be —

(A) 31st July of the assessment year

(B) 30th September of the assessment year

(C) 30th June of the assessment year

(D) 30th November of the assessment year in case it is required to furnish report referred to in Section 92E and 30th September of the assessment year in any other case

19. June 2016: For the previous year 2017-2018 an assessee suffered a business loss of ₹ 2,50,000. His income from other sources is ₹ 1,80,000. His due date of return was 31st July, 2018 but he submitted the return on 9th September 2018. The assessee in this case —

(A) Shall be allowed to carry forward the loss of ₹ 70,000

(B) Shall not be allowed to carry forward any loss

(C) Shall be allowed to set-off current year business loss to the extent of ₹ 1,80,000 but shall not be allowed to carry forward the balance loss of ₹ 70,000

(D) Shall not be allowed to set-off the business loss to the extent of ₹ 1,80,000 and would be liable to tax on ₹ 1,80,000

20. June 2016: The notice under Section 143(2) must be served within —

(A) 12 months from the date of filing of return

(B) 12 months from the due date of filing the return under Section 139(1) or from the date of filing of return of income

(C) 6 months from the end of the financial year in which the return was furnished

(D) 6 months from the end of month in which the return was furnished

21. Dec 2016: If there is an apparent error in the intimation dated 11th June, 2018 issued u/s 143(1), the time-limit for filing application for rectification u/s 154 is available up to —

(A) 31st March, 2022

(B) 31st March, 2023

(C) 31st March, 2019

(D) 31st October, 2018

22. Dec 2016: Quoting of PAN is not necessary in the case of -

(A) Purchase of immovable property valued at ₹ 50 lakh

(B) Payment of hotel bills ₹ 10,000

(C) Deposit of ₹ 75,000 into bank in a day

(D) Payment of ₹ 5,00,000 for purchase of shares of a company

23. Dec 2016: The last date of filing return by a company which is required to furnish report referred to in Section 92E is -

(A) 31st July of the relevant assessment year

(B) 30th September of the relevant assessment year

(C) 30th November of the relevant assessment year

(D) 31st of the relevant assessment year

24. June 2017: Zeet & Co. is a partnership firm whose turnover for the previous year 2018-2019 was ₹ 220 lakhs. The 'due date' for filing the return of income of the firm is:

(A) 31st July 2019
(B) 30th September, 2019
(C) 30th November, 2019
(D) 31st March, 2020

25. June 2017: Chatterjee filed his return of income for the assessment year 2019-2020 on 10.6.2019. He is eligible to revise his return:

(A) Up to the end of the assessment year 2020-2021
(B) Before the end of the assessment year 2019-2020
(C) Before completion of assessment u/s 153
(D) Before issue of notice u/s 148

26. June 2017: A fixed deposit of ₹ 90,000 made by Mr. P on 5.11.2013 was detected on 7.9.2018. The time limit for issue of notice u/s 148 is:

(A) 31.3.2019
(B) 31.3.2021
(C) 31.3.2023
(D) 31.3.2025

27. June 2017: An apparent error in the assessment order passed u/s 143(3) dated 15.11.2018 was noticed by the assessee in February, 2019. The time limit for seeking rectification of mistake is available up to:

(A) 31.3.2023
(B) 31.3.2022
(C) 31.3.2019
(D) 31.3.2020

28. Dec 2017: Mandatory filing of return of income by individuals will apply when the total income before deduction under the following section exceeds the basic limit chargeable to tax.

(A) Deduction under chapter VI-A
(B) Deduction under section 35

(C) Deduction under section 86

(D) Deduction under section 37

29. Dec 2017: Quoting of Permanent Account Number (PAN) mandatory when the cash deposit in a bank account exceeds:

(A) ₹ 9,999

(B) ₹ 19,999

(C) ₹ 49,999

(D) ₹ 99,999

ANSWERS:

1.	(C)	**2.**	(D)	**3.**	(C)	**4.**	(D)	**5.**	(A)	**6.**	(A)	**7.**	(D)
8.	(D)	**9.**	(C)	**10.**	(C)	**11.**	(B)	**12.**	(B)	**13.**	(D)	**14.**	(C)
15.	(D)	**16.**	(B)	**17.**	(D)	**18.**	(D)	**19.**	(C)	**20.**	(C)	**21.**	(B)
22.	(B)	**23.**	(C)	**24.**	(B)	**25.**	(B)	**26.**	(A)	**27.**	(A)	**28.**	(A)
29.	(C)												

CHAPTER 15

COMPUTATION OF TAX LIABILITY OF NON-RESIDENT ASSESSEE

MCQs ON THEORY

1. In the case of an individual, any income by way of interest on moneys standing to his credit in a _______ in any bank in India in accordance with the Foreign Exchange Management Act, 1999 is exempt.

(A) Resident (Foreign Currency) Account

(B) Non-Resident (External) Account

(C) Both (A) and (B)

(D) None of the above

2. What is the rate deemed income u/s 44B for non-resident assessee engaged in the business of operation of ships?

(A) 7.5%

(B) 10%

(C) 5%

(D) 8%

3. What is the rate deemed income u/s 44BB for non-resident assessee engaged in the business of exploration of mineral oils?

(A) 8%

(B) 10%

(C) 7.5%

(D) 5%

4. What is the rate deemed income u/s 44BBA for non-resident assessee engaged in business of operations of aircraft?

(A) 7.5%

(B) 10%

(C) 5%

(D) 8%

5. What is the rate deemed income u/s 44BBB for foreign company engaged in the business of civil construction?

(A) 10%

(B) 12%

(C) 15%

(D) 7.5%

6. Under Section 44C, deduction of head office expenditure in the case of non-residents is allowable to the extent of -

(A) 5% of gross total income

(B) 7.5% of total income

(C) 2.5% of book profit

(D) 5% of adjusted total income

7. As per Section 115A, tax rate for non-resident and a foreign company for dividend income other than dividends referred to in Section 115-O is -

(A) 20%

(B) 10%

(C) 5%

(D) 12.5%

8. As per Section 115A, tax rate for non-resident for dividend income other than dividends referred to in Section 115-O is -

(A) 20%

(B) 25%

(C) 10%

(D) 5%

9. What is the tax rate on income from bonds or GDR purchased in foreign currency or capital gains arising from their transfer as provided in Section 115AC?

(A) 10%

(B) 7.5%
(C) 8%
(D) 20%

10. What the tax rate is for non-resident sportsmen or sport associations as provided in Section 115BBA?

(A) 15%
(B) 12%
(C) 20%
(D) 17%

11. Which of the following statement is true?

(A) No basic exemption is available to non-resident individual.
(B) Capital gain to non-resident is liable to special rate of tax at 30%
(C) Transfer of bonds/GDR's by a non-resident to another non-resident outside India is not a transfer
(D) None of the above

12. Which of the following statement is true?

(A) As per Section 115AC, no deduction is allowed to non-resident in respect of any expenditure or allowance under sections 28 to 44C or section 57 and Chapter VI-A in computing his or its income.
(B) Scheme of deemed income as provided in Section 44DA to non-resident is optional.
(C) Both (A) and (B)
(D) Neither (A) nor (B)

PRACTICAL MCQs

13. A non-resident company assessee engaged in the business of operation of ships received ₹ 50,45,000 for carriage of goods, livestock, mail and passengers. Compute the tax payable by non-resident assessee?

(A) ₹ 3,78,375
(B) ₹ 3,89,726

(C) ₹ 1,51,350

(D) ₹ 1,57,400

14. Non-resident company assessee engaged in business of operations of aircraft received ₹ 1,25,45,000 for carriage of goods, livestock, mail and passengers in India. Its expense incurred in India are ₹ 15,25,000. Compute the tax payable by non- resident assessee?

(A) ₹ 6,27,750

(B) ₹ 6,46,070

(C) ₹ 2,51,100

(D) ₹ 2,60,940

ANSWERS:

1.	(B)	**2.**	(A)	**3.**	(B)	**4.**	(C)	**5.**	(A)	**6.**	(D)	**7.**	(A)
8.	(A)	**9.**	(A)	**10.**	(C)	**11.**	(C)	**12.**	(C)	**13.**	(D)	**14.**	(D)

PAST EXAMINATION MCQs

1. Dec 2014: In case of foreign companies having branches in India, maximum deduction (in respect of head office expenditure) allowed in computing their income u/s 44C is —

(A) An amount equal to 5% of the adjusted total income

(B) An amount equal to 5% of the total income

(C) An amount equal to 15% of the adjusted total income

(D) An amount equal to 15% of the total income

2. Dec 2015: The tax on the income of non-resident can be/may be recovered:

(1) By deduction of tax at source

(2) From his associates

(3) From his agents

Select the correct answer from the options given below—

(A) (1) only

(B) (1) & (2) only

(C) (1), (2) & (3)

(D) None of the above

3. June 2016: A non-resident Indian is not required to furnish his return of income under Section 139(1) if his total income in respect of which he is assessable under the Income Tax Act, 1961 during the previous year consists of —

(A) Investment income only

(B) Long-term capital gains only

(C) Short-term capital gains only

(D) Investment income and long-term capital gains only

4. June 2016: Where a non-resident/foreign company is liable to tax at special rate of 10% on account of royalty or fee for technical services, such assessee shall —

(A) Be eligible for deduction of any expenses from such income under sections 28 to 44C or section 57

(B) Not be eligible for any deduction under Chapter VI-A on account of such income

(C) Neither be eligible for deduction of any expenses under sections 28 to 44C or section 57 nor be eligible for any deduction under Chapter VI-A

(D) Not be eligible for deduction of any expense under sections 28 to 44C or section 57 but shall be eligible for deduction under Chapter VI-A

5. Dec 2016: Income of a non-resident from shipping business in India is computed at the rate —

(A) 5%

(B) 7.5%

(C) 10%

(D) 30%

6. Dec 2017: In the case of non-resident Indian having income by way of long term capital gains, the rate of tax on such income would be:

(A) 5%

(B) 10%

(C) 15%

(D) 20%

ANSWERS:

1.	(A)	**2.**	(C)	**3.**	(D)	**4.**	(D)	**5.**	(B)	**6.**	(B)

HINTS FOR PRACTICAL MCQs:

13. Total income = 50,45,000 × 7.5% = 3,78,375

Tax on total income = 3,78,375 × 41.6% (40% plus EC) = 1,57,404

Total income rounded up = 1,57,400

14. Total income = 1,25,45,000 × 5% = 6,27,250

Tax on total income = 6,27,250 × 41.6% (40% plus EC) = 2,60,936

Total income rounded up = 2,60,940

CHAPTER 16

APPEALS, REVISIONS, SETTLEMENT, PENALTIES, OFFENCES & RECOVERY OF TAX

MCQs ON THEORY

1. Who can file appeal before CIT (Appeals)?

(A) Assessee

(B) Department

(C) Assessee or Department

(D) Assessing officer

2. If total income of assessee exceeds ₹ 2,00,000 as computed by the Assessing Officer, the assessee is required to pay fee of ______ for filing appeal before Commissioner (Appeals).

(A) ₹ 250

(B) ₹ 500

(C) ₹ 1,000

(D) ₹ 5,000

3. Delay in filing appeal before ITAT or High Court can be condoned on showing ______

(A) Reasonable cause

(B) Appropriate cause

(C) Cause of action

(D) Sufficient cause

4. Appeal to High Court against the order of Income Tax Appellate Tribunal (ITAT) has to be filed in within _____ of receipt of order of ITAT.

(A) 60 days

(B) 90 days

(C) 120 days

(D) 180 days

5. Which of the following statement is false?

(1) An appeal to Commissioner (Appeals) once filed cannot be withdrawn.

(2) The right to file appeals against the orders of the Assessing Officer is not available to the Department.

Select the correct answer from the options given below -

(A) Neither (1) nor (2)

(B) (2) only

(C) (1) only

(D) Both (1) and (2)

6. Appeal before CIT (Appeals) has to be filed in _____

(A) Form No. 35

(B) Form No. 35A

(C) Form No. 36

(D) Form No. 36A

7. As per Section 263, the order for revision should be passed -

(A) within 2 years from the date of order of Assessing Officer.

(B) within 2 years from the end of the financial year in which the order sought to be revised was passed.

(C) within 1 year from the end of the assessment year relevant to previous year in which the order sought to be revised was passed.

(D) within 2 year from the end of the assessment year relevant to previous year in which the order sought to be revised was passed.

8. Match the following:

List I	*List II*
P. Section 263	1. Revisional powers of Commissioner, where the order of AO is erroneous and prejudicial to the interests of the revenue.
Q. Section 271B	2. Penalty for failure to furnish returns
R. Section 264	3. Revisional powers of Commissioner on application of assessee
S. Section 271F	4. Penalty for failure to get accounts audited
	5. Penalty for failure to collect tax at source

Select the correct answer from the options given below -

	P	**Q**	**R**	**S**
(A)	1	4	3	2
(B)	3	5	1	2
(C)	1	4	3	5
(D)	3	5	1	4

9. Appeal before Income Tax Appellate Tribunal (ITAT) has to be filed in _____

(A) Form No. 36A

(B) Form No. 37

(C) As per Code of Civil Procedure, 1908

(D) Form No. 36

10. While filing settlement application, in case of person on whom search or requisition is made, the additional amount of income-tax payable on the income disclosed in the application should exceeds

____

(A) ₹ 10 lakhs

(B) ₹ 50 lakhs

(C) ₹ 100 lakhs

(D) ₹ 60 lakhs

11. Appeal before CIT (Appeals) has to be filed in Form No. 35 in _____

(A) duplicate

(B) triplicate

(C) single copy

(D) quintuplicate

12. While filing settlement application, in case of relative of "specified person", the additional amount of income-tax payable on the income disclosed in the application should exceeds _________

(A) ₹ 5 lakhs

(B) ₹ 10 lakhs

(C) ₹ 15 lakhs

(D) ₹ 25 lakhs

13. Advance Ruling can be obtained by -

(A) A non-resident

(B) Notified category of residents

(C) Both (A) and (B)

(D) Neither (A) nor (B)

14. The application for Advance Ruling shall be made in _________

(A) duplicate

(B) triplicate

(C) quadruplicate

(D) quintuplicate

15. Appeal before Income Tax Appellate Tribunal (ITAT) has to be filed in Form No. 36 in _____

(A) quintuplicate

(B) duplicate

(C) in such copy as may specified by the Tribunal time to time

(D) triplicate

16. Appeal to Income Tax Appellate Tribunal (ITAT) has against the order of CIT (Appeals) has to be filed in -

(A) Within 60 days of communication of the order
(B) Within 60 days of the order
(C) Within 120 days of communication of the order
(D) Within 120 days of the order

17. An application to Settlement Commission shall be made in prescribed form with a fee of -

(A) ₹ 50
(B) ₹ 500
(C) ₹ 5,000
(D) ₹ 50,000

18. CIT (Appeals) shall wherever possible may hear and decide appeal ________

(A) within 1 year from the end of the month in which such appeal is filed before him
(B) within 4 years from the end of financial year in which such appeal was filed before him
(C) within 2 years from the end of financial year in which such appeal was filed before him
(D) within 1 year from the end of the financial year in which such appeal is filed before him

19. Which of the following statement is false?

(A) An appeal to Commissioner (Appeals) once filed cannot be withdrawn.
(B) An application of advance ruling once filed cannot be withdrawn.
(C) Settlement application once made cannot be withdrawn.
(D) All of the above

20. Appeal to Supreme Court against the order of High Court has to be filed in -

(A) Within 120 days of receipt of order
(B) Within 90 days from the date of receipt of order
(C) Within 90 days from the date of order
(D) Within 120 days from the date of order

21. As per Section 264, revision order can be passed by the Commissioner -

(A) own motion

(B) on request by assessing officer

(C) on an application by the assessee for revision

(D) either of his own motion or on an application by the assessee for revision

22. *Statement I:*

A Settlement application shall not be allowed to be withdrawn by the applicant.

Statement II:

No appeal can be filed against order passed by commissioner u/s 264.

Select the correct answer from the options given below -

(A) Statement I is true while Statement II is false

(B) Statement II is true while Statement I is false

(C) Both Statement I and Statement II are true

(D) Both Statement I and Statement II are false

23. The Appellate Tribunal may, at any time within ______ from the end of the month in which in which the order was passed, with a view to rectifying any mistake apparent from the record, amend any order passed by it and shall make such amendment if the mistake is brought to its notice by the assessee or the Assessing Officer.

(A) 4 years

(B) 4 months

(C) 6 months

(D) 90 days

24. Settlement commission shall issue notice to applicant within ______ from date of receipt of application requiring him to explain as to why application made by him be allowed to be proceeded with.

(A) 7 days

(B) 10 days

(C) 8 days

(D) 14 days

25. Time limit for rectification of settlement application is ______ from the end of the month in which final order is passed by the Settlement Commission.

(A) 3 months

(B) 6 months

(C) 12 months

(D) 9 months

26. When an appeal has been filed before the High Court, it shall be heard by a bench of ________ of the High Court, and shall be decided in accordance with the opinion of such Judges or of the majority of such Judges.

(A) not less than two Judges

(B) not less than three Judges

(C) two Judges

(D) three Judges

27. The Authority shall pronounce its advance ruling in writing within _____ of the receipt of application.

(A) 3 months

(B) 6 months

(C) 9 months

(D) 12 months

28. Settlement commission shall call for a report from Commissioner within ______ from date on which application was made in respect of an application which is allowed to be proceeded.

(A) 15 days

(B) 60 days

(C) 30 days

(D) 90 days

29. Income Tax Appellate Tribunal (ITAT) shall wherever possible may hear and decide appeal _______

(A) within 4 years from the end of financial year in which such appeal was filed

(B) within 4 years from the end of month in which such appeal was filed

(C) within 2 years from the end of financial year in which such appeal was filed

(D) within 1 years from the end of financial year in which such appeal was filed

30. If the assessee fails to pay tax payable as per an order under section 245D(4) within 35 days of receipt of copy of such order, simple interest _______ will be payable on unpaid amount from the date of expiry of 35 days.

(A) @ 1% p.a.

(B) @ 1.5% p.m. or part thereof

(C) @ 1.25% p.m. or part thereof

(D) @ 1.25% p.a.

31. Appeal before High Court has to be filed in _____

(A) Form No. 36

(B) Form No. 37

(C) Form No. 36A

(D) As per Code of Civil Procedure, 1908

32. After hearing the application, Settlement Commission shall pass a written order within _____ from the date of the application rejecting the application or allowing it.

(A) 7 days

(B) 10 days

(C) 14 days

(D) 21 days

33. The advance ruling pronounced by the Authority under section 245R shall be binding -

(A) On the applicant who had sought it

(B) On the Commissioner, and the income tax authorities subordinate to him

(C) Both (A) and (B)

(D) Neither (A) nor (B)

34. Under Section 264, the application must be made by the assessee within _____

(A) one year from the end of the financial year on which the order was communicated to him

(B) date on which he came to know of it

(C) one year from the date on which the order was communicated to him or the date on which he came to know of it, whichever is earlier

(D) one year from the end of the financial year on which the order was communicated to him or the date on which he came to know of it, whichever is earlier

35. Under Section 271(1)(*c*), concealment of the particulars of income or furnishing of in accurate particulars of income is liable to maximum penalty of -

(A) 100% of tax sought to be evaded

(B) Such amount as the Assessing Officer may impose

(C) 300% of the amount sought to be evaded

(D) ₹ 1,00,000

36. The Settlement Commission shall pass such order within _____ from the end of the month in which the application was made.

(A) 6 months

(B) 24 months

(C) 18 months

(D) 36 months

37. Application u/s 264 to Commissioner by the assessee must be accompanied by fees of -

(A) ₹ 50

(B) ₹ 500

(C) ₹ 5,000

(D) ₹ 1,000

38. Under Section 271A, failure to keep, maintain or retain books of account etc. as required under Section 44AA is liable to minimum penalty of -

(A) ₹ 1,00,000

(B) 0.5% of total sales, turnover

(C) ₹ 100 per day during which such failure continues

(D) ₹ 25,000

39. Under Section 271BA, failure to furnish report under Section 92E liable to penalty of --

(A) ₹ 1,00,000

(B) A sum equal to 2% of the value of each international

(C) ₹ 100 per day during which such failure continues

(D) ₹ 1,50,000

40. As per Section 164, in case of application by the assessee, the time-limit within which the order is to be passed by the Commissioner is within ______

(A) 1 year from the end of the financial year in which such application is made by the assessee

(B) 2 year from the end of the financial year in which such application is made by the assessee

(C) 1 year from the date the order sought to be revised is passed by assessing officer

(D) 2 year from the date the order sought to be revised is passed.

41. Under Section 271F, failure to furnish returns as required by Section 139(1) on or before due date is liable to penalty of --

(A) ₹ 100 per day during which such failure continues

(B) ₹ 1,00,000

(C) ₹ 25,000

(D) ₹ 5,000

42. Under 271AA, Failure to keep and maintain information and document in respect of international transaction or specified domestic transaction is liable to penalty of --

(A) ₹ 25,00,000

(B) A sum equal to 2% of the value of each international or specified domestic transaction

(C) (A) or (B) whichever is higher

(D) (A) or (B) whichever is less

43. If during the pendency of proceeding before it, the Settlement Commission is of the opinion that for the purpose of protecting the interests of the revenue it is necessary so to do, it may, attach provisionally any property belonging to the applicant in the manner provided in the ________ by passing appropriate order.

(A) First Schedule

(B) Second Schedule

(C) Third Schedule

(D) Fourth Schedule

44. Under Section 271B, failure to get accounts audited under Section 44AB or furnish audit report along with return of income is liable to penalty of --

(A) 0.5% of total sales/turnover

(B) ₹ 1,00,000

(C) ₹ 1,50,000

(D) (A) or (C)

45. Under section 272A(1)(*a*), failure to answer any question put to person legally bound to state the truth of any matter touching the subject of his assessment by an income-tax authority is liable to penalty of --

(A) ₹ 10,000 for each default

(B) ₹ 5,000 for each default

(C) ₹ 2,500 for each default

(D) ₹ 15,000 for each default

46. Every claim for refund shall be made in the prescribed ______

(A) Form No. 30

(B) Form No. 31

(C) Form No. 32

(D) Form No. 33

47. Every claim for refund shall be made within ________ from the last day of the assessment year to which the claim is related.

(A) one year

(B) six months

(C) two year

(D) three year

ANSWERS:

1.	(A)	**2.**	(C)	**3.**	(D)	**4.**	(C)	**5.**	(A)	**6.**	(A)	**7.**	(B)
8.	(A)	**9.**	(D)	**10.**	(B)	**11.**	(A)	**12.**	(B)	**13.**	(C)	**14.**	(C)
15.	(D)	**16.**	(A)	**17.**	(B)	**18.**	(D)	**19.**	(B)	**20.**	(B)	**21.**	(D)
22.	(C)	**23.**	(C)	**24.**	(A)	**25.**	(B)	**26.**	(A)	**27.**	(B)	**28.**	(C)
29.	(A)	**30.**	(C)	**31.**	(D)	**32.**	(C)	**33.**	(C)	**34.**	(C)	**35.**	(C)
36.	(C)	**37.**	(B)	**38.**	(D)	**39.**	(A)	**40.**	(A)	**41.**	(D)	**42.**	(B)
43.	(B)	**44.**	(D)	**45.**	(A)	**46.**	(A)	**47.**	(A)				

PAST EXAMINATION MCQs

1. Dec 2014: An appeal against the order of Tribunal to the High Court shall be filed within —

(A) 120 Days from the date of order

(B) 180 Days from the date of order

(C) 120 Days from the date on which such order is received

(D) 180 Days from the date of receipt of order

2. June 2015: The time-limit for revision by Commissioner of Income Tax (CIT) u/s 264 is—

(A) 3 Months

(B) 6 Months

(C) One year

(D) Two years

3. Dec 2015: The maximum penalty leviable for failure to get accounts audited or to furnish report u/s 44AB is —

(A) ₹ 75,000

(B) ₹ 1,00,000

(C) ₹ 1,50,000

(D) ₹ 3,00,000

4. Dec 2015: An order passed by the Commissioner (Appeals) should be communicated to —

(A) Assessee

(B) CIT who has jurisdiction over the case

(C) Both the assessee and CIT

(D) The assessee through CIT

5. Dec 2015: As per 234F of the Income Tax Act, 1961 maximum fee for failure to file return of income before the 31st day of December of the assessment year is —

(A) ₹ 1,000

(B) ₹ 10,000

(C) ₹ 5,000

(D) ₹ 2,000

6. Dec 2015: The premises of an assessee within the jurisdiction of an Assessing Officer can be surveyed by such Income-tax Authority —

(A) After sun-set and before sunrise

(B) After sunrise but before sun-set

(C) Any time during 24 hours

(D) After 11 AM

7. Dec 2015: The order passed by the Assessing Officer when challenged before the Commissioner (Appeals) under section 246A, memorandum of appeal should be filed in —

(A) Form No. 35

(B) Form No. 36

(C) Form No. 36A

(D) Form No. 38

8. Dec 2015: The Commissioner of Income-tax is empowered to revise the assessment order of the Assessing Officer when the same is erroneous and pre-judicial to the interest of revenue. Such power is vested in the Commissioner of Income-tax under —

(A) Section 263
(B) Section 246C
(C) Section 264
(D) Sections 263 and 264

9. Dec 2015: The income of non-resident from the business of operation of aircraft in respect of carrying of cargo or passenger in India shall be taxable as per section 44BBA @ —

(A) 5% of the amount received or receivable
(B) 10% of the amount received or receivable
(C) 15% of the amount received or receivable
(D) 7.5% of the amount received or receivable.

10. Dec 2015: Authority for Advance Rulings shall not allow an application where the question raised —

(A) Is already pending before the Supreme Court
(B) Involves determination of fair market value of any property
(C) Relates to a transaction designed *prima facie* for the avoidance of income tax
(D) All of the above

11. Dec 2015: The advance ruling pronounced by the Authority for Advance Ruling as per Section 245 is binding:

(1) In respect of transaction for which ruling has been sought
(2) On income-tax authorities
(3) On the applicant
(4) On all other persons having similar transaction.

Select the correct answer from the options given below —

(A) (1), (2) and (3)
(B) (1) and (3)
(C) (2) and (3)
(D) (1), (2), (3) and (4).

12. June 2016: The time-limit for making revisional order under Section 263(2) and 263(3) is —

(A) 6 months from the date of assessment
(B) 6 months from the date of order
(C) One year from the end of the financial year in which the order was passed
(D) None of the above

13. Dec 2016: Penalty for failure to collect tax at source, as a percentage of tax to be collected is -

(A) 25%
(B) 100%
(C) 75%
(D) 50%

14. Dec 2016: A survey is conducted in the premises of the assessee and assessments are reopened for some assessment years. An application for settlement could be made to the Settlement Commission when the additional amount of the income-tax payable on the income disclosed in the application exceeds —

(A) ₹ 50 lakh
(B) ₹ 25 lakh
(C) ₹ 10 lakh
(D) ₹ 100 lakh

15. Dec 2016: When an assessee fails to furnish any information relating to a specified domestic transaction, the quantum of penalty as a percentage of value of the transaction would be -

(A) 2%
(B) 1%
(C) 5%
(D) 3%

16. Dec 2016: The order of revision passed by Commissioner u/s 264 is -

(A) Appealable before Commissioner (Appeals)
(B) Appealable before Appellate Tribunal
(C) Appealable before High Court
(D) Not appealable

17. Dec 2016: Any person who is aggrieved by order passed by the Appellate Tribunal may make the appeal to High Court within -

(A) 30 days

(B) 60 days

(C) 90 days

(D) 120 days

18. Dec 2016: Revision of an order which is prejudicial to the revenue is made under -

(A) Section 264

(B) Section 260

(C) Section 263

(D) Section 262

19. Dec 2016: As per Section 271A, failures to keep, maintain or retain books of account would attract penalty of -

(A) ₹ 10,000

(B) ₹ 1,00,000

(C) ₹ 2,000

(D) ₹ 25,000

20. June 2017: Mr. Balwant received assessment order passed under section 143(3) on 10.1.2019. He wants to prefer an appeal before CIT (Appeals) against the assessment order. The time limit for preferring appeal is .... days from the date of receipt of assessment order.

(A) 15

(B) 30

(C) 35

(D) 60

21. June 2017: An assessment order under section 143(3) dated 15.9.2018 was served on the assessee on 25.9.2018. The Commissioner wants to make a revision of the order passed under section 143(3) by invoking section 263. The time limit for passing revision order under section 263 is:

(A) 31st March, 2019

(B) 31st March, 2020

(C) 31st March, 2021

(D) 26th September, 2022

22. June 2017: Mr. Rajan did not appear before the Assessing Officer in response to a notice issued under section 143(2). He repeatedly absented from appearing before the Assessing Officer. How much could be the quantum of penalty the Assessing Officer could levy on Mr. Rajan for the failure?

(A) ₹ 2,000

(B) ₹ 5,000

(C) ₹ 10,000

(D) ₹ 20,000

23. June 2017: Penalty for failure to furnish report under Section 92E is:

(A) ₹ 25,000

(B) 2% of the value of international transactions

(C) ₹ 1,00,000

(D) ₹ 1,50,000

24. Dec 2017: Padmaja Traders a partnership firm with turnover of ₹ 140 lakhs omitted to get the books of account audited under section 44AB. The amount of penalty leviable for failure to get the accounts audited under section 4AB is:

(A) ₹ 10,000

(B) ₹ 70,000

(C) ₹ 1,50,000

(D) ₹ 20,000

25. Dec 2017: The amount specified in notice of demand must be paid within .... days otherwise the assessee would be treated as assessee in default.

(A) 10

(B) 15

(C) 30

(D) 60

26. Dec 2017: Mr. Bimal received assessment order passed by the Assessing Officer on 10.1.2019. What is the time limit within which the appeal has to be filed to CIT (Appeals) in case the assessee wants to challenge the order of the Assessing Officer?

(A) 10 days after the receipt of order

(B) 15 days after the receipt of order

(C) 30 days after the date of order

(D) 30 days after the date of receipt

ANSWERS:

1.	(C)	2.	(C)	3.	(C)	4.	(C)	5.	(C)	6.	(B)	7.	(A)
8.	(A)	9.	(A)	10.	(D)	11.	(A)	12.	(C)	13.	(B)	14.	(A)
15.	(A)	16.	(D)	17.	(D)	18.	(C)	19.	(D)	20.	(B)	21.	(C)
22.	(C)	23.	(C)	24.	(B)	25.	(C)	26.	(D)				

HINTS FOR PAST EXAMINATION MCQs:

24. Failure to get accounts audited u/s 44AB or furnish audit report along with return of income is liable to penalty lower of the following two:

- 0.5% of total sales/turnover
- ₹ 1,50,000.

CHAPTER 17

TAX PLANNING, TAX MANAGEMENT & BASIC OF INTERNATIONAL TAXATION

MCQs ON THEORY

1. The basic objectives of tax planning are:

1. Minimization of litigation
2. Unproductive investment
3. Healthy growth of economy
4. Reduction of tax liability

Select the correct answer from the options given below -

(A) (1) & (3)

(B) (3) & (4)

(C) (2), (1) & (4)

(D) (3), (1) & (4)

2. Any income arising from an international transaction shall be computed having regard to the _____

(A) Uncontrolled price

(B) Resale price

(C) Identical goods price

(D) Arm's length price

3. GAAR means -

(A) General Anti-Avoidance Rules

(B) General Anti-Agreement Rules

(C) General Avoidance-Agreement Rules

(D) General Avoidance-Agreement Regulations

4. ________ refers to a situation where a person tries to reduce his tax liability by deliberately suppressing the income or by inflating the expenditure showing the income lower than the actual income and resorting to various types of deliberate manipulations.

(A) Tax avoidance

(B) Tax evasion

(C) Tax management

(D) Tax haven

5. Provisions of transfer pricing are not applicable if -

(A) in a case where the computation of income has the effect of reducing the income chargeable to tax

(B) in a case where the computation of income has the effect of increasing the loss

(C) Neither (A) nor (B)

(D) Both (A) and (B)

6. Any planning which, though done strictly according to legal requirements defeats the basic intention of the Legislature behind the statute could be termed as instance of ________

(A) Tax evasion

(B) Tax management

(C) Tax avoidance

(D) All of the above

7. Two enterprises shall be considered as associated enterprises if at any time during the previous year, following condition is satisfied -

(A) More than one third of the board of directors of one enterprise, is appointed by the other enterprise.

(B) One enterprise guarantees not less than 10% of the total borrowings of the other enterprise.

(C) One enterprise holds, directly or indirectly, shares carrying 25% of the voting power in the other enterprise.

(D) A loan advanced by one enterprise to the other enterprise constitutes less than 50% of the book value of the total assets of the other enterprise.

8. Permissive tax planning is -

(A) is tax planning under the express provisions of tax laws

(B) is based on the measures which circumvent the law.

(C) refers to year to year planning to achieve some specific or limited objective

(D) all of the above

9. Specified domestic transaction (not being an international transaction) in case of an assessee means any prescribed transactions where the aggregate of such transactions entered into by the assessee in the previous year exceeds a sum of _____

(A) ₹ 2 Crore

(B) ₹ 200 Crore

(C) ₹ 2,000 lakhs

(D) ₹ 5,000 lakhs

10. Under Sections 60 to 65 of the Income-tax Act, 1961 the income of the other persons is clubbed in the income of the assessee. If the assessee is in a position to plan in such a way that these provisions do not get attracted, such a plan would work in favour of the tax payer because it would increase his disposable resources. Such arrangement could be termed as ______

(A) Tax evasion

(B) Tax avoidance

(C) Purposive tax planning

(D) Long-range-planning

11. Which of the following is not method of calculating arm's length price?

(A) Resale price method

(B) Cost plus method

(C) Profit split method

(D) Repeated distribution method

12. ______ means systematic, well-organized steps taken by an organization in order to ensure compliance with tax laws within the specified time and in the specified manner with a view to minimize the tax cost.

(A) Tax evasion

(B) Tax avoidance

(C) Tax management

(D) All of the above

13. Match the following:

	List I		*List II*
P.	Double Taxation Relief	1.	Comparable uncontrolled price
Q.	Transfer pricing	2.	Section 90
R.	Unilateral Relief	3.	Tax credit method
S.	Deemed associated enterprise	4.	Shareholding by same person more than 26%
		5.	Section 91

Select the correct answer from the options given below -

	P	**Q**	**R**	**S**
(A)	3	1	2	1
(B)	2	4	5	4
(C)	3	1	5	4
(D)	2	4	4	5

14. If total value of international transactions as per books of account of assessee is up to ______, the assessee need not to maintain specified information and documents, but he will have to substantiate that income from international transactions computed as per Section 92.

(A) ₹ 1 lakhs

(B) ₹ 10 lakhs

(C) ₹ 1 Crore

(D) ₹ 2 Crore

15. Provisions relating to bilateral relief of double taxation are contained in -

(A) Section 90A

(B) Section 90

(C) Section 91

(D) Section 91A

16. As per Section 92D, the specified information and documents are to be maintained for a period of ______

(A) 8 years from the end of the relevant previous year

(B) 5 years from the end of the relevant Assessment Year

(C) 8 years from the end of the relevant assessment year

(D) 10 years from the end of the relevant previous year

17. Under ______ deduction is allowed of the tax paid in source country from the tax payable in India.

(A) Exemption method

(B) Tax credit method

(C) Relief method

(D) Any of the above

18. The Assessing Officer or the Commissioner (Appeals) may require person who has entered into an international transaction or specified domestic transaction to furnish specified information or documents within ________ from date of receipt of notice issued in this regard.

(A) 15 days

(B) 30 days

(C) 60 days

(D) 45 days

19. Provisions relating to unilateral relief of double taxation are contained in -

(A) Section 90

(B) Section 90A

(C) Section 91

(D) Section 92B

20. Which of the following condition(s) is/are essential for claiming unilateral relief of double taxation?

(1) Assessee is a resident in India during the relevant previous year.

(2) Income is deemed to accrue or arise in India during the previous year.

(3) Income in question has been subjected to income-tax in the foreign country in the hands of the assessee

(4) There is no agreement u/s 90 for the relief.

Select the correct answer from the options given below

(A) (3) and (4) only

(B) (3), (1) & (2)

(C) (1) & (3) only

(D) Except (2) all other

21. The assessee shall be entitled to a deduction from the Indian income-tax payable by him u/s 91 -

(I) Doubly taxed income × Indian rate of tax

(II) Doubly taxed income × Rate of tax paid in other country

Select the correct answer from the options given below -

(A) (I) only

(B) (I) or (II) whichever is greater

(C) (II) only

(D) (I) or (II) whichever is less

22. If any person fails to furnish audit report as required u/s 92E, he will be liable to penalty of ________

(A) ₹ 1 lakh

(B) 2% of value each international transaction

(C) Both (A) and (B)

(D) Both (A) and (B) whichever is more

23. For the purpose of unilateral relief, Indian rate of tax means -

(A) the rate determined by dividing the amount of Indian income-tax by the total income before giving deduction u/ss 80C to 80U

(B) the rate determined by dividing the amount of Indian income-tax by the total income before giving deduction u/ss 80C to 80U, u/s 90 & u/s 91.

(C) the rate determined by dividing the amount of Indian income-tax by the total income before giving relief u/s 91

(D) the rate determined by dividing the amount of Indian income-tax by the total income before giving relief u/ss 90 & 91

PRACTICAL MCQs

24. Hi-Fi Ltd., an Indian company and has following incomes:

Income from business in India	5,70,000
Income from business in foreign country	3,24,000

As per ADT agreement, ₹ 3,24,000 is taxable in India. However, it can also be taxed in the foreign country @ 11.85% which can be set off against Indian tax liability. Find out the Indian tax liability.

(A) ₹ 2,40,530

(B) ₹ 2,76,250

(C) ₹ 2,57,190

(D) ₹ 2,66,690

25. Natwarlal, aged 65 years is resident in India and his gross total income is 20,73,600. He has deposited ₹ 33,600 in PPF. His income from foreign country is ₹ 6,54,000 which is also taxable in India. Natwarlal has paid tax of 38,400 in foreign country. According to ADT agreement, income is taxable in the country in which it is earned and not in other country. However, in the other country, such income can be included for computation of tax rate. Find out the Indian tax liability.

(A) ₹ 6,28,200

(B) ₹ 4,86,950

(C) ₹ 4,90,010

(D) ₹ 6,47,050

26. Mr. Kharat, a resident Indian and aged 36 years, has following income for the previous year 2018-2019:

Income from business in India	2,75,000
Commission (gross) from a company in China	3,30,000
[Tax paid in China ₹ 66,000]	
Dividend (gross) from a company in China	99,000
[Tax paid in China ₹ 19,800]	
Interest on fixed deposit with banks in India	2,20,000

India has no double tax avoidance agreement with China. Compute the income and tax payable by Mr. Kharat for AY 2019-2020.

(A) 1,13,090

(B) 54,220

(C) 52,510

(D) 60,580

27. A sold a machine to B (Associated enterprise) and in turn B sold the same machinery to C (an independent party) at sale margin of 30% for ₹ 5,60,000 but B has incurred 5,600 in sending the machine to C. Here Arm's length price would be ______

(A) ₹ 3,86,400

(B) ₹ 5,60,000

(C) ₹ 5,54,400

(D) ₹ 3,92,000

ANSWERS:

1.	(D)	**2.**	(D)	**3.**	(A)	**4.**	(B)	**5.**	(D)	**6.**	(C)	**7.**	(B)
8.	(A)	**9.**	(C)	**10.**	(C)	**11.**	(D)	**12.**	(C)	**13.**	(C)	**14.**	(C)
15.	(B)	**16.**	(C)	**17.**	(B)	**18.**	(B)	**19.**	(C)	**20.**	(D)	**21.**	(D)
22.	(A)	**23.**	(C)	**24.**	(A)	**25.**	(B)	**26.**	(B)	**27.**	(A)		

PAST EXAMINATION MCQs

1. Dec 2014: An exercise undertaken to minimise tax liability through the best use of all available allowances, deductions, exclusions, exemptions, etc., to reduce income-tax liability is known as —

(A) Tax evasion

(B) Tax planning

(C) Tax avoidance

(D) Tax dodging

2. Dec 2014: According to the Organization for Economic Co-operation and Development (OECD), the following parameters are considered to decide whether a jurisdiction is tax haven or not —

(A) Rate of tax applicable

(B) Withholding personal financial information

(C) Lack of transparency

(D) All of the above

3. Dec 2014: Two enterprises shall be considered as associated enterprises if at any time during the previous year, following condition is satisfied —

(A) Holding 25% voting power in another enterprise

(B) Advancing of loan which is at least 51% of the book value of the assets of the borrower enterprise

(C) Providing guarantee for at least 5% of the total borrowings of enterprise

(D) Tapping at least 50% of raw material from the enterprise

4. Dec 2014: The following methods as per section 92C are used in determination of arm's length prices for international transactions and specified domestic transaction except —

(A) Comparable uncontrolled price method

(B) Resale price method

(C) Cost method

(D) Transactional net margin method

5. Dec 2014: A sold a machine to B (associated enterprise) and in turn B sold the same machinery to C (an independent party) at sale margin of 30% for ₹ 4,00,000 but B has incurred ₹ 4,000 in sending the machine to C. From the above data, determine arm's length price —

(A) ₹ 2,76,000

(B) ₹ 2,80,000

(C) ₹ 4,00,000

(D) ₹ 1,20,000

6. Dec 2014: GAAR stands for —

(A) Government anti-avoidance rules

(B) General anti-avoidance rules

(C) General agreement-avoidance rules

(D) Government anti-agreement rules

7. June 2015: The Income-tax Act, 1961 empowers the Central Government to enter into double taxation avoidance agreements with other countries u/s —

(A) 87

(B) 88

(C) 90

(D) None of the above

8. June 2015: Which of the following double taxation avoidance agreement (DTAA) emphasises on residence principle —

(A) UN Model

(B) US Model

(C) OECD Model

(D) Andean Model

9. June 2015: As per transfer pricing provisions, an advance pricing agreement (APA) is valid for —

(A) Such period as specified in the APA, but not exceeding 3 consecutive years

(B) Such period as specified in the APA, but not exceeding 5 consecutive years

(C) 2 Years

(D) None of the above

10. Dec 2015: A legal entity that exists in one jurisdiction but is owned or controlled primarily by taxpayers of different jurisdiction is called —

(A) Collaborative foreign corporation

(B) Controlled foreign corporation

(C) Customised future company

(D) Co-operative control society

11. Dec 2015: Double taxation relief for incomes taxed in the countries with which no agreement exists is governed by —

(A) Section 91

(B) Section 89

(C) Section 93

(D) None of the above

12. Dec 2015: Tax planning is honest and right approach to attain the maximum benefit of taxation laws within its framework only. Objectives of tax planning are:

(1) Productive investment

(2) Un-healthy growth of economy

(3) Minimisation of litigation

(4) Increase in tax liability

Select the correct answer from the options given below —

(A) (1), (2) and (3)

(B) (1) and (3)

(C) (1), (2) and (4)

(D) (1), (2), (3) and (4)

13. Dec 2015: The provisions of transfer pricing are applicable with effect from 1st April, 2012 to specified domestic transactions entered into by the assessee in the previous year in aggregate of —

(A) ₹ 300 lakh

(B) ₹ 500 lakh

(C) ₹ 2,000 lakh

(D) ₹ 1,000 lakh

14. Dec 2015: XYZ has sold a machine to ABC (associate enterprise) for ₹ 3 lakh which was sold by ABC to PQR, an unrelated party, on the sale margin of 30% for ₹ 5,00,000 and has also incurred an amount of ₹ 10,000 in sending the machine to PQR. The arm's length price of this transaction will be —

(A) ₹ 3,40,000

(B) ₹ 3,50,000

(C) ₹ 3,00,000

(D) ₹ 5,00,000

15. Dec 2015: ABC Ltd. entered into international transactions with Allen Inc. of USA during the year ended on 31st March, 2019 totalling ₹ 1,000 lakh, but failed to keep and maintain the information and documents in respect of such international transactions. The Assessing Officer can levy a penalty on ABC Ltd. for this default u/s 271AA up to —

(A) ₹ 10,00,000

(B) ₹ 20,00,000

(C) ₹ 50,00,000

(D) ₹ 1,50,000

16. June 2016: Acrylic Ltd. sourced its new materials from Breeze Ltd. The relationship of associated enterprises would be established when Acrylic Ltd. buys raw material from Breeze Ltd. exceeding —

(A) 50% of total raw material purchased

(B) 90% of total raw material purchased

(C) 25% of total raw material purchased

(D) 35% of total payments for purchases

17. June 2016: Which of the following person is eligible to seek advance ruling —

(A) Senior citizens

(B) Professional

(C) Foreign companies

(D) Non-residents

18. June 2016: Anand, a resident in India, has a total income of ₹ 10,00,000 during the previous year 2018-2019. This income includes foreign income of ₹ 3,00,000 from a country with which India does not have agreement to avoid double taxation. Tax levied by the foreign country on that foreign income was ₹ 40,000 and the tax payable as per the Indian rate on the total income amounts to ₹ 2,50,000. The double taxation relief allowable to Anand shall be—

(A) ₹ 40,000

(B) ₹ 75,000

(C) ₹ 35,000

(D) ₹ 25,000

19. June 2016: The authority for advance ruling in income-tax is appointed by —

(A) The President of India

(B) The Central Board of Direct Taxes

(C) The Central Government

(D) The Chief Commissioner of Income-tax

20. June 2016: The validity period of advance pricing agreement (APA) is -

(A) 2 Years

(B) 3 Years

(C) 5 Years

(D) 7 Years

21. Dec 2016: One of the benefits of advance pricing agreement is —

(A) Minimum tax

(B) Certainty in tax liability

(C) Exemption from tax

(D) Exemption from penalty

22. Dec 2016: When an advance ruling is obtained, it is applicable to —

(A) All assessees

(B) The applicant who sought it

(C) Those notified

(D) None of the above

23. Dec 2016: Assessee who are eligible to approach Dispute Resolution Panel regardless of the transfer pricing adjustment are -

(A) Co-operative societies

(B) Foreign companies

(C) Domestic companies

(D) Firms and LLPs

24. Dec 2016: The monetary limit for aggregate transactions between two enterprises to fall in the category of specified domestic transaction is -

(A) ₹ 5 Crore

(B) ₹ 3 Crore

(C) ₹ 20 Crore

(D) ₹ 25 Crore

25. Dec 2016: An advance pricing agreement shall not be valid for more than -

(A) 3 Years

(B) 5 Years

(C) 4 Years

(D) 7 Years

26. Dec 2016: Payment of advance tax on or before due date is termed as -

(A) Tax planning

(B) Tax management

(C) Tax evidence

(D) None of the above

27. Dec 2016: Two enterprises will be said to be associate enterprises if one enterprise holds -

(A) 25%

(B) 51%

(C) 26%

(D) 30%

28. June 2017: Tax heaven does not have the following feature:

(A) There is no income-tax

(B) There is lack of transparency

(C) It is an island owned by certain individual

(D) There is no exchange of information

29. June 2017: Mr. Anuj (Age 65) resident of India has total income in India of ₹ 6 lakhs. His income from a foreign country with which there is no DTAA between India and that country, was ₹ 2 lakhs (converted). He paid income-tax at 20% on the foreign income in that country. His net tax liability for the assessment year 2019-2020 after relief under section 91 is:

(A) ₹ 54,600

(B) ₹ 61,800

(C) ₹ 72,100

(D) ₹ 82,400

30. June 2017: Which of the following powers is not vested with the Transfer Pricing Officer?

(A) Power of search and seizure under section 132

(B) Power of survey under section 133A

(C) Power of levy penalty under section 271G

(D) Power to call for information under 133(6)

31. June 2017: The monetary limit for international transaction for getting exemption from documentations prescribed in Section 92D is:

(A) ₹ 500 lakhs

(B) ₹ 300 lakhs

(C) ₹ 2000 lakhs

(D) ₹ 100 lakhs

32. June 2017: Which of the following persons is not eligible to seek advance ruling?

(A) Non-resident

(B) Resident having transaction with non-resident

(C) A resident in respect of impermissible avoidance agreement

(D) Resident having transaction with not ordinarily resident

33. June 2017: General Anti Avoidance Rules (GAAR) is applicable from the assessment year:

(A) 2015-2016

(B) 2017-2018

(C) 2020-2021

(D) 2016-2017

34. Dec 2017: When the international transaction involves transfer of unique intangibles, the method to be applied for the purpose of determining arm's length price would be:

(A) Comparable uncontrolled price method

(B) Resale price method

(C) Profit split method

(D) Cost plus method

35. Dec 2017: The provisions of specified domestic transactions will apply where the aggregate of transactions covered by criteria as given in section 92BA exceeds:

(A) ₹ 1 Crore in a year

(B) ₹ 3 Crores in a year

(C) ₹ 5 Crores in a year

(D) ₹ 20 Crores in a year

36. Dec 2017: The advance pricing agreement is valid for not more than .... consecutive previous years.

(A) 3

(B) 5

(C) 7

(D) 9

ANSWERS:

1.	(B)	2.	(D)	3.	(B)	4.	(C)	5.	(A)	6.	(B)	7.	(C)
8.	(B)	9.	(B)	10.	(B)	11.	(A)	12.	(B)	13.	(C)	14.	(A)
15.	(B)	16.	(A)	17.	(D)	18.	(A)	19.	(C)	20.	(C)	21.	(B)
22.	(B)	23.	(B)	24.	(C)	25.	(B)	26.	(B)	27.	(C)	28.	(C)
29.	(A)	30.	(A)	31.	(D)	32.	(D)	33.	(**)	34.	(D)	35.	(D)
36.	(B)												

** *MCQs are wrongly drafted. For further clarification please see the hints.*

HINTS FOR PRACTICAL MCQs:

24.

Income from business in India	5,70,000
Income from a business in a foreign country	3,24,000
Total Income	8,94,000
Total Tax Payable in India (8,94,000 × 31.2%)	2,78,928
(-) Tax paid in foreign country (3,24,000 × 11.85%)	(38,394)
Net Indian tax Liability	2,40,534
Rounded off	2,40,530

25.

Gross total income	20,73,600
(-) Deduction u/s 80C (PPF)	(33,600)
Total income	20,40,000
(+) Foreign income	6,54,000
Total income for tax purpose	26,94,000
Tax on total income (*basic exemption ₹ 3,00,000*)	6,18,200
(+) Education cess @ 4%	24,728
Total tax	6,42,928

$$\text{Average rate of tax} = \frac{6,42,928}{26,94,000} \times 100 = 23.87\%$$

Indian tax liability = 20,40,000 × 23.87% = 4,86,948

Rounded up = 4,86,950

26.

Income from business in India	2,75,000
Commission (gross) from a company in China	3,30,000
Dividend (gross) from a company in China	99,000
Interest on fixed deposit with banks in India	2,20,000
Total income	9,24,000
Tax on total income (*basic exemption ₹ 2,50,000*)	97,300
(+) Education cess @ 4%	3,892
Total tax	1,01,192

$$\text{Indian rate of tax} = \frac{1,01,192}{9,24,000} \times 100 = 10.95\%$$

$$\text{Foreign rate of tax} = \frac{85,800}{4,29,000} \times 100 = 20\%$$

Total tax		1,01,192
(-) Relief u/s 91; Lower of following two		
- Doubly taxed income × Indian rate of tax (4,29,000 × 10.95%)	46,975	
- Doubly taxed income × Rate of tax paid in other country (4,29,000 × 20%)	85,800	(46,975)
Indian tax liability		54,217
Rounded up		54,220

27.

Resale price	5,60,000
(-) Margin @ 30%	(1,68,000)
	3,92,000
(-) Expenses	(5,600)
	3,86,400

PAST EXAMINATION MCQs HINTS:

18.

Relief u/s 91: Lower of following two

- Doubly taxed income × Indian rate of tax (3,00,000 × 25%)	75,000
- Doubly taxed income × Rate of tax paid in other country (3,00,000 × 13.3333%)	40,000

$$\text{Indian rate of tax} = \frac{2,50,000}{10,00,000} \times 100 = 25\%$$

$$\text{Foreign rate of tax} = \frac{40,000}{3,00,000} \times 100 = 13.3333\%$$

29.

Income in India	6,00,000
Income from foreign country	2,00,000
Total income	8,00,000
Tax on total income (*basic exemption ₹ 3,00,000*)	70,000
(+) Education cess @ 4%	2,800
Total tax	72,800

$$\text{Indian rate of tax} = \frac{72,800}{8,00,000} \times 100 = 9.1\%; \text{Foreign rate of tax} = 20\%$$

Total tax		72,800
(-) Relief u/s 91; Lower of following two		
- Doubly taxed income × Indian rate of tax (2,00,000 × 9.1%)	18,200	
- Doubly taxed income × Rate of tax paid in other country (2,00,000 × 20%)	40,000	(18,200)
Indian tax liability		54,600

33. GAAR Provisions are applicable from PY 2017-2018 *i.e. AY 2018 - 2019*. Question asks for assessment year but AY 2018-2019 is not given in any option and ***hence none of the given option is correct.***

PART B

INDIRECT TAX (30 MARKS)

CHAPTER 18

GOODS & SERVICES TAX (GST)

MCQs ON THEORY

Introduction

1. GST is one of the widely accepted indirect taxation system prevalent in more than _____ countries across the globe.

(A) 60

(B) 110

(C) 130

(D) 140

2. Which country first introduced GST?

(A) America

(B) France

(C) Egypt

(D) Italy

3. Which of the following statement is correct?

(A) GST is based on principle of 'pay as you earn'.

(B) GST is a destination based tax.

(C) GST is technically paid by consumers but it is actually funded by suppliers.

(D) All of the above

4. In Australian model of GST, _____

(A) Tax is collected by the Centre and State respectively.

(B) Tax is collected by States only.

(C) Tax is collected by the Centre and distributed to the States.

(D) Tax is collected by States and agreed share is given to the Centre.

5. _____ envisages a combination of Central Excise, Service Tax and VAT to make it a common base of GST to be levied both by the Centre and the States separately.

(A) Kelkar-Shah Model

(B) Bagchi-Poddar Model

(C) Modi-Shah Model

(D) Canada Model

6. Which of the following Country follows dual GST model?

(A) Brazil

(B) Canada

(C) India

(D) All of the above

7. GST is a _____ based tax.

(A) Consumption

(B) Destination

(C) Consumption or destination

(D) None of the above

8. GST is a comprehensive tax regime covering ____

(A) Goods

(B) Services

(C) Both goods and services

(D) Goods, services & imports

9. Goods and Services Tax is a tax levied on goods and services imposed at each point of -

(A) Demand

(B) Cash sale

(C) Supply

(D) Manufacturing

10. Which of the following statement is correct?

(I) GST is technically paid by suppliers but it is actually funded by consumers.

(II) Under GST, input tax credit is provided throughout the value chain for creditable acquisition.

Select the correct answer from the options given below -

(A) (I) only

(B) (II) only

(C) Both (I) and (II)

(D) Neither (I) nor (II)

11. Which of the following taxes have been subsumed under GST?

(1) Central Excise Duty

(2) Service Tax

(3) VAT

(4) Luxury Tax

Select the correct answer from the options given below -

(A) (1) & (2)

(B) (3), (1) & (2)

(C) (4), (1), (3) & (2)

(D) None of the above

12. Which of the following taxes have been subsumed under GST?

(*i*) Entertainment tax

(*ii*) Entry tax

(*iii*) Gift tax

(*iv*) Basic custom duty

Select the correct answer from the options given below -

	(*i*)	**(*ii*)**	**(*iii*)**	**(*iv*)**
(A)	✓	×	✓	×
(B)	×	✓	✓	×
(C)	×	✓	×	✓
(D)	✓	✓	×	×

13. Who among the following suggested a comprehensive Goods & Services Tax based on VAT principle?

(A) Empowered Committee State Finance Ministers

(B) Kelkar Task Force

(C) Committee headed by Pranav Mukherjee

(D) Committee of Commissioners of Trade Taxes

14. A special purpose vehicle setup by the Government to provide IT infrastructure and services to the Central and State Governments, tax payers and other stakeholders for implementation of the GST is -

(A) Non-Government company

(B) Private limited company

(C) Non-profit making company

(D) All of the above

15. On which date the Constitution (One Hundred & Twenty-Second Amendment) Bill seeking to amend the Constitution to introduce the GST and subsume state Value Added Tax, octroi and entry tax, luxury tax, etc. was introduced in the Lok Sabha on _____ by the Honourable Minister of Finance, Mr. Arun Jaitley.

(A) December 19, 2014

(B) December 25, 2014

(C) June 21, 2014

(D) June 14, 2016

16. On _______, the Ministry of Finance released draft model law on GST in public domain for views and suggestion.

(A) June 14, 2015

(B) June 14, 2016

(C) June 21, 2016

(D) August 8, 2016

17. Which of the following is the main decision-making body that was formed to finalize the design of GST?

(A) GST Company

(B) Empowered Council

(C) Empowered Committee
(D) GST Council

18. Who is the Chairman GST Council?
(A) Vice President of India
(B) Union Finance Minister
(C) Leader of opposition
(D) Chief Justice of Supreme Court

19. In the GST Council, a decision will be taken by a _____ majority with the Centre having a _____ and the states the remaining ______
(A) three-fourth; one-third vote; two-third
(B) one-third; three-fourth vote; two-third
(C) one-half; one-third vote; two-third
(D) three-fourth; two-third vote; one-third

20. GST was first levied by France in _____
(A) 1947
(B) 2001
(C) 1954
(D) 1979

21. Under GST the taxable event is _____
(A) Sale of goods
(B) Provision of services
(C) Sale of goods or provision of services or both
(D) Supply of goods or services or both

22. India has chosen ____ model of dual GST.
(A) USA
(B) UK
(C) Canadian
(D) Japan

23. Which of the following country has maximum GST tax slab?
(A) Australia

(B) China

(C) Greece

(D) India

24. What does "I" stand for IGST?

(A) International

(B) Integral

(C) Integrated

(D) Intra

25. The headquarter of GST Council is at _____

(A) Mumbai

(B) New Delhi

(C) Hyderabad

(D) Ahmadabad

26. Which of the following goods have been kept out of GST?

1. Alcoholic liquor for human consumption
2. Readymade garments
3. Natural gas
4. Treadmill
5. Aviation turbine fuel
6. Petrol
7. Air conditioner
8. High speed diesel
9. Electricity
10. Cycle

Select the correct answer from the options given below -

(A) 1, 6, 2, 5, 3, 9 & 5

(B) 5, 4, 9, 5, 3, 6 & 5

(C) 9, 1, 7, 5, 3, 5 & 6

(D) 3, 6, 5, 1, 9 & 5

27. On Intra-State supply of goods or services which of the following type of GST can be levied?

(A) State GST (SGST)

(B) Central GST (CGST)

(C) Integrated GST (IGST)

(D) (A) & (B)

28. Under the GST regime, liability to pay tax arises when a person crosses the turnover threshold of_____ and _____ for North Eastern & Special Category States.

(A) ₹ 20 lakhs; ₹ 10 lakhs

(B) ₹ 10 lakhs; ₹ 20 lakhs

(C) ₹ 50 lakhs; ₹ 20 lakhs

(D) ₹ 25 lakhs; ₹ 15 lakhs

29. Which of the following type of GST is payable on all Inter-State supply of goods and/or services?

(A) State GST (SGST)

(B) State GST (SGST) & Integrated GST (IGST)

(C) Central GST (CGST) & Integrated GST (IGST)

(D) Integrated GST (IGST)

30. Under the GST regime, a Composition Scheme, which is mainly devised for small taxpayers, provides concessional rate of tax and filing of _____

(A) Monthly returns

(B) Quarterly returns

(C) Yearly returns

(D) No return at all

31. To be eligible for registration under Composition scheme it is required that the aggregate turnover of a registered taxpayer should not exceed ______ in the preceding financial year. (The limit is _____ for North Eastern & Special Category States)

(A) ₹ 1,00,00,000; ₹ 75,00,000

(B) ₹ 75,00,000; ₹ 75,00,000

(C) ₹ 50,00,000; ₹ 25,00,000

(D) ₹ 30,00,000; ₹ 40,00,000

32. Which of the following country has second highest maximum GST tax slab after India?

(A) Netherland

(B) Argentina

(C) South Korea

(D) Ireland

33. Match the following identifying taxable event for each type of duty/tax:

List I	*List II*
(P) Excise Duty	1. Sale
(Q) GST	2. Manufacture
(R) Service Tax	3. Supply
(S) VAT	4. Gift
	5. Provided or agreed to be provided

Select the correct answer from the options given below -

	(P)	**(Q)**	**(R)**	**(S)**
(A)	2	3	1	5
(B)	3	2	5	1
(C)	2	3	1	4
(D)	2	3	5	1

The CGST Act, 2017

34. The Union Government ***presented*** the Central Goods and Services Tax Bill, 2017 in Lok Sabha on _______

(A) 27th March, 2017

(B) 29th March, 2017

(C) 7th March, 2016

(D) 22nd March, 2017

35. Central Goods and Services Tax Bill, 2017 was ***passed*** by Lok Sabha on -

(A) 27th March, 2017

(B) 29th March, 2017

(C) 7th March, 2016

(D) 22nd March, 2017

36. The CGST Act, 2017 extends to -

(A) Whole of India excluding the State of Jammu & Kashmir

(B) Whole of India

(C) Whole of India excluding the State of Jammu & Kashmir and Union territories

(D) Whole of India excluding the State of Jammu & Kashmir but including Union territories

37. Which of the following authority is appointed or authorized to pass order or decision under the CGST Act, 2017?

(A) Adjudicating Authority

(B) Assessing Authority

(C) GST Council

(D) Revisional Authority

38. As per CGST Act, 2017 "Adjudicating Authority" include -

I. Revisional Authority

II. Authority for Advance Ruling

III. CBEC

Select the correct answer from the options given below -

(A) I

(B) III

(C) II

(D) None of the above

39. The Rajya Sabha *passed* the Central Goods and Services Tax Bill, 2017 on -

(A) 6th April, 2017

(B) 13th April, 2017

(C) 4th April, 2017

(D) 20th April, 2017

40. As per the CGST Act, 2017, "business" includes -

(*a*) Adventure not for a pecuniary benefit

(*b*) Any activity or transaction undertaken by the Central Government, a State Government or any local authority in which they are engaged as public authorities.

Select the correct answer from the options given below -

(A) (b) only

(B) Both (a) and (b)

(C) Neither (a) nor (b)

(D) (a) only

41. The President *assented* the Central Goods and Services Tax Bill, 2017 on -

(A) 8th April, 2017

(B) 10th April, 2017

(C) 6th April, 2017

(D) 13th April, 2017

42. Composite supply is similar to the concept of ________ which is under service tax laws earlier.

(A) Mixed service

(B) Mixed service where one service is taxable while other service is exempt.

(C) Bundled service

(D) None of the above

43. As per CGST Act, 2017, ________ means a distinguishable component of an enterprise that is engaged in the supply of individual goods or services or a group of related goods or services which is subject to risks and returns that are different from those of the other business verticals.

(A) Business

(B) Business vertical

(C) Organization

(D) Continuous business

44. In mixed supply -

(A) goods or services are naturally bundled and usually provided together in normal course of business.

(B) the goods or services can be sold separately

(C) consist of two or more taxable supplies of goods or services

(D) (C) & (B)

45. As per the CGST Act, 2017, "continuous supply of goods" means -

(1) Supply of goods on recurrent basis

(2) Supply of goods as the Government may specify by notification

Select the correct answer from the options given below -

(A) (1) only

(B) Neither (1) nor (2)

(C) Both (1) and (2)

(D) (2) only

46. As per the CGST Act, 2017, "exempt supply" means supply of any goods or services -

(*i*) Which attracts nil rate of tax

(*ii*) Which may be wholly exempt from tax u/s 11 or u/s 6 of the IGST Act

(*iii*) Which is non-taxable supply

Select the correct answer from the options given below -

(A) (ii)

(B) (i)

(C) (iii)

(D) All of the above

47. Which of the following can be treated as "goods" under the CGST Act, 2017?

I. Movable property

II. Money and securities

III. Actionable claim

Select the correct answer from the options given below -

	I	II	III
(A)	✓	×	✓
(B)	×	✓	✓
(C)	×	✓	×
(D)	✓	×	×

48. As per the CGST Act, 2017, "input" -

(1) Includes capital goods to be used by a supplier in the course or furtherance of business

(2) Means any service used or intended to be used by a supplier in the course or furtherance of business

Select the correct answer from the options given below -

(A) (2) is correct but not (1)

(B) (1) is correct but not (1)

(C) Both (1) and (2)

(D) (A) and (B) both are incorrect

49. ______ is a supply made by a taxable person to a recipient consisting of two or more taxable supplies of goods or services or both, or any combination thereof, which are naturally bundled and supplied in conjunction with each other in the ordinary course of business, one of which is a principal supply.

(A) Mixed supply

(B) Composite supply

(C) Integrated supply

(D) Mixed demand

50. According to Section 2(6) of the CGST Act, 2017 "aggregate turnover" -

(A) means value of all taxable supplies

(B) includes the value of inward supplies on which tax is payable by a person on reverse charge basis

(C) includes exempt supplies, exports of goods or services or both and Inter-State supplies

(D) (A) and (C)

51. Identify which of the following is *"Composite Supply"* and which is *"Mixed Supply"* as per the provisions of the CGST Act, 2017:

(1) Where goods are packed and transported with insurance

(2) A supply of a package consisting of canned foods, sweets, chocolates, cakes, dry fruits, aerated drinks and fruit juices which are supplied for a single price

Select the correct answer from the options given below -

	(1)	**(2)**
(A)	Mixed Supply	Composite Supply
(B)	Composite Supply	Mixed Supply
(C)	Mixed Supply	Mixed Supply
(D)	Composite Supply	Composite Supply

52. Supply has been very subjectively and inclusively defined in the CGST Act, 2017 and _____ of the said Act specifies the scope of supply.

(A) Section 7

(B) Section 5

(C) Section 8

(D) Section 4

53. Provisions relating to "Composition levy" are contained in _____ of the CGST Act, 2017.

(A) Section 11

(B) Section 10

(C) Section 15

(D) Section 12

54. ______ of the CGST Act, 2017 lists activities that are to be treated as supply even if they are without a consideration.

(A) Schedule II

(B) Schedule I

(C) Schedule III

(D) Schedule IV

55. As per Section 12 of the CGST Act, 2017 where the supplier of taxable goods receives an amount up to ₹ 1,000 in excess of the amount indicated in the tax invoice, the time of supply to the extent of such excess amount shall, at the option of the said supplier, be the ______ in respect of such excess amount.

(A) date of issue of invoice

(B) date of payment

(C) date of dispatch of goods

(D) earlier of the above three

56. Some activities are to be treated as supply under GST even if they are without a consideration.

(A) False

(B) True

(C) Partly incorrect

(D) None of the above

57. Section 15 of the CGST Act states that, the value of taxable supply under GST is the -

(A) Transaction value

(B) Total sales or services value

(C) Value as determined by the Assessing Officer and accepted by the assessee

(D) None of the above

58. Which of the following is deemed to be supply and liable to GST as per the Schedule I to the CGST Act, 2017?

(I) Gifts from an employer to an employee of ₹ 40,000.

(II) XYZ Ltd. gives laptops to office staff on which it had already availed ITC in past.

Select the correct answer from the options given below -

(A) (I) but not (II)

(B) (II) but not (I)

(C) Both (I) and (II) are supply and liable to GST

(D) Both (I) and (II) are not supply and not liable to GST

59. Consider following statements.

Statement I:

In the previous indirect tax regime, supply of goods between principal to his agent or agent to his principal was taxable but under GST, such a supply will not be taxable.

Statement II:

Any services imported by a taxable person from a related person or from any of his other establishments, will attract GST.

Select the correct answer from the options given below -

(A) Statement I is correct but Statement II is incorrect

(B) Statement II is correct but Statement I is incorrect

(C) Both Statements I & II are correct

(D) Both Statements I & II are incorrect

60. As per Section 10 of the CGST Act, a registered person, whose aggregate turnover in the preceding financial year did not exceed ____ may opt to composite tax.

(A) ₹ 20 lakhs

(B) ₹ 50 lakhs

(C) ₹ 75 lakhs

(D) ₹ 100 lakhs

61. Transaction value means the price actually paid or payable for the supply of goods or services or both where -

(A) the supplier and the recipient of the supply are not related

(B) the price is the sole consideration for the supply.

(C) (A) or (B)

(D) (A) and (B)

62. ______ of the CGST Act, 2017 specifies activities to be treated as supply of goods or supply of services.

(A) Schedule IV

(B) Schedule II

(C) Schedule I

(D) Schedule III

63. As per Section 8 of the CGST Act, 2017, a mixed supply comprising two or more supplies shall be treated as a supply of that particular supply which attracts the -

(A) Lowest rate of tax

(B) Average rate of tax

(C) Highest rate of tax

(D) Any of the above

64. Match the following with reference to provisions of the CGST Act, 2017:

List I	*List II*
P. Composition levy	1. Section 14
Q. Scope of supply	2. Section 12
R. Time of supply of goods	3. Section 10
S. Change in rate of tax	4. Section 7
	5. Section 11

Select the correct answer from the options given below -

	P	*Q*	*R*	*S*
(A)	3	4	1	2
(B)	5	4	2	1
(C)	3	4	2	1
(D)	5	3	1	2

65. A deposit given in respect of the supply of goods or services or both shall not be considered as payment made for supply and hence cannot be included in transaction value.

(A) True

(B) False

(C) Partly true

(D) None of the above

66. Which of the following is/are included in 'value of supply' under the CGST Act, 2017?

1. Commission and packing expenses
2. Discount recorded in invoice
3. taxes, duties, cesses, fees and charges levied under any law for the time being in force
4. Subsidies provided by the Central Government and State Government

Select the correct answer from the options given below -

(A) 1 & 2

(B) 2 & 3

(C) 1 & 3

(D) 2 & 4

67. As per Section 15 of the CGST Act, 2017, which of the following persons shall be deemed to be "related persons"?

(*a*) Employer and employee

(*b*) Person directly or indirectly holding 21% share in company

(*c*) Members of the same family

Select the correct answer from the options given below -

(A) (a) & (b)

(B) (b) & (c)

(C) (a) & (c)

(D) All of the above

68. Activities which are neither supply of goods nor supply of services are specified in _____ to the CGST Act, 2017.

(A) Schedule III

(B) Schedule V

(C) Schedule I-A

(D) Schedule II-A

69. Is it mandatory to capitalize the capital goods in books of account?

(A) Yes

(B) No

(C) Optional

(D) None of the above

70. Which of the following activity is deemed to be supply and liable to GST under the CGST Act, 2017?

(A) Services by employee to employer

(B) Functions performed by the Members of Parliament

(C) Supply of goods by unincorporated association to a member thereof

(D) Services of funeral

71. For a special category States (Assam, Arunachal Pradesh, Manipur, Meghalaya, Mizoram, Nagaland, Tripura, Sikkim and Himachal Pradesh) a registered person having aggregate turnover up to ______ can opt composition scheme. However, for other States such limit is ______ or such amount as may be recommended by the GST Council.

(A) ₹ 5 lakh; ₹ 50 lakh

(B) ₹ 50 lakh; ₹ 1 Crore

(C) ₹ 100 lakh; ₹ 500 lakh

(D) ₹ 500 lakh; ₹ 5,000 Crore

72. Under the GST, whether credit on capital goods can be taken immediately on receipt of the goods?

(A) After usage of such capital goods

(B) No

(C) Yes

(D) None of the above

73. Which of the following activity does not amounts to supply of goods or service and hence not liable to GST under the CGST Act, 2017?

(A) Licence to occupy land

(B) Renting of immovable property

(C) Works Contract

(D) Services by any Court or Tribunal

74. The term *"used in the course or furtherance of business"* in definition of capital goods under the CGST Act, 2017 means?

(A) It should be directly correlated to output supply

(B) It is planned to use in the course of business

(C) It is used in the course of business

(D) It is used in the course of business for making outward supply

75. Which of the following is included (✓) and which is excluded (×) from the definition of "aggregate turnover" as defined in CGST Act, 2017?

(1) Exempt supplies

(2) Central tax

(3) Exports of goods or services

(4) Union territory tax

Select the correct answer from the options given below -

	(1)	**(2)**	**(3)**	**(4)**
(A)	×	✓	×	✓
(B)	✓	✓	×	×
(C)	✓	×	✓	×
(D)	×	×	✓	✓

76. Credit on inputs should be availed based on -

(A) Receipt of goods

(B) Receipt of Documents

(C) Both

(D) Either receipt of documents or Receipt of goods

77. As per Section 10 of the CGST Act, 2017, a registered person, whose aggregate turnover in the preceding financial year did not exceed ₹ 50 lakh, may opt to pay, in lieu of the tax payable by him, an amount calculated at such rate as may be prescribed, but not exceeding, - (*a*)_____ of the turnover in State or turnover in Union territory in case of a manufacturer, (*b*)_____ of the turnover in State or turnover in Union territory in case of persons engaged in making supplies referred to in clause (*b*) of paragraph 6 of Schedule II, and (*c*)_____ of the turnover in State or turnover in Union territory in case of other suppliers, subject to such conditions and restrictions as may be prescribed.

(A) 1%; 2.5%; 0.5%

(B) 2.5%; 2.5%; 1%

(C) 0.5%; 1%; 2.5%

(D) 1%; 2%; 0.5%

78. Input tax credit on capital goods and Inputs can be availed -

(A) In thirty six instalments

(B) In twelve instalments

(C) In one instalment

(D) In six instalments

79. Which of the following is included in the definition of "aggregate turnover" as defined in CGST Act, 2017?

(I) Value of inward supplies on which tax is payable by a person on reverse charge basis

(II) Inter-State supplies of persons having the same Permanent Account Number

Select the correct answer from the options given below -

(A) Neither (II) nor (I)

(B) Both (I) and (II)

(C) (I) only

(D) (II) only

80. Who among the following is included in definition of "Agriculturist" as defined in Section 2(7) of the CGST Act, 2017?

I. Individual

II. HUF

III. Partnership Firm

IV. Company

Select the correct answer from the options given below -

(A) I

(B) I & II

(C) I, II & III

(D) I, II, III & IV

81. Which of the following statement is true?

(A) Composite tax scheme is not available for services sector except restaurants.

(B) A registered person under composition scheme is not permitted to collect tax and neither he will be eligible for any input tax credit.

(C) Both (A) and (B)

(D) Neither (A) nor (B)

82. The tax-paying documents in Section 16(2) is -

(A) Supply invoice by the recipient

(B) Acknowledged copy of tax paid to department

(C) Bill of entry, Invoice raised on RCM supplies, etc.

(D) Any of the above

83. Point of taxation means -

(A) the point in time when GST is actually paid by the supplier of goods or services

(B) the point in time when GST is actually paid after taking input credit by the supplier of goods or services

(C) the point in time when goods have been deemed to be supplied or services have been deemed to be provided

(D) the point in time when GST return is filed by the supplier of goods or services

84. Who can avail the benefit of Input Tax Credit (ITC) under the GST?

(A) Registered person

(B) Person who has applied for registration and his application is pending

(C) Unregistered person

(D) Any of the above

85. The point of taxation enables us to determine -

(A) Tax

(B) Value

(C) Due date for payment of tax

(D) All of the above

86. Which of the following section of the CGST Act, 2017 deals with provisions relating to *"time of supply of goods"*?

(A) Section 11

(B) Section 12

(C) Section 13

(D) Section 14

87. Which of the following section of the CGST Act, 2017 deals with provisions relating to *"time of supply of services"*?

(A) Section 12

(B) Section 13

(C) Section 14

(D) Section 15

88. Which of the following condition is required to be fulfilled to avail Input Tax Credit (ITC)?

1. Registered taxable person should be in possession of tax invoice or debit note.
2. Registered taxable person should have received the goods or services or both.
3. Registered taxable person should have furnished the return u/s 39.
4. Supplier should have actually paid the tax charged in respect of the supply to the Government.

Select the correct answer from the options given below -

(A) 1 only

(B) 1 and 2 only

(C) 1, 2 & 3 only

(D) 1, 2, 3 & 4

89. If a recipient fails to pay the amount of supply along with tax payable thereon within ______ from the date of issue of invoice, the recipient will be liable to pay along with the output tax liability an amount equal to the input tax credit availed by the recipient along with interest thereon

(A) 3 months

(B) 2 months

(C) 4 months

(D) 6 months

90. Which of the following section makes the provisions relating to "*apportionment of credit and blocked credits* (*i.e. restriction on utilization of credit*)"?

(A) Section 17

(B) Section 18

(C) Section 16A

(D) Section 19

91. Where goods or services or both are used partly for taxable supplies including zero rated supplies and partly for exempted supplies then input tax credit is available in respect that input which is attributable to the -

(A) Taxable supplies

(B) Taxable supplies & exempted supplies

(C) Taxable supplies & zero rated supplies

(D) Both (B) & (C)

92. Is a composition dealer registered under the old law required to obtain final GST registration?

(A) No, old number will continue

(B) Yes, mandatory for all Composition dealers

(C) Yes, subject to the turnover crossing the GST Turnover limit

(D) No, will be governed by old law

93. In which of the following case input tax credit (ITC) under the GST is allowed?

i. Input tax on motor vehicle and other conveyance used for taxable supply of transportation of such vehicles or conveyances

ii. Input tax on motor vehicle and other conveyance are used for making available transportation facility to officers and directors of the company

Select the correct answer from the options given below -

(A) i only

(B) ii only

(C) Both i and ii

(D) Neither i nor ii

94. Input tax credit as per the VAT law will be carried forward as:

(A) CGST

(B) SGST

(C) IGST

(D) CGST or SGST at the option of the supplier

95. In which of the following case(*s*) Input Tax Credit (ITC) under the GST is not available?

(1) Caterer using a service of another caterer

(2) Travel benefits extended to employees on vacation such as leave or home travel concession.

(3) Input service used for further supply of works contract service.

(4) Input tax credit on goods or services by a person for construction of immovable property.

Select the correct answer from the options given below -

(A) (2) & (4)

(B) (1) & (3)

(C) (2) & (1)

(D) (3) & (2)

96. Whether credit brought forward under the old law is eligible as input tax credit under GST law?

(A) Yes, without any restrictions

(B) Credit irregularly taken under the earlier law will also be available

(C) Eligible credit under the earlier law will be available only if it is also admissible as input tax credit under the GST law

(D) Eligible credit under the earlier law is available on a proportionate basis

97. Unavailed CENVAT Credit on Capital Goods will be carried forward as _______ under the GST Law.

(A) CGST

(B) SGST

(C) IGST

(D) CGST or SGST at the option of the supplier

98. In which of the following case input tax credit (ITC) under the GST is allowed?

(*i*) Input tax paid under Composition Scheme.

(*ii*) Input tax on goods or services used for personal consumption.

(*iii*) Input tax with respect to goods lost.

(*iv*) Input tax on goods given as gifts or free samples.

Select the correct answer from the options given below -

(A) (i)

(B) (ii)

(C) (iii)

(D) None of the above

99. The inputs in stock should be used or intended to be used for making:

(A) Taxable supplies

(B) Exempt supplies

(C) Either taxable or exempt supplies

(D) Both taxable and exempt supplies

100. Which of the following will not be considered as eligible duties and taxes for availing input tax credit?

(A) Additional duty leviable u/s 3(5) of the CTA

(B) Basic Customs Duty

(C) Central Excise

(D) Service Tax

101. If the principal send 'input' to job worker but does not received the same within _____ then input tax credit allowed to him will be reversed.

(A) 3 years

(B) 1 year

(C) 2 years

(D) 6 months

102. Which of the following section makes the provisions relating to maintenance of "accounts and other records" under the CGST Act, 2017?

(A) Section 35

(B) Section 34

(C) Section 36

(D) Section 40

103. Where supply has been made before the date of implementation of GST, no tax shall be payable -

(A) If tax/duty has been paid under the earlier law

(B) If goods were exempted under the earlier law

(C) If the goods were non-taxable under the earlier law

(D) All of the above

104. Match the following with reference to provisions of CGST Act, 2017.

List I	*List II*
1. Persons not liable for registration	P. Section 21
2. Procedure for registration	Q. Section 22
3. Persons liable for registration	R. Section 23
4. Compulsory registration in certain cases	S. Section 24
5. Deemed registration.	T. Section 25
	U. Section 26

Select the correct answer from the options given below -

	1	*2*	*3*	*4*	*5*
(A)	R	T	U	S	Q
(B)	T	R	U	S	Q
(C)	R	T	Q	S	U
(D)	R	T	Q	U	S

105. The time duration for retention of accounts and records under GST is until expiry of ______ from the due date of furnishing of annual return for the year pertaining to such accounts and records.

(A) seventy-two months (i.e. 6 years)

(B) thirty six months (i.e. 3 years)

(C) sixty months (i.e. 5 years)

(D) ninety six months (i.e. 8 years)

106. As per Section 2(47) of the CGST Act, 2017, "exempt supply" means supply of any goods or services or both -

(A) Which attracts nil rate of tax

(B) Which may be wholly exempt from tax

(C) Includes non-taxable supply

(D) All of the above

107. Continuous supply of services means a supply of services which is provided, or agreed to be provided, continuously or on recurrent basis, under a contract, for a period exceeding ______ with periodic payment obligations and includes supply of such services as the Government may, subject to such conditions, as it may, by notification, specify.

(A) 3 months
(B) 5 months
(C) 2 months
(D) 6 months

108. The time duration for retention of accounts and records under the CGST Act, 2017 is until expiry of seventy-two months from -

(A) Expiry of year to which accounts and records pertains
(B) End of two year for the year pertaining to such accounts and records
(C) End of six months to which accounts and records pertains
(D) The due date of furnishing of annual return for the year pertaining to such accounts and records.

109. ________ of the CGST Act, 2017 specifies the time limit for raising invoice for goods.

(A) Section 31
(B) Section 30
(C) Section 32
(D) Section 28

110. The tax invoice should contain the _____, the tax charged thereon and such other particulars as may be prescribed.

(A) Description
(B) Quantity
(C) Value of goods
(D) All of the above

111. As per Section 2(12) of the CGST Act, 2017, "associated enterprises" shall have the same meaning as assigned to it in _______ of the Income-tax Act, 1961.

(A) Section 93A
(B) Section 93
(C) Section 92
(D) Section 92A

112. Which of the following person is/are included in definition of "family" as defined under Section 2(49) of the CGST Act, 2017 —

(i) Spouse

(ii) Children of the person

(iii) Dependent parents

(iv) Dependent grand-parents

(v) Dependent brothers and sisters

Select the correct answer from the options given below -

(A) (i), (ii) & (iii) only

(B) (i), (ii), (iii) & (iv) only

(C) All except (iii) & (iv)

(D) All (i) to (v)

113. Every supplier shall be liable to be registered under the CGST Act, 2017 in the State or Union territory, from where he makes a taxable supply of goods or services or both, if his aggregate turnover in a financial year exceeds ______.

However, where such person makes taxable supplies of goods or services or both from any of the Special Category States, he shall be liable to be registered if his aggregate turnover in a financial year exceeds ______.

(A) ₹ 10 lakh; ₹ 20 lakh

(B) ₹ 50 lakh; ₹ 20 lakh

(C) ₹ 20 lakh; ₹ 50 lakh

(D) ₹ 20 lakh; ₹ 10 lakh

114. As per Section 2(79) of the CGST Act, 2017, non-taxable territory means -

(A) the territory within the India but declared by Government as territory not liable to GST

(B) the territory which is inside the taxable territory

(C) the territory which is outside the taxable territory

(D) the territory which is outside the India with which government of India has bilateral agreement

115. Which of the following persons are required to be registered under the GST?

1. Supplier of taxable goods or services
2. Every person who holds a license under an existing law
3. An agriculturist
4. Any person engaged exclusively in the business of supplying goods or services or both that are not liable to tax or wholly exempt from tax

Select the correct answer from the options given below -

(A) 1 & 2

(B) 2 & 3

(C) 1, 2 & 4

(D) All of the above option are correct

116. Which of the following products is/are presently not covered under the GST regime?

(a) Alcoholic liquor

(b) Petrol

(c) Natural gas

(d) Aviation turbine fuel

Select the correct answer from the options given below -

(A) (a) & (b)

(B) (b) & (c)

(C) (a), (b) & (d)

(D) All of the above

117. Which of the following is/are included in definition of "Goods" as defined under Section 2(52) of the CGST Act, 2017 --

I. Money

II. Actionable claim

III. Securities

IV. Growing crops

Select the correct answer from the options given below -

(A) IV only

(B) II & III

(C) II & IV

(D) I & II

118. As per Section 22(3) of the CGST Act, where a business carried on by a taxable person registered is transferred, whether on account of succession or otherwise, to another person as a going concern, the transferee or the successor, as the case may be, -

(A) shall not be liable to take fresh registration again under the GST.

(B) shall be liable to be registered at the option of such transferee or successor

(C) shall be liable to be registered with effect from the date of such transfer or succession

(D) shall be liable to be registered within 1 year from the date of transfer

119. "Council" means the Goods & Services Tax Council established under _____ of the Constitution of India.

(A) Article 278

(B) Article 278B

(C) Article 279

(D) Article 279A

120. As per Section 2(37) of the CGST Act, 2017, "credit note" means a document issued by a registered person under -

(A) Section 34(1)

(B) Section 35(1)

(C) Section 36(2)

(D) Section 37(3)

121. Which of the following persons are required to be registered under the GST?

I. Inter-State supplier

II. Persons who are required to pay tax under reverse charge mechanism

III. Input Service Distributor

IV. Electronic Commerce Operator

Select the correct answer from the options given below -

(A) I only

(B) I and II only

(C) I, II & III except IV

(D) All I, II, III & IV

122. Where the goods against an invoice are received in lots or instalments, the registered person shall be entitled to take credit upon receipt of the -

(A) First lot or instalment

(B) Last lot or instalment

(C) 50% goods

(D) (A) or (B) at the option of such registered person

123. Where the goods or services or both are used by the registered person partly for the purpose of any business and partly for other purposes -

(A) the amount of credit shall be restricted to 50% of the input tax

(B) the amount of credit shall be 100%

(C) the amount of credit shall be restricted to 60% of the input tax

(D) the amount of credit shall be restricted to so much of the input tax as is attributable to the purposes of his business

124. Annual return u/s 44 of the CGST Act, 2017 is required to filed -

(A) Physically

(B) Electronically

(C) Physically or electronically

(D) Electronically but if online submission is not possible then with permission of proper officer physical return can be filed.

125. A banking company or a financial institution including a non-banking financial company, engaged in supplying services by way of accepting deposits, extending loans or advances shall have the option to either comply with the provisions of Section 17(2), or avail of, every month, an amount equal to ______ of the eligible input tax credit on inputs, capital goods and input services in that month and the rest shall lapse.

(A) 75%

(B) 50%

(C) 25%

(D) 80%

126. Where the inputs sent for job work are not received back by the principal after completion of job work or otherwise or are not supplied from the place of business of the job worker in accordance with Section 143(1) within ______ of being sent out, it shall be deemed that such inputs had been supplied by the principal to the job worker on the day when the said inputs were sent out.

(A) One year

(B) 180 days

(C) Two year

(D) 200 days

127. Which of the following person is not liable to be registered under the CGST Act, 2017?

1. Person engaged exclusively in the business of supplying goods or services or both that is not liable to tax
2. Person engaged exclusively in the business of supplying goods or services or both that is wholly exempt from tax

Select the correct answer from the options given below -

(A) 1 only

(B) 2 only

(C) Both 1 and 2

(D) Neither 1 nor 2

128. Every person who is liable to be registered under Section 22 or 24 shall apply for registration in every such State or Union territory in which he is so liable within _______ from the date on which he becomes liable to registration, in such manner and subject to such conditions as may be prescribed.

(A) 30 days
(B) 20 days
(C) 10 days
(D) 60 days

129. As per Section 25 of the CGST Act, 2017, a casual taxable person or a non-resident taxable person shall apply for registration at least _____ prior to the commencement of business.

(A) 5 days
(B) 10 days
(C) 7 days
(D) 30 days

130. Which of the following person/entities shall be granted a Unique Identity Number u/s 25 of the CGST Act, 2017?

(I) Specialized agency of the United Nations Organization
(II) Embassy of foreign countries
(III) Specialized branches of non-resident large taxpayer
(IV) Multilateral Financial Institution

Select the correct answer from the options given below -

(A) (I) only
(B) (I) and (II) only
(C) All (I) to (IV)
(D) (I), (II) & (III)

131. As per Section 27 of the CGST Act, 2017, the certificate of registration issued to a casual taxable person or a non-resident taxable person shall be valid for the period specified in the application for registration or ______ from the effective date of registration, whichever is earlier and such person shall make taxable supplies only after the issuance of the certificate of registration.

(A) 180 days

(B) 90 days

(C) 100 days

(D) 60 days

132. Where the capital goods sent for job work are not received back by the principal within a period of ____ of being sent out, it shall be deemed that such capital goods had been supplied by the principal to the job worker on the day when the said capital goods were sent out.

(A) One year

(B) Two years

(C) Three years

(D) Four years

133. As per Section 44 of the CGST Act, 2017 every registered person, *other than an Input Service Distributor, a person paying tax u/s 51 or 52, a casual taxable person and a non-resident taxable person,* shall furnish an annual return for every financial year electronically in such form and manner as may be prescribed on or before the ____

(A) 31st December of financial year.

(B) 31st March following the end of such financial year.

(C) One month before the start of each financial year.

(D) 31st December following the end of such financial year.

134. Application for cancellation of registration shall be filed electronically in -

(A) Form GST REG-16

(B) Form GST REG-17

(C) Form GST REG-15

(D) Form GST REG-14

135. The invoice in case of taxable supply of services shall be issued within a period of ______ from the date of supply of service. However, if the supplier is an insurance company or banking company or a financial institution or NBFC, invoice can be issued within ____ from the date of supply of service.

(A) 30 days; 45 days

(B) 45 days; 30 days
(C) 60 days; 90 days
(D) 90 days; 60 days

136. A registered person may, within _____ from the date of issuance of certificate of registration and in such manner as may be prescribed, issue a revised invoice against the invoice already issued during the period beginning with the effective date of registration till the date of issuance of certificate of registration to him.

(A) 1 month
(B) 2 month
(C) 3 month
(D) 4 month

137. Application for cancellation of voluntary registration shall not be considered before the expiry of _____ form the effective date of registration.

(A) 5 year
(B) 1 year
(C) 182 days
(D) 200 days

138. A registered person may not issue a tax invoice if the value of the goods or services or both supplied is less than _____ subject to such conditions and in such manner as may be prescribed.

(A) ₹ 100
(B) ₹ 200
(C) ₹ 500
(D) ₹ 1,000

139. The Proper Officer may cancel *suo motu* the registration where a person paying tax has not furnished returns for _____

(A) 3 consecutive tax periods
(B) 4 consecutive tax periods
(C) 2 consecutive tax periods
(D) 5 consecutive tax periods

140. Where the goods being sent or taken on approval for sale or return are removed before the supply takes place, the invoice shall be issued before or at the time of supply or ______ from the date of removal, whichever is earlier.

(A) 2 months

(B) 6 months

(C) 3 months

(D) 4 months

141. The Proper Officer may cancel *suo motu* the registration where any person who has taken voluntary registration has not commenced business within _____ from the date of registration.

(A) 3 months

(B) 6 months

(C) 4 months

(D) 12 months

142. Keeping prescribed books of account is compulsory under ______ of the CGST Act, 2017.

(A) Section 30

(B) Section 35

(C) Section 33

(D) Section 38

143. Any registered person, whose registration is cancelled by the proper officer on his own motion, may apply to such officer for revocation of cancellation of the registration in the prescribed manner within _____ from the date of service of the cancellation order.

(A) 180 days

(B) 120 days

(C) 90 days

(D) 30 days

144. As per Section 37(1) of the CGST Act, 2017, every registered person shall furnish electronically the details of outward supplies of goods or services or both effected during a tax period on or before the _______ and such details shall be communicated to the recipient of the said supplies within such time and in such manner as may be prescribed.

(A) 10th day of the next month
(B) 15th day of the quarter
(C) 15th day of the next month
(D) 10th day of the quarter

145. A dealer who has opted for composition scheme is required to file _____ as per Section 39 of the CGST Act, 2017.

(A) Monthly return
(B) Quarterly return
(C) Half yearly return
(D) Yearly return

146. Every registered person whose aggregate turnover during a financial year exceeds _____ shall get his accounts audited

(A) ₹ 1 Crore
(B) ₹ 2 Crore
(C) ₹ 5 Crore
(D) ₹ 10 Crore

147. As per Section 39 of the CGST Act, 2017, every taxable person registered as an Input Service Distributor shall, for every calendar month or part thereof, furnish, in such form and manner as may be prescribed, a return, electronically, within ______ after the end of such month.

(A) 10 days
(B) 15 days
(C) 13 days
(D) 20 days

148. If any registered person after furnishing a return discovers any omission or incorrect particulars therein, other than as a result of scrutiny, audit, inspection or enforcement activity by the tax authorities, he shall rectify such omission or incorrect particulars in the return to be furnished for the month or quarter during which such omission or incorrect particulars are noticed, subject to payment of interest. However, no such rectification of any omission or incorrect particulars shall be allowed after the due date for furnishing of return for the month of ________ following the end of the financial year, or the actual date of furnishing of relevant annual return, whichever is earlier.

(A) October or first quarter

(B) October or second quarter

(C) September or first quarter

(D) September or second quarter

149. Every registered person required audit his accounts shall furnish a copy of audited annual accounts and a reconciliation statement, duly certified, in ________, electronically through the common portal either directly or through a Facilitation Centre notified by the Commissioner.

(A) Form GSTR-9

(B) Form GSTR-8C

(C) Form GSTR-9C

(D) Form GSTR-8

150. Who is authorized to conduct audit under Section 35(5) of the CGST Act, 2017?

1. Chartered Accountant
2. Any person having master degree in finance of recognized university
3. Cost Accountant
4. Company Secretary

Select the correct answer from the options given below -

(A) 1, 3 & 4

(B) 4, 2, 3 & 1

(C) 1 only

(D) 1 or 3 only

151. Every registered person who is required to furnish a return u/s 39(1) and whose registration has been cancelled shall furnish a final return within ______ of the date of cancellation or date of order of cancellation, whichever is later, in such form and manner as may be prescribed.

(A) 6 months

(B) 3 months

(C) 2 months

(D) 4 months

152. Section 46 of the CGST Act, 2017 provides that where a registered person fails to furnish a return u/s 39 or 44 or 45, a notice shall be issued requiring him to furnish such return within ______ in such form and manner as may be prescribed.

(A) 10 days

(B) 15 days

(C) 30 days

(D) 60 days

153. Any registered person who fails to furnish the details of outward or inward supplies required u/s 37 or 38 or returns required u/s 39 or 45 by the due date shall pay a late fee of -

(A) ₹ 5,000

(B) ₹ 100 for every day during which such failure continues

(C) ₹ 200 for every day during which such failure continues

(D) ₹ 10,000

154. What is the maximum late fee for not furnishing the details of outward or inward supplies required u/s 37 or 38 or required returns u/s 39 or 45?

(A) ₹ 10,000

(B) ₹ 2,000

(C) ₹ 5,000

(D) ₹ 50,000

155. A Company Secretary can act as GST Practitioner?

(A) True

(B) False

(C) Partly true

(D) None of the above

156. Which of the following person can act as GST Practitioner?

1. Retired officer of the Commercial Tax Department of any State Government
2. Retired officer of nationalized banks
3. Sales Tax Practitioner having 6 years experience after his enrolment
4. A person working as Tax Return Preparer for 2 years from the date of his enrolment

Select the correct answer from the options given below -

	1	*2*	*3*	*4*
(A)	✓	✓	×	×
(B)	×	×	✓	✓
(C)	✓	×	×	✓
(D)	✓	×	✓	×

157. In which sequence IGST input credit has to be utilized?

(A) In sequence of IGST, CGST & SGST

(B) In sequence of SGST, CGST & IGST

(C) In sequence of CGST, IGST & SGST

(D) In sequence of UTGST, CGST, SGST & IGST

158. Section 50 of the CGST Act, 2017 provides that every person who is liable to pay tax but fails to pay the tax or any part thereof within the period prescribed, shall for the period for which the tax or any part thereof remains unpaid, pay, on his own, interest at such rate, not exceeding ______, as may be notified by the Government on the recommendations of the Council.

(A) 12%

(B) 18%

(C) 24%

(D) 28%

159. Application to work as GST Practitioner has to be made in -

(A) FORM GST PCT-5

(B) FORM GST PCT-2

(C) FORM GST PCT-4

(D) FORM GST PCT-1

160. As per GST Law only citizen of India can at as GST Practitioner.

(A) False

(B) True

(C) Partly true

(D) None of the above

161. Section 50 of the CGST Act, 2017 provides that taxable person who makes an undue or excess claim of input tax credit or undue or excess reduction in output tax liability, shall pay interest on such undue or excess claim or on such undue or excess reduction, as the case may be, at such rate not exceeding _____, as may be notified by the Government on the recommendations of the Council.

(A) 6%

(B) 24%

(C) 18%

(D) 30%

162. GST TDS provisions can apply where total value of supply, under a contact exceeds _____

(A) ₹ 2,50,000

(B) ₹ 5,00,000

(C) ₹ 10,00,000

(D) ₹ 2,00,000

163. In which sequence CGST input credit has to be utilized?

(A) In sequence of CGST, IGST & SGST

(B) In sequence of CGST & IGST

(C) In sequence of CGST, SGST & IGST

(D) CGST input credit can only be utilized against CGST and not against IGST or SGST.

164. The Government may mandate to deduct GST TDS @ _____ of taxable goods or services or both.

(A) 1%

(B) 2%

(C) 1.5%

(D) 0.5%

165. What is time limit for claiming refund under the GST Law?

(A) 1 year

(B) 2 year

(C) 180 days

(D) 5 years

166. A specialized agency of the United Nations Organization or any Multilateral Financial Institution and Organization, Consulate or Embassy of foreign countries or any other person or class of persons, as notified u/s 55, entitled to a refund of tax paid by it on inward supplies of goods or services or both, may make an application for refund, in prescribed form, before the expiry of _____ from the last day of the quarter in which such supply was received.

(A) 6 months

(B) 1 year

(C) 2 year

(D) 10 months

167. Unjust enrichment means -

(A) getting loss due to benefit of another.

(B) getting refund under indirect taxes.

(C) getting benefit at the expenses of another.

(D) increase in taxes due fault of another.

168. Section 60(3) of the CGST Act, 2017 provides that on sufficient cause being shown and for reasons to be recorded in writing, period stated in order to pay tax on provisional basis be extended by the *Joint or Additional Commissioner* for a further period not exceeding _____

(A) 12 months

(B) 8 months

(C) 3 months

(D) 6 months

169. Section 60(3) of the CGST Act, 2017 provides that on sufficient cause being shown and for reasons to be recorded in writing, period stated in order to pay tax on provisional basis be extended by the *Commissioner* for such further period not exceeding ____

(A) 4 years

(B) 1 year

(C) 2 years

(D) 5 years

170. Under GST Law refund will be normally paid by crediting tax to _____

(A) Customer Welfare Fund

(B) Consumer Welfare Fund

(C) State Welfare Fund

(D) Investors Welfare Fund

171. Where a registered person fails to furnish the return u/s 39 or 45, even after the service of a notice, the proper officer may proceed to assess the tax liability of the said person to the best of his judgment taking into account all the relevant material which is available or which he has gathered and issue an assessment order within a period of ______ from the date specified u/s 44 for furnishing of the annual return for the financial year to which the tax not paid relates.

(A) 5 years

(B) 4 years

(C) 3 years

(D) 8 years

172. In which sequence SGST input credit has to be utilized?

(A) In sequence of CGST, IGST & SGST

(B) In sequence of SGST & IGST

(C) In sequence of CGST, SGST & IGST

(D) SGST input credit can only be utilized against SGST and not against IGST or CGST.

173. In case of audit by tax authorities, the registered person shall be informed by way of a notice not less than _____ prior to the conduct of audit.

(A) 15 working days

(B) 30 working days

(C) 10 working days

(D) 45 working days

174. In which of the following case(*s*) GST refund is possible?

I. Zero rated supplies made without payment of tax

II. Supply of exempted goods

III. Excess input credit due to inverted duty structure

IV. Exporting the goods by availing duty drawback.

Select the correct answer from the options given below -

(A) II & IV

(B) I & III

(C) III & IV

(D) III & I

175. In which sequence UTGST input credit has to be utilized?

(A) In sequence of CGST, IGST & SGST

(B) In sequence of UTGST, CGST, IGST & SGST

(C) Only against CGST

(D) In sequence of UTGST & IGST

176. As per Section 60 of the CGST Act, 2017, in which of the following case provisional assessment is possible?

(1) Where taxable person is unable to determine the value of goods or services or both

(2) Where taxable person is unable to determine the rate of tax applicable

Select the correct answer from the options given below -

(A) (2) only

(B) Both (1) and (2)

(C) (1) only

(D) Neither (1) nor (2)

177. The person claiming refund has to establish that the incidence of such tax and interest had not been passed on to any other person. However, where the amount claimed as refund is less than ________, it shall not be necessary for the applicant to furnish any documentary and other evidences but he may file a declaration, based on the documentary or other evidences available with him, certifying that the incidence of such tax and interest had not been passed on to any other person.

(A) ₹ 2,000

(B) ₹ 20,000

(C) ₹ 2,00,000

(D) ₹ 20,00,000

178. Taxable person may request the proper officer in writing giving reasons for payment of tax on a provisional basis and the proper officer shall pass an order within a period of _____ from the date of receipt of request, allowing payment of tax on provisional basis at rate specified him.

(A) 60 days

(B) 90 days

(C) 120 days

(D) 30 days

179. The proper officer may, in the case of any claim for refund on account of zero-rated supply of goods or services or both, refund on a provisional basis, _____ of amount claimed, excluding the amount of input tax credit provisionally accepted for final settlement of the refund claim after due verification of documents furnished by the applicant.

(A) 95%

(B) 90%

(C) 80%

(D) 75%

180. The proper officer shall, within a period not exceeding ______ from the date of the communication of the order issued of provisional assessment, pass the final assessment order after taking into account required information for finalizing the assessment.

(A) 2 months

(B) 4 months

(C) 6 months

(D) 8 months

181. The proper officer shall issue the refund order refusing or accepting refund claim within ______ from the date of receipt of application complete in all respects.

(A) 15 days

(B) 45 days

(C) 60 days

(D) 30 days

182. Which of the following section of the CGST Act, 2017 makes the provisions relating to 'audit by tax authorities'?

(A) Section 64

(B) Section 65

(C) Section 66

(D) Section 67

183. Where a refund is withheld, the taxable person shall be entitled to interest at such rate not exceeding _____ as may be notified on the recommendations of the Council, if as a result of the appeal or further proceedings he becomes entitled to refund.

(A) 8%

(B) 6%

(C) 4%

(D) 9%

184. What is the time limit for completion of audit ordered by Commissioner under Section 65 of the CGST Act, 2017?

(A) 60 days
(B) 3 months
(C) 180 days
(D) 9 months

185. As per Section 54 of the CGST Act, 2017, if the amount of refund is less than ______ then refund will not be granted.

(A) ₹ 100
(B) ₹ 1,000
(C) ₹ 10,000
(D) ₹ 1,00,000

186. Which of the following section of the CGST Act, 2017 makes the provisions relating to 'special audit'?

(A) Section 64
(B) Section 65
(C) Section 66
(D) Section 68

187. Which of the following type of punishment can be imposed under GST Law?

(A) Civil punishment
(B) Criminal punishment
(C) Both (A) and (B)
(D) (A) only but not (B)

188. Section 56 of the CGST Act, 2017 provides that if any tax ordered to be refunded to any applicant is not refunded within ______ from the date of receipt of application, interest at such rate not exceeding ______ as may be specified in the notification issued by the Government on the recommendations of the Council shall be payable till the date of refund of such tax.

(A) 60 days; 6%
(B) 30 days; 9%
(C) 60 days; 9%
(D) 45 days; 12%

189. The audit ordered by Commissioner under Section 65 of the CGST Act, 2017 shall be completed within a period of 3 months from the date of commencement of the audit. Where the Commissioner is satisfied that audit in respect of such registered person cannot be completed within 3 months, he may, for the reasons to be recorded in writing, extend the period by a further period not exceeding ______

(A) 3 months

(B) 6 months

(C) 9 months

(D) 12 months

190. Where any claim of refund arises from an order passed by an adjudicating authority or Appellate Authority or Appellate Tribunal or Court which has attained finality and the same is not refunded within 60 days from the date of receipt of application filed consequent to such order, interest at such rate not exceeding ______ as may be notified by the Government on the recommendations of the Council shall be payable in respect of such refund from the date immediately after the expiry of 60 days from the date of receipt of application till the date of refund.

(A) 9%

(B) 12%

(C) 18%

(D) 24%

191. As per Section 132 of the CGST Act, 2017, where the amount of tax evaded or the amount of input tax credit wrongly availed or utilized or the amount of refund wrongly taken exceeds ₹ 500 lakh, the punishment is -

(A) Imprisonment for a term which may extend to 5 years and fine.

(B) Imprisonment for a term which may extend to 3 years and fine.

(C) Imprisonment for a term which may extend to 5 years or fine.

(D) Imprisonment for a term which may extend to 3 years or fine.

192. As per Section 132 of the CGST Act, 2017, where the amount of tax evaded or the amount of input tax credit wrongly availed or utilized or the amount of refund wrongly taken exceeds ₹ 200 lakh but does not exceed ₹ 500 lakh, the punishment is -

(A) Imprisonment up to 3 years or fine

(B) Imprisonment up to 3 years and fine

(C) Imprisonment up to 2 years and fine

(D) Imprisonment up to 2 years or fine

193. As per Section 132 of the CGST Act, 2017, where the amount of tax evaded or the amount of input tax credit wrongly availed or utilized or the amount of refund wrongly taken exceeds ₹ 100 lakh but does not exceed ₹ 200 lakh, the punishment is -

(A) Imprisonment only

(B) Fine only

(C) Imprisonment or fine

(D) Imprisonment and fine

194. Where any person convicted of an offence under section 132 is again convicted of an offence, then, he shall be punishable for the second and for every subsequent offence with imprisonment for a term which may extend to -

(A) 5 years or with fine

(B) 3 years and with fine

(C) 5 years and with fine

(D) 2 years or with fine

195. As per Section 132(3) of the CGST Act, 2017, in the absence of special and adequate reasons to the contrary to be recorded in the judgment of the Court punishment given above in Section 132(1) cannot be for a term not less than ______

(A) 2 months

(B) 3 months

(C) 4 months

(D) 6 months

196. As per the provisions of the CGST Act, 2017, the offences specified in Section 132(1)(*a*) to (*d*) and punishable under section 132(1)(*i*) shall be -

(A) cognizable

(B) bailable

(C) non-cognizable

(D) none of the above

197. Input tax credit as per the VAT law will be carried forward as -

(A) CGST

(B) SGST

(C) IGST

(D) CGST or SGST at the option of the supplier

198. Section 69 of the CGST Act, 2017 provides that all arrests should be made as per the provisions of -

(A) Code of Criminal Procedure, 1973

(B) Civil Procedure Code, 1908

(C) Indian Penal Code, 1860

(D) Foreign Exchange Management Act, 1999

199. Power of inspection, search and seizure under Section 69 of the CGST Act, 2017 can be initiated by Proper Officer not below the rank of -

(A) Superintendent

(B) Inspector

(C) Joint Commissioner

(D) Commissioner

200. The tax authorities may conduct audit u/s 65 at -

(A) the place of business of the registered person

(B) the place of residence of the registered person

(C) the office of the tax authorities

(D) (A) or (C)

IGST Act, 2017 & UTGST Act, 2017

201. The IGST Act, 2017 extends to the -

(A) whole of India except the State of Jammu & Kashmir.

(B) whole of India.

(C) whole of India except the State of Jammu & Kashmir & Pondicherry

(D) none of the above

202. The IGST Act, 2017 came into force on -

(A) 1st July, 2017

(B) 1st April, 2017

(C) 2nd July, 2017

(D) 13th April, 2017

203. The IGST Act, 2017 has -

(A) 8 Chapters

(B) 9 Chapters

(C) 10 Chapters

(D) 7 Chapters

204. The IGST Act, 2017 has total -

(A) 52 Sections

(B) 25 Sections

(C) 20 Sections

(D) 22 Sections

205. What is the maximum rate of tax that can be levied as IGST?

(A) 20%

(B) 28%

(C) 30%

(D) 40%

206. IGST has to be levied on value to be determined as per -

(A) Provisions of respective state laws from where movement of goods start

(B) Section 15 of the SGST Act, 2017

(C) Notification issued by Central Government from time to time

(D) Section 15 of the CGST Act, 2017

207. The IGST on goods imported into India shall be levied and collected in accordance with the provisions of ______ of the Customs Tariff Act, 1975 on the value as determined under the said Act at the point when duties of customs are levied on the said goods u/s 12 of the Customs Act, 1962.

(A) Section 3

(B) Section 4

(C) Section 5

(D) Section 6

208. A supply of goods shall be treated as supply of goods in the course of Inter-State trade or commerce where the location of the supplier and the place of supply are in -

(A) Two different States

(B) Two different Union territories

(C) A State and a Union territory

(D) Any of the above

209. Which of the following section of the IGST Act, 2017 makes provisions relating to "place of supply of goods"?

(A) Section 9

(B) Section 10

(C) Section 12

(D) Section 8

210. The place of supply of goods imported into India shall be -

(A) the location of the importer

(B) the location of the receiver of goods

(C) the location of the exporter

(D) all of the above

211. Which article mentions distribution of IGST among Centre and State?

(A) Article 246A

(B) Article 269A

(C) Article 279A

(D) Article 271A

212. IGST shall be levied and collected by the

(A) State Governments

(B) Government of India

(C) Partly by State Governments and partly by Central Government

(D) None of the above

213. The UTGST Act, 2017 has _____ covering _____

(A) 9 Chapters; 26 Sections

(B) 8 Chapters; 20 Sections

(C) 9 Chapters; 20 Sections

(D) 8 Chapters; 26 Sections

214. There shall be levied a tax called the Union Territory tax on all Intra-State supplies of goods or services or both, except on the supply of alcoholic liquor for human consumption, on the value determined u/s 15 of the CGST Act, 2017 and at such rates, not exceeding _____, as may be notified by the Central Government on the recommendations of the Council and collected in such manner as may be prescribed and shall be paid by the taxable person.

(A) 40%

(B) 20%

(C) 28%

(D) 10%

215. GST Compensation Law provides for compensating states that incur losses because of implementation of the Goods & Service Tax (GST) in first _____

(A) 3 years

(B) 5 years

(C) 10 years

(D) 12 years

216. The financial year ______ shall be taken as base year for the purpose of calculating compensation amount payable to the States.

(A) 2016-2017

(B) 2015-2016

(C) 2018-2019

(D) 2014-2015

217. As per Section 3 of the Goods & Services Tax (Compensation to States) Act, 2017, the projected nominal growth rate of revenue subsumed for a State during the transition period shall be -

(A) 10% p.a.

(B) 12% p.a.

(C) 14% p.a.

(D) 16% p.a.

PRACTICAL MCQs

218. If value of capital goods is ₹ 1,00,000 plus GST ₹ 18,000. Input credit of ₹ 18,000 on capital goods is taken. What will be the depreciable value of capital goods under the GST Law?

(A) ₹ 1,18,000

(B) ₹ 1,00,000

(C) ₹ 82,000

(D) ₹ 1,09,000

219. X sales goods to Y for ₹ 2,61,800 inclusive of SGST & CGST @ 5% each. Both X and Y are registered dealers. Net GST payable by X -

(A) ₹ 26,180

(B) ₹ 23,800

(C) ₹ 12,467

(D) ₹ 13,090

220. Mr. X purchases a product for ₹ 7,48,000 plus SGST & CGST @ 10% each from Mr. Y. He adds ₹ 57,200 as his profit and sells the customer by levying SGST & CGST @ 10%.

Cost to consumer = ?

Net GST payable by Mr. X = ?

(A) ₹ 9,66,240; ₹ 11,440

(B) ₹ 11,45,760; ₹ 41,360

(C) ₹ 9,66,240; ₹ 5,720

(D) ₹ 7,48,000; ₹ 1,49,600

221. Mr. X of Maharashtra, purchased Raw Material A from Maharashtra for ₹ 7,200 (inclusive SGST & CGST @ 10%) and Raw Material B for ₹ 1,24,000 plus SGST & CGST @ 10%. His expenses are ₹ 2,70,000. Margin is 20% on cost. SGST & CGST rate is 10% each on supply. How much net GST is payable by the trader?

(A) SGST = 35,000; CGST = 35,000

(B) SGST = 48,000; CGST = 48,000

(C) SGST = 35,144; CGST = 35,144

(D) SGST = 30,000; CGST = 30,000

222. A registered dealer of Maharashtra purchased goods from registered dealer of Delhi for ₹ 5,70,000 inclusive of IGST @ 20% and sold the same to registered dealer in Karnataka for ₹ 6,80,000 plus IGST @ 20%. How much IGST is payable by dealer in Maharashtra?

(A) ₹ 41,000

(B) ₹ 1,36,000

(C) ₹ 95,000

(D) ₹ 19,000

223.

Particulars	₹
Value of receipt of goods & services	3,60,000
Value of supply of goods & services	4,32,000

SGST & CGST rate is 10% each on input as well as output. Net GST payable = ?

(A) ₹ 36,000

(B) ₹ 14,400

(C) ₹ 43,200

(D) ₹ 7,200

224. Z Ltd. supplies the following information to you:

Particulars	₹
Value of receipt of goods & services	5,52,000
Value of supply of goods & services	4,60,000

SGST & CGST rate is 10% on input.

SGST & CGST rate is 6% on output.

(A) Excess credit of ₹ 27,600 each of SGST and CSGT can be refunded if eligible as per refund provisions.

(B) Excess credit of ₹ 27,600 each of SGST and CSGT should be written to profit & loss account.

(C) Excess credit of ₹ 27,600 each of SGST and CSGT can be carried forward in 'electronic credit ledger'.

(D) Any of the above depend on situation

225. Y Ltd. supplies the following information to you:

Particulars	₹
Value of receipt of goods & services	5,40,000
Value of supply of goods & services	3,24,000

Y Ltd. had supplied only 50% of goods and services out of goods and services received by it. SGST & CGST rate is 10% on input & output.

(A) SGST & CGST payable each ₹ 21,600.

(B) SGST & CGST each refundable ₹ 21,600.

(C) The excess credit of ₹ 21,600 each in SGST & CGST can be carried forward in 'electronic credit ledger' and utilized in subsequent period.

(D) None of the above is correct.

226. XYZ Ltd. is engaged in sale of Product X. All the sales are made *outside the State.*

Particulars	₹
Value of receipt of goods & services (SGST & CGST 10%)	7,00,000
Value of Product X sold (IGST 20%)	8,40,000

Select the correct answer from the options given below:

(A) Net IGST payable is ₹ 28,000.

(B) Net IGST payable is ₹ 1,68,000.

(C) Net IGST payable is ₹ 98,000 after setting-off CGST of ₹ 70,000 as SGST cannot be set-off against IGST.

(D) None of the above the correct.

227. Value of receipt of goods and services within the State: ₹ 7,00,000

Value of supply of goods and services within the State: ₹ 4,20,000

Value of supply of goods and services in Inter-State sale: ₹ 4,20,000

IGST rate for supply of goods and services is 20%.

SGST and CGST rate on receipt and supply of goods and services is 10% each.

How much GST is payable?

	SGST	*CGST*	*IGST*
(A)	42,000	42,000	84,000
(B)	42,000	42,000	28,000
(C)	-	-	84,000
(D)	-	-	28,000

228. Value of receipt of goods and services Inter-State: ₹ 10,00,000

Value of supply of goods and services within the State : ₹ 12,00,000

IGST rate on receipt is 20%. SGST and CGST is 10% each.

	SGST	*CGST*	*IGST*
(A)	1,20,000	1,20,000	-
(B)	40,000	1,20,000	-
(C)	40,000	-	-
(D)	40,000	-	(2,00,000)

229. From the following details find out the total GST collection by the State Government & Central Government?

Seller	*Purchaser*	₹
Sagar	Ritesh	1,35,000
Ritesh	Madan	1,87,500
Madan	Consumer	2,25,000

The SGST & CGST rate on purchase and sales is 12% each. Price shown above are exclusive of GST.

	SGST	*CGST*
(A)	21,600	21,600
(B)	30,000	30,000
(C)	27,000	27,000
(D)	36,000	36,000

230. A sale goods to B for ₹ 55,000 (inclusive of SGST & CGST 5% each). B sale to C for ₹ 82,500 (inclusive of SGST & CGST 5% each). C sales the goods to consumer for ₹ 1,15,500 (inclusive of SGST & CGST 5% each).

Total GST collection by the State Government & Central Government = ?

	SGST	*CGST*
(A)	10,500	10,500
(B)	7,500	7,500
(C)	5,250	5,250
(D)	5,000	5,000

231. Determine the time of supply (TOS) *of goods* from the following details.

Date of removal	1.1.2019
Date of invoice	2.1.2019
Date when goods are made available to recipient	3.1.2019
Date of receipt of payment	15.2.2019

Select the correct answer from the options given below -

(A) 1.1.2019

(B) 1.2.2019

(C) 3.1.2019

(D) 15.3.2019

232. Determine the time of supply (TOS) *of goods* from the following details.

Date of removal	3.1.2019
Date of invoice	1.1.2019
Date when goods are made available to recipient	4.1.2019
Date of receipt of payment	25.2.2019

Select the correct answer from the options given below -

(A) 3.1.2019

(B) 1.1.2019

(C) 4.1.2019

(D) 25.2.2019

233. Determine the time of supply (TOS) *of goods* from the following details.

Date of removal	4.1.2019
Date of invoice	4.1.2019
Date when goods are made available to recipient	6.2.2019
Date of receipt of payment	1.10.2019

Select the correct answer from the options given below -

(A) 4.1.2019

(B) 6.2.2019

(C) 1.10.2019

(D) None of the above

234. Determine the time of supply (TOS) *of goods* in case the recipient of goods is liable to pay tax under Reverse Charge Mechanism (RCM).

Date of invoice	1.1.2019
Date of receipt of goods	5.1.2019
Date of payment in the books	10.1.2019
Date when payment is debited in bank account	12.1.2019

Select the correct answer from the options given below -

(A) 1.1.2019

(B) 5.1.2019

(C) 10.1.2019

(D) 12.1.2019

235. Determine the time of supply (TOS) *of goods* in case the recipient of goods is liable to pay tax under Reverse Charge Mechanism (RCM).

Date of invoice	1.1.2019
Date of receipt of goods	15.1.2019
Date of payment in the books	10.1.2019
Date when payment is debited in bank account	12.1.2019

Select the correct answer from the options given below -

(A) 1.1.2019

(B) 15.1.2019

(C) 10.1.2019

(D) 12.1.2019

236. Determine the time of supply (TOS) *of goods* in case the recipient of goods is liable to pay tax under Reverse Charge Mechanism (RCM).

Date of invoice	1.1.2019
Date of receipt of goods	15.1.2019
Date of payment in the books	18.1.2019
Date when payment is debited in bank account	20.2.2019

Select the correct answer from the options given below -

(A) 15.1.2019

(B) 18.1.2019

(C) 20.2.2019

(D) 1.2.2019

237. Determine the time of supply *of service* from the following details.

Date of actual provision of service	10.1.2019
Date of invoice	31.1.2019
Date of receipt of payment	15.2.2019

Select the correct answer from the options given below -

(A) 10.1.2019

(B) 31.1.2019

(C) 15.2.2019

(D) 9.2.2019

238. Determine the time of supply *of service* from the following details.

Date of actual provision of service	10.1.2019
Date of invoice	12.2.2019
Date of receipt of payment	30.6.2019

Select the correct answer from the options given below -

(A) 10.1.2019

(B) 12.2.2019

(C) 30.6.2019

(D) 9.2.2019

239. Determine the time of supply *of service* from the following details.

Date of actual provision of service	10.1.2019
Date of invoice	30.1.2019
Date of receipt of part payment	15.1.2019
Date of receipt of remaining part payment	10.3.2019

For part payment received on 15.1.2019 time of supply will be _____ and for part payment received on 10.3.2019 time of supply will be ______

Select the correct answer from the options given below -

(A) 15.1.2019 & 30.1.2019 respectively

(B) 15.1.2019 & 10.3.2019 respectively

(C) 10.1.2019 & 10.3.2019 respectively
(D) 10.1.2019 & 30.1.2019 respectively

240. Determine the time of supply *of service* from the following details.

Date of actual provision of service	10.1.2019
Date of invoice	12.2.2019
Date of receipt of part payment	5.1.2019
Date of receipt of remaining part payment	25.2.2019

For part payment received on 5.1.2019 time of supply will be _____ and for part payment received on 25.2.2019 time of supply will be _____

Select the correct answer from the options given below -

(A) 10.1.2019 & 5.1.2019 respectively
(B) 5.1.2019 & 12.2.2019 respectively
(C) 5.1.2019 & 10.1.2019 respectively
(D) 5.1.2019 & 25.2.2019 respectively

241. Determine the time of supply (TOS) *of service* in case the recipient of goods is liable to pay tax under Reverse Charge Mechanism (RCM).

Date of payment of receipt of service	10.3.2019
Date of issue of invoice by supplier of service	29.1.2019

Select the correct answer from the options given below -

(A) 10.3.2019
(B) 29.1.2019
(C) 30.3.2019
(D) Data given is insufficient

242. Determine the time of supply (TOS) *of service* in case the recipient of goods is liable to pay tax under Reverse Charge Mechanism (RCM).

Date of payment of receipt of service	10.3.2019
Date of issue of invoice by supplier of service	1.1.2019

Select the correct answer from the options given below -

(A) 10.3.2019

(B) 1.1.2019

(C) 3.3.2019

(D) Data given is insufficient

243. XX Ltd. purchased goods from ZZ Ltd. in the month of Jan 2019 but the goods were received in the month of March 2019. XX Ltd. can take the GST credit in the month of -

(A) Against GST payable for the month of Jan 2019

(B) Against GST payable for the month of Feb 2019

(C) Against GST payable for the month of April 2019

(D) Against GST payable for the month of March 2019

ANSWERS:

1.	(D)	**2.**	(B)	**3.**	(B)	**4.**	(C)	**5.**	(B)	**6.**	(D)	**7.**	(C)
8.	(C)	**9.**	(C)	**10.**	(C)	**11.**	(C)	**12.**	(D)	**13.**	(B)	**14.**	(D)
15.	(A)	**16.**	(B)	**17.**	(D)	**18.**	(B)	**19.**	(A)	**20.**	(C)	**21.**	(D)
22.	(C)	**23.**	(D)	**24.**	(C)	**25.**	(B)	**26.**	(D)	**27.**	(D)	**28.**	(A)
29.	(D)	**30.**	(B)	**31.**	(A)	**32.**	(B)	**33.**	(D)	**34.**	(A)	**35.**	(B)
36.	(B)	**37.**	(A)	**38.**	(D)	**39.**	(A)	**40.**	(B)	**41.**	(D)	**42.**	(C)
43.	(B)	**44.**	(D)	**45.**	(C)	**46.**	(D)	**47.**	(A)	**48.**	(A)	**49.**	(B)
50.	(D)	**51.**	(B)	**52.**	(A)	**53.**	(B)	**54.**	(B)	**55.**	(A)	**56.**	(B)
57.	(A)	**58.**	(B)	**59.**	(B)	**60.**	(B)	**61.**	(D)	**62.**	(B)	**63.**	(C)
64.	(C)	**65.**	(A)	**66.**	(C)	**67.**	(C)	**68.**	(A)	**69.**	(A)	**70.**	(C)
71.	(B)	**72.**	(C)	**73.**	(D)	**74.**	(C)	**75.**	(C)	**76.**	(C)	**77.**	(A)
78.	(C)	**79.**	(D)	**80.**	(B)	**81.**	(C)	**82.**	(C)	**83.**	(C)	**84.**	(A)
85.	(D)	**86.**	(B)	**87.**	(B)	**88.**	(D)	**89.**	(A)	**90.**	(A)	**91.**	(C)
92.	(C)	**93.**	(A)	**94.**	(B)	**95.**	(A)	**96.**	(C)	**97.**	(A)	**98.**	(D)
99.	(A)	**100.**	(B)	**101.**	(B)	**102.**	(A)	**103.**	(C)	**104.**	(C)	**105.**	(A)
106.	(D)	**107.**	(A)	**108.**	(D)	**109.**	(A)	**110.**	(D)	**111.**	(D)	**112.**	(D)
113.	(D)	**114.**	(C)	**115.**	(A)	**116.**	(D)	**117.**	(C)	**118.**	(C)	**119.**	(D)

120.	(A)	**121.**	(D)	**122.**	(B)	**123.**	(D)	**124.**	(B)	**125.**	(B)	**126.**	(A)
127.	(C)	**128.**	(A)	**129.**	(A)	**130.**	(D)	**131.**	(B)	**132.**	(A)	**133.**	(D)
134.	(A)	**135.**	(A)	**136.**	(A)	**137.**	(B)	**138.**	(B)	**139.**	(A)	**140.**	(B)
141.	(B)	**142.**	(B)	**143.**	(D)	**144.**	(A)	**145.**	(B)	**146.**	(B)	**147.**	(C)
148.	(D)	**149.**	(C)	**150.**	(D)	**151.**	(B)	**152.**	(B)	**153.**	(B)	**154.**	(C)
155.	(A)	**156.**	(D)	**157.**	(A)	**158.**	(B)	**159.**	(D)	**160.**	(B)	**161.**	(B)
162.	(A)	**163.**	(B)	**164.**	(A)	**165.**	(B)	**166.**	(A)	**167.**	(C)	**168.**	(D)
169.	(A)	**170.**	(B)	**171.**	(A)	**172.**	(B)	**173.**	(A)	**174.**	(D)	**175.**	(D)
176.	(B)	**177.**	(C)	**178.**	(B)	**179.**	(B)	**180.**	(C)	**181.**	(C)	**182.**	(B)
183.	(B)	**184.**	(B)	**185.**	(B)	**186.**	(C)	**187.**	(C)	**188.**	(A)	**189.**	(B)
190.	(A)	**191.**	(A)	**192.**	(B)	**193.**	(D)	**194.**	(C)	**195.**	(D)	**196.**	(A)
197.	(B)	**198.**	(A)	**199.**	(C)	**200.**	(D)	**201.**	(B)	**202.**	(A)	**203.**	(B)
204.	(B)	**205.**	(D)	**206.**	(D)	**207.**	(A)	**208.**	(D)	**209.**	(B)	**210.**	(A)
211.	(B)	**212.**	(B)	**213.**	(A)	**214.**	(B)	**215.**	(B)	**216.**	(B)	**217.**	(C)
218.	(B)	**219.**	(B)	**220.**	(A)	**221.**	(A)	**222.**	(A)	**223.**	(B)	**224.**	(D)
225.	(C)	**226.**	(A)	**227.**	(D)	**228.**	(C)	**229.**	(C)	**230.**	(C)	**231.**	(A)
232.	(B)	**233.**	(D)	**234.**	(B)	**235.**	(C)	**236.**	(D)	**237.**	(B)	**238.**	(A)
239.	(A)	**240.**	(C)	**241.**	(A)	**242.**	(C)	**243.**	(D)				

PAST EXAMINATION MCQs

1. Dec 2017: Which of the following countries was the first to introduce GST?

(A) United States

(B) Britain

(C) Canada

(D) France

2. Dec 2017: All decisions of GST Council must have .... majority in order to implement the same.

(A) One-half

(B) Three-fourth

(C) 60%

(D) 90%

3. Dec 2017: A service would be called as "continuous supply of service", if the service under a contract is provided continuously or on recurrent basis exceeding:

(A) One year

(B) 6 months

(C) 3 months

(D) 1 month

4. Dec 2017: Which law will govern the inter-state supply of goods or services?

(A) CGST

(B) SGST

(C) UTGST

(D) IGST

5. Dec 2017: Which of the following has been kept out of the GST Levy?

(A) Generator

(B) Computer

(C) Jewellery

(D) Electricity

6. Dec 2017: Threshold limit of turnover for levy of GST in the case of a person earning on business in Gujarat is:

(A) ₹ 10 lakhs

(B) ₹ 20 lakhs

(C) ₹ 30 lakhs

(D) ₹ 40 lakhs

7. Dec 2017: Abhijit Sen is engaged in running a textile showroom at Gangtok (Sikkim). In order to avail composition scheme under GST law, his "aggregate turnover" in the preceding financial year should not have exceeded:

(A) ₹ 10 lakhs

(B) ₹ 20 lakhs

(C) ₹ 50 lakhs

(D) ₹ 75 lakhs

8. Dec 2017: When employer gifts goods to his employees, it will not be considered as taxable supply for the purpose of GST if the value of supply to an employee does not exceed:

(A) ₹ 5,000

(B) ₹ 20,000

(C) ₹ 50,000

(D) ₹ 1,00,000

9. Dec 2017: Which of the following incomes/activities is liable for GST?

(A) Salary

(B) Salary and allowances of MPs

(C) Services by Court

(D) Sale of jewellery

10. Dec 2017: Which of the following represents composite supply?

(A) Doctor's service with medicines

(B) Package with fruits and chocolates

(C) Coaching centre with monthly excursions on trekking

(D) Supply of computer printer and laptop

11. Dec 2017: In the case of a manufacturer who opts for composition scheme the rate of GST (including CGST and IGST) is:

(A) 1%

(B) 2%

(C) 3%

(D) 5%

12. Dec 2017: Who among the following is eligible for availing composition scheme under GST?

(A) Supply through e-commerce operators

(B) Service supply like Company Secretary

(C) Goods not taxable under CGST/SGST/ UTGST/IGST

(D) Restaurants

13. Dec 2017: Mr. Ram supplied goods to Mr. Laxman. The invoice is dated 30.7.2018. Payment was received for the supply on 30.10.2018. The goods were dispatched on 5.8.2018. What is time of supply under CGST Act?

(A) 5.8.2018

(B) 30.7.2018

(C) 30.10.2018

(D) None of the above

14. Dec 2017: Mani gave goods for processing by Murali. While Mani is registered in GST, Murali is not registered in GST. Both are at Chennai. The processing is liable for GST @ 5%. The goods were received after processing on 11.7.2018. Entries in the books were made by Mr. Mani on 12.7.2018. The delivery challan was also received on 11.7.2018. Job work charges amount to ₹ 1,00,000 (without GST). When and how much is the GST liability? And who must pay?

(A) 11.7.2018; ₹ 5,000 and Murali must pay

(B) 12.7.2018; ₹ 1,050; and Murali must pay

(C) 11.7.2018; ₹ 5,000 and Mani must pay

(D) 12.7.2018; ₹ 2,500 and Mani must pay

15. Dec 2017: Which of the following though shown in Bill will not be included in determining the value of supply for the purpose of GST?

(A) Packing

(B) Discount

(C) Interest for late payment

(D) Installation charges

16. Dec 2017: Which of the following expenditure is eligible for input tax credit?

(A) Membership fee of a club

(B) Home travel concession extended to employees

(C) Goods given as free gifts

(D) Caterer using the service another caterer

17. Dec 2017: XYZ Co. Ltd. registered under GST has to maintain accounts and records until the expiry of .... months from the due date furnishing the annual return for the year.

(A) 36 months
(B) 84 months
(C) 72 months
(D) 60 months

18. Dec 2017: Debit note is issued by the supplier of goods when:

(A) Tax charged in the invoice is excessive
(B) When the goods are returned by recipient
(C) Tax charged is less than the tax payable
(D) When the goods supplied are deficient

19. Dec 2017: Madan is located in Chennai. He has a branch office in Cochin. He wants to transfer goods. His turnover was always below ₹ 10 lakhs. His registration under GST is:

(A) Voluntary
(B) Compulsory
(C) Compulsory only when turnover exceeds ₹ 20 lakhs
(D) As and when deemed by the Revenue

20. Dec 2017: A taxable person whose registration has been cancelled or surrendered must file the final return of GST within:

(A) 6 months of the cancellation
(B) 6 months after the end of the financial year
(C) 3 months after the end of the financial year
(D) 3 months after the date of cancellation

21. Dec 2017: Who must perform the function of Tax Collection at Source (TCS) under GST?

(A) E-commerce operator
(B) Transport operator
(C) Job workers
(D) Input service distributor

22. Dec 2017: When a person liable to pay tax under GST claims excess input tax credit or excess reduction in output tax liability, he shall pay interest not exceeding:

(A) 12%

(B) 15%

(C) 24%

(D) 21%

23. Dec 2017: When a special audit is directed under GST with the prior approval of Commissioner the audit report signed and certified must be submitted within .... days.

(A) 15

(B) 45

(C) 90

(D) 150

24. Dec 2017: When a person evades GST or avails input tax credit exceeding ₹ 500 lakhs he is liable for the following punishment:

(A) Imprisonment for 5 years and with fine

(B) Imprisonment for 3 years and with fine

(C) Imprisonment for 3 years

(D) Imprisonment for 5 years

25. Dec 2017: Online information and database access or retrieval service does include the following:

(A) Online gaming

(B) Cloud services

(C) Advertising on the internet

(D) Physical delivery of goods

26. Dec 2017: Refreshments were supplied on board in an aircraft proceeding from Chennai to Delhi. It had a stop at Hyderabad. The refreshments were taken on board at Hyderabad. The place of supply is:

(A) Delhi

(B) Chennai

(C) Hyderabad

(D) None of the above

27. Dec 2017: For the purpose of calculating the compensation payable to the States under the Goods and Service Tax (Compensation to States) Act, 2017 the base year for reckoning the Revenue is:

(A) 31.3.2014

(B) 31.3.2015

(C) 31.3.2016

(D) 31.3.2017

28. Dec 2017: Which of the following GST model is adopted in India?

(A) Australian model

(B) Bagchi-Poddar model

(C) Dual model

(D) American model

29. Dec 2017: For the purpose of deciding "aggregate turnover" in order to determine the GST payable under composition scheme, which of the following is to be excluded?

(A) Exemption supply

(B) Export of goods

(C) Inter-state branch transfer

(D) CGST

30. Dec 2017: Export of service does not include:

(A) the supplier of service located outside India

(B) the recipient of service located outside India

(C) the place of supply of service is outside India

(D) the supplier of service is located in India

ANSWERS:

1.	(D)	2.	(B)	3.	(C)	4.	(D)	5.	(D)	6.	(B)	7.	(C)
8.	(C)	9.	(D)	10.	(A)	11.	(B)	12.	(D)	13.	(B)	14.	(C)
15.	(B)	16.	(D)	17.	(C)	18.	(C)	19.	(B)	20.	(D)	21.	(A)

22.	(C)	23.	(C)	24.	(A)	25.	(**)	26.	(C)	27.	(C)	28.	(C)
29.	(D)	30.	(A)										

**MCQ's are wrongly drafted.

25. Online information and database access or retrieval services includes all the four option given in the MCQ and hence MCQ itself is wrong.

HINTS FOR PRACTICAL MCQs:

219. $2,61,800 \times \frac{10}{110} = 23,800$

220.

Purchase cost (8,97,600 - 74,800 - 74,800)	7,48,000
(+) Profit	57,200
Sale price	8,05,200
(+) SGST @ 10%	80,520
(+) CGST @ 10%	80,520
Invoice price/cost to customer	9,66,240

Calculation of net GST payable:

Particulars	SGST	CGST
Output GST	80,520	80,520
(-) Input GST	(74,800)	(74,800)
Net GST payable	5,720	5,720

Short cut method to calculate GST:

GST is payable on value addition. Value addition made by trader is 'profit' *i.e.* ₹ 57,200.

SGST = 57,200 × 10% = 5,720

CGST = 57,200 × 10% = 5,720

221.

Raw Material A (7,200 - 600 - 600)	6,000
Raw Material B (1,48,800 - 12,400 - 12,400)	1,24,000
Other expenses	2,70,000
Total cost	4,00,000
(+) Profit @ 20%	80,000
Sale price	4,80,000
(+) SGST @ 10%	48,000
(+) CGST @ 10%	48,000
Invoice price	5,76,000

Calculation of Net GST payable by Mr. X:

Particulars	SGST	CGST
Output GST	48,000	48,000
(-) Input GST	(13,000)	(13,000)
Net GST payable	35,000	35,000

Short cut method to calculate GST:

GST is payable on value addition. Value addition made by trader is 'other expenses' and 'profit' i.e. ₹ 3,50,000.

SGST = 3,50,000 × 10% = 35,000

CGST = 3,50,000 × 10% = 35,000

Note: *Short method works accurately only if input and output rate of GST is same.*

222.

Output IGST	1,36,000
(-) Input IGST (5,70,000 × 20/120)	(95,000)
Net IGST payable	41,000

223.

SGST & CGST rate is 10% each. Thus, total rate will be 20%.

(4,32,000 - 3,60,000) × 20% = 14,400

225.

Particulars	SGST	CGST
Output GST	32,400	32,400
(-) Input GST	(54,000)	(54,000)
Net GST payable	Nil	Nil
Excess credit	21,600	21,600

The excess credit of ₹ 21,600 each in SGST & CGST can be carried forward in 'electronic credit ledger' and utilized in subsequent period.

226.

Particulars	SGST	CGST	IGST
Output GST on Product X @ 20%	-	-	1,68,000
(-) Input SGST @ 10%	-	-	(70,000)
(-) Input CGST @ 10%	-	-	(70,000)
Net GST payable	-	-	28,000

The entire input credit of SGST and CGST can be utilized for payment of IGST.

229.

Details of sales	Calculation	SGST	CGST
Sagar to Ritesh	(1,35,000 × 12%)	16,200	16,200
Ritesh to Madan	(1,87,500 - 1,35,000) × 12%	6,300	6,300
Madan to Consumer	(2,25,000 - 1,87,500) × 12%	4,500	4,500
		27,000	27,000

Shortcut method for calculation of net GST collected by Government:
Last sale *i.e.* 2,25,000 × 12% = 27,000 (However, this shortcut method gives accurate result only if rate of GST is same in all sales)

231 to 233.

As per Section 12 of the CGST Act, 2017, the time of supply of goods shall be the **earlier** of the following dates:

(1) The date of issue of invoice by the supplier or the last date on which he is required, to issue the invoice with respect to the supply u/s 31(1) or

(2) The date on which the supplier receives the payment with respect to the supply.

Tax invoice in respect of goods [Section 31(1)]: A registered person supplying taxable goods shall, ***before or at the time of removal of goods*** for supply to the recipient, where the supply involves movement of goods or delivery of goods or making available thereof to the recipient, issue a tax invoice showing the description, quantity and value of goods, the tax charged thereon and other prescribed particulars.

In simple words earliest of - date of removal, date of invoice, date of receipt of goods or date of receipt of payment has to taken as date of time of supply.

234 to 236.

In case of supplies in respect of which tax is paid or liable to be paid on reverse charge basis, the time of supply shall be the earliest of the following dates:

(1) The date of the receipt of goods or

(2) The date of payment as entered in the books of account of the recipient or the date on which the payment is debited in his bank account, whichever is earlier or

(3) The date immediately following 30 days from the date of issue of invoice or any other document, by whatever name called, in lieu thereof by the supplier.

However, where it is not possible to determine the time of supply as stated above, the time of supply shall be the date of entry in the books of account of the recipient of supply.

237.

Time of supply of services [Section 13(1)]: The liability to pay tax on services shall arise at the time of supply.

The time of supply of services shall be the earliest of the following dates:

(4) The date of issue of invoice by the supplier, if the invoice is issued within the period Section 31(2) or the date of receipt of payment, whichever is earlier or

(5) The date of provision of service, if the invoice is not issued within the period prescribed Section 31(2) or the date of receipt of payment, whichever is earlier or

(6) The date on which the recipient shows the receipt of services in his books of account, in a case where the provisions of clause (1) or clause (2) do not apply.

If advance up to ₹ 1,000 is received, GST can be paid at the time of issue of invoice: Where the supplier of taxable service receives an amount up to ₹ 1,000 in excess of the amount indicated in the tax invoice, the time of supply to the extent of such excess amount shall, at the option of the said supplier, be the date of issue of invoice relating to such excess amount. (*If advance up to₹ 1,000 is received, GST is not payable at that stage. In that case, GST will be payable when invoice is raised.*)

Explanation:

The supply shall be deemed to have been made to the extent it is covered by the invoice or, as the case may be, the payment.

"The date of receipt of payment" shall be the date on which the payment is entered in the books of account of the supplier or the date on which the payment is credited to his bank account, *whichever is earlier.*

Tax invoice in respect of services [Section 31(2)]: A registered person supplying taxable services shall, before or after the provision of service but within a prescribed period, issue a tax invoice, showing the description, value, tax charged thereon and such other particulars as may be prescribed.

Time limit for issuing tax invoice for services [Rule 47 of the CGST Rules, 2017]: The invoice in case of taxable supply of services shall be issued within a period of **30 days** from the date of supply of service. However, if the supplier is an insurance company or banking company or a financial institution or NBFC, invoice can be issued within **45 days** from the date of supply of service.

241 & 242.

Time of supply of service when GST payable on reverse charge basis [Section 13(3)]: In case of supplies in respect of which tax is paid or liable to be paid on reverse charge basis, the time of supply shall be the earlier of the following dates:

(1) The date of payment as entered in the books of account of the recipient or the date on which the payment is debited in his bank account, whichever is earlier or

(2) The date immediately following 60 days from the date of issue of invoice or any other document, by whatever name called, in lieu thereof by the supplier.

However, where it is not possible to determine the time of supply under clause (1) or clause (2), the time of supply shall be the date of entry in the books of account of the recipient of supply.

CHAPTER 19

CUSTOMS ACT, 1962

MCQs ON THEORY

1. Customs Act, 1962 extends to –

(A) Whole of India excluding Jammu & Kashmir

(B) Whole of India

(C) Whole of India excluding Jammu & Kashmir and Union Territories

(D) Whole of India excluding Jammu & Kashmir and Special Economic Zones

2. As per Section 2(1) of the Customs Act, 1962, ______ means any authority competent to pass any order or decision under this Act, but does not include the Board, Commissioner (Appeals) or Appellate Tribunal.

(A) Adjudicating Authority

(B) Proper Authority

(C) Proper Officer

(D) Custom Authority

3. As per Section 2(2) of the Customs Act, 1962, "assessment" includes –

(I) Provisional assessment

(II) Self assessment

(III) Re-assessment

(IV) Any assessment in which the duty assessed is NIL.

Select the correct answer from the options given below:

(A) (I) & (II)

(B) (I), (II) & (IV)

(C) (I), (II) & (III)

(D) All (I) to (IV)

4. The Customs Act, 1962, not only regulates the levy and collection of duties, but also, serves equally important purposes like –

(A) Regulation of imports & exports.

(B) Protection of domestic industry

(C) Prevention of smuggling

(D) Conservation & augmentation of foreign exchange

Select the correct answer from the options given below:

(A) All (A) to (D)

(B) All except (A)

(C) All except (B)

(D) All except (C)

5. It is Section 12 of the Customs Act, 1962 that provides duties of customs to be levied at such rates as may be specified under the _____ or other applicable Acts on goods imported into or exported from India.

(A) Customs Tariff Act, 1962

(B) Customs Tariff Act, 1975

(C) Customs Rates & Tariff Act, 1975

(D) Customs Rate Act, 1962

6. Under the Customs Act, 1962, the *rule making* power is delegated to –

(A) Central Board of Indirect Taxes and Customs (CBITC)

(B) Central Government

(C) Respective State Governments

(D) Partly to the Central Government and partly to the respective State Governments

7. Under the Customs Act, 1962, the *regulations making* power is delegated to –

(A) Central Board of Indirect Taxes and Customs (CBITC)

(B) Respective State Governments

(C) Partly to the Central Government and partly to the respective State Governments

(D) Central Government

8. For which of the following Rules can be made by the Central Government u/s 156 of the Customs Act, 1962?

(A) Transaction Value

(B) Form of Bill of Entry

(C) Import & export manifest

(D) Conditions for transhipment & removal of goods without payment of duty

9. As per Section 2(3) of the Customs Act, 1962, "baggage" includes –

(P) unaccompanied baggage

(Q) motor vehicles

Select the correct answer from the options given below:

(A) (Q) only

(B) Both (P) & (Q)

(C) (P) but not (Q)

(D) None of the above

10. As per Section 2(4) of the Customs Act, 1962, "bill of entry" means a bill of entry referred to in ______

(A) Section 45

(B) Section 46

(C) Section 47

(D) Section 48

11. As per Section 2(5) of the Customs Act, 1962, "bill of export" means a bill of export referred to in ______

(A) Section 53

(B) Section 52

(C) Section 51

(D) Section 50

12. "Board" means the Central Board of Indirect Taxes and Customs constituted under the ______

(A) Central Boards Indirect Taxes Act, 1963

(B) Central Boards of Revenue Act, 1963

(C) Central Boards Indirect Taxes & Customs Act, 1963

(D) Central Boards of Taxation Act, 1963

13. "Coastal goods" means –

(A) goods, other than imported goods, transported in a vessel from one port in India to another.

(B) any goods including imported goods, transported in a vessel from one port in India to another.

(C) goods, other than imported goods, transported in a vessel from one port in India to place outside India.

(D) any goods including imported goods, transported in a vessel from one port in India to place outside India.

14. As per Section 2(7A) of the Customs Act, 1962, Commissioner (Appeals) means a person appointed to be a Commissioner of Customs (Appeals) under sub-section (1) of –

(A) Section 3

(B) Section 4

(C) Section 5

(D) Section 7

15. As per Section 2(9) of the Customs Act, 1962, "conveyance" includes –

(I) Vessel

(II) Aircraft

(III) Vehicle

(IV) Animal

Select the correct answer from the options given below:

	(I)	**(II)**	**(III)**	**(IV)**
(A)	✓	✓	✓	✓

	(I)	(II)	(III)	(IV)
(B)	✓	✓	✓	✓
(C)	✓	✓	×	×
(D)	✓	×	×	×

16. "Customs Area" means –

(A) Area of a Customs Station

(B) Area of a warehouse

(C) Any area in which imported goods or export goods are ordinarily kept before clearance by Customs Authorities

(D) All of the above

17. "Customs Station" means –

(A) Any customs port

(B) Any customs airport

(C) Any international courier terminal

(D) All of the above

18. Which of the following is not included within the definition of "Customs Station" as defined in the Customs Act, 1962?

(A) Land customs station

(B) International courier terminal

(C) Foreign post office

(D) Are where goods are kept after custom clearance

19. "Dutiable Goods" means –

(A) All imported goods.

(B) Any goods which are chargeable to duty and on which duty has been paid.

(C) Any goods which are chargeable to duty and on which duty has not been paid.

(D) Any goods which are chargeable to duty and on which proper amount duty has been paid.

20. "Entry" in relation to goods means an entry made in _______ and includes the entry made under the regulations made under section 84

(A) Ahe case of goods imported or to be exported by post, the entry referred to in section 82

(B) A bill of entry, shipping bill or bill of export

(C) Bill of entry, import report or bill of export

(D) Import report, bill of export, bill of entry & import manifest

21. As per Section 2(17) of the Customs Act, 1962, "examination", in relation to any goods, includes _____

(A) Measurement

(B) Weighment

(C) Measurement and weighment

(D) Measurement or weighment

22. "Export goods" means –

(A) Any goods which are to be taken out of India

(B) Any goods which are to be taken out of India to a place outside India

(C) Which exporter desires to take outside India

(D) None of the above

23. Foreign-going vessel or aircraft means any vessel or aircraft for the time being engaged in the carriage of _____ between any port or airport in India and any port or airport outside India.

(A) Goods

(B) Passengers

(C) Goods or passengers

(D) None of the above

24. Which of the following is included within the definition of "foreign-going vessel or aircraft" as defined in Section 2(21) of the Customs Act, 1962?

(A) Any naval vessel of any foreign government taking part in any naval exercises

(B) Any vessel engaged in fishing or any other operations in territorial waters of India

(C) Both (A) and (B)

(D) Neither (A) nor (B)

25. As per Section 2(22) of the Customs Act, 1962, "goods" includes –

(A) Vessels, aircrafts and vehicles

(B) Currency & negotiable instruments

(C) Stores, baggage

(D) Any of the above

26. Imported goods means –

(A) Any goods brought into India from a place outside India.

(B) Any goods brought into India from a place outside India and include goods which have been cleared for home consumption.

(C) Any goods brought into India from a place outside India but does not include goods which have been cleared for home consumption.

(D) None of the above is correct.

27. Which of the following can be treated as Adjudicating Authority under the Customs Act, 1962?

(i) Board [Central Board of Indirect Taxes & Customs (CBITC)]

(ii) Commissioner (Appeals)

(iii) Appellate Tribunal

(iv) Authority competent to pass any order or decision under the Act.

Select the correct answer from the options given below:

(A) (i), (ii) & (iii)

(B) (i), (ii), (iii) & (iv)

(C) (ii) & (iv)

(D) (iv)

28. Which of the following statement is *correct*?

(A) All imported goods are dutiable goods.

(B) Market price, in relation to any goods, means the retail price of the goods in the ordinary course of trade in India.

(C) All dutiable goods are imported goods.

(D) All of the above

29. Which of the following is included within the definition of "foreign-going vessel or aircraft" as defined in Section 2(21) of the Customs Act, 1962?

(A) Any naval vessel of any foreign government taking part in any naval exercises.

(B) Any vessel engaged in fishing or any other operations outside the territorial waters of India.

(C) Any vessel or aircraft proceeding to a place outside India for any purpose whatsoever.

(D) All of the above

30. Prohibited goods means any goods –

(A) The import or export of which is subject to any prohibition under the Act

(B) The import or export of which is subject to any prohibition any other law for the time being in force

(C) Any such goods in respect of which the conditions subject to which the goods are permitted to be imported or exported have not been complied with

(D) All of the above

31. Proper officer –

(A) In relation to any functions to be performed under the Act, means the officer of customs who is assigned those functions by the Board

(B) Includes Principal Commissioner of Customs

(C) Includes Commissioner of Customs

(D) All of the above

32. As per Section 2(37) of the Customs Act, 1962, "Shipping bill" means a shipping bill referred to in ______

(A) Section 56

(B) Section 50

(C) Section 62

(D) Section 60

33. As per Section 2(38) of the Customs Act, 1962, "Stores" –

(A) Means goods for use in a vessel or aircraft

(B) Includes fuel and spare parts and other articles of equipment, whether or not for immediate fitting

(C) Both (A) and (B)

(D) (A) but not (B)

34. Smuggling, in relation to any goods, means any act or omission which will render such goods liable to confiscation under _____ or _____

(A) Section 111; Section 113

(B) Section 110; Section 111

(C) Section 113; Section 114

(D) Section 111; Section 115

35. A warehouse –

(A) is a designated area where goods are allowed to be stored after landing, without the payment of duty.

(B) is a designated area where goods are allowed to be stored after payment of proper amount of duty.

(C) is a designated area where goods are allowed to be stored after landing, without the payment of duty and in certain cases after payment of proper amount of duty.

(D) is a designated area where imported goods are kept if the importer is unable to pay for the proper amount of duty.

36. Identify which of the following statement is correct (✓) and which is incorrect (✕).

(P) An exemption notification can be withdrawn.

(Q) Duty can be demanded with retrospective effect.

(R) The goods imported in to India, are now subject to IGST and not CVD or SAD.

(S) General basic rate of basic custom duty is 15%.

Select the correct answer from the options given below:

	(P)	(Q)	(R)	(S)
(A)	✓	✓	✓	×
(B)	×	×	✓	×
(C)	✓	×	✓	×
(D)	✓	✓	×	✓

37. Match the following:

List I	***List II***
(P) Petroleum Product	1. IGST is not leviable
(Q) Schedule I of the Customs Tariff Act, 1975	2. Applies when goods can't be classified under rule 3(a) or 3(*b*)
(R) Alcoholic liquor for human consumption	3. CVD & SAD are applicable
(S) Latter the Better Principle	4. Rates for imports
	5. Rates for exports

Select the correct answer from the options given below:

	(P)	(Q)	(R)	(S)
(A)	3	4	1	2
(B)	3	5	1	2
(C)	2	4	3	1
(D)	3	5	2	1

38. Levy is the stage –

(A) Where the declaration of such liability is made and the persons/properties in respect of which the duty is to be levied is identified.

(B) Where actually import or export duties are paid.

(C) Where bill of entry is submitted for duty assessment before goods come to India by sea.

(D) Where imported goods are kept before payment of duty.

39. General basic rate of basic customs duty is –

(A) 5%

(B) 10%

(C) 15%

(D) 7.5%

40. Basic Customs Duty could be levied at –

(A) Standard Rate

(B) Preferential Rate

(C) Both (A) and (B)

(D) Either (A) or (B)

41. Onus is on the _____ to substantiate with the supporting evidence that the goods are chargeable with a preferential rate of duty.

(A) Person (owner)

(B) Government

(C) Custom Officials

(D) (B) or (C)

42. Countervailing Duty (CVD) is subsumed under –

(A) GST

(B) Excise

(C) Income Tax

(D) Local Duties

43. Which of the following statement(s) is/are correct?

(A) The goods imported in to India, are now subject to IGST and not CVD or SAD.

(B) Petroleum is outside the scope of GST, and hence CVD and SAD are applicable to them.

(C) IGST is now payable on Assessable Value + Basic Customs Duty.

(D) All of the above

44. Classification –

(A) Enables categorizing the goods into groups/sub-groups, in order to apply a different rate of duty on goods following within the same group.

(B) Enables the proper officer to recover the duties of custom.

(C) Enables categorizing the goods into groups/sub-groups, in order to apply a single rate of duty on each group/sub-group.

(D) Is based on the concept of MAT.

45. Schedule II of the Customs Tariff Act, 1975 specifies –

(A) Rate applicable to imported goods

(B) Preferential rate of duty

(C) Rate applicable for export of goods

(D) List out the goods which are exempt from import or export duty as the case may be.

46. There are _____ Interpretation Rules under the Customs Tariff Act, 1975.

(A) Four

(B) Eight

(C) Six

(D) Three

47. Rule 2(*a*) of the Interpretation Rules under the Customs Tariff Act, 1975 states that –

(A) Goods shall be classified under the heading which is closest to the specific description.

(B) Any reference in a heading to an article, shall be deemed to include a reference to that article in an unfinished stage too, as long as in the present stage, the incomplete article exhibits the essential character of that article in complete/finished form.

(C) Goods which cannot be classified in accordance with Rule 1 shall be classified under the heading which includes goods that are the most "akin or similar".

(D) Any reference in a heading to a material or substance, shall be deemed to include a reference to the mixtures and combinations of that material/substance with other materials/substances.

48. Which of the following example is best suitable to the "Specific Identification Rule" of the Interpretation Rules under the Customs Tariff Act, 1975?

(A) Car without tyres or without seats would be still construed as Cars, but not Cars without engines.

(B) Natural rubber would include its mixture with synthetic or other forms of rubber.

(C) If one imports 'Liquor Gift Sets' that have both, liquor and glasses, it should be classified under the heading, 'Liquor'.

(D) Mint Tea is not separately classified, but the classification should be tea as the product is closest to the one under the heading "tea", mint is only a flavour.

49. If composite goods cannot be classified as per Rule 3(*a*) of the Interpretation Rules, then, shall be classified on the basis of material/substance. This rule is known as –

(A) Latter the Better Principle

(B) Most Suitable Rule

(C) Essential Character Rule

(D) Akin Principle

50. Rule 2(*b*) of the Interpretation Rules states that any reference in a heading to a material or substance, shall be deemed to include a reference to the mixtures and combinations of that material/substance with other materials/substances. You are required to state which of the following example of this rule –

(A) Natural rubber would include its mixture with synthetic or other forms of rubber

(B) Scooter without tyres is classified as Scooter.

(C) Mint Tea is not separately classified, but the classification should be tea as the product is closest to the one under the heading "tea", mint is only a flavour.

(D) All of the above

51. ______ states that the goods which cannot be classified in accordance with Rule 1, 2 or 3, shall be classified under the heading which includes goods that are the most similar.

(A) Residual Rule

(B) Akin Rule

(C) Standard Rule

(D) Sub-heading Rule

52. Which of the following is covered under the Rule 3 of the Interpretation Rules?

(A) Specific Identification Rule

(B) Essential Character Rule

(C) Latter the Better Rule

(D) All of the above

53. Valuation for Customs Duty begins with –

(A) Determination of Import Value

(B) Determination of Transaction Value

(C) Determination of Invoice Value

(D) Interrogation of Importer.

54. The custom value fixed as per Section 14 is the value that would be used for calculating the customs duty payable. This is also called –

(A) Standard Value

(B) Assessable Value

(C) Nominal Value

(D) Any of the above

55. Mr. Ramsay imported some goods from USA of US $ 1,00,000. Advice him the exchange applicable for converting foreign currency value in to Indian currency?

(A) Rate of exchange in force as notified by RBI and approved by CBITC as on the date when the bill of entry is presented is considered for imports.

(B) Rate of exchange notified by the Government of India from time to time is relevant.

(C) Rate of exchange in force as notified by CBITC as on the date when the bill of entry is presented is considered for imports.

(D) Telegraphic transfer rate as notified by RBI as on the date when the bill of entry is presented is considered for imports.

56. Which of the following factor(s) is/are essential to determine assessable value in case of import and export under the Customs Act, 1962?

(1) Price at which such or like goods are ordinarily sold or offered for sale.

(2) Discount given by the exporter when goods are imported in to India.

(3) Fact that Seller and Buyer are not be related to each other.

(4) Exchange rate prescribed by the RBI when the bill of entry is presented.

Select the correct answer from the options given below:

(A) (2) & (1)

(B) (4) & (2)

(C) (3) & (1)

(D) (4), (1) & (3)

57. In case of exports –

(A) Rate of exchange in force as notified by CBEC as on the date on which is shipping bill is submitted to the Proper Officer makes the clearance order is relevant.

(B) Rate of exchange in force as notified by RBI as on the date on which bill of export is submitted to the Proper Officer is relevant.

(C) Rate of exchange in force as notified by CBEC as on the date on which bill of export is submitted to the Proper Officer is relevant.

(D) Rate of exchange in force as notified by CBITC as on the date on which the Proper Officer makes the clearance order is relevant.

58. Value of Imported Goods shall be the Transaction Value adjusted in accordance with provisions of –

(A) Rule 8

(B) Rule 10

(C) Rule 6

(D) Rule 12

59. CIF Value means –

(A) Price paid/payable for delivery at the time and place of importation, which essentially implies that the price up to a port in India when goods are imported.

(B) Price paid/payable for delivery at the time and place of exportation, which essentially implies that the price up to a port in India when goods are exported

(C) Both (A) and (B)

(D) None of the above

60. CIF Value = _____

(A) FOB Value – Cost of Transport + Insurance

(B) FOB Value + Cost of Transport – Insurance

(C) FOB Value – Cost of Transport – Insurance

(D) FOB Value + Cost of Transport + Insurance

61. Insurance to be taken at actual capped to a maximum of –

(A) 1.125% of FOB

(B) 1.125% of CIF

(C) 1.25% of FOB

(D) 1.25% of CIF

62. FOB Value = ?

(A) CIF Value – Cost of Transport – Insurance

(B) CIF Value + Cost of Transport + Insurance

(C) CIF Value – Cost of Transport + Insurance

(D) CIF Value + Cost of Transport – Insurance

63. Transaction Value = ?

(A) CIF + 1% of CIF as Landing Charges

(B) FOB + 1% of CIF as Landing Charges

(C) CIF + 1% of FOB as Landing Charges

(D) FOB + 1% of FOB as Landing Charges

64. In case of export if transaction value is not acceptable then value as per Export Valuation Rules has to be taken. Determine the proper sequence of such values.

1. Value arrived by Residual Method
2. Value of Similar Goods
3. Value of Identical Goods

Select the correct answer from the options given below:

(A) 3, 2, 1

(B) 1, 2, 3

(C) 2, 1, 3

(D) 3, 1, 2

65. If more than one transaction value of identical goods is found then which of the following shall be used to determine the value of imported goods?

(A) Value which importer agrees to apply with the permission of Proper Officer.

(B) Highest of such value.

(C) Value which Proper Officer deems fit.

(D) Lowest such value

66. Computed Value= ?

(A) Cost of production + Reasonable profit + Post importation transport charges

(B) Cost of production + Charges for design or brand + Reasonable profit

(C) Cost of production + Charges for design or brand + Actual profit earned by importer on resale in domestic market

(D) Cost of production + Charges for design or brand + Reasonable profit + Actual profit earned by importer on resale in domestic market – Marketing charges

67. Safeguard duty is a duty paid on ____.

(A) Import of goods into India

(B) Export of goods out of India

(C) (A) or (B)

(D) (A) and (B)

68. Safeguard duty is levied on goods imported into India –

(A) When such goods are imported from countries listed as non co-operative countries.

(B) When Central Government introduces an ordinance in the Parliament and goods are imported from countries listed as non co-operative countries.

(C) To protect the domestic industries in India from goods imported in mass quantities from China and other countries listed as non co-operative countries and later appropriate Act is passed by the Central Government with two third majority in the Parliament.

(D) When such goods are already manufactured in India, but the cost is higher as compared to import prices. It is levied to ensure that the Indian manufacturers don't suffer owing to import of cheaper goods from outside and therefore aims to create a level playing field for the Indian manufacturers and importers, thereby with the intent of safeguarding the National interest.

69. Anti-dumping duty –

(A) Prevents the predatory pricing measures/discriminatory pricing, that could be unfair for the local goods and markets

(B) Is levied on goods imported into India, when such goods are already manufactured in India, but the costs are higher as compared to import prices.

(C) Both (A) and (B)

(D) Either (A) or (B)

70. Central Government may, by special order, exempt from duty, any goods, on which duty is leviable only under exceptional circumstances. Further, no duty is to be collected, if the amount of duty leviable is less than or equal to ___

(A) US $ 100

(B) INR 100

(C) INR 1,000

(D) US $ 1,000

71. Match the following in relation to person in charge as defined in the Customs Act, 1962:

List I	***List II***
(P) Master	1. In case of an aircraft
(Q) Commander or Pilot	2. In case of a Vessel
(R) Conductor, guard or any other person having the chief direction of the train	3. In case of any other conveyance
(S) Driver or other person in charge of the conveyance	4. In case of a train

Select the correct answer from the options given below:

	(P)	**(Q)**	**(R)**	**(S)**
(A)	2	1	4	3
(B)	1	2	3	4
(C)	1	2	4	3
(D)	2	1	3	4

72. Which of the following is duty or responsibility of a person in charge under the Customs Act, 1962?

1. To submit Import/Export Manifest.
2. To pay import duty on all goods contained in vessel or ship.

3. To ensure that the conveyance lands at the appropriate place
4. Ensure that the Goods are loaded or unloaded only after proper permissions or orders.

Select the correct answer from the options given below:

(A) 1, 2 & 3

(B) 4, 2 & 1

(C) 2, 3 & 4

(D) 3, 1 & 4

73. As per Section 4 of the Customs Act, 1962, who may appoint persons as officers of customs?

(A) Board

(B) Central Government

(C) Board with prior approval of the Central Government

(D) Board with prior approval of the respective State Governments

74. As per Section 6 of the Customs Act, 1962, to whom the Central Government may, by notification in the Official Gazette, entrust either conditionally or unconditionally any functions of the Board or any officer of customs under the Act.

(A) to any officer of the Central Government

(B) to any officer the State Government

(C) to any officer of a local authority

(D) any of the above

75. Which of the following is the charging section of the Customs Act, 1962 for levy of customs duty?

(A) Section 12

(B) Section 13

(C) Section 11

(D) Section 10

76. The Import Manifest or Import Report is required to be delivered under –

(A) Section 29

(B) Section 30

(C) Section 31

(D) Section 35

77. In case of vessel or the aircraft Import Manifest is required to be delivered –

(A) Within twelve hours after its arrival in the customs station

(B) Prior to the arrival of the vessel or the aircraft, as the case may be

(C) Within twelve hours after its arrival in the customs water

(D) None of the above

78. In case of vehicle Import Report is required to be delivered –

(A) Within twelve hours after its arrival in the customs water

(B) Within twelve hours after its arrival in the customs station

(C) Within twelve hours after proper officer pass appropriate order

(D) Within twenty four hours after its arrival in the customs station.

79. Custom ports or airports are appointed by the –

(A) Central Government

(B) Board [CBITC]

(C) Respective State Governments with prior approval of Central Government

(D) Either (A) or (B)

80. Entry Inward granted by the Customs –

(A) Acts as permission for unloading the goods.

(B) Is the date which is construed as the relevant date for arrival of goods in India.

(C) Both (A) and (B).

(D) Only (A) but not (B)

81. The Custodian –

(A) Would be responsible for keeping proper record of unloaded goods.

(B) Is responsible to ensure that the goods don't leave the customs area without proper authorization from the Customs Officer

(C) Is appointed by the Principal Commissioner of Customs or Commissioner of Customs

(D) all of the above

82. Assessed duty is paid *vide* –

(A) TR-6 Challan

(B) TR-5 Challan

(C) TR-6A Challan

(D) TR-5A Challan

83. Demurrage charges are levied by the port authorities, if goods are not cleared within _____ of unloading.

(A) 3 days

(B) 5 days

(C) 7 days

(D) 10 days

84. Export General Manifest (EGM) is generally filed on the basis of –

(A) Bill of Entry

(B) Bill of Lading

(C) Airway Bill

(D) Either (B) or (C)

85. As per provisions of Chapter VIII of the Customs Act, 1962, in ______, the goods remain in the same vessel and consequently reach the port of clearance.

(A) Transhipment

(B) Transit

(C) Transport

(D) Travelling

86. As per provisions of Chapter VIII of the Customs Act, 1962, in ______, the vessel after reaching an intermediate port, transfers the goods to another vessel and the second vessel into which the goods are transferred (loaded) from the first vessel, carries the goods to the destination port.

(A) Transit

(B) Transhipment

(C) Travelling

(D) Transport

87. As per Section 53 of the Customs Act, 1962, subject to the provisions of section 11, where any goods imported in a conveyance and mentioned in the arrival manifest or import manifest or the import report, as for transit in the same conveyance to any place outside India or to any customs station, the Proper Officer may allow the goods and the conveyance to transit ________, subject to such conditions, as may be prescribed.

(A) Without payment of duty

(B) After payment of duty

(C) Without filing bill of transit

(D) After filing bill of transit

88. Which of the following section of the Customs Act, 1962 deals with transhipment of goods without payment of duty?

(A) Section 53

(B) Section 54

(C) Section 55

(D) Section 56

89. In transhipment –

(A) Goods are transferred to a different vessel at the intermediate port.

(B) Bill of Transhipment/declaration is also required to be submitted.

(C) A different vessel reaches the destination port

(D) All of the above

90. In transit –

(A) Goods remain in the same vessel at the intermediate port.

(B) Import manifest is not required to be submitted for entry.

(C) Double duty bond would also be required.

(D) All of the above

91. Which of the following types of goods can be warehoused?

(A) Only dutiable goods

(B) All types of imported goods whether dutiable or not

(C) Only goods to be exported

(D) Only prohibited goods

92. Section 57 of the Customs Act, 1962 provides that the ______ may, subject to such conditions as may be prescribed, licence a public warehouse wherein dutiable goods may be deposited.

(A) Principal Commissioner of Customs or Commissioner of Customs

(B) Central Government

(C) Central Government or Commissioner of Customs

(D) Commissioner (Appeal) or Commissioner of Customs

93. As per Section 58B(4) of the Customs Act, 1962, where the licence issued u/s 57 or 58 or 58A is cancelled, the goods warehoused shall, within ______ from the date on which order of such cancellation is served on the licensee or within such extended period as the proper officer may allow, be removed from such warehouse to another warehouse or be cleared for home consumption or export

(A) Seven days

(B) Ten days

(C) Thirty days

(D) One month

94. The importer of any goods in respect of which a bill of entry for warehousing has been presented u/s 46 and assessed to duty u/s 17 or 18 shall execute a bond in a sum equal to –

(A) thrice the amount of the duty assessed on such goods

(B) twice the amount of the duty assessed on such goods

(C) thrice the amount of assessable value of such goods

(D) twice the amount of assessable value of such goods

95. In the case of capital goods intended for use in any 100% EOU, such goods can be stored up to a period of ______

(A) 1 year

(B) Till the clearance of such goods from warehouse

(C) 3 years

(D) Till the expiry of 1 year from the date of order u/s 60(1) permitting removal of goods from customs station for deposit in warehouse

96. In the case of goods other than capital goods intended for use in any 100% EOU, such goods can be stored up to a period of ______

(A) Till the clearance of such goods from warehouse

(B) Till the consumption of such goods from warehouse

(C) Till the clearance or consumption of such goods from warehouse

(D) 3 years

97. In the case of any goods not intended for use in any 100% EOU, such goods can be stored up to a period of ______

(A) 2 years

(B) 1 year

(C) 6 months

(D) 3 months

98. What is the maximum rate of drawback of duty as per Section 74 of the Customs Act, 1962?

(A) 90%

(B) 80%

(C) 95%

(D) 98%

99. The owner of any warehoused goods may, after warehousing the same –

(a) Inspect the goods

(b) Sale the goods

(c) Deal with their containers to prevent loss/deterioration/ damage to the goods

(d) Consume the goods

(e) Sort the goods

(f) Show the goods for sale.

Select the correct answer from the options given below:

(A) (a), (c), (e) & (f)

(B) (a), (b), (d) & (f)

(C) (a), (b), (c), (e) & (f)

(D) (a), (e) & (f)

100. As per Section 74 of the Customs Act, 1962, duty drawback is allowed –

(A) On re-export of duty paid goods

(B) On material used in the manufacture of exported goods.

(C) Only respect of notified goods.

(D) As per All Industry Rate.

101. As per Section 74 of the Customs Act, 1962, duty drawback is allowed –

(A) Only respect of notified goods.

(B) As per All Industry Rate.

(C) If minimum value addition is achieved

(D) All of the above

102. Which of the following is eligible condition for availing drawback u/s 74?

(A) The goods must be capable of being easily identified.

(B) The goods must be exported within 2 years from the date of payment of duty.

(C) There is no requirement of value addition.

(D) All of the above

103. If goods are used for less than 3 months then how much percentage of import duty can be paid as drawback as per the rate notified by the Central Government u/s 74(2)?

(A) 98%
(B) 95%
(C) 90%
(D) 88%

104. If goods are used more than 3 months but for less than 6 months then how much percentage of import duty can be paid as drawback as per the rate notified by the Central Government u/s 74(2)?

(A) 95%
(B) 85%
(C) 80%
(D) 75%

105. If goods are used more than 18 months then how much percentage of import duty can be paid as drawback as per the rate notified by the Central Government u/s 74(2)?

(A) 60%
(B) 50%
(C) 10%
(D) Nil

106. Which of the following goods are not eligible for drawback?

(I) Wearing apparel
(II) Tea chests
(III) Exposed cinematograph film
(IV) Unexposed cinematograph film

Select the correct answer from the options given below:

(A) (I)
(B) (I), (II)
(C) (I), (II), (III)
(D) (I), (II), (III) & (IV)

107. Where any drawback payable to a claimant under section 74 or section 75 is not paid within a period of one month from the date of filing a claim for payment of such drawback, there shall be paid to that claimant in addition to the amount of drawback, interest at the rate of –

(A) 12%

(B) 15%

(C) 10%

(D) 6%

108. Where any drawback has been paid to the claimant erroneously or it becomes otherwise recoverable under the Act or the rules made thereunder, the claimant shall, within a period of 2 months from the date of demand, pay in addition to the said amount of drawback, interest at the rate of –

(A) 15%

(B) 12%

(C) 10%

(D) 8%

109. No drawback shall be allowed –

(A) In respect of any goods the market price of which is less than the amount of drawback due thereon

(B) Where the drawback due in respect of any goods is less than ₹ 50

(C) Both (A) and (B)

(D) None of the above

110. Where any duty has not been levied or not paid or short-levied or short-paid or erroneously refunded, or any interest payable has not been paid, part-paid or erroneously refunded, for any reason other than the reasons of collusion or any wilful misstatement or suppression of facts, the proper officer shall, within ______ from the relevant date, serve notice on the person chargeable with the duty or interest which has not been so levied or paid or which has been short-levied or short-paid or to whom the refund has erroneously been made, requiring him to show cause why he should not pay the amount specified in the notice.

(A) 1 year

(B) 2 years

(C) 3 years

(D) 6 months

111. Section 28(1) of the Customs Act, 1962 provides that the proper officer shall not serve such show cause notice, where the amount involved is less than ____

(A) ₹ 10

(B) ₹ 100

(C) ₹ 1,000

(D) ₹ 10,000

112. Generally, the show cause notice, should be served within ____ from the relevant date as provided in Section 28(1)(*a*).

(A) 1 year

(B) 3 years

(C) 4 years

(D) 2 years

113. In specific cases, where the duty or interest is not paid, or short paid, by reason of collusion, wilful suppression of facts, or misstatement, then the notice could be served within a period of –

(A) 5 years

(B) 4 years

(C) 3 years

(D) 2 years

114. Where notice has been served and the Proper Officer is of the opinion that the amount of duty along with interest payable thereon u/s 28AA or the amount of interest, as specified in the notice, has been paid in full within ______ from the date of receipt of the notice, no penalty shall be levied and the proceedings against such person or other persons to whom the said notice is served shall be deemed to be concluded.

(A) 30 days

(B) 15 days

(C) 60 days

(D) 45 days

115. As per Section 28(7A) of the Customs Act, 1962, the proper officer may issue a ______ under such circumstances and in such manner as may be prescribed.

(A) Show cause notice

(B) Proper notice

(C) Supplementary notice

(D) Demand notice

116. Which of the following section of the Customs Act, 1962 deals with *"confiscation of improperly imported goods"*?

(A) Section 110

(B) Section 111

(C) Section 111A

(D) Section 112

117. As per Section 112 of the Customs Act, 1962, what is the penalty for 'prohibited goods'?

(A) Value of goods or ₹ 5,000, whichever is higher.

(B) 10% of the duty sought to be evaded or ₹ 5,000, whichever is higher.

(C) Value of goods or ₹ 10,000, whichever is higher.

(D) 10% of the duty sought to be evaded or ₹ 10,000, whichever is higher.

118. As per Section 112 of the Customs Act, 1962, what is the penalty for 'dutiable goods' other than prohibited goods?

(A) 10% of the duty sought to be evaded or ₹ 10,000, whichever is higher.

(B) Value of goods or ₹ 10,000, whichever is higher.

(C) 10% of the duty sought to be evaded or ₹ 5,000, whichever is higher.

(D) Value of goods or ₹ 5,000, whichever is higher.

119. As per Section 112 of the Customs Act, 1962, what is the minimum penalty for 'prohibited goods'?

(A) ₹ 5,000

(B) ₹ 10,000

(C) ₹ 50,000

(D) ₹ 1,00,000

120. As per Section 112 of the Customs Act, 1962, what is the penalty for "Goods for which value stated in Bill of Entry or baggage declaration is greater than actual value"?

(A) Actual Value *less* Declared Value, or ₹ 5,000, whichever is higher.

(B) Actual Value of the goods, or Declared Value *less* Actual Value, or ₹ 5,000, whichever is higher.

(C) Actual Value *less* Declared Value, or ₹ 10,000, whichever is higher.

(D) Declared Value *less* Actual Value, or ₹ 5,000, whichever is higher.

121. As per Section 112 of the Customs Act, 1962, what is the penalty for "Prohibited goods in respect of which value stated in Bill of Entry or baggage declaration is greater than actual value"?

(A) Actual Value of the goods, or Declared Value *less* Actual Value, or ₹ 5,000, whichever is higher.

(B) Value of goods or ₹ 5,000, whichever is higher.

(C) Declared Value *less* Actual Value, or ₹ 10,000, whichever is higher.

(D) Actual Value of the goods, or Declared Value *less* Actual Value, or ₹ 10,000, whichever is higher.

122. As per Section 112 of the Customs Act, 1962, what is the penalty for "Prohibited goods (not dutiable) in respect of which value stated in Bill of Entry or baggage declaration is greater than actual value"?

(A) Actual Value of the goods, or Declared Value *less* Actual Value, or ₹ 5,000, whichever is higher.

(B) Duty sought to be evaded, or Declared Value *less* Actual Value, or ₹ 5,000, whichever is higher.

(C) Duty sought to be evaded, or Actual Value of the goods, whichever is higher.

(D) Duty sought to be evaded, or Actual Value of the goods, or ₹ 5,000, whichever is higher.

123. Section 123 clearly states that if goods are seized, the onus is on the –

(A) Owner to prove that they were not smuggled

(B) Person in possession of the goods to prove that they were not smuggled

(C) Proper officer prove that goods are smuggled goods

(D) CBITC to prove that goods are smuggled goods

124. Central Government may prohibit, _______, the import/export of goods of the specified description

(A) absolutely

(B) subject to such conditions specified in the notification

(C) either absolutely or subject to such conditions specified in the notification

(D) none of the above

125. Which of the following section of the Customs Act, 1962 deals with option to pay fine in lieu of confiscation?

(A) Section 121

(B) Section 123

(C) Section 125

(D) Section 127

126. Section 125 of the Customs Act, 1962 provides that redemption fine shall not exceed the –

(A) Market price of the goods confiscated

(B) Declared Value *less* Actual Value

(C) Actual Value of the goods

(D) Market price of the goods confiscated, less in the case of imported goods the duty chargeable thereon

127. Refund application must be filed within ______ from the date of payment of duty.

(A) 1 year

(B) 6 months

(C) 2 years

(D) 3 months

128. _____ of the Customs Act, 1962 prescribes the method for self-assessment of duty.

(A) Section 15

(B) Section 17

(C) Section 19

(D) Section 16

129. Self-assessed goods may be ____ by the proper officer.

(A) Verified

(B) Examined

(C) Tested

(D) Verified, examined or tested

130. Which of the following can be classified as 'criminal liability' under the Customs Act, 1962?

(A) Recovery of duties short paid

(B) Punishment up to 7 years

(C) Confiscation of import/export goods

(D) Interest charge

131. Which of the following can be classified as 'civil liability' under the Customs Act, 1962?

(A) Recovery of duties short paid

(B) Confiscation of import/export goods

(C) Confiscation of conveyances used for smuggling

(D) All of the above

132. Advance Ruling refers to the determination, by the authority, of a _____ specified in the application, regarding the liability to pay duty in relation to an activity proposed to be undertaken by an applicant.

(A) Question of law

(B) Question of fact

(C) Any question raised by the applicant

(D) Either (A) or (B)

133. Advance ruling application can be withdrawn within ______ of the application.

(A) 10 days

(B) 60 days

(C) 30 days

(D) 45 days

134. Advance ruling must be made within ______ of the application.

(A) 90 days

(B) 120 days

(C) 60 days

(D) 180 days

135. The Central Government may if it deems necessary to do so in the general interest of the public, exempt goods –

(A) Generally

(B) Specifically

(C) Generally or specifically

(D) By passing appropriate order

136. Offences under the Customs Act, 1962 could attract –

1. Civil Liabilities

2. Criminal Liabilities

Select the correct answer from the options given below:

(A) 1 only

(B) Either 1 or 2

(C) 2 only

(D) Either 1 or 2 or both

137. Which of the following duty is/are now subsumed under GST?

(I) Countervailing duty (CVD)

(II) Special Additional Duty (SAD)

Select the correct answer from the options given below:

(A) (II) only

(B) (I) only

(C) Both (I) or (II)

(D) Neither (I) nor (II)

138. Under the Customs Act, 1962, the relevant date for determining the rate of exchange in case of imported goods is:

(A) Date when the vessel arrives in India

(B) Date of presentation of bill of entry

(C) Date of examination of goods by proper officer

(D) Date of deposit of duty

139. Anti-Dumping duty is calculated as –

(A) Higher of margin of dumping or injury margin

(B) Lower of margin of dumping or injury margin

(C) Higher of export price or normal value

(D) Lower of export price or normal value

140. Which of the following can be taken as assessable value under the Customs Act, 1962?

(A) FOB Value

(B) CIF Value

(C) Landed Value

(D) Import Value

141. If the goods are imported by Air, the freight cannot exceed –

(A) 20% of FOB Value

(B) 20% of CIF Value

(C) 10% of FOB Value

(D) 15% of CIF Value

142. In which of the following cases, the refund under section 27 of the Customs Act, 1962 is credited to the Consumer Welfare Fund?

(A) If the importer proves that there is no unjust enrichment.

(B) Where goods are imported for non-personal use of an individual.

(C) If the amount of refund relates to drawback under sections 74 and 75 of the Customs Act, 1962.

(D) If the amount relates to export duty paid on goods which have been returned to exporter as specified under section 26 of the Customs Act, 1962

143. Which of the following goods are not mandatorily required to be deposited in a special warehouse under section 58A of the Customs Act, 1962?

(A) Gold and silver articles

(B) Supply as stores to vessels/aircrafts

(C) Supply to duty free shops in a customs area

(D) Supply meant for Government use

144. The integrated tax leviable on imported goods is levied –

(A) As an additional duty of customs u/s 3(7) of the Customs Tariff Act, 1975

(B) As integrated tax u/s 5 of the IGST Act, 2017

(C) As a duty of customs under the Customs Tariff Act, 1975 read with IGST Act, 2017

(D) None of the above

145. Which of the following statement is correct?

I. Customs area does not include a warehouse.

II. A beneficial owner of imported goods is a person on whose behalf the goods are being imported but cannot be exported.

III. Customs station includes international courier terminal but does not include the foreign post office.

Select the correct answer from the options given below:

(A) I

(B) II

(C) III

(D) None of the above

146. The Supreme Court in ______ has held that importation gets complete when goods become part of mass of goods within the country.

(A) Weston Components Ltd. v. CC

(B) Graden Silk Manufacturing Ltd. v. UOI

(C) Graden Silk Mills v. UOI

(D) Weston Silk Mills v. UOI

147. Which of the following statement is correct?

(A) Proper officer has right to reject transactional value.

(B) Transactional value shall be accepted even where the buyer and seller are related if relationship has not influenced the price.

(C) A bill of entry shall include all the goods mentioned in the bill of lading.

(D) All of the above

148. What is the interest rate for late payment of customs duty?

(A) 10%

(B) 12%

(C) 15%

(D) 22%

149. Which of the following statement is incorrect?

(I) Transit is allowed in every port normally.

(II) Transhipment is allowed in specified ports only.

Select the correct answer from the options given below:

(A) (II) only

(B) Both (I) and (II)

(C) (I) only

(D) Neither (I) nor (II)

150. Warehouse means –

(A) A public warehouse licensed u/s 57

(B) A private warehouse licensed u/s 58

(C) A special warehouse licensed u/s 58A

(D) (A) or (B) or (C)

PRACTICAL MCQs

151. Following data is available for import from USA:

FOB Value = ₹ 12,70,000

Freight = ₹ 2,54,000

Insurance = ₹ 6,000

Calculate CIF Value.

(A) ₹ 10,10,000

(B) ₹ 15,18,000

(C) ₹ 10,22,000

(D) ₹ 15,30,000

152. Following data is available for import from USA:

CIF Value = US $ 5,400

Freight = US $ 600

Insurance = US $ 1,800

Calculate FOB Value.

(A) US $ 3,000

(B) US $ 7,800

(C) US $ 4,200

(D) US $ 6,600

153. KPMG Ltd. imports equipment by Air. CIF price is US $ 6,000, freight paid is US $ 1,200 and insurance is US $ 1,800. RBI prescribes the exchange rate as ₹ 68. CBITC notifies the exchange rate as ₹ 65. What is assessable value under the Customs Law?

(A) ₹ 3,90,000

(B) ₹ 1,95,000

(C) ₹ 3,51,000

(D) ₹ 2,80,000

154. Parag International Ltd. exported some goods to USA by air at an FOB price of US $ 1,00,000. Other details are as follows:

Particulars	*Presentation of shipping bill*	*Let export order*
Date	16th April	18th May
Rate of duty	12%	10%
Exchange rate notified by CBITC	1 US $ = 65	1 US $ = 64
Exchange rate prescribed by RBI	1 US $ = 68	1 US $ = 66

The basic export duty payable by Parag International Ltd. is:

(A) ₹ 6,50,000

(B) ₹ 7,80,000

(C) ₹ 7,68,000

(D) ₹ 6,40,000

155. Shubham Ltd. has imported a machine from UK. Details of Import as follows:

Particulars	***Amount***
Price of the machine	£ 10,000
Freight (air)	£ 3,000
Engineering and design charges paid to a firm in UK	£ 500
License fee payable by the buyer as a condition of sale	20% of price
Materials and components supplied in UK by the buyer free of cost	₹ 20,000
Insurance paid to insurer in India	₹ 6,000

Particulars	*Amount*
Buying commission paid by the buyer to his agent in UK	£ 100

Inter-bank exchange rate: £ 1 = ₹ 98

CBITC notified exchange rate: £ 1 = ₹ 100

Importer paid ₹ 5,000 towards demurrage charges for delay in clearing the machine from the airport. Assessable value = ?

(A) ₹ 12,70,000

(B) ₹ 15,30,000

(C) ₹ 15,70,000

(D) ₹ 12,30,000

156. A person makes an unauthorized import of goods liable to confiscation. After adjudication, Assistant Commissioner provides an option to the importer to pay fine in lieu of confiscation. It is proposed to impose fine (in lieu of confiscation) equal to 50% of margin of profit. The following particulars are made available:

(i) Assessable value : ₹ 65,000

(ii) Total duty payable : ₹ 15,808

(iii) Market value : ₹ 1,00,000

What is the maximum amount of fine that can be levied u/s 125 of the Customs Act, 1962?

(A) ₹ 1,00,000

(B) ₹ 84,702

(C) ₹ 15,808

(D) ₹ 19,192

157. A person makes an unauthorized import of goods liable to confiscation. After adjudication, Assistant Commissioner provides an option to the importer to pay fine in lieu of confiscation. It is proposed to impose fine (in lieu of confiscation) equal to 50% of margin of profit. The following particulars are made available:

(i) Assessable value : ₹ 65,000

(ii) Total duty payable : ₹ 15,808

(iii) Market value : ₹ 1,00,000

Calculate total payment to be made by importer to clear the consignment.

(A) ₹ 19,192

(B) ₹ 9,596

(C) ₹ 15,808

(D) ₹ 25,404

158. Certain goods were imported by air. The free on board value of goods is ₹ 100. The cost of transport, loading, unloading and handling charges up to place of importation is ₹ 25. The cost of insurance is ₹ 10. For the purposes of Rule 10(2) of the Customs Valuation (Determination of Value of Imported Goods) Rules, 2007, which of the following shall be added to the value of imported goods?

(A) Cost of transport, loading, unloading & handling charges – ₹ 25 and Cost of insurance ₹ 10.

(B) Cost of transport, loading, unloading & handling charges – ₹ 25 and Cost of insurance ₹ 1.125.

(C) Cost of transport, loading, unloading & handling charges – ₹ 20 and Cost of insurance ₹ 1.125.

(D) Cost of transport, loading, unloading & handling charges – ₹ 20 and Cost of insurance ₹ 10.

159. ABC Ltd. imports equipment by air. CIF price of the equipment is US$ 6,000, freight paid is US$ 1,200 and insurance cost is US$ 1,800. CBITC notifies the exchange rate as ₹ 70 per $. ABC Ltd. expends ₹ 56,000 in India for certain development activities with respect to the imported equipment. Basic customs duty is 10%, Integrated tax is leviable @ 12% and social welfare surcharge is 10% on duty. *Ignore GST Compensation Cess.* Compute the amount of total duty and integrated tax payable by ABC Ltd. under Customs law.

(A) ₹ 91,930

(B) ₹ 50,350

(C) ₹ 37,800

(D) ₹ 40,900

160. From the following information you are required to determine the basic Export Duty:

(i) FOB Price of goods US $ 1,20,000

(ii) Shipping Bill presented electronically on 26th April

(iii) Proper officer passed the order permitting clearance and loading of goods for export on 5th May.

(iv) Rate of exchange and rate of export duty are as under:

Date	*Rate of exchange*	*Rate of Export Duty*
26th April	1 US $ = ₹ 60	9%
5th May	1 US $ = ₹ 61	10%

(A) ₹ 6,48,000

(B) ₹ 7,20,000

(C) ₹ 7,32,000

(D) ₹ 6,58,800

161. Priya imported certain goods weighing 1,000 kgs. having CIF value of US $ 40,000. Exchange rate of 1 US $ was ₹ 65 on the date of presentation of bill of entry. Basic customs duty chargeable is @ 10% and social welfare surcharge as applicable. There is no Integrated tax and GST compensation payable on these goods, if supplied in India. However, vide Notification issued by the Government of India, anti-dumping duty has been imposed on these goods. The anti-dumping duty will be equal to the difference between amount calculated @ US $ 60 per kg and the 'landed value' of goods. You are required to compute the amount of customs duty and of the anti-dumping duty payable by Priya.

(A) ₹ 10,14,000

(B) ₹ 12,67,800

(C) ₹ 2,86,000

(D) ₹ 13,00,000

162. Jaggi Mehta imported a car from UK for his personal use and paid ₹ 4,50,000 as import duty on the car. However, the car was being re-exported immediately without bringing it into use by Mr. Mehta. Calculate the amount of duty drawback allowable under the Customs Act, 1962.

(A) ₹ 4,41,000

(B) ₹ 4,50,000

(C) ₹ 4,27,500

(D) ₹ 3,60,000

163. Meenakshi imported a music player from Dubai and paid ₹ 12,000 as import duty. She used it for 4 months and thereafter re-exported the same after 4 months. Calculate the amount of duty drawback allowable under the Customs Act, 1962.

(A) ₹ 12,000

(B) ₹ 11,040

(C) ₹ 960

(D) Nil

164. Bholaram imported certain goods in November, and an 'into bond' bill of entry was presented on 28th November. Assessable value was US $ 1,00,000. Order permitting the deposit of goods in warehouse for 3 months was issued on 2nd Dec. Bholaram neither obtained extension of warehousing period nor cleared the goods within the permitted warehousing period of 1st March. Only after a notice was issued under section 72 of the Customs Act, 1962 demanding duty and other charges, Bholaram removed the goods on 15th April.

No additional duty or special additional duty is payable. You are supplied with the following information:

Particulars	28th Nov	1st March	15th April
Rate per US $	66	65	64

Calculate Assessable Value.

(A) ₹ 66,00,000

(B) ₹ 65,00,000

(C) ₹ 64,00,000

(D) ₹ 63,00,000

165. Calculate FOB Value, Cost of Insurance, Cost of Freight and Assessable Value where only the CIF value is given as US $ 5,000. Exchange rate notified by RBI and CBEC are ₹ 70 and ₹ 68 respectively for one US $.

(A) ₹ 2,17,600; ₹ 43,520; ₹ 2,448

(B) ₹ 2,41,264; ₹ 48,253; ₹ 2,714

(C) ₹ 2,80,702; ₹ 56,140; ₹ 3,158

(D) ₹ 2,69,144; ₹ 53,829; ₹ 3,028

166. From the following details calculate total custom duty payable:

Particulars	***(US $)***
Cost of the machine	20,000
Transport charges from the factory of the exporter, to the port for shipment	800
Handling charges paid for loading the machine in the ship	50
Buying commission paid by importer	100
Lighterage charges	200
Freight incurred from port of entry to Inland Container depot	1,000
Ship demurrage charges	400
Freight from exporting country to India	5,000

Date of bill of entry: 20th February

(BCD 20%; Exchange rate ₹ 60 per US $)

Date of entry inward: 25th January

(BCD 12%; Exchange rate ₹ 65 per US $)

Rate of IGST = 12%.

(A) ₹ 5,86,633

(B) ₹ 5,86,366

(C) ₹ 5,68,633

(D) ₹ 5,68,366

167. Sai Cars Ltd. is a dealer in cars. They import cars from abroad and sell it to customers in India. On 20th March, they have imported cars from Japan, as per following details:

Customs duty	10%
IGST	28%
Compensation cess	20%

Assessable value of cars = ₹ 4,00,00,000

Sai Cars Ltd. is eligible to claim input tax credit (ITC). Their output IGST liability, before taking credit for ITC is ₹ 130 lakh. Compute the net liability towards customs duty and IGST.

(A) ₹ 2,57,12,000; ₹ 1,24,32,000

(B) ₹ 2,57,12,000; ₹ 5,68,000

(C) ₹ 1,24,32,000; ₹ 1,24,32,000

(D) ₹ 88,80,000; ₹ 5,68,000

ANSWERS:

1.	(B)	**2.**	(A)	**3.**	(D)	**4.**	(A)	**5.**	(B)	**6.**	(B)	**7.**	(A)
8.	(A)	**9.**	(C)	**10.**	(B)	**11.**	(D)	**12.**	(B)	**13.**	(A)	**14.**	(B)
15.	(B)	**16.**	(D)	**17.**	(D)	**18.**	(D)	**19.**	(C)	**20.**	(B)	**21.**	(C)
22.	(B)	**23.**	(C)	**24.**	(A)	**25.**	(D)	**26.**	(C)	**27.**	(D)	**28.**	(C)
29.	(D)	**30.**	(D)	**31.**	(D)	**32.**	(B)	**33.**	(C)	**34.**	(A)	**35.**	(A)
36.	(B)	**37.**	(A)	**38.**	(A)	**39.**	(B)	**40.**	(D)	**41.**	(A)	**42.**	(A)
43.	(D)	**44.**	(C)	**45.**	(C)	**46.**	(C)	**47.**	(B)	**48.**	(D)	**49.**	(C)
50.	(A)	**51.**	(B)	**52.**	(D)	**53.**	(B)	**54.**	(C)	**55.**	(C)	**56.**	(C)
57.	(D)	**58.**	(B)	**59.**	(A)	**60.**	(D)	**61.**	(A)	**62.**	(A)	**63.**	(A)
64.	(A)	**65.**	(D)	**66.**	(B)	**67.**	(A)	**68.**	(D)	**69.**	(A)	**70.**	(B)
71.	(A)	**72.**	(D)	**73.**	(A)	**74.**	(D)	**75.**	(A)	**76.**	(B)	**77.**	(B)
78.	(B)	**79.**	(B)	**80.**	(C)	**81.**	(D)	**82.**	(A)	**83.**	(A)	**84.**	(D)
85.	(B)	**86.**	(B)	**87.**	(A)	**88.**	(B)	**89.**	(D)	**90.**	(A)	**91.**	(A)
92.	(A)	**93.**	(A)	**94.**	(A)	**95.**	(B)	**96.**	(C)	**97.**	(B)	**98.**	(D)
99.	(A)	**100.**	(A)	**101.**	(D)	**102.**	(D)	**103.**	(B)	**104.**	(B)	**105.**	(D)

106.	(D)	**107.**	(D)	**108.**	(A)	**109.**	(C)	**110.**	(B)	**111.**	(B)	**112.**	(D)
113.	(A)	**114.**	(A)	**115.**	(C)	**116.**	(B)	**117.**	(A)	**118.**	(C)	**119.**	(A)
120.	(D)	**121.**	(A)	**122.**	(B)	**123.**	(A)	**124.**	(C)	**125.**	(C)	**126.**	(D)
127.	(A)	**128.**	(B)	**129.**	(D)	**130.**	(B)	**131.**	(D)	**132.**	(D)	**133.**	(C)
134.	(A)	**135.**	(C)	**136.**	(D)	**137.**	(C)	**138.**	(B)	**139.**	(B)	**140.**	(B)
141.	(A)	**142.**	(B)	**143.**	(D)	**144.**	(D)	**145.**	(D)	**146.**	(C)	**147.**	(D)
148.	(C)	**149.**	(D)	**150.**	(D)	**151.**	(D)	**152.**	(A)	**153.**	(C)	**154.**	(A)
155.	(B)	**156.**	(B)	**157.**	(D)	**158.**	(D)	**159.**	(A)	**160.**	(B)	**161.**	(D)
162.	(A)	**163.**	(B)	**164.**	(A)	**165.**	(C)	**166.**	(A)	**167.**	(B)		

HINTS FOR IMPORTANT PRACTICAL MCQs

151. CIF Value = FOB Value + Cost of Transport + Insurance

= 12,70,000 + 2,54,000 + 6,000

= 15,30,000

152. FOB Value = CIF Value – Cost of Transport – Insurance

= 5,400 – 600 – 1,800

= 3,000

153.

Particulars	**Amount**
FOB value	\$ 3,000
(+) Freight (20% of FOB value) [Note 1]	\$ 600
(+) Insurance (actual)	\$ 1,800
CIF	\$ 5,400
Exchange rate as per CBIC [Note 2]	₹ 65 per \$
Assessable value = ₹ 65 × \$ 5,400	₹ 3,51,000

Note 1: If the goods are imported by air, the freight cannot exceed 20% of FOB price [Fifth proviso to Rule 10(2) of the Customs (Determination of Value of Imported Goods) Rules, 2007].

Note 2: Rate of exchange determined by CBITC is considered [Clause (*a*) of the *explanation* to section 14 of the Customs Act, 1962].

155.

Particulars	**Amount (£)**
Price of the machine	10,000
(+) Engineering and design charges paid in UK [Note 1]	500
(+) License fee payable by the buyer as a condition of sale (20% of price of machine) [Note 1]	2,000
Total	12,500

Particulars	**Amount (₹)**
Value in Indian currency [£ 12,500 × ₹ 100] [Note 2]	12,50,000
(+) Materials and components supplied by the buyer free of cost [Note 1]	20,000
FOB	12,70,000
(+) Freight [Note 3]	2,54,000
Insurance paid to the insurer in India [Note 1]	6,000
CIF value	15,30,000
Assessable value (rounded off)	15,30,000

Notes:

1. Engineering and design charges paid in UK, licence fee relating to imported goods payable by the buyer as a condition of sale, materials and components supplied by the buyer free of cost and actual insurance charges paid are all includible in the assessable value [Rule 10 of the Customs (Determination of Value of Imported Goods) Rules, 2007].
2. As per explanation to section 14(1) of the Customs Act, 1962, assessable value should be calculated with reference to the rate of exchange notified by the CBIC.
3. If the goods are imported by air, the freight cannot exceed 20% of FOB value [Fifth proviso to rule 10(2) of the Customs (Determination of Value of Imported Goods) Rules, 2007].

4. Buying commission is not included in the assessable value [Rule 10(1)(*a*) of the Customs (Determination of Value of Imported Goods) Rules, 2007].
5. Only ship demurrage charges on chartered vessels are included in the cost of transport of the imported goods. Thus, demurrage charges for delay in clearing the machine from the airport will not be includible in the assessable value [*Explanation* to rule 10(2) of the Customs (Determination of Value of Imported Goods) Rules, 2007].

156. & 157.

Option to pay fine in lieu of confiscation [Section 125]: Whenever confiscation of any goods is authorized by the Act, the officer adjudging it may give to the owner of the goods or where such owner is not known, the person from whose possession or custody such goods have been seized an option to pay in lieu of confiscation such fine as the said officer thinks fit.

However, such fine shall not exceed the 'market price of the goods confiscated' *less* 'import duty'.

Assessable value	65,000
(+) Duty payable	15,808
Total cost	80,808
Market value	1,00,000
Profit (25,00,000 – 21,00,000)	19,192
Proposed fine = 50% of margin of profit	9,596
Maximum fine 'market price of the goods confiscated' *less* 'import duty' [1,00,000 – 15,808]	84,702

Since the proposed fine is less than maximum fine permissible, the redemption fine payable by the importer would be ₹ 9,596.

Total payment to be made by the importer = ₹ 15,808 (Duty) + ₹ 9596 (Fine) = ₹ 25,404.

159.

Particulars	**Amount ($)**
CIF	6,000
(-) Freight	1,200
(-) Insurance	1,800
FOB	3,000
Add: Freight (20% of FOB value) [Note 1]	600
Add: Insurance (actual)	1,800
CIF Value	5,400

Particulars	**Amount (₹)**
Assessable value = $ 5,400 × ₹ 70	3,78,000.00
(+) Basic customs duty @ 10%	37,800.00
(+) Social Welfare Surcharge @ 10%	3,780.00
Sub-total	4,19,580.00
Integrated tax u/s 3(7) of the Customs Tariff Act @ 12% of 4,19,580 [Note 4]	50,349.60
Total customs duty and integrated tax payable [37,800 + 3,780 + 50,349.60]	91,929.60
Total customs duty and integrated tax payable (rounded off)	91,930

Notes:

1. If the goods are imported by air, the freight cannot exceed 20% of FOB price.
2. Rate of exchange determined by CBIC is considered.
3. Rule 10(1)(*b*)(*iv*) of the Customs Valuation (Determination of Value of Imported Goods) Rules, 2007 *inter alia* provides that value of development work undertaken elsewhere than in India is includible in the value of the imported goods. Thus, development charges of ₹ 56,000 paid for work done in India have not been included for the purposes of arriving at the assessable value.

4. Integrated tax leviable u/s 3(7) of the Customs Tariff Act, 1975 is levied on the sum total of the assessable value of the imported goods, customs duties and applicable social welfare surcharge.

160. Transactional value = FOB Price of goods = $ 1,20,000.

Rate of exchange will be the date of presentation of Shipping Bill *i.e.* 26.4.2018: 1$ = ₹ 60.

Value in Indian currency = $ 1,20,000 × ₹ 60 = ₹ 72,00,000.

Rate of export duty will be the date on which proper officer passed the order permitting clearance and loading of goods for export *i.e.* 5.5.2018 = 10%

Basic Export Duty = ₹ 72,00,000 × 10% = ₹ 7,20,000.

Note: *Education cess is not levied on export duty.*

161.

Assessable value i.e. CIF Value [$ 40,000 ×65]	26,00,000
(+) Basic Customs Duty @ 10%	2,60,000
(+) Social Welfare Charge @ 10% of basic duty	26,000
Landed value/cost of the goods	28,86,000
Cost of Goods for anti-dumping duty [1,000 kg × $ 60 × $ 65]	39,00,000
Anti-dumping duty [39,00,000 – 28,86,000]	10,14,000
Total customs duty [2,60,000 + 26,000 + 10,14,000]	13,00,000

Notes:

- *As per question only basic customs duty (including cess) and anti-dumping duty are leviable on goods. Additional duty u/s 3(5) is not leviable.*
- *Cess is not levied on anti-dumping duty.*
- *Landed value includes all duties of custom except duties levied under sections 3, 8B, 9 & 9A.*

162. As per **Section 74** of the Customs Act, 1962, when any goods capable of being easily identified which have been imported into India and upon which any duty has been paid on importation, are to be exported, 98% of duty shall be re-paid as drawback, if –

(i) the goods are identified to the satisfaction of the AC/DC as the goods which were imported; and

(ii) the goods are entered for export within 2 years from the date of payment of duty on the importation thereof.

Thus, Jaggi Mehta can claim drawback of ₹ 4,41,000 i.e. 98% of ₹ 4,50,000.

163. In respect of a **motor car** or **goods imported for personal use**, drawback of duty shall be allowed equal to import duty paid as reduced by 4%, 3%, 2.5% & 2% respectively for use for each quarter or part thereof during the first year, second year, third year and fourth year respectively. Thus, Meenakshi will be allowed drawback as calculated below:

Duty paid	12,000
(-) Reduction for two quarters of first year [12,000×8%]	(960)
	11,040

164. Rate of exchange = Rate of exchange in force on the date of presentation of bill of entry for warehousing shall apply i.e. $ 1 = ₹ 66. **[Section 14]**

Rate of duty = Goods are deemed to be removed on expiry of warehousing period i.e. on 1.3.2017 and hence rate of duty will be 10% including cess of 3%. Net rate = 10.3%. **[Section 72]**

Assessable value = $1,00,000 × 66 = ₹ 66,00,000.

165. CIF Value in Indian currency = $ 5,000 × 68 = ₹ 3,40,000.

CIF Value = FOB Value + Cost of transport + Cost of Insurance

Let the FOB value be 'x'.

FOB Value	x
(+) Cost of transport [Note 1]	$0.2x$
(+) Cost of Insurance [Note 2]	$0.01125x$
CIF Value	3,40,000

$1.21125x = 3,40,000$

x = FOB Value = 2,80,702

Cost of transport = 2,80,702 × 20% = 56,140

Cost of Insurance = 2,80,702 × 1.125% = 3,158

Note 1: Cost of transport will be 20% of FOB Value if not ascertainable.

Note 2: Cost of insurance will be 1.125% of FOB Value if not ascertainable

166. *Computation of assessable value:*

Particulars	$
Cost of the machine at the factory of the exporter	20,000
(+) Transport charges	800
(+) Handling charges	50
FOB Value	20,850
(+) Lighterage charges paid by the importer	200
(+) Ship demurrage charges	400
(+) Freight charges from exporting country to India	5,000
(+) Insurance @ 1.125% of FOB Value	234.5625
CIF Value/Assessable value	26,684.5625

Computation of total customs duty payable:

Particulars	₹
Assessable value in Indian currency [26,684.5625 × 60]	16,01,073.75
(+) Basic customs duty [16,01,073.75 × 20%]	3,20,214.75
(+) Social Welfare Charge [3,20,214.75 × 10%]	32,021.48
	19,53,309.98
(+) Integrated tax u/s 3(7) [19,53,309.98 × 12%]	2,34,397.20
Total cost of import	21,87,707.18
Total Customs Duty Payable [3,20,214.75 + 32,021.48 + 2,34,397.20]	5,86,633

Notes:

- Buying commission is not includible in assessable value.

- Freight incurred from port of entry to Inland Container depot is not includible in assessable value.
- No landing charges are added to the CIF Value due to amendment in Rule 10(2).

167. *Computation of total customs duty payable:*

Particulars	₹
Assessable value in Indian currency	4,00,00,000
(+) Basic customs duty [4,00,00,000 × 10%]	40,00,000
(+) Social Welfare Charge [40,00,000 × 10%]	4,00,000
	4,44,00,000
(+) Integrated tax u/s 3(7) [4,44,00,000 × 28%]	1,24,32,000
(+) Compensation cess [4,44,00,000 × 20%]	88,80,000
Total cost of import	6,57,12,000
Total Customs Duty Payable	2,57,12,000

True Sai Cars Pvt. Ltd. can take credit of integrated tax paid of ₹ 1,24,32,000.

Computation of net IGST payable:

Particulars	₹
Output IGST liability	1,30,00,000
(-) Integrated tax paid on import	(1,24,32,000)
	5,68,000

Solved Paper
CS Executive - June 2018

(AS PER LAW APPLICABLE FOR AY 2019-2020)

PART A

1. Which out of the following elements you find are sufficient for bringing to tax as income from business or profession :

(*i*) Ownership of the business is not necessary

(*ii*) Business must be legal

(*iii*) Income may be earned in cash or kind

(*iv*) Profit motive is the sole consideration

(A) (*i*), (*ii*) and (*iv*)

(B) All the four

(C) (*i*) and (*iii*)

(D) (*ii*), (*iii*) and (*iv*)

2. Sakshita Pvt. Ltd., has spent a sum of ₹ 30 lakh towards meeting its Corporate Social Responsibility (CSR) obligation. The amount of deduction available while computing the business income is ₹ :

(A) 30 lakh

(B) Nil

(C) 37.5 lakh

(D) 45 lakh

3. Expenses not specifically being allowed under any of sections 30 to 36 and incurred for the purpose of business or profession are allowable as per section 37(1) of the Act. The following expenses are allowable under this section :

(*i*) Expenditure on issue of share capital

(*ii*) Expenses for the installation of new telephone

(*iii*) Annual listing fees paid to stock exchange

(*iv*) Loss caused by robbery or dacoity incidental to business

(A) (*i*) and (*iv*)

(B) (*ii*), (*iii*) and (*iv*)

(C) (*ii*) and (*iii*)

(D) All the four

4. John Miller & Co. of UK is maintaining and operating a branch in India for sale of its garment products. The adjusted total income of the branch for the year prior to charge of H.O. expenses of ₹ 20 lakh is of ₹ 100 lakh. Indian branch intends to know the maximum amount of H.O. expenses as allowable during the year under the Act. Specify the amount:

(A) ₹ 20 lakh

(B) Nil as HO is non-resident

(C) ₹ 5 lakh

(D) 8% of adjusted total income

5. The additional depreciation on the factory building constructed during the P.Y. 2018-2019 and put to use for manufacturing of garments on 1st Feb., 2019 having cost of ₹ 100 lakh shall be allowed in A.Y. 2019-2020 at a rate of :

(A) 5%

(B) 10%

(C) 15%

(D) Nil

6. Out of the following, which income is chargeable as capital gain :

(*i*) from transfer of self generated goodwill of profession

(*ii*) from transfer of personal jewellery

(*iii*) from transfer of paintings and art-work

(*iv*) from transfer of furniture utilised for personal use

(A) (*i*) and (*ii*)

(B) (*ii*) and (*iii*)

(C) (*i*), (*ii*) and (*iii*)

(D) All the four

7. Land or building, or both, if transferred on or after 1st April, 2018 shall be treated as a long term capital asset, if it is being held immediately prior to the date of its transfer for more than :

(A) 36 months

(B) 12 months

(C) 24 months

(D) None of the above

8. Base year for the purpose of calculation of indexed cost of acquisition or the cost of improvement in respect of long term capital asset acquired prior to 1st April, 2001 shall be taken as :

(A) 1981-82

(B) 2001-02

(C) 1991-92

(D) 2011-12

9. X entered into an agreement for sale of his house located at Jaipur to Y on 1st April, 2017 for a total sale consideration of ₹ 90 lakh. Y paid an amount of ₹ 20 lakh by account payee cheque to X on the date of agreement and balance was to be paid at the time of registration of deed. However, the conveyance deed could not be executed till 1st Sept., 2018. The Stamp Valuation Authority determined the value of the property on the date of registration of conveyance deed at ₹ 120 lakh and the value determined by the Stamp Valuation Authority on the date of agreement was ₹ 100 lakh. The value for the purpose of capital gain u/s 50C shall be taken :

(A) ₹ 90 lakh

(B) ₹ 120 lakh

(C) ₹ 20 lakh

(D) ₹ 100 lakh

10. The cost of improvement in relation to the capital asset being goodwill of the business shall be taken to be as :

(A) Cost incurred by the previous owner

(B) Actual cost incurred by the assessee

(C) Incurred cost after indexation

(D) None of the above

11. In the hands of Mr. Sarath, a salaried employee, the following income shall be chargeable to tax as income under the head "Income from other sources" :

(*i*) Dividend

(*ii*) Income from hiring of machinery

(*iii*) Winning from Lottery

(*iv*) Interest on securities

(A) (*i*) and (*iii*)

(B) (*iii*) and (*iv*)

(C) All the four above

(D) (*i*), (*iii*) and (*iv*)

12. Babu Lal won a prize of ₹ 1,00,000 in Rajasthan State Lottery and Lottery Department paid him an amount of ₹ 70,000 after deduction of tax at source of ₹ 30,000. He had purchased lottery tickets for ₹ 8,000. The amount chargeable to tax in the hands of Babu Lal under other sources shall be :

(A) ₹ 70,000

(B) ₹ 1,00,000

(C) ₹ 92,000

(D) None of the above

13. Mr. Pankaj, a salaried employee, has taken a house on rent of ₹ 12,000 p.m. which was sub-let by him for ₹ 15,000 p.m. He has incurred miscellaneous expenses in relation to sub-let of the house of ₹ 1,000. How much income from the sub-letting of house shall be taxable in the A.Y. 2019-2020 where the house was taken on rent and also sub-let by him from 1st April, 2018 onwards :

(A) ₹ 36,000

(B) ₹ 26,000

(C) ₹ 1,44,000

(D) None of the above

14. Ram has gifted an amount of ₹ 10,00,000 to his wife Sita without consideration (but not to live apart), which was invested by his wife in interest bearing security. She earned interest of ₹ 1,00,000. The interest of ₹ 1,00,000 was further invested by her in the business from which she earned a profit of ₹ 15,000. The income which is to be included out of this gifted amount in the hands of Ram is :

(A) ₹ 1,15,000

(B) ₹ 15,000

(C) ₹ 1,00,000

(D) Nil, because gift is to relative

15. In which case a partnership firm is not entitled to carry forward and set off so much of the losses proportionate to the share of a retired or deceased person exceeding his/her share of profits, if any, in the firm in respect of the previous year :

(A) When the public are not substantially interested in firm

(B) When the business or profession is succeeding by another person

(C) When a change occurred in constitution of the firm

(D) None of the above

16. Deduction u/s 80C from the gross total income of an amount equal to the eligible investment made subject to a maximum amount of ₹ 1,50,000 is allowed to the assessee who is :

(A) A Hindu Undivided Family

(B) Any person

(C) An individual

(D) Both (A) and (C)

17. 50% deduction of the eligible amount is allowed u/s 80CCG, provided some of the conditions out of the following are to be fulfilled:

(*i*) The assessee is a resident Individual

(*ii*) The gross total income does not exceed ₹ 12 lakh

(*iii*) He has acquired listed shares or listed units of an equity oriented funds in accordance with a notified scheme

(*iv*) The investment is locked in for a period of 3 years from the date of acquisition in accordance with the equity oriented scheme

(A) (*i*), (*ii*) and (*iv*)

(B) All the four above

(C) (*i*) and (*iii*)

(D) (*i*), (*ii*) and (*iii*)

18. An assessee can avail the deduction in respect of rent paid u/s 80GG of the Act subject to a maximum amount of:

(A) ₹ 5,000 p.m.

(B) 25% of the adjusted total income

(C) ₹ 3,000 p.m.

(D) None of the above

19. The profits of a co-operative society engaged in (*i*) Carrying out the business of banking, (*ii*) A cottage industry and (*iii*) Collective disposal of labours of its member are eligible for deduction u/s 80P up to

(A) 75% of the profits

(B) 100% of the profits

(C) 50% of the profits

(D) None of the above

20. Maximum amount of deduction (in terms of ₹) in the case of an individual who is resident in India, a patentee and in receipt of income by way of royalty in respect of a patent registered on or after first day of April, 2003 under the Patents Act, 1970 is allowed :

(A) 100% of such income

(B) 50% of such income

(C) ₹ 3 lakh

(D) No such deduction under the Act

21. Ram & Co., a partnership firm, worked out total book profits for the year ended 31st March, 2019 at ₹ 5,00,000. The firm has made payment of salary of ₹ 4,60,000 authorized by the deed to the working partners wants to know that how much amount of salary paid to partners is allowable:

(A) Actual salary paid of ₹ 4,60,000

(B) ₹ 3,90,000

(C) ₹ 2,70,000

(D) ₹ 2,50,000

22. The provisions of AMT under Chapter XII-BA shall not apply to an individual, a HUF, etc., if the adjusted total income of such person does *not* exceed :

(A) ₹ 10,00,000

(B) ₹ 25,00,000

(C) ₹ 5,00,000

(D) ₹ 20,00,000

23. RS HUF consists of R Karta, Y and S co-parceners, D, the daughter of a co-parcener and W, the wife of Karta as members. The following can demand the partition of RS HUF :

(A) D

(B) R, Y and S

(C) W

(D) (A) and (B) above

24. Total income of XYZ Limited includes the income of dividend of ₹ 10 lakh paid by a U.K. based foreign company in which XYZ Limited holds 30% of the equity share capital. ₹ 50,000 has been spent for earning such dividend. The dividend income so received by the company from the U.K. based foreign company and the tax rate shall be :

(A) Not taxable being exempt u/s 10(34)

(B) Taxable @ 15% of ₹ 10 lakh

(C) Taxable @ 15% of ₹ 9.5 lakh

(D) Taxable @ 10% of ₹ 9.5 lakh

25. MAT credit can be carried forward for a period of following number of assessment years :

(A) 5

(B) 8

(C) 10

(D) No time limit

26. A non-resident (other than company) and a foreign company will pay tax on the income of interest received from an infrastructure debt fund referred to in section 10(47) at the rate of:

(A) 20%

(B) 5%

(C) 10%

(D) 7.5%

27. ABC Limited has paid amount of royalty of ₹ 30 lakh in September, 2018 to John Miller Company of USA in pursuance of an agreement approved by the Central Government in the previous year 2016-2017. The royalty so received by the foreign company shall be subject to tax in A.Y. 2019-2020 and the amount of tax payable by the foreign company shall be :

(A) ₹ 9.27 lakh

(B) ₹ 4.635 lakh

(C) ₹ 3 lakh

(D) None of the above

28. LM, a co-operative society, has paid interest of ₹ 1,05,000 to PQ, another co-operative society. The tax to be deducted at source u/s 194A is :

(A) ₹ 10,500

(B) ₹ 10,815

(C) ₹ 5,250

(D) Nil

29. Mr. Rajesh had a turnover of ₹ 3 crore during the year ended 31st March, 2018. During the F.Y. 2018-2019, he paid a sum of ₹ 10 lakh to E, an Engineer for construction of his self-occupied residence and ₹ 25 lakh to E, for construction of office building. The amount of tax to be deducted at source from payments made to E is :

(A) ₹ 3 lakh

(B) ₹ 50,000

(C) ₹ 2.5 lakh

(D) None of the above

30. Where the advance tax paid on or before March, 2019 is less than 100% of the tax due on the total income declared in the return of income, as reduced by tax deducted at source, the assessee shall be making payment of interest on the amount of shortfall on the returned income so declared at the rate of .... per month for the period of delay.

(A) 2%

(B) 1%

(C) Nil

(D) 1.5%

31. Finance Act, 2017 has inserted the provision for charging of fees for delay in furnishing the return of income and as per this section, be the amount of fee payable for the return declaring income of ₹ 25 lakh to be filled by 'X' on 28th January, 2020 instead of due date of filing of return u/s 139(1) for A.Y. 2019-2020:

(A) ₹ 1,000

(B) ₹ 5,000

(C) ₹ 10,000

(D) ₹ 3,000

32. ABC Limited has filed its return of income for A.Y. 2019-2020 as per section 139(1) but had failed to make the payment of tax on the returned income as per section 140A. The return so filed by ABC Limited shall be treated as :

(A) A defective return u/s 139(9)

(B) A valid return

(C) A *non-est* return

(D) None of the above

33. The time limit prescribed u/s 153 for completion of the regular assessment u/s 143(3) and a best judgment assessment u/s 144 is of .... months from the end of the assessment year in which the income was first assessable.

(A) 24

(B) 9

(C) 18

(D) 3

34. An appeal against the order passed by the Assessing Officer u/s 143(3) read with section 148 can be filed by an aggrieved assessee before the :

(A) Addl. Commissioner of Income Tax

(B) Commissioner of Income Tax

(C) ITAT

(D) Commissioner of Income Tax (Appeals)

35. The Assessing Officer, while scrutinizing the return of an assessee, finds under-reporting of income for the reason of misreporting of facts of such income. He can levy penalty on such under-reported income resulting from misreporting of income upto .... of tax payable on such under-reported or misreported income.

(A) 50%

(B) 100%

(C) 200%

(D) 300%

36. Avinash Enterprises sold a machine to Bimlesh LLP (Associated Enterprises) at sale margin of 25% for ₹ 4,00,000 which was actually to be sold to Chetan Enterprises. Bimlesh LLP, after receipt of machine, has incurred amount of ₹ 10,000 in sending the same to Chetan Enterprises. The arm's length price of the transaction is :

(A) ₹ 3,00,000

(B) ₹ 4,10,000

(C) ₹ 2,90,000

(D) Insufficient information

37. ABC Pvt. Ltd. has a business loss of ₹ 10 lakh. There is unexplained share application money to the tune of ₹ 25 lakh. The total income of the company will be :

(A) ₹ 15 lakh

(B) ₹ 35 lakh

(C) ₹ 25 lakh

(D) None of the above

38. Provisions of Minimum Alternate Tax (MAT) are applicable to the companies which are :

(*i*) Indian companies

(*ii*) Foreign companies in certain situations

(*iii*) LLP

(A) (*i*) and (*iii*)

(B) (*i*) and (*ii*)

(C) All the three

(D) None of the above

39. Mr. Soloman, a resident in India, aged 70 and has the following income for the previous year 2018-2019. (All the incomes given below are the computed income) :

(*i*) Net taxable pension under the head 'salary' from employer ₹ 2,30,000

(*ii*) Rental Income under House Property ₹ 2,00,000

(*iii*) Agricultural income from a land in Jaipur ₹ 60,000

His total tax liability for A.Y. 2019-2020 is :

(A) ₹ 14,420

(B) ₹ 3,240 after rebate u/s 87A

(C) ₹ 8,240

(D) Nil, because total income is less than ₹ 5,00,000

40. The Principal Commissioner of Income-tax is empowered to revise the assessment order of the Assessing Officer when the same is found to be erroneous and pre-judicial to the interest of Revenue. Such power is vested in the Principal Commissioner of Income-tax u/s :

(A) 263

(B) 246C

(C) 264

(D) Both 263 and 264

41. First appeal can be filed by :

(A) Department only

(B) Assessee only

(C) (A) or (B)

(D) None of the above

42. The A.O. can complete the assessment u/s 144 of the Act even though there is no failure on the part of assessee u/s 139(1), 139(4), 139(5), 142(1), 142(2A) or 143(2) of the Act. Such powers by the A.O. may be exercised in the following situations :

(A) Where the A.O. is not satisfied about the correctness or completeness of the accounts of the assessee.

(B) Where the method of accounting has not been regularly followed by the assessee.

(C) Where the income has not been computed in accordance with "ICDS" notified by the Central Government u/s 145(2).

(D) Any of above three or in all three above situations.

43. The respondent is having right to file Memorandum of Cross Objections before the ITAT after receipt of the Memorandum of Appeal filed by the appellant. Such Memorandum of Cross Objections is to be filed by the respondent within a period of:

(A) 45 days

(B) 60 days

(C) 30 days

(D) 15 days

44. Income-tax Appellate Tribunal cannot grant stay either under the original order or any other subsequent order in aggregate beyond the period of :

(A) 180 days

(B) 365 days

(C) 90 days

(D) 240 days

45. Rahim has shown an air-conditioner installed at his residence as having been installed at his factory, and claimed depreciation thereon. This is an act of :

(A) Tax planning

(B) Tax management

(C) Tax evasion

(D) None of the above

46. An appeal from the order of ITAT lies before the High Court and the same is to be filed within the period of........ days from the date on which the order appealed against is received by the assessee or the CIT.

(A) 60

(B) 90

(C) 120

(D) 180

47. Tax planning is honest and right approach to attain the maximum benefit of taxation laws within its framework only. Objectives of tax planning are :

(*i*) Productive investment

(*ii*) Un-healthy growth of economy

(*iii*) Minimization of litigation

(*iv*) Increase in the tax liability

(A) (*i*), (*ii*) and (*iii*)

(B) (*i*) and (*iii*)

(C) (*i*), (*ii*) (*iv*)

(D) All the four

48. The factor/factors to be considered in taking the decision or deciding whether a country is being tax haven or not is/are :

(*i*) Nil rate of tax

(*ii*) Lack of transparency

(*iii*) Limited regulatory supervision

(*iv*) Lack of co-operation

(A) (*ii*) and (*iv*)

(B) (*i*), (*ii*) and (*iv*)

(C) (*i*), (*ii*) and (*iii*)

(D) (*i*), (*ii*), (*iii*) and (*iv*)

49. The provisions of transfer pricing are applicable relating to specified domestic transactions entered into by the assessee in the previous year when the aggregate amount of such transactions is ₹:

(A) 300 lakh

(B) 500 lakh

(C) 2,000 lakh

(D) 1,000 lakh

50. The advance ruling pronounced by the Authority for Advance Ruling as per section 245 is binding :

(*i*) in respect of transaction for which ruling has been sought

(*ii*) on Income-tax Authorities

(*iii*) on the Applicant

(*iv*) on all other persons having similar transactions

(A) (*i*), (*ii*) and (*iii*)

(B) (*i*) and (*iii*)

(C) (*ii*) and (*iii*)

(D) All the four

51. Income chargeable to tax under the Income-tax Act, 1961 in the Assessment Year has been defined in section 2(24) to include :

(*i*) Voluntary contribution received by an electoral trust

(*ii*) Profits of insurance business

(*iii*) Amounts received under Keyman Insurance Policy [except where it is exempt u/s 10(10D)]

(*iv*) Gift from non-relative of an amount exceeding ₹ 50,000

(A) (*ii*) and (*iv*)

(B) (*i*) and (*iv*)

(C) (*ii*) and (*iii*)

(D) All the four above

52. Amount of ₹ 5,00,000 received by Ram & Co., as a compensation for premature termination of contract of agency in the month of April, 2018 is to be treated as :

(A) Income from other sources

(B) Taxable under section 28(*ii*)(*c*)

(C) Revenue receipt which is exempt

(D) Capital receipt which is not chargeable to tax

53. John is a foreign citizen born in USA. His father was born in Delhi in 1960 and his grand-father was born in Lahore in 1935 but his mother was born in UK in 1963. John came to India for the first time on 1st June, 2018 and stayed in India for 183 days and then left for USA. His residential status for the A.Y. 2019-2020 shall be :

(A) Resident

(B) Resident but not ordinary resident

(C) Non-resident

(D) Foreign national

54. In the case of a co-operative society, surcharge is levied, where its total income exceeds ₹ .... crore.

(A) 1

(B) 5

(C) 10

(D) None of the above

55. The following income of Ms. Nargis who is a non-resident shall be included in her total income:

(*i*) Salary for 2 months received in Delhi ₹ 40,000.

(*ii*) Interest on Savings Bank Account in Mumbai ₹ 2,100.

(*iii*) Agricultural income in Bangladesh and Invested in shares in Bangladesh.

(*iv*) Amount brought into India out of past non-taxed profits earned in USA.

(A) (*i*), (*iii*) and (*iv*)

(B) (*i*) and (*ii*)

(C) (*i*), (*ii*) and (*iv*)

(D) All the four above

56. The income earned during the previous year is subject to tax under the Act on the basis of residential status of an assessee. However, the residential status of an assessee .... every year.

(A) will not change

(B) will certainly change

(C) may change

(D) None of the above

57. The income derived from growing, manufacturing and sale of Centrifuged latex or Cenex or Latex based crops as per Rule 7A of the Income-tax Rules, 1962 shall be taken as agricultural and non-agricultural income in the following ratio :

(A) 75% and 25%

(B) 60% and 40%

(C) 65% and 35%

(D) None of the above

58. The following incomes derived, received and earned during the previous year are not subject to tax being exempt under the Act :

(*i*) Money received by an individual as a member of HUF

(*ii*) Share of profit received by partner from LLP

(*iii*) Interest on Savings bank account

(*iv*) Income of SAARC Fund

(A) (*i*) and (*ii*)

(B) (*i*), (*ii*) and (*iv*)

(C) None of the above

(D) All of the above

59. Ram Kripa Charitable Trust owns a capital asset of ₹ 2,00,000 and half of the income from such asset is utilized for charitable purposes. The asset was sold for ₹ 3,50,000 and from the sale proceeds, the trust bought another asset for ₹ 2,90,000. The amount of capital gain deemed to have been applied for charitable purposes is :

(A) ₹ 45,000

(B) ₹ 30,000

(C) ₹ 75,000

(D) None of the above

60. For employee who is covered under the Payment of Gratuity Act, 1972 the maximum amount of gratuity exempt and the maximum amount of leave encashment exempt under the Act respectively are :

(A) ₹ 2,50,000 in each case

(B) ₹ 20,00,000 and ₹ 3,00,000

(C) ₹ 5,00,000 and ₹ 2,50,000

(D) None of the above

61. HSP, a LLP had taken Key Men insurance policy on the life of its Managing Partner. The policy got matured on 13th September, 2017 and amount of ₹ 75 lakh was paid by the insurers to the Managing Partner. The amount so received on maturity of the policy by the managing partner :

(A) is exempt in full u/s 10(10D)

(B) 50% of ₹ 75 lakh is exempt

(C) ₹ 75 lakh is taxable

(D) ₹ 25 lakh is exempt and balance is taxable

62. In a scheme of buy back of shares, XYZ Ltd., a listed company, paid ₹ 6 lakh to a shareholder X on 12-3-2019. The buy back was through recognized stock exchange. The sum of ₹ 6 lakh received by X who had bought these shares 2 years back will be :

(A) Taxable in full

(B) Fully exempt

(C) Taxable @ 20%

(D) Taxable at normal rate of tax

63. The loss derived from a house property can be set off during the year against :

(A) the income of any other house property
(B) the capital gain
(C) the income under other sources
(D) (A) and (C) above

64. The WDV of a block of asset depreciated @ 15% as on 1st April, 2018 was of ₹ 3,00,000. Out of this block, one machine was sold for ₹ 2,00,000 on 1st July, 2018 and a new machine of ₹ 6,00,000 added on 1st August, 2018 was put to use only from 1st Sept., 2018.

The amount of depreciation to be claimed (in the manner most beneficial to the assessee) in the A.Y. 2019-2020 shall be :

(A) ₹ 1,20,000
(B) ₹ 96,000
(C) ₹ 1,05,000
(D) ₹ 60,000

65. Zing Zang is an individual, manufacturing a product. He has turnover of ₹ 98,50,000 which is inclusive of amount of ₹ 25 lakh received through electronic clearing system. The accounts are not properly maintained and you have advised him to pay tax u/s 44 AD of the Act. On how much income he will pay tax for A.Y. 2019-2020 :

(A) ₹ 7,88,000
(B) ₹ 7,38,000
(C) Manufacturers not allowed u/s 44AD
(D) ₹ 5,91,000

66. XYZ Ltd., engaged in manufacture of a product, has incurred an expenditure of ₹ 3 lakh on notified skill development project u/s 35CCD. The deduction available for such expenditure is ₹ .... lakh.

(A) 3
(B) 3.75
(C) 4.5
(D) None of the above

67. Mr. Zen owns a flat in Mumbai which was let out by him in the previous year 2018-2019 on a rent of ₹ 20,000 p.m. upto December, 2018 and for ₹ 30,000 p.m. thereafter. The annual municipal value is of ₹ 3,00,000, Fair Rent is ₹ 2,50,000 and Standard Rent is ₹ 2,90,000. The gross Annual Value of the flat shall be taken as :

(A) ₹ 2,70,000

(B) ₹ 3,00,000

(C) ₹ 2,50,000

(D) ₹ 2,90,000

68. Santhnam purchased in October, 2018, a flat in Chennai, to be used for his own residential purposes with the financial assistance of housing loan taken from PNB Housing Finance Ltd. He has paid interest on such loan till March, 2019 of ₹ 1,78,780. The amount of interest paid on such loan allowed u/s 24 is :

(A) ₹ 1,25,000

(B) ₹ 1,78,780

(C) ₹ 1,50,000

(D) None of the above

69. SH made three different cash payments of ₹ 10,000, ₹ 10,000 and of ₹ 11,500 to a supplier for purchase of goods and material on 11th Sept., 2018. The payments were made during different times in the day. Amount to be disallowed u/s 40A(3) is :

(A) ₹ 11,500

(B) ₹ 31,500

(C) ₹ NIL

(D) None of the above

70. Radhey has sold his house on 11th August, 2018 for ₹ 80 lakh. The value applied by Stamp Valuation Authority is ₹ 100 lakh. He disputed this valuation and the departmental valuation cell made the valuation at ₹ 110 lakh. The value to be taken for calculation of capital gain as per section 50C is ₹:

(A) 80 lakh

(B) 110 lakh

(C) 100 lakh

(D) None of the above

PART B

71. GST Council comprises of various persons from Union and States and is being headed by a Chair Person who is :

(A) Finance Secretary to Government of India

(B) Union Finance Minister

(C) Any State Finance Minister

(D) Union Revenue Minister

72. XYZ Limited engaged in various activities, is having a garment show-room in Allahabad and a leather processing unit in Kanpur. Both these units of XYZ Limited under section 2 of the CGST Act, 2017 shall be treated as :

(A) Business Partners

(B) Business units

(C) Show-room and Factory

(D) Business Verticals

73. Construction of a complex, building, civil structure or the part thereof including a complex or building intended for sale to a buyer, wholly or partly except where the entire consideration has been received after issuance of completion certificate, where required, by a competent authority or after its first occupation, whichever is earlier for the purpose of taxability under the CGST Act, 2017 shall be treated as supply of:

(A) Goods

(B) Both goods and services

(C) Services

(D) Contract work

74. The following categories of registered persons are not being eligible for the Composition Scheme under the CGST Act, 2017 :

(*i*) Supplier of the Restaurant Services

(*ii*) Manufacturer of notified goods

(*iii*) Non-resident taxable persons

(*iv*) Casual taxable person

(A) (*iii*) and (*iv*)

(B) (*ii*), (*iii*) and (*iv*)

(C) (*ii*) and (*iv*)

(D) (*i*), (*iii*) and (*iv*)

75. Section 2(62) of the CGST Act, 2017 specifies input tax in relation to a registered person to mean Central Tax, State Tax, Integrated Tax or Union Territory Tax charged on any supply of goods or services or both and also include :

(*i*) Integrated goods and services, tax charged on import of goods

(*ii*) Tax under the provisions of section 9(3) and 9(4)

(*iii*) Tax paid under composition levy

(*iv*) Tax under Union Territory Goods and Services Tax Act

(A) All the above four

(B) (*i*), (*ii*) and (*iv*)

(C) (*i*) and (*ii*)

(D) (*ii*), (*iii*) and (*iv*)

76. Mr. Pankaj of Delhi supplied goods to Mr. Krishna of Delhi for ₹ 1 lakh, on which total GST was charged @ 12%. Mr. Krishna, after purchase of goods, added 20% margin of profit (on cost) and sold the entire goods to Mr. Ravi of Delhi. The total amount of tax payable after claiming input tax on such transaction by Mr. Krishna is :

(A) ₹ 12,000

(B) ₹ 14,400

(C) ₹ 2,400

(D) None of the above

77. Raj & Co., applied for voluntary registration under CGST Act, 2018 on 5th July, 2018 and the registration was granted on 15th July, 2018. Raj & Co., was having the stock available against the invoices for a period of 3 months old. Raj & Co., shall be eligible for input tax credit on such stock as held as on :

(A) 30th June, 2018

(B) 05th July, 2018

(C) 15th July, 2018

(D) 14th July, 2018

78. A registered person as per section 35 of the CGST Act, 2017 is required to maintain proper accounts and records, and keep at his registered, principal place of business. Following are the records specified under this section are to be maintained by the registered person :

(*i*) Production or manufacturing of goods

(*ii*) Inward and Outward supply of goods or services or both

(*iii*) Stock of goods

(*iv*) Input credit availed

(*v*) Output tax payable and paid

(*vi*) Such other particulars as may be prescribed

(A) (*i*), (*iii*) and (*iv*)

(B) All the six as given in above

(C) (*i*), (*ii*), (*iii*) and (*v*)

(D) (*i*), (*iii*) (*iv*), (*v*) and (*vi*)

79. Time duration as per section 36 of the CGST Act, 2017 for retention of accounts and records under GST is until expiry of .... months from the due date of furnishing of annual return for the year pertaining to such accounts and record.

(A) 72

(B) 84

(C) 60

(D) None of the above

80. A casual taxable person or a non-resident taxable person shall be required to apply for registration at least .... days prior to the commencement of business.

(A) 30

(B) 5

(C) 15

(D) 7

81. Mr. Bala has made supply (within State) of taxable goods to the tune of ₹ 17 lakh, export supplies of ₹ 3 lakh and intra-State supply of exempt services of ₹ 4 lakh. His aggregate turnover as per section 2(6) of the CGST/ SGST Act, 2017 is :

(A) ₹ 17 lakh

(B) ₹ 20 lakh

(C) ₹ 24 lakh

(D) None of the above

82. Non-resident taxable person is required to provide details in the return for non-resident foreign taxable person in the Return Form No. :

(A) GSTR-3

(B) GSTR-5

(C) GSTR-8

(D) None of the above

83. Input Service Distributor shall file the return in GSTR-6 for the input service distributed by:

(A) 10th of the next month

(B) 18th of the next month

(C) 13th of the next month

(D) 20th of the next month

84. A taxable person who makes an excess claim of input tax credit or excess reduction in output tax liability shall pay interest at such rate not exceeding :

(A) 18%

(B) 24%

(C) 20%

(D) 21%

85. Section 56 of the CGST Act, 2017 specifies that if any tax ordered to be refunded after the order of an Appellate Authority is not refunded within 60 days from the date of application filed consequent to such order, interest as such rate not exceeding .... shall be payable in respect of such refund.

(A) 90%

(B) 6%

(C) 12%

(D) 18%

86. A supply made by a taxable person to a recipient consisting of two or more taxable supply of goods or services of both or any combination thereof which are only bundled and supplied in conjunction with each other in the ordinarily course of business out of which one is a principal supply has been defined u/s 2(3) of CGST Act, 2017 to mean :

(A) Mixed supply

(B) Composite supply

(C) Bundled supply

(D) Both (A) and (B)

87. Tax on inter-State supplies, import into India, supplies made outside India and supplies made in SEZ shall be charged to :

(A) CGST and SGST

(B) CGST and UTGST

(C) CGST and IGST

(D) IGST

88. Provision for levy and collection of tax on intra-State supply of goods or services or both by the Union Territory and for matters connected therewith or incidental thereto are being enumerated in:

(A) CGST Act, 2017

(B) IGST Act, 2017

(C) UTGST Act, 2017

(D) None of the above

89. The highest enabling limit of tax rate of IGST has been prescribed at :

(A) 20%

(B) 14%

(C) 28%

(D) None of the above

90. The base Financial Year for the purpose of calculating compensation amount payable to the State as per Goods and Services Tax (Compensation to States) Act, 2017 shall be taken :

(A) 2014-15

(B) 2016-17

(C) 2012-13

(D) 2015-16

91. The proceeds of the cess and such other amounts as being recommended by the GST Council shall be credited to a non-lapsable fund known as :

(A) Goods and Services Tax Compensation Fund

(B) Goods and Services Tax Cess Fund

(C) Goods and Services Tax Welfare Fund

(D) None of the above

92. A proper Officer not below the rank of Joint Commissioner or an Officer authorized by such Proper Officer can make an order of seizure in Form :

(A) GST INS-01

(B) GST INS-02

(C) GST INS-03

(D) None of the above

93. Goods seized by a Proper Officer or an Authorized Officer can be released on a provisional basis upon execution of a bond for the value of goods and furnishing of security. The bond so executed will be in Form :

(A) GST INS-06

(B) GST INS Bond-03

(C) GST INS-01

(D) GST INS-4

94. Taxes that were replaced by GST legislation are :

(A) Purchase tax

(B) Luxury tax

(C) Central Sales tax

(D) Options (A) and (B) above

95. A registered supplier under composition levy can withdraw at any time and be required to file the Form for withdrawal from composition levy in :

(A) GST CMP-3

(B) GST CMP-4

(C) GST MIS-1

(D) GST PCT-2

96. Goods and Services Tax (GST) noted to be a greatest tax reform in India and therefore was rolled-out with effect from 1st July, 2017. It transforms a system of taxation and administration into the digital world by adopting latest information technology. The GST model rolled out in India has been adopted from :

(A) France

(B) Canada

(C) Argentina

(D) None of the above

97. Special purpose vehicle to cater the IT needs of GST is called :

(A) HSN

(B) GSTN

(C) IGSTN

(D) SGSTN

98. GST in India is levied on the basis of :

(A) Consumption principle

(B) Set-off against that payable principle

(C) Destination base principle

(D) Both consumption and destination base principle

99. The tax under GST legislation in India is being levied:

(A) Exclusively by Union and State Laws

(B) Simultaneously by Union and State Laws

(C) Only by Union Laws

(D) Only by State Laws

100. Inter-State supply of service is primarily covered in section .... of the CGST Act, 2017.

(A) 12

(B) 14

(C) 8

(D) 18

ANSWERS:

1.	(C)	**2.**	(B)	**3.**	(C)	**4.**	(C)	**5.**	(D)	**6.**	(C)	**7.**	(C)
8.	(B)	**9.**	(D)	**10.**	(D)	**11.**	(C)	**12.**	(B)	**13.**	(D)	**14.**	(C)
15.	(C)	**16.**	(D)	**17.**	(B)	**18.**	(A)	**19.**	(B)	**20.**	(C)	**21.**	(B)
22.	(D)	**23.**	(D)	**24.**	(B)	**25.**	(**)	**26.**	(B)	**27.**	(D)	**28.**	(D)
29.	(D)	**30.**	(B)	**31.**	(C)	**32.**	(B)	**33.**	(C)	**34.**	(D)	**35.**	(C)
36.	(D)	**37.**	(C)	**38.**	(B)	**39.**	(**)	**40.**	(A)	**41.**	(B)	**42.**	(D)
43.	(C)	**44.**	(A)	**45.**	(C)	**46.**	(C)	**47.**	(B)	**48.**	(C)	**49.**	(C)
50.	(A)	**51.**	(D)	**52.**	(B)	**53.**	(B)	**54.**	(A)	**55.**	(B)	**56.**	(C)
57.	(C)	**58.**	(B)	**59.**	(A)	**60.**	(B)	**61.**	(C)	**62.**	(C)	**63.**	(**)
64.	(C)	**65.**	(B)	**66.**	(C)	**67.**	(D)	**68.**	(B)	**69.**	(B)	**70.**	(C)
71.	(B)	**72.**	(D)	**73.**	(C)	**74.**	(A)	**75.**	(B)	**76.**	(C)	**77.**	(D)
78.	(B)	**79.**	(A)	**80.**	(B)	**81.**	(C)	**82.**	(B)	**83.**	(C)	**84.**	(B)
85.	(**)	**86.**	(B)	**87.**	(D)	**88.**	(C)	**89.**	(D)	**90.**	(D)	**91.**	(A)
92.	(B)	**93.**	(D)	**94.**	(**)	**95.**	(B)	**96.**	(B)	**97.**	(B)	**98.**	(D)
99.	(B)	**100.**	(**)										

** *MCQs are wrongly drafted. For further clarification please see the hints.*

HINTS FOR PRACTICAL MCQs:

4. The head office expenditure is allowable to the extent of the *lower of the following* -

(*a*) 5% of adjusted total income (100 lakh × 5%) *or*	₹ 5 lakh
(*b*) The amount of so much of the expenditure in the nature of head office expenditure incurred by the assessee as is attributable to the business or profession of the assessee in India.	₹ 20 lakh

Thus, deduction available will be ₹ 5 lakh.

5. Additional depreciation is available for 'Plant & Machinery' not for 'Building'.

13.

Income from sub-letting (3,000 × 12)	36,000
(-) Expenses	(1,000)
Net income	35,000

Hence, Option (D) is correct.

21. *Remuneration to working partners:*

(A)

Book Profits	*Allowable Remuneration*		
On first ₹ 3,00,000 of book profits or in case of a loss.	₹ 1,50,000 or 90% of book profits, whichever is more.	2,70,000	3,90,000
On balance book profits	60% of the book profits.	1,20,000	
(B) Remuneration as per partnership deed			4,60,000

(A) or (B) whichever is less.

Hence, remuneration allowed as per Section 40(*b*) is ₹ 3,90,000.

25. The amount of tax credit shall be carried forward up to **15 years** immediately succeeding the assessment year in which tax credit becomes available. **[Section 115JAA]**

'15 years' do appear in option and hence wrong MCQ.

28. If interest is paid by one co-operative society to another co-operative society, no TDS is required to be deducted.

29. Rate of TDS is 1% where the payment is made to an individual or HUF for any contract [Section 194C].

Thus, TDS required to be deducted for payment to E = 25,00,000 × 1% = 25,000. Hence, Option (D) is correct.

39.

Pension from employer	2,30,000
Income from house property	2,00,000
Total income	4,30,000

Step 1: Calculate tax on: Agricultural income + Non-agricultural income

60,000 + 4,30,000 = 4,90,000

On first	3,00,000		Nil
On next	1,90,000	@ 5%	9,500
	4,90,000		9,500

Step 2: Calculate tax on: Agricultural income + Basic exemption limit

60,000 + 3,00,000 = 3,60,000

On first	3,00,000		Nil
On next	60,000	@ 5%	3,000
	3,60,000		3,000

Step 3:

Tax as per Step 1	9,500
(-) Tax as per Step 2	(3,000)
	6,500
(+) Education cess @ 4%	260
	6,760

None of the options contains 6,760; hence question itself is wrong.

63. Loss from house property can be set-off against - (A) income from any other house property (B) capital gain (C) income under other sources.

Option (D) needs to be corrected - "(D) All of the above".

Hence, question itself is wrong.

65. (73,50,000 × 8%) + (25,00,000 × 6%) = 7,38,000.

76.

Purchase cost (1,12,000 - 6,000 - 6,000)	1,00,000
(+) Margin @ 20%	20,000
Sale price	1,20,000
(+) CGST @ 6%	7,200
(+) SGST @ 6%	7,200
Invoice price	1,34,400

Calculation of Net GST payable by Mr. Krishna:

Particulars	SGST	CGST
Output GST	7,200	7,200
(-) Input GST	(6,000)	(6,000)
Net GST payable	1,200	1,200

Total GST = 1,200 + 1,200 = 2,400

Short cut method to calculate GST:

GST is payable on value addition. Value addition made by trader is 'profit' *i.e.* ₹ 20,000.

SGST = 20,000 × 6% = 1,200

CGST = 20,000 × 6% = 1,200

85. Interest rate is 9% for delayed refunds in case of order of adjudicating authority or Appellate Authority or Appellate Tribunal or Court. ***Option (A) needs to be corrected. Hence, question is wrong.***

100. Inter-State supply of service is covered in Section 7(3) of the IGST Act, 2017.

None of the option covers Section 7 and hence Question itself is wrong.

Important Note:

- **MCQs No. 36, 45, 47 & 49** are not relevant for New Syllabus of CS Executive as these questions relates to topics that are not in syllabus.
- All MCQs are relevant for Old Syllabus of CS Executive.

Solved Paper
CS Executive - December 2018

(AS PER LAW APPLICABLE FOR AY 2019-2020)

PART A

1. Income earned in the other contracting state trout the operation of ships in international traffic as per Double Taxation Avoidance Agreements (DTAA), will be taxed in that contracting State where …………

(A) PE (Permanent Establishment) is situated

(B) the place of effective management (POEM) of enterprises is situated

(C) the business of air and shipping originated

(D) none of the above

2. General Anti Avoidance Rule (GAAR) though were announced in the Finance Act, 2012 but had been deferred and been made applicable in India from :

(A) Assessment year 2017-18

(B) Assessment year 2018-19

(C) Assessment year 2019-20

(D) None of the above

3. State the relevant Form No. for filing an application to Authority for Advance Ruling by a resident having transactions with a non-resident and the amount of fees to be paid for filing such application :

(A) 34EA & ₹ 5,000

(B) 34C & ₹ 2,500

(C) 34D & ₹ 10,000

(D) 34E & ₹ 5,000

4. Qualification prescribed for appointment as a Chairman of Authority for Advance Ruling (AAR) as specified under the Income Tax Act, 1961 in Section 245-O is

(A) Judge of High Court

(B) A Law Member from Indian Legal Service

(C) Judge of the Supreme Court

(D) A Revenue Member from Indian Revenue Service

5. Depreciation whether to be allowed on the purchase and installation of a fire extinguisher by a practicing CS in his office, even when the same is not put to use or used during the year of acquisition as stipulated under section 32 of Income Tax Act, 1961 :

(A) No, Failure to use for the profession or business

(B) Yes, Safety measures and kept standby, treated as passive use and eligible for depreciation

(C) Yes, Allowable @ 10% of the cost

(D) Yes, Allowable @ 50% of the cost

6. XYZ Pvt. Ltd. had distributed income of ₹ 9,00,000 to Rajesh for the reason of buy back of its shares from him on 1st March, 2019. These shares were purchased by him for ₹ 5,00,000 on 1st March, 2013. The income out of the amount received by Rajesh against the buyback of shares from the company XYZ Pvt. Ltd. shall be subject to tax in A. Y. 2019-2020 shall be of __________.

(A) ₹ 4 lakh

(B) ₹ 9 lakh

(C) Nil being exempt u/s 10(34A) of Act

(D) None of the above

7. Radhey has sold his residential house on 11th Sept., 2018 for ₹ 75 lakh. Value applied by the Stamp Valuation Authority on the date of registration of the Conveyance Deed on 15th Sept., 2018 was of ₹ 115 lakh. Radhey disputed the valuation made by the Stamp Valuation Authority and asked the departmental valuation officer to determine the value of the house on the date of registration of deed. The departmental valuation officer determined the value of the house on the date of registration of the deed at ₹ 120 lacs. Sale value of the house to be taken for calculation of capital gain in A.Y. 2019-2020 as per section shall be of ______________

(A) 50C, ₹ 115 lakh

(B) 50C, ₹ 120 lakh

(C) 48, ₹ 75 lakh

(D) 45, Indexed cost of ₹ 75 lakh

8. DJPA, LLP, resident in India has received dividend of ₹ 15 lakh from R Ltd., an Indian company, on which the company R Ltd. had paid Dividend Distribution Tax (DDT) under section 115-O of the Income-Tax Act, 1961. The amount of tax payable by DJPA, LLP in respect of such dividend income for A.Y. 2019-2020 shall be :

(A) ₹ 5 lakh

(B) ₹ 10 lakh

(C) ₹ 52,000

(D) ₹ 78,000

9. Radha engaged in the trading business and had contributed a sum of ₹ 1 lakh to an approved university in July, 2018 to be used for scientific research, which is not related to her business. The amount of deduction for which she is eligible under section 35 of Income-Tax Act, 1961 for assessment year 2019-2020 would be :

(A) ₹ 1 lakh

(B) ₹ 1.5 lakh

(C) ₹ 1.75 lakh

(D) ₹ 2 lakh

10. All income which arises or accrues to the minor child (not suffering from any disability as specified in section 80U) shall be clubbed with the income of parent whose total income excluding the income to be included of the minor not derived from any activity involving application of his skill, talent or specialized knowledge:

(A) in the hands of father only

(B) in the hands of mother only

(C) equally in the hands of both mother and father

(D) with the income of that parent whose total income is greater before clubbing of such income

11. The loss computed under the head "Income from house property" can be set-off by intra head adjustment during the same year from :

(A) any other head of income upto maximum of ₹ 2,50,000

(B) any other head of income upto maximum of ₹ 3,00,000

(C) any other head of income upto maximum of ₹ 5,00,000

(D) any other head of income upto maximum of ₹ 2,00,000

12. An assessee is not eligible to claim any relief under section 89 of Income Tax Act, 1961, when he is in receipt of income as arrears or in advance during the previous year from his employer:

(A) in respect of gratuity

(B) in respect of commutation of pension

(C) in respect of arrears of family pension

(D) in respect of amount received on voluntary retirement or termination of services

13. SJG Ltd., a manufacturer of leather goods in a factory located at Noida having an annual turnover of ₹ 50 crore. The company, during the year, employed 200 new regular workers in the factory, which was 20% of the existing work-force employed on the last day of the preceding year. It paid ₹ 30 lakh to the new workers during the year as additional wages. All workmen were employed from 1st May, 2018. The eligible amount of deduction which the company can claim under section 80JJAA of Income-Tax Act, 1961 is :

(A) ₹ 30 lakh

(B) ₹ 15 lakh

(C) ₹ 9 lakh

(D) ₹ 18 lakh

14. The quantum of deduction available to Offshore Banking Units under section 80LA of Income-Tax Act, 1961 located in Special Economic Zone (SEZ) and satisfying all conditions from the Gross Total Income is :

(A) 100% of such income for five consecutive assessment years, relating to the previous year in which the permission was obtained

(B) 50% of such income for next five consecutive years

(C) 25% of such income for next ten years

(D) both (A) and (B)

15. Ram & Co., a proprietorship firm has paid tax for the assessment year 2019-2020 as per section 115JC of the Income Tax Act, 1961. Credit of such paid tax can be carried forward by the proprietor for a period of following number of assessment years immediately succeeding the assessment year 2019-2020 :

(A) 8 years

(B) 5 years

(C) 10 years

(D) 15 years

16. Which out of the following income is not to be clubbed while computing income of the Hindu Undivided Family (HUF) for the assessment year 2019-2020 ?

(A) Fees or remuneration received by the member as a director or a partner in the company or firm if the funds of the HUF are invested in a company or firm

(B) Income from 'stridhan' and personal income of the members

(C) Income of minor sons out of the investments of the family funds

(D) None of the above

17. The assessee opting to pay tax under the provisions of section 44ADA is not be required to maintain books of account as per section 44AA and gets the accounts audited under section 44AB of the Income Tax Act, 1961 where ______________

(A) It claims that the profit and gains from the profession is higher than the deemed profit and gains

(B) Total gross receipts should not exceed ₹ 60 lakh

(C) Its income does not exceed the maximum amount which is not chargeable to income tax

(D) Both (A) and (C)

18. The lock in period under the scheme of presumptive taxation based on the tonnage of the ship, in case of Shipping Company, under the provisions of sections 115 to 115VZC is :

(A) 5 years
(B) 7 years
(C) 10 years
(D) 3 years

19. Which of the undermentioned incomes of a Co-operative Society is not eligible for deduction under section 80P of the Income Tax Act, 1961 when the gross total income of the society exceeds ₹ 20,000 ?

(A) Agency business
(B) Income from letting of godown
(C) Income from house property
(D) Dividend from other Co-operative Societies

20. Tax shall be charged on the total income of the AOP at the maximum marginal rate under the provisions of section 167B of Income Tax Act, 1961 :

(A) where individual shares of the members of an association or body are indeterminable or unknown in relation to the whole of income
(B) where members share equally
(C) where the individual shares of the members of an associate or body are indeterminable or unknown relating to any part of income
(D) both (A) and (C)

21. Income tax on the income from the transfer of Carbon Credit under section 115BBG of Income Tax Act, 1961 derived/earned during the previous year 2018-2019 shall be taxable :

(A) At normal rate of tax
(B) At concessional rate of 10% only
(C) At concessional rate of 10% + HEC
(D) At 20% of concessional rate

22. Income Tax Act, 1961 distinguished a closely held company from widely held company significantly from the viewpoint of:

(A) tax levied at different rates

(B) section 2(22)(*e*) where certain payments made to shareholders are treated as deemed dividend

(C) allowed to carry forward its business losses only if the conditions specified in section 79 are satisfied

(D) both (B) and (C)

23. While calculating Book Profits under section 115JB of Income Tax Act, 1961, which of the following is not to be added ?

(A) The amount of dividend upto ₹ 10 lakh

(B) Interest on Income tax including surcharge and cess

(C) The amounts carried to any reserves

(D) The amount by way of provision for losses of subsidiary companies

24. While calculating book profits under section 115JB of Income Tax Act, 1961 which of the following is not to be deducted ?

(A) The amount withdrawn from any reserve or provision if any such amount is credited to the Profit & Loss Account

(B) The amount of income by way of royalty in respect of patent chargeable to tax under section 115BBF

(C) Long term capital gain referred under section 10(38) of the Act

(D) Brought forward loss/unabsorbed depreciation whichever is less

25. Income of a non-resident from airline business under section 44BBA of Income Tax Act, 1961 is calculated at the rate of percentage of the aggregate amounts specified, on presumptive basis.

(A) 7.5%

(B) 5%

(C) 10%

(D) 15%

26. Royalty of ₹ 105 lakh received by a foreign company from an Indian concern in pursuance of an agreement approved by the Central Government in the previous year 2018-19. The amount of tax payable on such royalty Income for Asst. Year 2019-20 is :

(A) ₹ 10 lakh

(B) ₹ 11.1384 lakh

(C) ₹ 20 lakh

(D) ₹ 22.2768 lakh

27. Nargis during the previous year 1st April, 2018 to 31st March, 2019 had donated the amount of ₹ 50,000 each in Africa Fund, National Children Fund, National Illness Assistance Fund and further amount of ₹ 30,000 in Rajiv Gandhi Foundation. The amount of deduction eligible to be claimed by her as per section.......... in A.Y. 2019-2020 shall be of ....

(A) 80GG, ₹ 1,80,000

(B) 80G, ₹ 1,65,000

(C) 80GGB, ₹ 1,50,000

(D) 80G, ₹ 90,000

28. Payment of ₹ 2,00,000 was made to Krishna Roadways Pvt. Ltd. owning nine heavy goods carriages and having PAN which was furnished by them to the payer of freight GG Carriers. The amount of tax to be deducted by the payer on such amount is .... as per section ....

(A) ₹ 2,000, 194C

(B) ₹ 10,000, 194C

(C) ₹ 4,000, 194C

(D) Nil because PAN furnished, 194C(6)

29. State whether tax is required to be collected at source (TCS) under the provision of section 206C of Income Tax Act, 1961 by a person making

(A) Payment of dividend

(B) Winning from horse races

(C) Sale of motor vehicle of the value exceeding ₹ 10 lakh by a dealer to the customer

(D) Payment to non-resident

30. It is obligatory for an assessee to make payment of tax under section 208 of Income Tax Act, 1961

(A) Where the advance tax payable is ₹ 10,000 or more

(B) Where the advance tax payable is ₹ 2,500 or more

(C) Where the advance tax payable is ₹ 5,000 or more

(D) Where the advance tax payable is ₹ 1,000 or more

31. Interest is payable to an assessee on the amount of refund under the Income Tax Act, 1961 where the amount of refund is

(A) more than ten percent of the tax as determined on regular assessment

(B) more than five percent of the tax as determined on regular assessment

(C) more than fifteen percent of the tax as determined on regular assessment

(D) more than twenty percent of the tax as determined on regular assessment

32. Any person who has not filed the return within the time allowed under section 139(1) may file a belated return :

(A) at any time before the end of the relevant previous year

(B) at any time before the end of the relevant assessment year

(C) before the completion of assessment

(D) at any time before the end of the relevant assessment year or before the completion of the assessment whichever is earlier

33. The self-assessment tax computed u/s 140A by an individual assessee is ₹ 1,50,000 which includes ₹ 15,000 as interest for late filing of return as per section 234A. The assessee has deposited ₹ 75,000 as self-assessment tax. In this case :

(A) ₹ 75,000 so deposited shall be adjusted in the proportion of 9 : 1 towards tax and interest

(B) ₹ 15,000 shall be adjusted towards interest due and balance of ₹ 60,000 shall be adjusted towards tax due

(C) ₹ 75,000 so deposited shall be adjusted towards tax due

(D) None of the above

34. The assessee can file an application for rectification of mistake as per section 154 of the Act when it is

(*i*) a mistake of fact

(*ii*) a mistake of law

(*iii*) glaring obvious or apparent from the records

(*iv*) a decision on debatable point of law

(A) (*i*) and (*iii*)

(B) (*i*), (*ii*) and (*iv*)

(C) (*i*), (*ii*) and (*iii*)

(D) all of the above

35. The time limit for completion of Assessment/Re-assessment under sections 143 and 144 of the Income Tax Act, 1961 is

(A) 24 months from the end of relevant assessment year

(B) 18 months from the end of relevant assessment year

(C) 12 months from the end of relevant assessment year

(D) 9 months from the end of relevant assessment year

36. What are the items taken into consideration by Assessing Officer (AO) while processing a return at Centralised Processing Centre (CPC) ?

(A) the total income or loss after making adjustments for any arithmetical error in the return

(B) an incorrect claim, if such incorrect claim is apparent from any information in the return

(C) the fee payable under section 234F (fee for default in furnishing return of income) in computing the tax

(D) all of the above

37. The maximum penalty leviable for under reporting of income which results from misreporting of income by the assessee

(A) Two hundred percent of the tax payable

(B) One hundred percent of the tax payable

(C) Fifty percent of the tax payable

(D) Three hundred percent of the tax payable

38. The rationale behind power of revision of orders prejudicial to the interest of revenue conferred on the Commissioner of Income Tax under section 263 of Income Tax Act, 1961 is that :

(A) the order passed is without inquiries or verification which should have been made

(B) the order is passed allowing any relief without inquiring into the claim

(C) the department has no right of appeal to the Commissioner (Appeals) against any order passed by the Assessing Officer

(D) the order has not been made in accordance with any order, direction or instruction issued by the Board under section 119

39. The Patna High Court following the decision laid down by the Bombay High Court in the case of Mahindra Sintered Products Ltd. held that to claim special deduction u/s 80 J, the assessee has to establish the fact/facts relating to ....

(A) investment of substantial fresh capital in the new industrial undertaking so set up

(B) earning of profits clearly attributable to the said undertaking

(C) manufacture or production of articles on the said undertaking

(D) all of the above

40. The provisions of "deemed dividend" under section 2(22)(*e*) of the Income Tax Act, 1961, in respect of advances or loans to shareholders, or any payment on behalf of shareholders or any payment for the individual benefit of a shareholder are applicable to:

(A) A Public Limited Listed Company

(B) A Public Limited Unlisted Company

(C) A Closely held Company

(D) None of the above

41. The benefit of carry forward and set-off of losses under section 79 of Income Tax Act, 1961, by a closely held Indian Company which is a subsidiary of a foreign company as a result of amalgamation or demerger, is subject to the condition that specified percentage of the shareholders of the amalgamating or demerged foreign company continue to be the shareholders of the amalgamated or the resulting foreign company which is :

(A) 51%

(B) 10%

(C) 26%

(D) 100%

42. A resident individual can avail the benefit of rebate of ₹ 2,500 or 100% of Income Tax whichever is less under section 87A of Income Tax Act, 1961 for the assessment year 2019-2020 on fulfilling the condition that total income does not exceed :

(A) ₹ 2.50.000

(B) ₹ 3.50.000

(C) ₹ 5,00.000

(D) ₹ 3,00,000

43. Surcharge on the amount of tax is to be levied at specified percentage when an individual is having income exceeding specified limits:

(A) @ 7% having income exceeding ₹ 1 crore and @ 12% if the income exceeds ₹ 10 crores

(B) @ 2% having income exceeding ₹ 1 crore and @ 12% if the income exceeds ₹ 10 crores

(C) @ 15% having income exceeding ₹ 1 crore and @ 10% if the income exceeds ₹ 50 lakh but does not exceed ₹ 1 crore

(D) None of the above

44. D an individual resident of India, aged 62 years, received after IDS of professional fees of ₹ 2,50,000 on 1st July, 2018 and ₹ 3,00,000 on 1st March, 2019 for rendering services in Hong Kong on which TDS of ₹ 50,000 and ₹ 60,000 have been deducted respectively. He incurred ₹ 2,60,000 as expenditure for earning this fees. He deposited ₹ 1,00,000 in PPF account. His income from other sources is ₹ 1,50,000. Tax liability including cess of D for Asst. Year 2019-2020 will be assuming that India do not have any tax treaty with Hong Kong :

(A) ₹ 10,300

(B) Nil

(C) ₹ 7,725

(D) None of the above

45. The equalization levy would be applicable from a non-resident having permanent establishment in India, on gross consideration payable for a "specified service" at a specified percentage. The applicable rate of equalization levy is

(A) 10%

(B) 5%

(C) 2%

(D) 6%

46. Engineering Instruments Ltd. is a 100% Indian subsidiary of a USA company. The parent company sells one of its products to the Indian subsidiary at a price of $ 200 per unit. The same product is sold to unrelated buyers in India at a price of $ 250 per unit. The Arm Length Price (ALP) of the product so sold to the Indian subsidiary by the parent company shall be taken in the case when there is no functional differences in both the prices at

(A) $ 50 per unit

(B) $ 250 per unit

(C) $ 200 per unit

(D) $ 450 per unit

47. How the relief of double taxation is allowed when a person resident in India, in any previous year, has paid tax in any country with which India has no bilateral agreement under section 90 ?

(A) Lower of tax paid in India and tax paid in foreign country

(B) Higher of tax paid in India and tax paid in foreign country

(C) Lower of average Indian Income tax rate or the average Foreign tax rate

(D) Higher of average Indian Income tax rate or the average Foreign tax rate

48. Which amongst the following is *not* a power of Authority for Advance Ruling (AAR) ?

(A) Power to arrest

(B) Compelling the production of books of account and other documents

(C) Discovery and inspection

(D) Enforcing the attendance of any person including any officer of a banking company and examining him on oath

49. Find out from the following, when shall an arrangement be deemed to be lacking in commercial substance so as to invoke provisions of General Anti Avoidance Rule (GAAR) under the Income Tax Act, 1961

(*i*) not a round trip financing

(*ii*) an accommodation party

(*iii*) elements having effect of offsetting or cancelling each other

(A) (*i*) and (*ii*)

(B) (*ii*) and (*iii*)

(C) (*ii*)

(D) all the three above in (*i*), (*ii*) and (*iii*)

50. An application for Advance Pricing Agreement (APA) was filed on 28th Feb., 2016 covering a period from financial years 2016-2017 to 2020-2021. The applicant applies for roll back of such APA. The roll back years can cover the period from

(A) F.Ys. 2016-2017 to 2019-2020

(B) F.Ys. 2014-2015 to 2017-2018

(C) F.Ys. 2013-2014 to 2016-2017

(D) F.Ys. 2012-2013 to 2015-2016

51. An employee director of a company was paid ₹ 5 lakh as a lump sum consideration for resigning from the directorship by XYZ Ltd. The amount so paid shall be treated in the accounts of the company as

(A) Deferred Revenue expenses

(B) Revenue expenses

(C) Capital expenses

(D) Gift to employee director

52. The basic exemption limit in case of a non resident individual being a senior citizen for assessment year 2019-2020 is :

(A) ₹ 5,00,000

(B) ₹ 3,00,000

(C) ₹ 2,50,000

(D) ₹ 1,80,000

53. Contribution made or given other than by way of cash by an Indian company in the previous year to any political party or to an electoral trust shall be allowed as deduction while computing its total income under section 80GGB of Income Tax Act, 1961 of an amount maximum or upto :

(A) ₹ 50,000

(B) ₹ 1,50,000

(C) No monetary ceiling limit

(D) None of the above

54. Total income-tax including education cess payable in case of a resident individual aged 58 years, whose computed total income is ₹ 3,40,000 for assessment year 2019-2020 shall be :

(A) ₹ 9,360

(B) ₹ 2,080

(C) ₹ 4,160

(D) ₹ 4,680

55. Hari Krishna Vidhyut Company Ltd. engaged in the business of generation and distribution of power and electricity has opted WDV method for claiming depreciation on its assets. Opening balance of the block of Plant and Machinery depreciated @ 15% on 1st April 2018 was ₹ 15,00,000. New machines of an amount of₹ 25,00,000 were purchased on 15th Nov. 2018 but put to use from 1st December, 2018. Computers for ₹ 2,00,000 were purchased on 9th Sept. 2018 and put to use in business since that date. The depreciation including the additional depreciation available to the company on plant and machinery and on the computers shall be of an amount of .... for A.Y. 2019-2020.

(A) ₹ 4,92,500

(B) ₹ 5,32,500

(C) ₹ 7,82,500

(D) ₹ 7,42,500

56. Radhey a trader having turnover of ₹ 90,00,000 from textile business inclusive of turnover of ₹ 20,00,000 carried through banking channel by way of drafts and online payments had opted to pay tax as per section 44AD of the Income Tax Act. The amount of income which shall be taken for the purpose of tax for AY 2019-2020 under the head income from business and profession is

(A) ₹ 9,00,000

(B) ₹ 6,80,000

(C) ₹ 7,20,000

(D) ₹ 5,40,000

57. Sardar Sukhdev Singh engaged in the business of plying, hiring or leasing of goods carriages owned 6 vehicles during the period 1st April, 2018 to 31st March, 2019 which were given on lease for plying to GS Transport Company on a fixed rate of ₹ 5,000 p.m. per vehicle for whole year. He had opted to pay tax as per section 44AE of the Income Tax Act. The amount of income which shall be taken for all such trucks for the purpose of tax for Asst. Year 2019-2020 is

(A) ₹ 5,40,000

(B) ₹ 3,60,000

(C) ₹ 6,48,000

(D) ₹ 6,84,000

58. A capital asset purchased on 11th Sept., 2013 for ₹ 2,00,000 was sold for ₹ 3,00,000 on 18th Dec, 2018 by a Charitable Trust registered under section 12AA of the Income Tax Act. New capital assets after the sale was purchased on 1st January, 2019 for ₹ 2,60,000. The amount of capital gain arising from the sale of capital asset utilized in purchase of new asset for the AY. 2019-2020 shall be .... and taxable amount shall be

(A) ₹ 40,000 and ₹ 60,000

(B) ₹ 1,00,000 and ₹ 2,60,000

(C) ₹ 2,60,000 and ₹ 1,00,000

(D) ₹ 60,000 and ₹ 40,000

59. The base for determination of notional income arising from the operation of a ship, in case of Indian Shipping Company under sections 115V to 115VZC of the Income Tax Act, 1961 is taken :

(A) Aggregate turnover/receipt/sales of the ship

(B) Tonnage of the ship

(C) @ 8% of turnover/receipts/sales of the ship

(D) Gross profit rate of preceding year

60. Which out of the following criteria determines the Place of Effective Management (POEM) in order to treat a foreign company as resident in India (resident company) during the previous year as per guidelines issued by CBDT and the provisions contained under the Income Tax Act, 1961

(A) General Meeting held in India

(B) Research and Development work is done in India

(C) Board Meetings are held in India

(D) None of the above

61. DAS Pvt. Ltd. fulfilling all the conditions as being specified in section 35AD of the Income Tax Act, 1961 has incurred capital expenditure of ₹ 30 lakh on purchase of land, ₹ 80 lakh (₹ 75 lakh by cheque and ₹ 5 lakh in cash) on construction of building and ₹ 10 lakh on the plant and machinery during the previous year 2018-2019 for setting up and operating a warehouse for the storage of sugar. The warehouse became operational on 1st March, 2019. The amount of deduction which the company can claim for such capital expenditure as per section 35AD in A.Y. 2019-2020 shall be

(A) ₹ 120 lakh

(B) ₹ 180 lakh

(C) ₹ 85 lakh

(D) ₹ 90 lakh

62. Anand, a resident individual having computed for the previous year 1st April, 2018 to 31st March, 2019 his business loss at ₹ 60,000, short term capital gain on sale of gold of ₹ 40,000 long term capital gain on sale of house property of ₹ 3,60,000. The amount of total income to be declared in the return for the assessment year 2019-2020 by Anand shall be

(A) ₹ 4,00,000

(B) ₹ 3,40,000

(C) ₹ 4,00,000 and carry forward loss of ₹ 60,000

(D) None of the above

63. State which out of the following gifts received during the year by Girish from different persons shall be subject to tax in the assessment year 2019-2020 :

(*i*) Wrist watch of ₹ 75,000 given by a non-resident friend.

(*ii*) Cash of ₹ 51,000 given by elder brother.

(*iii*) Cash of ₹ 21,000 each given by 4 friends on his birthday.

(*iv*) Painting of ₹ 30,000 given by employer on his birthday.

(A) (*iii*) and (*iv*)

(B) (*i*), (*iii*) and (*iv*)

(C) (*ii*) and (*iii*)

(D) All the four in (*i*), (*ii*), (*iii*) and (*iv*)

64. Kapoor gifted ₹ 10,00,000 to his wife Sunita Kapoor on 15th May, 2018. The amount of gift of ₹ 10,00,000 was invested by his wife in debentures of a company on 1st June, 2018 earning interest @ 12% p.a. The income of interest of .... from the debentures earned by Sunita Kapoor shall be .... with the income of Kapoor in A.Y. 2019-2020.

(A) ₹ 1,20,000, not clubbed

(B) ₹ 1,00,000, clubbed

(C) ₹ 1,00,000, not clubbed

(D) ₹ 1,20,000, clubbed

65. The assessee who has filed a return of income for A.Y. 2018-19 as per section 139(1) can file revise return any time :

(A) before 1 year from the end of the relevant assessment year

(B) before the end of the relevant assessment year or before the completion of assessment whichever is earlier

(C) before the expiry of the relevant assessment year or before the completion of assessment whichever is later

(D) before the completion of the assessment year

66. The time limit for filing an appeal by person denying liability to deduct tax in respect of payments payable to non-resident or a foreign company as provided in section 249(2)(*a*) of the Income Tax Act, 1961 is within :

(A) 30 days from the date of payment of tax deducted at source to the credit of Central Government

(B) 35 days from the date of payment of tax deducted at source to the credit of Central Government

(C) 45 days from the date of payment of tax deducted at source to the credit of Central Government

(D) 60 days from the date of payment of tax deducted at source to the credit of Central Government

67. The due date for e-filing of return of income by a Charitable Trust claiming exemption u/ss 11 and 12 for assessment year 2018-19 is :

(A) 31st March, 2018

(B) 30th September, 2018

(C) 31st August, 2018

(D) Between any time specified in (B) and (C)

68. An application for stay of demand to be filed before the Income Tax Appellate Tribunal (ITAT) has to be accompanied by requisite fee of :

(A) ₹ 1,000

(B) ₹ 500

(C) ₹ 1,500

(D) ₹ 10,000

69. Which planning is based on the measures which circumvent the law ?

(A) Long-range tax planning

(B) Purposive tax planning

(C) Short range planning

(D) Permissive tax planning

70. R sold a machine to H (Associated Enterprise) and in turn H sold the same machinery to N (an independent party) at sale margin of 40% for ₹ 6,00,000 but H has incurred ₹ 8,000 in sending the machine to N. The "Arm Length Price" (ALP) in respect of the machine sold on the basis of Retail Price Method as per provisions of the Income Tax Act, 1961 shall be :

(A) ₹ 6 lakh

(B) ₹ 3.6 lakh

(C) ₹ 3.52 lakh

(D) ₹ 6.08 lakh

PART B

71. Mr. S a manufacturer of medicines, whose turnover for financial year 2018-2019 was of ₹ 70 lakh opted to pay tax under GST as per composition scheme from 1st April, 2019. His turnover crosses ₹ 1 crore on 30 November, 2018. Will he be allowed to pay tax under composition scheme for the remainder of year i.e. from 1st December, 2019 to 31st March, 2020 ?

(A) Yes, he can avail the benefit till 31st March, 2020

(B) No, the option availed shall lapse from the day on which his aggregate turnover during the financial year 2018-19 exceeds ₹ 1 crore

(C) Yes, the option can be availed upto completion of half financial year i.e. till 30th September, 2019

(D) None of the above

72. A supply made by a taxable person to a recipient of goods being buyer consisting of two or more taxable supplies of goods or services or of both or any combination thereof which are only bundled and supplied in conjunction with each other in the ordinarily course of business out of which one is a principal supply has been defined u/s 2(3) of CGST Act, 2017 as

(A) Composite supply

(B) Mixed supply

(C) Higher rate tax supply

(D) Bundled supply

73. Taxable person whose registration has been surrendered or cancelled is required to file the return within 3 months of the date of cancellation or date of cancellation order whichever is later in Form Number

(A) GSTR-13

(B) GSTR-10

(C) GSTR-7

(D) GSTR-9

74. The payment of tax by electronic operator who does not have physical presence in taxable territory in India be made by

(A) e-commerce operator himself

(B) his appointed representative in India

(C) the person who receives supply

(D) either (A) or (B)

75. The time of supply "where goods or services or both have been supplied in a situation where the invoice issued before the change in the rate of tax but payment received after the change in rate of tax" as per section 14 of the CGST Act, 2017 shall be :

(A) Date of issue of invoice

(B) Date of receipt of payment or the date of issue of invoice whichever is earlier

(C) Date of receipt of payment

(D) None of the above

76. State the "Base Year" and "Projected Growth Rate" for the purpose of calculating the compensation amount payable by the Centre on account of revenue loss to the States as specified under the Goods and Services Tax (Compensation to States) Act, 2017 :

(A) Financial Year 2014-15, @ 14%

(B) Financial Year 2015-16, @ 14%

(C) Financial Year 2016-17, @ 14%

(D) Financial Year 2017-18, @ 14%

77. The limit of nautical miles from base line of sea coast into the sea in order to determine the supply in territorial water as per section 9 of the IGST Act, 2017 is :

(A) Upto 7 nautical miles

(B) Upto 10 nautical miles

(C) Upto 12 nautical miles

(D) Upto 20 nautical miles

78. Which of the following called the Union territory as being covered under Union Territory Goods and Services Tax Act (UTGST), 2017 ?

(A) Andaman and Nicobar Island

(B) Puducherry

(C) Daman and Diu

(D) None of the above

79. Subsidy given by the Central Government or a State Government while determining value of taxable supply under Goods and Services Tax (GST) as per section 15 of the CGST Act, 2017 :

(A) included in the transaction value i.e. (value of taxable supply)

(B) just ignored no treatment

(C) shall not be included in transaction value i.e. (value of taxable supply)

(D) deducted from the transaction value i.e. (value of taxable supply)

80. Patel of Surat, Gujarat supplied goods to Patil of Mumbai, Maharashtra for ₹ 1,20,000 (excluding GST) but after adding 30% profit margin (on cost). Patil is also a taxable person. IGST rate is 18%. The amount of input tax credit that can be availed and the maximum time limit for availing such input tax credit by Patil of Mumbai, Maharashtra as per CGST Act, 2017 is ....

(A) ₹ 28,080 and within 6 months from the date of issue of tax invoice

(B) ₹ 7,020 and within next quarter from the date of issue of tax invoice

(C) ₹ 21,600 and within 1 year from the date of issue of tax invoice

(D) None of the above

81. The stipulated time limit within which inputs and capital goods sent to a job worker in a job work, shall be brought back and beyond that period it will be treated as supply and tax is payable by the principal as per CGST Act, 2017 is ....

(A) 6 months and 1 year in case of inputs and capital goods respectively

(B) 1 year and 2 years in case of inputs and capital goods respectively

(C) 1 year and 3 years in case of inputs and capital goods respectively

(D) None of the above

82. The credit of tax paid on input services used by more than one supplier be distributed as per provisions of the CGST Act, 2017 ....

(A) only to one supplier

(B) equally among all the suppliers

(C) among the suppliers who used such input service on *pro rata* basis of turnover in such state

(D) cannot be distributed

83. The GST Council for ensuring single interface has distributed the administrative control of taxpayers of certain percentage with Central Tax Administration:

(A) 5% of taxpayers having turnover below ₹ 1 crore

(B) 10% of taxpayers having turnover below ₹ 1.5 crores

(C) 10% of taxpayers having turnover below ₹ 1 crore

(D) 20% of taxpayers having turnover below ₹ 1.5 crores

84. The time duration for retention of accounts and records under Goods and Services Tax (GST) as per section 36 of the CGST Act, 2017 is :

(A) Until expiry of 36 months from the due date of furnishing of annual return for the year pertaining to such accounts and records

(B) Until expiry of 48 months from the due date of furnishing of annual return for the year pertaining to such accounts and records

(C) Until expiry of 60 months from the due date of furnishing of annual return for the year pertaining to such accounts and records

(D) Until expiry of 72 months from the due date of furnishing of annual return for the year pertaining to such accounts and records

85. Find out from the following, who are the persons not liable for registration under section 23 of the CGST Act, 2017 :

(A) non-resident making taxable supply

(B) person supplying exempted goods and services or goods or services which are not liable for tax under GST

(C) an agriculturist to the extent of supply of produce out of cultivation of land

(D) both (B) and (C)

86. Maximum validity period of certificate of registration issued to a casual and non-resident taxable person as per section 27 of the CGST Act, 2017 is :

(A) 90 days from the effective date of registration

(B) 180 days from the effective date of registration

(C) 365 days from the effective date of registration

(D) none of the above

87. The quantum of punishment "where any person convicted of an offence under section 132(2) of the CGST Act, 2017 and again convicted of an offence under this section" is :

(A) imprisonment for a term which may extent to five years and with fine

(B) imprisonment for a term which may extent to four years and with fine

(C) imprisonment for a term which may extent to three years and with fine

(D) imprisonment for a term which may extent to two years and with fine

88. The validity period specified for an e-way bill or a consolidated e-way bill under E-way rules as specified in rule 138 for

(A) distance upto 1 km—half day

(B) distance upto 10 km—1 day

(C) for every 100 km or part thereof thereafter—one additional day

(D) both (B) and (C) above

89. Grounds which leads a Commissioner to order for a special audit in case of a registered person by a communication in writing for getting his records including books of account examined and audited and by a person who

(A) supplies any goods or service or both without issue of any invoice by Cost Accountant or Company Secretary

(B) avail input tax credit with bogus invoice by Company Secretary or Cost Accountant

(C) has not correctly declared the value or the credit availed is not within the normal limits, by a Chartered Accountant or a Cost Accountant

(D) none of the above

90. State the default committed on the part of a registered person which attracts an action by the proper officer to make best judgment assessment and also state the time limit within which such assessment is to be made :

(A) furnish inaccurate data in return and within 2 years from the due date of annual return of the period to which the tax not paid relates

(B) fails to file general return under section 39 and within 5 years from the due date of annual return of the period to which tax not paid relates

(C) fails to file final return under section 45 even after notice under section 46 and within 5 years from the due date of annual return of the period to which tax not paid relates

(D) both (B) and (C) above

91. Section 51 of the CGST Act, 2017 mandates deduction of tax at source (TDS) at a specified percentage by the Government or Local Authorities from the payments made or credited to the supplier where the value of supply under a contract exceeds specified limit. State the specified percentage of TDS and the threshold limit of taxable goods or services or both under the contract

(A) 0.50% & ₹ 1,00,000

(B) 0.75% & ₹ 1,50,000

(C) 2% & ₹ 5,00,000

(D) 2% & ₹ 2,50,000

92. Who is authorized under Integrated Goods and Services Tax (IGST) Act, to levy tax :

(A) State

(B) Centre

(C) Union Territory

(D) Both (A) and (B)

93. State which shall be taken as the effective date of registration as per CGST Act, 2017 where the aggregate turnover of Madhur Company engaged in supply of taxable services in the State of Rajasthan exceeded ₹ 20 lakh during the year on 25th September, 2018, the application for registration under GST was filed on 19th October, 2018 and the registration certificate was granted on 29th October, 2018 by the authority :

(A) 25-9-2018

(B) 19-10-2018

(C) 24-10-2018

(D) 29-10-2018

94. Consumer Welfare Fund has been constituted by the Government of India and as per section 57 of the CGST Act, 2017, the following amounts will be credited to this fund :

(*i*) amount referred to in section 54(5)

(*ii*) refund of tax in pursuance of section 77

(*iii*) income from investment of the fund amount

(*iv*) refund of unutilized input tax credit

(A) (*ii*) and (*iii*)

(B) (*i*) and (*iii*)

(C) (*i*), (*ii*) and (*iv*)

(D) All the four above

95. The available balance of input tax credit in the electronic ledger of the registered person on account of Union territory tax shall be utilized as per section 9 of UTGST Act, 2017

(A) first towards payment of central tax

(B) first towards payment of integrated tax

(C) first towards payment of union territory tax and the amount remaining, if any towards payment of integrated tax

(D) none of the above

96. Find out from the following, who will be the member in GST Council on behalf of each of the Slate :

(A) Chief Minister of the State

(B) Home Minister of the State

(C) The Minister in charge of Finance or Taxation or any other Minister nominated by the State Government

(D) Chief Secretary of the State

97. The assessee is required mandatorily to mention the Harmonized System Nomenclature (HSN) or Service Accounting Code (SAC) on the tax invoice of the product or service supplied under GST:

(A) having a turnover of ₹ 2 crore and above

(B) having a turnover of ₹ 3 crore and above

(C) having a turnover of ₹ 4 crore and above

(D) having a turnover of ₹ 5 crore and above

98. GST Council is being constituted for making recommendation on various issues relating to policy making, formulation of principle and implementation of policies relating to CGST Act, 2017. It is thus

(A) An administrative body

(B) A Central level body

(C) A Committee of Finance Ministers

(D) An Apex Body

99. Exempt supply means supply of any goods or services or both which may be wholly exempt from tax under section 11 or under section 6 of the IGST Act and includes.

(*i*) Non-taxable supply

(*ii*) Zero rated supply

(*iii*) Supply having Nil rate of tax

(*iv*) Composite supply

(A) (*i*), (*ii*) and (*iii*)

(B) (*i*) and (*iv*)

(C) (*i*) and (*iii*)

(D) All the four above

100. The exception to the general rule that "normally, the supplier of goods and services is liable to pay tax on supply, even if he does not collect from his customer i.e. recipient of supply of goods or services" shall be applicable where there are :

(A) supply from an unregistered dealer to registered dealer

(B) specified services through an e-commerce operator

(C) both (A) and (B)

(D) none of the above

ANSWERS:

1.	(B)	**2.**	(B)	**3.**	(C)	**4.**	(C)	**5.**	(B)	**6.**	(C)	**7.**	(A)
8.	(C)	**9.**	(B)	**10.**	(D)	**11.**	(D)	**12.**	(D)	**13.**	(C)	**14.**	(D)
15.	(C)	**16.**	(B)	**17.**	(D)	**18.**	(C)	**19.**	(C)	**20.**	(D)	**21.**	(C)
22.	(D)	**23.**	(**)	**24.**	(C)	**25.**	(B)	**26.**	(B)	**27.**	(B)	**28.**	(D)
29.	(C)	**30.**	(A)	**31.**	(A)	**32.**	(D)	**33.**	(B)	**34.**	(B)	**35.**	(C)
36.	(D)	**37.**	(A)	**38.**	(C)	**39.**	(D)	**40.**	(**)	**41.**	(A)	**42.**	(B)
43.	(C)	**44.**	(D)	**45.**	(D)	**46.**	(C)	**47.**	(C)	**48.**	(A)	**49.**	(D)

50.	(D)	**51.**	(B)	**52.**	(C)	**53.**	(C)	**54.**	(B)	**55.**	(C)	**56.**	(B)
57.	(A)	**58.**	(D)	**59.**	(B)	**60.**	(C)	**61.**	(C)	**62.**	(B)	**63.**	(B)
64.	(B)	**65.**	(B)	**66.**	(A)	**67.**	(B)	**68.**	(B)	**69.**	(B)	**70.**	(C)
71.	(B)	**72.**	(A)	**73.**	(B)	**74.**	(B)	**75.**	(A)	**76.**	(B)	**77.**	(C)
78.	(B)	**79.**	(C)	**80.**	(C)	**81.**	(C)	**82.**	(C)	**83.**	(B)	**84.**	(D)
85.	(D)	**86.**	(A)	**87.**	(A)	**88.**	(C)	**89.**	(C)	**90.**	(D)	**91.**	(D)
92.	(B)	**93.**	(A)	**94.**	(B)	**95.**	(C)	**96.**	(C)	**97.**	(D)	**98.**	(D)
99.	(C)	**100.**	(C)										

HINTS FOR IMPORTANT PRACTICAL MCQs

23. All the amounts given in options are added and hence none of the given option is correct.

40. Option (B) and Option (C) both are correct and hence MCQ itself is wrong.

44.

Professional fees for rendering service in Hong Kong (2,50,000 + 3,00,000 + 50,000 + 60,000)	6,60,000	
Expenses	(2,60,000)	4,00,000
Income from other sources		1,50,000
Gross total income		5,50,000
(-) Deduction u/s 80C [PPF]		(1,00,000)
Total income		4,50,000
Tax on total income *(basic exemption ₹ 3,00,000 as age is above 60 years)*		7,500
(+) Education cess @ 3%		225
Total tax		7,725

$$\text{Tax on doubly taxed income in India} = \frac{4{,}00{,}000 \times 7{,}725}{4{,}50{,}000} \times 100 = 6{,}866$$

$$\text{Tax on doubly taxed income in foreign country} = \frac{4{,}00{,}000 \times 1{,}10{,}000}{6{,}60{,}000} \times 100 = 66{,}666$$

Total tax	7,725
(-) Relief u/s 91; Lower of ₹ 6,866 or ₹ 66,666	(6,866)
Indian tax liability	859
Rounded up	860

₹ 860 do not appear in any option and hence Option (D) is correct.

Alternatively relief can be calculated as follows:

$$\text{Indian rate of tax} = \frac{7{,}725}{4{,}50{,}000} \times 100 = 1.7166\%$$

$$\text{Foreign rate of tax} = \frac{50{,}000 + 60{,}000}{6{,}60{,}000} \times 100 = 16.6666\%$$

Total tax		7,725
(-) Relief u/s 91; Lower of following two		
- Doubly taxed income × Indian rate of tax (4,00,000 × 1.7166%)	(6,866)	
- Doubly taxed income × Rate of tax paid in other country (4,00,000 × 16.6666%)	(66,666)	(6,866)
Indian tax liability		859
Rounded up		860

50. In many countries the APA scheme provides for "roll back" mechanism for dealing with ALP issues relating to transactions entered into during the period prior to APA. The "roll back" provisions refers to the applicability of the methodology of determination of ALP, or the ALP, to be applied to the international transactions which had already been entered into in a period prior to the period covered under an APA. However, the "roll back" relief is provided on case to case basis subject to certain conditions. Providing of such a mechanism in Indian legislation would also lead to reduction in large scale litigation which is currently pending or may arise in future in respect of the transfer pricing matters.

Therefore, it is proposed to amend the Act to provide roll back mechanism in the APA scheme. The APA may, subject to such prescribed conditions, procedure and manner, provide for determining the arm's length price or for specifying the manner in which arm's length price is to be determined in relation to an international transaction entered into by a person during any period not exceeding **4 previous years preceding the first of the previous years for which the advance pricing agreement applies** in respect of the international transaction to be undertaken in future.

This amendment is effective from 1st October, 2014.

52. Basic exemption for senior citizen is ₹ 3,00,000; however, for non-resident senior citizen basis exemption limit is **₹ 2,50,000** and hence option (C) correct.

55.

Particulars	Plant & Machinery 15%	Computer 40%
Opening WDV 1.4.2018	15,00,000	–
(+) Assets put to use more than 180 days	–	2,00,000
(+) Assets put to use less than 180 days	25,00,000	–
(-) Sold during the year	–	–
WDV for charging depreciation	40,00,000	2,00,000
Regular depreciation		
- On assets put to use less than 180 days	1,87,500	–
- On balance	2,25,000	80,000
Additional depreciation		
- On assets put to use less than 180 days @ 10%	2,50,000	–
- On assets put to use more than 180 days @ 20%	–	40,000
Total depreciation	6,62,500	1,20,000

Total = 6,62,500 + 1,20,000 = 7,82,500.

'Computer' also comes in block of 'plant & machinery' and eligible for additional depreciation.

It is assumed that computers are not used in office.

56. (70,00,000 × 8%) + (20,00,000 × 6%) = 6,80,000

57. 6 × 7,500 × 12 = 5,40,000.

58.

Full value of consideration		3,00,000
(-) Cost of acquisition		(2,00,000)
Capital gain		1,00,000
(-) Exemption: Lower of the following two –		
- Capital gain	1,00,000	
- Cost of new asset – Cost of asset transferred	60,000	
(2,60,000 – 2,00,000)		(60,000)
		40,000

70.

Resale price	6,00,000
(-) Margin @ 40%	(2,40,000)
	3,60,000
(-) Expenses	(8,000)
	3,52,000

Important Note:

- **MCQs No. 1, 2, 3, 4, 18, 46, 47, 48, 49, 50, 59, 69 & 70** are not relevant for New Syllabus of CS Executive as these questions relates to topics that are not in syllabus.
- All MCQs are relevant for Old Syllabus of CS Executive.

Solved Paper
CS Executive - June 2019

(AS PER LAW APPLICABLE FOR AY 2019-2020)

PART A: INCOME TAX

1. When a person, who has entered into an international transaction, fails to furnish information or document in relation to his international transaction to the Assessing Officer, he is liable to pay penalty of:

(A) 1% of the value of International transaction

(B) 2% of the value of International transaction

(C) ₹ 1,50,000

(D) ₹ 5,00,000

2. In the case of an individual who is not an ordinarily resident in India, the income chargeable to tax in India out of the following shall be:

(A) Rental income in foreign country

(B) Interest income in foreign country

(C) Income from outside India from a business controlled in India

(D) All the three above in (A), (B) & (C)

3. Which of the following is not the objective of safe harbour rules:

(A) Compliance and Simplicity

(B) Reduce Litigation

(C) Administration Simplicity

(D) Higher collection of Taxes

4. Anil made following transaction for the year ended 31st March, 2019:

(A) Acquired immovable property for ₹ 6 lakh;

(B) Made a term deposit (TDR) of ₹ 30,000 in a bank;

(C) Paid ₹ 75,000 to a hotel for his birthday party and

(D) Deposited ₹ 45,000 cash in his Savings Bank (SB) account..

Quoting of PAN is mandatory in which of these transactions:

(A) Purchase of immovable property

(B) TDR with bank and deposit of cash in bank

(C) Payment to hotel for birthday party

(D) All the three above in (A), (B) & (C)

5. M Ltd. has Minimum Alternative Tax (MAT) credit of ₹ 5,20,000 of the assessment year 2019-2020. It can carry forward this MAT credit up to _____ assessment years immediately succeeding the assessment year 2019-2020.

(A) 5

(B) 10

(C) 15

(D) 20

6. The monetary limit for specified domestic transaction in order to be liable for transfer pricing provision should exceed, in aggregate, in a year:

(A) ₹ 20 Crore

(B) ₹ 10 Crore

(C) ₹ 5 Crore

(D) ₹ 3 Crore

7. Tom (P) Ltd. availed the services of a foreign company for online advertisement of its products. It has to pay a levy @ ______ % of the gross amount paid/payable to the foreign company when it has no permanent establishment in India.

(A) 2

(B) 5

(C) 6

(D) 10

8. Kadam sold a vacant land for ₹ 15 lakh on 20th March, 2019. The indexed cost of acquisition of the land is ₹ 12,00,000. He received ₹ 3 lakh being part of the sales consideration in cash and the balance through Electronic Clearance System (ECS). The AO can levy penalty in such case on Kadam of an amount of:

(A) ₹ 12,00,000

(B) NIL

(C) ₹ 15,00,000

(D) ₹ 3,00,000

9. When an Indian company holds 30% of the nominal value of equity capital of a foreign company, the amount of dividend received from the foreign company in the hands of Indian company is:

(A) Exempt from Tax

(B) Taxable @ 15%

(C) Taxable @ 10%

(D) Taxable @ 30%

10. The secondary adjustment in certain international transaction is required to be made when the amount of primary adjustment exceeds:

(A) ₹ 10 Crore

(B) ₹ 5 Crore

(C) ₹ 3 Crore

(D) ₹ 1 Crore

11. The total income of Ram is ₹ 4,90,000 and due date of filing the return of income for AY 2019-2020 is 31st July, 2019. The return by Ram shall be filed on 20th September, 2019. The late fee payable for late filing of return of income shall be:

(A) ₹ 1,000

(B) ₹ 5,000

(C) ₹ 10,000

(D) No late fee up to income of ₹ 5 lakh

12. Notice for assessment or re-assessment of the escaped income of non-resident can not be issued to the statutory agent of the non-residential after expiry of......... years from the end of the relevant assessment year.

(A) 4

(B) 6

(C) 2

(D) 16

13. Ashish, director of PQR Ltd. is eligible for board sitting fees of ₹ 10,000 for every meeting attended by him. During the year 2018-2019, he had attended six meetings. The amount of tax required to be deducted from such sitting fees to be paid to Ashish by the company shall be:

(A) ₹ 12,000 @ 20%

(B) ₹ 1,200 @ 2%

(C) ₹ 3,000 @ 5%

(D) ₹ 6,000 @ 10%

14. Advance Pricing Agreement (APA) shall be valid for a period as specified in the Advance Pricing Agreement but this period will not be for more than ______ consecutive previous years.

(A) 5

(B) 3

(C) 2

(D) 10

15. Any payment in commutation of pension received from a pension fund setup by the Life Insurance Corporation of India in terms of section 10(23AAB) of the Income-tax Act, 1961, is:

(A) Liable for tax

(B) Fully exempt from tax

(C) Partly liable for tax

(D) Taxable @ 10%

16. Find out from the following income derived from house property which is being exempt from Income Tax:

(A) Income from property of a trust for charitable or religious purposes

(B) Income from property of a housing society

(C) Income from property of a trade association

(D) Income from property of a sports association

17. Z an assessee incurs expenditure for acquisition of an asset in respect of which payment (or aggregate of payment made to a person in a day), otherwise than by an account payee cheque/draft or use of ECS through a bank, exceeds ₹ ...., such payment shall not be eligible for claiming the amount of depreciation on such asset.

(A) ₹ 50,000

(B) ₹ 20,000

(C) ₹ 10,000

(D) ₹ 2,00,000

18. Exemption under section 54G on fulfilling of specified conditions is available on:

(A) Shifting of industrial undertaking from urban area to a Special Economic Zone (SEZ)

(B) Shifting of industrial undertaking from urban Area by government

(C) Compulsory acquisition of land and building

(D) Transfer of certain capital assets as specified

19. Business loss can be set off from income of any other business but cannot be set off from:

(A) Salary Income

(B) House Property Income

(C) Long Term Capital Gains

(D) Income from derivatives specified in section 43(5)

20. 100% deduction in respect of donations as per section 80G without any qualifying amount or limit is available in the case of:

(A) Prime Minister Drought Relief Fund

(B) Jawaharlal Nehru Memorial Fund

(C) Payment to local authority for promotion of family planning

(D) Africa Fund

21. Alternate Minimum Tax (AMT) under section 115JC is payable by a person other than a company on the adjusted total income at the rate of:

(A) 20% plus cess

(B) 18% plus cess

(C) 18.5% plus cess

(D) 20.5% plus cess

22. Dividend distribution tax by a domestic company under section 115-O shall be paid within........... days of declaration of dividend.

(A) 30 days

(B) 15 days

(C) 10 days

(D) 14 days

23. A non-resident is not required to furnish return of income under section 139(1) if his total income during the previous year consists of:

(A) Income from Technical fee

(B) Income from Interest/Dividends

(C) Income from Royalty

(D) Income from House Rent

24. An income tax authority referred to in section 116 of the Income-tax Act, 1961 may amend with a view to rectify any mistake apparent from the records in respect of:

(A) Any intimation under sub-section (1) of section 200A

(B) Any dispute raised by the assessee in respect of an issue having two views

(C) Any order passed by its higher authorities

(D) Any section, if required by law

25. X filed his return of income for the AY 2018-2019 on 31st July, 2018. The return so filed was selected for scrutiny assessment.

The notice under section 143(2) for making scrutiny assessment can be served by:

(A) 30th September, 2019

(B) 31st December, 2018

(C) 31st March, 2019

(D) 31st December, 2019

26. Income Tax Appellate Tribunal (ITAT) as per section 254(2A) may hear and decide any appeal within a period of:

(A) 1 year from the end of financial year in which appeal is filed

(B) 2 years from the end of financial year in which appeal is filed

(C) 3 years from the end of financial year in which appeal is filed

(D) 4 years from the end of financial year in which appeal is filed

27. Application to settlement commission can be made only:

(A) Where the additional amount of income tax payable exceeds ₹ 10 lakh

(B) Where the additional amount of income tax payable exceeds ₹ 5 lakh

(C) Where the additional amount of income tax payable exceeds ₹ 3 lakh

(D) Where the additional amount of income tax payable exceeds ₹ 1 lakh

28. Maximum amount of penalty for failure to get accounts audited required as per section 44AB of the Act from an accountant is:

(A) ₹ 1,50,000

(B) ₹ 1,00,000

(C) ₹ 50,000

(D) ½% of turnover or gross receipts of the business or profession or ₹ 50,000

29. Which one is not a method under transfer pricing for calculating Arm's Length Price (ALP) of the transactions:

(A) Comparable Uncontrolled Price method (CUP)

(B) Profit Method (PM)

(C) Resale Price Method (RPM)

(D) Profit Split Method (PSM)

30. Agriculture income from agriculture land located in a foreign country is taxable in the case of:

(A) Non-resident

(B) Not ordinarily resident

(C) Resident

(D) In all cases stated in (A), (B) & (C)

31. Mohan, retried from Y & Company Ltd. on 31.8.2018 after rendering services for 31 years and 7 months. He was paid ₹ 11 lakhs as gratuity under the Payment of Gratuity Act, 1972. His last drawn salary was ₹ 52,000. How much of the amount of gratuity would be exempt?

(A) ₹ 10,00,000

(B) ₹ 20,00,000

(C) ₹ 9,30,000

(D) ₹ 9,60,000

32. Green Wood Plantation Ltd. is engaged in cultivation and processing of Tea. Their net income during AY 2019-2020 is to the tune of ₹ 20 Lakhs. What proportion out of the income of ₹ 20 lakhs would be treated as agriculture income?

(A) 10%

(B) 25%

(C) 40%

(D) 60%

33. Application filed before Authority for Advance Ruling (AAR) may be withdrawn within ______ from the date of application.

(A) 15 days

(B) 30 days

(C) 60 days

(D) 90 days

34. Short term capital loss can be set-off as per provisions of section 72 of the Income Tax Act, 1961 from:

(A) Short term capital gain

(B) Short term capital gain and Long term capital gain

(C) Long term capital gain

(D) Short term capital gain and profit & gain from business

35. Nair, a retired person of 68 years of age obtained ₹ 10,000 per month from 1st April, 2018 on reverse mortgage of his self-occupied residential property from a bank. The fair rent of the property is ₹ 15,000 per month. The income chargeable to tax in respect of amount received on reverse mortgage for his self-occupied house property for the FY 2018-2019 would be:

(A) ₹ 1,20,000

(B) ₹ 1,26,000

(C) NIL

(D) (15,000 – 10,000) × 12 = 60,000

36. Rohan, an employee of State Government received ₹ 1,000 per month as entertainment allowance during the financial year 2018-2019. His salary excluding any allowance, benefit or other perquisite for the year is ₹ 8,40,000. The amount of entertainment allowance eligible for deduction is:

(A) ₹ 12,000

(B) 1% of salary of ₹ 8,400

(C) ₹ 5,000

(D) (12,000 – 8,400) = 3,600

37. Appeal against the order of Appellate Tribunal (ITAT) can be filed in High Court within................ days.

(A) 30 days from the date of order

(B) 60 days from the date of receipt of order by the assessee

(C) 120 days from the date of receipt of order by the assessee

(D) 180 days from the date of order

38. Narendra engaged in retail trade let out his fully furnished house with lift, air conditioners, fridge, security staff and gardener at a rent of ₹ 1,00,000 per month. The agreement did not provide for separate rent for various facilities but is a composite agreement. The amount received by him would be chargeable to tax under the head:

(A) Other Sources

(B) Business Income

(C) Income from House Property

(D) Capital Gains

39. John, who recently retired from service of a company on 31st March, 2019 is eligible for a monthly pension of ₹ 20,000. He has received gratuity on his retirement also. He wants to commute 50% of his pension for ₹ 6.00 lakh. How much amount of this commuted pension shall be subject to tax in AY 2019-2020?

(A) ₹ 6,00,000

(B) ₹ 2,00,000

(C) ₹ 3,00,000

(D) ₹ 3,50,000

40. Revision order of the Commissioner of Income Tax passed under section 264 of the Income-tax Act, 1961 can be challenged by the assessee by filing an appeal to:

(A) Income Tax Appellate Tribunal (ITAT)

(B) High Court

(C) Commissioner Appeals

(D) Dispute Resolution Penal (DRP)

41. A registered political party have income during the year 2018-2019 of banks interest ₹ 5,00,000, rent from letting of building ₹ 3,00,000 and voluntary contribution by cheque ₹ 8,00,000. Total income chargeable to tax under section 13A of the Income-tax Act, 1961 for the AY 2019-2020 of the political party shall be:

(A) ₹ 5,00,000

(B) ₹ 8,00,000

(C) ₹ 16,00,000

(D) NIL

42. Raghav Housing Finance Ltd., a NBFC is eligible to claim deduction in the case of provision made for bad and doubtful debts to the extent of .... total income.

(A) 10%

(B) 5%

(C) 2%

(D) 1%

43. XYZ Ltd. paid ₹ 5 lakh on 22.1.2019 to a national level laboratory for carrying scientific research unrelated to the business of the company. The amount of deduction eligible under section 35(2AA) of the Income-tax Act, 1961 is:

(A) ₹ 5,00,000 @ 100%

(B) ₹ 6,25,000 @ 125%

(C) ₹ 7,50,000 @ 150%

(D) ₹ 10,00,000 @ 200%

44. Patel, a textile dealer, purchases goods worth ₹ 65,000 from Anand and made the payments: (*i*) ₹ 12,000 by account payee cheque on 5th June, 2018, (*ii*) ₹ 8,000 by cash on 16th August, 2018, (*iii*) ₹ 15,000 by bearer cheque on 7th November, 2018 and (*iv*) ₹ 30,000 by ECS on 21st March, 2019. The amount of expenditure not allowable as per provisions of section 40A(3) would be:

(A) NIL

(B) ₹ 8,000

(C) ₹ 23,000

(D) ₹ 38,000

45. Deccan Ltd. incurred an amount of ₹ 16 lakh as preliminary expenses for setting up a project costing ₹ 100 lakh during financial year 2018-2019. The amount of amortization available as deduction during the AY 2019-2020 for the preliminary expenses would be:

(A) ₹ 1,60,000

(B) ₹ 3,20,000

(C) ₹ 16,00,000

(D) ₹ 1,00,000

46. Tulip & Co. is a partnership firm of two partners. Total turnover of the firm during financial year 2018-19 is ₹ 160 lakh inclusive of ₹ 60 lakh made through account payee cheques and ECS. The partnership deed provided for monthly working salary of ₹ 30,000 to each of the partners. The income of the firm by applying section 44AD for AY 2019-2020 would be:

(A) ₹ 11,60,000

(B) ₹ 12,80,000

(C) ₹ 5,00,000

(D) ₹ 4,40,000

47. Employer's contribution to Recognized Provident Fund (RPF) in excess of 12% of salary income of an employee shall be treated as:

(A) Taxable income from salaries

(B) Deemed income from salaries

(C) Exempted income

(D) Income of other sources

48. Zed Ltd. a domestic company engaged in manufacturing activity at Mumbai acquired a plant for ₹ 5 lakh on 7th January, 2019 which is eligible for depreciation @ 15%. It paid ₹ 4 lakh through ECS system from bank and balance ₹ 1 lakh in cash on 23rd February, 2019. The plant was put to use on 12.3.2019. The amount of depreciation (normal and additional) on this plant for AY 2019-20 shall be:

(A) ₹ 40,000

(B) ₹ 30,000

(C) ₹ 70,000

(D) ₹ 60,000

49. A professional is required to get his accounts audited under section 44AB of the Income-tax Act, 1961 where the gross receipts from profession during the financial year 2018-2019:

(A) Exceeds ₹ 100 lakhs

(B) Equals to or exceeds ₹ 50 lakh

(C) Equals to or exceeds ₹ 100 lakh

(D) Exceeds ₹ 50 lakhs

50. 'A' Transport company engaged in the business of plying goods carriage with 4 heavy vehicles and 3 non-heavy vehicles. All the non-heavy vehicles were sold on 10th May, 2018 and 2 heavy vehicles were acquired on the same date. Transporter wants to declare its income for A.Y. 2019-20 as per provisions of section 44AE and the same would be:

(A) ₹ 5,70,000

(B) ₹ 5,47,500

(C) ₹ 5,55,000

(D) ₹ 3,60,000

51. As per Income-tax Act, 1961 surcharge @ 12% is payable by a domestic company if the total income exceeds:

(A) ₹ 10 lakh

(B) ₹ 1 Crore

(C) ₹ 10 Crore

(D) ₹ 100 Crore

52. B joined Avtar & Co. as a partner on 1st June, 2018. He contributed his vacant land in the firm as his capital which was recorded in the books of the firm at ₹ 5 lakh. The land was inherited by B from his father in April, 2010 and the Fair Market Value (FMV) on that date was ₹ 2 lakh. The land was originally acquired by his father in August, 2005 for ₹ 1 lakh. The Fair Market Value (FMV) on 1st June, 2018 was ₹ 10 lakh. The full value of consideration received as a result of transfer of land by B as capital would be taken as :

(A) ₹ 1 lakh

(B) ₹ 2 lakh

(C) ₹ 5 lakh

(D) ₹ 10 lakh

53. Maintenance of books of account in the case of an HUF carrying business is mandatory, if the turnover or gross receipts in any one of the three years immediately preceding the previous year exceeds:

(A) ₹ 10 lakh

(B) ₹ 15 lakh

(C) ₹ 25 lakh

(D) ₹ 100 lakh

54. A company engaged in manufacturing of steel balls acquired computers at a cost of ₹ 3 lakh on 10th July, 2018. The depreciation allowance for the AY 2019-2020 under Income-tax Act, 1961 would be:

(A) ₹ 1,80,000

(B) ₹ 1,20,000

(C) ₹ 3,00,000

(D) ₹ 45,000

55. Durafon (P) Ltd., engaged in steel industry, acquired a vacant piece of land on 15th May, 2016. The company sold the said land in December, 2018. The profit earned on sale of vacant land of ₹ 10 lakh shall be taxable as:

(A) Business income

(B) Income from other sources

(C) Short term capital gain

(D) Long term capital gain

56. Aiyer gifted 100 shares to his wife on 1st August, 2013. She received 200 bonus shares from the company in April, 2017. All the shares were sold to a friend for ₹ 1,50,000 in May, 2018. The 100 shares were originally acquired by Aiyer for ₹ 5,000. The capital gain on sale of shares in the month of May, 2018 shall be chargeable to tax:

(A) Fully in the hands of Aiyer

(B) Fully in the hands of Mrs. Aiyer

(C) For 100 shares in the hands of Aiyer and balance 200 shares in the hands of Mrs. Aiyer

(D) For 200 shares in the hands of Aiyer and balance 100 shares in the hands of Mrs. Aiyer

57. The loss from activity of owning and maintaining race horses is eligible for carry forward and set off for a maximum period of:

(A) 8 Assessment years

(B) 6 Assessment years

(C) 4 Assessment years

(D) 2 Assessment years

58. D transferred Zero Coupon Bonds on 20th August 2018. These bonds were acquired during the financial year 2010-2011. The capital gain computed on the redemption with indexation benefit is ₹ 2 lakh and without indexation benefit is ₹ 3 lakh. The long term capital gain would be chargeable to tax on such Zero Coupon Bonds in AY 2019-2020:

(A) @ 5%

(B) @ 10%

(C) @ 20%

(D) @ 30%

59. Objective of tax planning cell in an organization is to:

(A) Improve tax collection

(B) Take advantages of various allowances and deductions

(C) Make tax avoidance

(D) Have inflation management

60. The total income of Mrs. Rose for the financial year 2018-2019 is ₹ 3,40,000. Her tax liability for AY 2019-2020 on the income of ₹ 3,40,000 shall be:

(A) ₹ 2,080

(B) NIL

(C) ₹ 2,500

(D) ₹ 4,700

61. Rao, carrying a business, contributed ₹ 40,000 in the National Pension Trust account. He also made a tax saving deposit of ₹ 1,20,000 in his PPF account and ₹ 40,000 in LIC Premium. The total amount eligible for deduction under various sections enumerated in Chapter VI-A shall be:

(A) ₹ 1,90,000

(B) ₹ 1,50,000

(C) ₹ 1,20,000

(D) ₹ 2,00,000

62. Timir, (aged 51 years) subscribed to health insurance for him, wife and son and paid premium of ₹ 28,000. He also incurred medical expenditure for his parents during the year amounting to ₹ 32,000. He can claim deduction for these expenses as per section 80D of the Income-tax Act, 1961, of:

(A) ₹ 57,000

(B) ₹ 30,000

(C) ₹ 28,000

(D) ₹ 55,000

63. In the case of a non-resident, which of the following income is not taxable in his hand:

(A) Interest received from Government of India

(B) Capital gain on transfer of capital assets situated in India

(C) Interest received from a person resident in India on money borrowed and used outside India for carrying a business

(D) Royalty received from a person resident in India for the patent rights used in India

64. Kant, is engaged in the business of purchase and sale of pieces of various lands. During the FY 2018-2019, he sold pieces of lands for ₹ 32 lakh. All these sales were made through cheques and Electronic Clearing System (ECS). The valuation of these pieces of lands for stamp duty purpose was ₹ 41 lakh. He wants to pay tax on the income as per section 44AD. The income as per this section for AY 2019-2020 shall be:

(A) ₹ 2,46,000

(B) ₹ 3,28,000

(C) ₹ 2,56,000

(D) ₹ 1,92,000

65. Time limit for completion of Assessment/Re-assessment under section 147 of the Income-tax Act, 1961 is:

(A) 9 months from the end of the financial year in which notice for re-assessment is served

(B) 6 months from the end of the financial year in which notice for re-assessment is served

(C) 12 months from the end of the financial year in which notice for re-assessment is served

(D) 15 months from the end of the financial year in which notice for re-assessment is served

66. Prakash maintained a recurring deposit by paying ₹ 20,000 per month in a bank. The interest accrued and credited during 2018-2019 on such deposit is ₹ 15,000. The amount of TDS required to be deducted by the bank would be:

(A) NIL

(B) ₹ 1,500 @ 10%

(C) ₹ 3,000 @ 20%

(D) ₹ 500 @ 10% over ₹ 10,000

67. Sagar engaged in a business, booked a marriage hall of Yash having PAN for conducting mega sale during festival season of FY 2018-2019 and paid rent of ₹ 55,000 for 3 days period. His total turnover for financial year 2018-2019 is ₹ 85 lakh. The amount of Tax Deduction at Source (TDS) to be made by Sagar on the amount of rent paid will be:

(A) NIL

(B) ₹ 5,500

(C) ₹ 2,750

(D) ₹ 11,000

68. Hindu Undivided Family (HUF) of Vinay consisted of himself, his major son, minor son and his wife. At the time of filing of return of income of the HUF for AY 2019-2020, Vinay was out of country. The return of income of the HUF can be signed in this case by:

(A) Karta

(B) Authorized Tax Consultant

(C) Major Son

(D) Minor Son

69. A taxpayer wants to prefer an appeal against the order of the Assessing Officer. He received the order dated 30th April, 2019 on 5th May, 2019. He must prefer an appeal before the CIT (Appeals) under section 246A of the Income-tax Act, 1961, within:

(A) 30 days from the date of order

(B) 30 days from the date of receipt of order

(C) 60 days from the date of order

(D) 60 days from the date of receipt of order

70. An advance ruling can be sought from the Authority for Advance Ruling (AAR) by:

(A) Non-resident having transaction with resident

(B) Resident having transaction with another resident

(C) Foreign Government

(D) A Listed Company

PART B: GST

71. Supplier registered under composition scheme must file return within:

(A) 7 days after end of every month

(B) 20 days after end of every month

(C) 18 days after end of every quarter

(D) 20 days after end of every quarter

72. When the goods are sent to job worker input tax credit will be reversed if the goods are not received back by the principal after completion of job work within .... of being sent out.

(A) 3 months

(B) 6 months

(C) 1 year

(D) 3 years

73. Mr. Pandit is engaged in trading of gifts articles and his annual turnover will exceeds ₹ 200 lakh. The due date for filing annual return would be .... of the following financial year.

(A) 31st October

(B) 31st December

(C) 30th September

(D) 30th November

74. When a movement of goods is of more than........... in value, the e-way bill must accompany the goods.

(A) ₹ 20,000

(B) ₹ 50,000

(C) ₹ 1,00,000

(D) ₹ 2,00,000

75. A registered person of Delhi is buying and selling goods only in Delhi and Puducherry. The applicable law for GST in his case will be:

(A) State GST

(B) UTGST Act, 2017

(C) GST (Compensation to States) Act, 2017

(D) CGST Act, 2017

76. When the goods are dispatched to a destination which is 280 kms from the place of dispatch, the e-way bill generated is valid for:

(A) 1 day

(B) 3 days

(C) 2 days

(D) 5 days

77. Which of the following goods is not exempt from GST:

(A) Fish seed

(B) Ice cream

(C) Pappad

(D) Plastic Bangles

78. Power to declare certain activities/transactions as neither supply of goods nor of services is given in:

(A) Schedule IV

(B) Schedule III

(C) Schedule II

(D) Schedule I

79. Input Service Distributor (ISD) may distribute the CGST credit within the State as:

(A) UTGST

(B) CGST

(C) SGST

(D) Any of the above

80. The proper officer may cancel the GST registration, if any registered person other than a person paying tax under section 10 of CGST Act, 2017 has not furnished the returns for a continuous period of:

(A) 12 months

(B) 9 months

(C) 6 months

(D) 3 months

81. Goods and Services to be supplied chargeable under the CGST Act, 2017 have been classified under different specified Code Number/s which are known as Harmonized System Nomenclature (HSN) Codes. These HSN Codes have been evolved and developed by:

(A) GST Council

(B) HSN/SAC Codes Committee

(C) Customs Cooperation Council of Belgium

(D) None of the above

82. ABC Ltd. of Mumbai supplied goods to XYZ Ltd. of Delhi under a contract for the goods to be delivered at the factory of the buyers. Goods removed from the factory of ABC Ltd. on 9.8.2018 and were delivered in the factory of XYZ Ltd. of Delhi on 16.8.2018. Invoice for the supplies was raised by ABC Ltd. on 18.8.2018. Payment of the bill was received on 20.9.2018. The time of supply in this case under GST be taken as:

(A) 9.8.2018

(B) 16.8.2018

(C) 18.8.2018

(D) 20.9.2018

83. The registered person, in case of supply of capital goods or of plant and machinery on which input tax credit (ITC) has been availed/taken shall pay an amount equal to the Input Tax Credit on such capital goods or plant and machinery which is being arrived at by reducing the Input-tax at percentage points for every quarter or part thereof from the date of issue of invoice of such goods or the tax on the transaction value of such capital goods, whichever is higher.

(A) 3

(B) 5

(C) 6

(D) 2

84. Section 24 of the CGST Act, 2017 lists categories of persons who are required to take registration even if they are not covered under section 22 of the Act. Find out from the following categories of persons who are being required to take registration as per section 24 of the CGST Act, 2017:

(i) Casual taxable person

(ii) Non-resident taxable person

(iii) Recipient of service under reverse charge

(iv) Inter-State supplier

(v) Input service distributor

Select the correct answer from the options given below:

(A) (*i*), (*iii*) and (*v*)

(B) (*i*), (*ii*), (*iv*) and (*v*)

(C) (*i*), (*ii*) and (*v*)

(D) All the 5 in (*i*) to (*v*)

85. Section 2(6) of the CGST/SGST Act, 2017 defines aggregate turnover which is being computed on all India basis excluding the taxes charged under CGST Act, SGST Act, UTGST Act and IGST Act. Aggregate turnover shall include all supplies made by a taxable person comprising of:

(*i*) Taxable supply

(*ii*) Exempt supply

(*iii*) Export of goods and/or services

(*iv*) All inter-State supply of person having same PAN

(*v*) Supply on which tax is levied on reverse charge basis

(*vi*) Value of all inward supply

Select the correct answer from the options given below

(A) (*i*), (*iii*), (*iv*) and (*v*)

(B) (*i*), (*iii*), (*iv*) and (*vi*)

(C) All the above in (*i*) to (*vi*)

(D) (*i*), (*ii*), (*iii*) and (*iv*)

86. The certificate of registration issued to casual taxable person or to a non-resident taxable person shall be valid for the period specified in the application for registration or for ______ days from the effective date of registration whichever is earlier. The validity of registration period on a request made by such taxable person may be further extended by the Proper Officer for a period not exceeding ______ days.

(A) 60, 45

(B) 90, 60

(C) 90, 90

(D) 90, 30

87. The Proper Officer may make the best judgment assessment of the registered person where he fails to file general return under section 39 or final return under section 45 even after notice given under section 46 of the CGST Act, 2017 within............. years from the due date of annual return of the period to which the tax not paid relates.

(A) 5

(B) 3

(C) 2

(D) 1

88. Refund order should be made by the Proper Officer within .... days from the date of receipt of application which is complete in all respects and where the Proper Officer is satisfied with the amount so refundable is payable to the applicant, he shall make an order in Form .... which shall be credited to the account of the applicant.

(A) 45, GST-RFD-5

(B) 90, GST-RFD-4

(C) 60, GST-RFD-6

(D) 90, GST-RFD-6

89. President of India gave assent to (*i*) Central Goods and Services Tax Act, 2017 (*ii*) Integrated Goods and Services Tax Act, 2017 (*iii*) Union Territory Goods and Services Tax Act, 2017 and (*iv*) Goods and Services Tax (Compensation to State) Act, 2017 on:

(A) 13th May, 2017

(B) 13th April, 2017

(C) 16th April, 2017

(D) 6th June, 2017

90. Radhey & Company registered supplier paying GST under regular scheme had made Inter-State Taxable Supply of ₹ 8,00,000 and Intra-State Taxable Supply of ₹ 6,00,000 chargeable under CGST, SGST and IGST at the rates of 9%, 9% and 18% respectively. He is having available amount of ITC under CGST of ₹ 30,000 and under SGST of ₹ 20,000. Supplies made are exclusive of taxes. Amount of the total tax payable as CGST, SGST and IGST after availing the amount of ITC by Radhey & Company on such supplies shall be of:

(A) ₹ 2,30,000

(B) ₹ 2,00,000

(C) ₹ 2,22,000

(D) ₹ 2,26,000

91. Decision of the GST Council will be adopted when it has the support of:

(A) One-third majority

(B) Two-third majority

(C) Three-fourth majority

(D) Simple majority

92. The Compensation to States for loss of revenue on account of implementation of GST is for _____ years.

(A) 2

(B) 5

(C) 8

(D) 10

93. When agriculturist supplies tobacco leaves to a factory, registered under to pay GST is on:

(A) Tobacco leaves seller

(B) The buyer under reverse charge

(C) The agriculturist

(D) Consumer of tobacco leaves

94. When an unregistered dealer supplied goods to a registered dealer, the time of supply under reverse charge shall be earliest of the:

(A) date of receipt of goods

(B) date of supply of goods

(C) date of loading of goods in transport

(D) date of intimation of supply of goods

95. Composition scheme is not applicable to service providers except the following:

(A) Consultancy Service

(B) Restaurant Service

(C) Beauty Parlours

(D) Cleaning work

96. To avail input tax credit, which of the following factors is not relevant:

(A) Tax invoice

(B) Furnishing of return by supplier

(C) Receipt of goods and services

(D) Payment by buyer for supply received

97. Input tax credit cannot be availed after the expiry of _____ from the date of issue of tax invoice of supply.

(A) 6 months

(B) 3 months

(C) 1 year

(D) 2 years

98. When goods are packed and transported with insurance, the supply of goods, packing materials, transport and insurance as per provisions of the CGST Act, 2017, is called as:

(A) Mixed Supply

(B) Uniform Supply

(C) Complex Supply

(D) Composite Supply

99. A service shall be a continuous supply of service agreed to be provided continuously or on recurrent basis under a contract when the period of service exceeds:

(A) 1 month

(B) 3 months

(C) 6 months

(D) 1 year

100. Which of the following is not liable to be registered as per provisions of the CGST Act, 2017:

(A) Person supplying exempted goods

(B) Non-resident making taxable supplies

(C) Deductor of tax at source

(D) Supplier on behalf of other person

ANSWERS:

1.	(D)	2.	(C)	3.	(D)	4.	(C)	5.	(C)	6.	(A)	7.	(C)
8.	(D)	9.	(B)	10.	(D)	11.	(A)	12.	(B)	13.	(D)	14.	(A)
15.	(B)	16.	(A)	17.	(C)	18.	(B)	19.	(A)	20.	(D)	21.	(C)

22.	(D)	23.	(B)	24.	(A)	25.	(A)	26.	(D)	27.	(A)	28.	(A)
29.	(B)	30.	(C)	31.	(D)	32.	(D)	33.	(B)	34.	(B)	35.	(C)
36.	(C)	37.	(C)	38.	(C)	39.	(B)	40.	(B)	41.	(D)	42.	(B)
43.	(C)	44.	(**)	45.	(D)	46.	(A)	47.	(A)	48.	(C)	49.	(D)
50.	(**)	51.	(C)	52.	(C)	53.	(C)	54.	(A)	55.	(D)	56.	(C)
57.	(C)	58.	(B)	59.	(B)	60.	(A)	61.	(B)	62.	(A)	63.	(C)
64.	(A)	65.	(C)	66.	(B)	67.	(C)	68.	(C)	69.	(B)	70.	(A)
71.	(C)	72.	(C)	73.	(B)	74.	(B)	75.	(**)	76.	(B)	77.	(B)
78.	(B)	79.	(B)	80.	(C)	81.	(C)	82.	(A)	83.	(B)	84.	(D)
85.	(D)	86.	(C)	87.	(A)	88.	(C)	89.	(B)	90.	(**)	91.	(C)
92.	(B)	93.	(B)	94.	(A)	95.	(B)	96.	(D)	97.	(C)	98.	(D)
99.	(B)	100.	(A)										

** *MCQs are wrong; for further clarification please refer hints.*

Important Note:

- **MCQ Nos. 1, 3, 6, 10, 14, 27, 29, 33 & 70 are not relevant for New Syllabus of CS Executive as these questions relates to topics that are not in syllabus.**
- **All MCQs are relevant for Old Syllabus of CS Executive.**

HINTS FOR IMPORTANT THEORY AND PRACTICAL MCQS [JUNE 2019 PAPER]

1.

Section	Type of Default	Minimum Penalty	Maximum Penalty
271AA	Failure to keep and maintain information and document in respect of international transaction or specified domestic transaction	A sum equal to 2% of value of each international or specified domestic transaction	–
	Failure to *furnish* information and document as required u/s 92D(4)	₹ 5,00,000	–

Hence, Option (D) is correct.

4. ***Relevant Transactions given in MCQ*** **where quoting of PAN made compulsory [Rule 114B]**

Nature of transaction	Value of transaction
Payment to a hotel or restaurant against a bill or bills at any one time.	Payment in cash of an amount exceeding ₹ 50,000.
Deposit with – (*i*) banking company or a co-operative bank to which the Banking Regulation Act, 1949, applies (including any bank or banking institution referred to in section 51 of that Act); (*ii*) Post Office.	Cash deposits exceeding ₹ 50,000 during any one day.
A time deposit with,— (*i*) a banking company or a co-operative bank to which the Banking Regulation Act, 1949, applies (including any bank or banking institution referred to in section 51 of that Act); (*ii*) a Post Office; (*iii*) a Nidhi referred to in section 406 of the Companies Act, 2013; or (*iv*) a non-banking financial company which holds a certificate of registration under section 45-IA of the RBI Act, 1934, to hold or accept deposit from public.	*Amount exceeding* ₹ 50,000 *or aggregating to more than* ₹ 5,00,000*during a financial year.*
Sale or purchase of any immovable property.	Amount exceeding ₹ 10,00,000 or valued by stamp valuation authority referred to in Section 50C at an amount exceecing ₹ 10,00,000 .

Hence, Option (C) is correct.

7. Equalization Levy: Equalization levy was introduced in India by Finance Act, 2016, with the intention of taxing the digital transactions *i.e.* the income accruing to foreign e-commerce companies from India. It is aimed at taxing business to business transactions.

Applicability of equalization levy: Equalization Levy is a direct tax, which is withheld at the time of payment by the service recipient. The two conditions to be met to be liable to equalization levy

- The payment should be made to a non-resident service provider;

- The annual payment made to one service provider exceeds **₹ 1,00,000** in one financial year.

Services covered under equalization levy: Currently, not all services are covered under the ambit of equalization levy. The following services covered:

- Online advertisement;
- Any provision for digital advertising space or facilities/ service for the purpose of online advertisement;

Rate of tax: Currently the applicable rate of tax is **6%** of the gross consideration to be paid.

8. Restriction on cash transactions [Section 269ST]: No person shall receive an amount of **₹ 2,00,000 or more** – (*a*) in aggregate from a person in a day; or (*b*) in respect of a single transaction; or (*c*) in respect of transactions relating to one event or occasion from a person, otherwise than by an account payee cheque or an account payee bank draft or use of electronic clearing system through a bank account.

However, the provisions of this section shall not apply to –

(*i*) any receipt by – (*a*) Government; (*b*) Any banking company, post office savings bank or co-operative bank;

(*ii*) transactions of the nature referred to in Section 269SS;

(*iii*) such other persons or class of persons or receipts, which the Central Government may, by notification in the Official Gazette, specify.

Penalty for failure to comply with Section 269ST [Section 271DA]: If a person receives any sum in contravention of the provisions of section 269ST, he shall be liable to pay, by way of penalty, a **sum equal to the amount of such receipt**. However, no penalty shall be imposable if such person proves that there were good and sufficient reasons for the contravention. Any penalty imposable as above shall be imposed by the Joint Commissioner.

9. Dividend received by Indian Companies from specified foreign companies [Section 115BBD]:

Tax rate = 15% *plus* Surcharge *plus* Education Cess. *Specified foreign company means company in which Indian company holds 26% or more nominal value of equity share capital.*

11. Fee for default in furnishing return of income [Section 234F]: Where a person required to furnish a return of income u/s 139, fails to do so within the prescribed time, he shall pay, by way of fee, a sum of —

(a) **₹ 5,000**, if the return is furnished on or before the 31st day of December of the assessment year;

(b) **₹ 10,000** in any other case.

However, if the total income of the person does not exceed **₹ 5,00,000**, the fee payable under this section shall not exceed **₹ 1,000**.

12. If the person on whom a notice under section 148 is to be served is a person treated as the agent of a non-resident u/s 163 and the assessment, reassessment or re-computation to be made in pursuance of the notice is to be made on him as the agent of such non-resident, the notice shall not be issued after the expiry of a period of **six years** from the end of the relevant assessment year. **[Section 149(3)]**

17. Where the assessee incurs any expenditure for acquisition of any asset or part thereof in respect of which a payment or aggregate of payments made to a person in a day, otherwise than by *an account payee cheque* drawn on a bank or an *account payee bank draft* or use of *electronic clearing system* through a bank account, exceeds **₹ 10,000**, such expenditure shall be ignored for the purposes of determination of actual cost.

24. Rectification of mistake [Section 154(1)]: With a view to rectifying any mistake apparent from the record an income-tax authority referred to in section 116 may –

(*a*) amend any order passed by it under the provisions of the Act;

(*b*) amend any intimation or deemed intimation u/s 143(1);

(*c*) amend any intimation u/s 200A(1);

(*d*) amend any intimation u/s 206CB(1).

25. In case of scrutiny assessment notice shall be served on the assessee before the expiry of **6 months from the end of the financial year in which the return is furnished. [Section 143(2)]**

31. *Minimum of following three is exempt gratuity:*

(1) Amount received	11,00,000
(2) [Last Salary $\times \frac{15}{26} \times$ Completed year of service] [52,000 $\times \frac{15}{26} \times 32$]	**9,60,000**
(3) Amount specified	20,00,000

39.

Commuted pension received		6,00,000
(-) Exempt	$\left[\frac{1}{3} \times \frac{6,00,000}{50\%}\right]$	(4,00,000)
Taxable amount		2,00,000

44. Expenditure exceeding ₹ 10,000 [Section 40A(3)]: Where assessee incurs an expenditure, which is allowable and claimed as deduction and the payment or aggregate of payments made to a person in a day in respect of such expenditure, otherwise than by an account payee cheque drawn on a bank or account payee bank draft or use of electronic clearing system exceeds ₹ **10,000** then no deduction shall be allowed in respect of such expenditure.

In the case of payment made for plying, hiring or leasing goods carriages, the aforesaid limit shall be ₹ ***35,000*** *instead of* ₹ *10,000.*

If payment is made for any liability of earlier years in current year otherwise than account payee cheque and such payment exceeds ₹ 10,000 then such expenditure is not allowed to be deducted while computing profits and gains of business and profession.

As per data given in question ₹ 15,000 paid by bearer cheque will be disallowed u/s 40A(3). However, no option contains figure of ₹ 15,000 and hence question itself is wrong.

45. As per **Section 35D**, minimum of following two will qualify for deduction:

(1) Aggregate amount of eligible expenditure	16,00,000
(2) Higher of 5% of Cost of the project or 5% of Capital employed	5,00,000

Deduction = 5,00,000 × 1/5 = 1,00,000

46. (100 lakh × 8%) + (60 lakh × 6%) = 11.6 lakh.

Deduction for remuneration of partners is not available while computing deemed income u/s 44AD.

48. Where the assessee incurs any expenditure for acquisition of any asset or part thereof in respect of which a payment or aggregate of payments made to a person in a day, otherwise than by *an account payee cheque* drawn on a bank or an *account payee bank draft* or use of *electronic clearing system* through a bank account, exceeds ₹ **10,000**, such expenditure shall be ignored for the purposes of determination of actual cost. *Thus depreciation cannot be claimed on such amount.*

Depreciation rate = 7.5% (regular) + 10% (additional) = 17.5% [As put to use less than 180 days]

4,00,000 × 17.5% = 70,000

50. Section 44AE is ***amended by Finance Act, 2018*** whereas question is designed as per old provisions and hence question itself is wrong.

54. Depreciation rate = 40% (regular) + 20% (additional) = 17.5% [As put to use more than 180 days]

3,00,000 × 60% = 1,80,000

55. In case of following assets if period of holding is **less than 24 months** then they will be treated as short term capital assets –

- Unlisted shares;
- An immovable property being land or building or both.

As per data given in question, vacant land (non depreciable asset) was sold after holding more than 24 months and hence gain arising on such sale will be long term capital gain.

56. Income from **accretion** to gifted asset cannot be clubbed in the hands of person who transfer the asset by way of gift. Thus, if husband transfers 100 shares to wife and wife received 200 bonus shares then capital gain arising on transfer of 300 shares by wife will be taxed as follows:

- Capital gain on 100 shares will be taxable in the hands of husband and
- Capital gain on 200 shares will be taxable in the hands of wife.

58. In case of *zero coupon bonds,* capital gain tax shall be lower of following:

(1) 10% of (Net consideration – Cost of acquisition without indexation)

(2) 20% of LTCG (Net consideration – Indexed cost of acquisition)

60.

On first	2,50,000		Nil
On balance	90,000	@ 5%	4,500
	3,40,000		4,500
(-) Rebate u/s 87A			(2,500)
			2,000
(+) Cess @ 4%			80
			2,080

61. The maximum amount of deduction u/ss 80C and 80CCC and u/s 80CCD(1) (*i.e.* employee's contribution or an individual assessee's contribution to pension scheme of Central Government), is restricted to ₹ **1,50,000**.

62.

For Timir and his family	25,000
For parent (senior citizen)	32,000
	57,000

64. 41,00,000 × 6% = 2,46,000

Special provision for full value of consideration for transfer of assets other than capital assets [Section 43CA]

[Amended by Finance Act, 2018]

Stamp duty value deemed to be full value of consideration: If the sale price of land and building (not being capital asset) is less than stamp duty value then for the purpose of computing profits and gains of such asset stamp value has to be taken as full value of consideration.

However, where the value adopted or assessed or assessable by the authority for the purpose of payment of stamp duty does not exceed 105% of the consideration received or accruing as a result of the transfer, the consideration so received or accruing as a result of the transfer shall, for the purposes of computing profits and gains from transfer of such asset, be deemed to be the full value of the consideration.

Stamp duty value on the date of agreement to be considered: If the date of agreement and the date of registration of asset are not the same, then value at the date of agreement has to be taken as stamp duty value and not on the date of registration. However, this provision shall apply only in a case where the amount of consideration or a part thereof has been received by way of an account payee cheque or an account payee bank draft or by use of electronic clearing system through a bank account on or before the date of agreement for transfer of the asset.

Special provision for computing profits and gains on presumptive basis [Section 44AD]

The scheme shall be applicable to an individual, HUF or partnership firm who is a resident. The scheme is not applicable to LLP, company or AOP/BOI.

The scheme is applicable for any business (excluding a business of plying, hiring or leasing goods carriages referred to u/s 44AE) whose total turnover gross receipts in the previous year does not exceed an amount of **₹ 2 Crore**.

A sum equal to **8%** of the total turnover or gross receipts of the assessee in the previous year on account of such business *(6% in respect of the amount of total turnover or gross receipts which is received by an account payee cheque or an account payee bank draft or use of electronic clearing system through a bank account during the previous year or before the due date specified in Section 139(1) in respect of that previous year)* shall be deemed to be the profits and gains of such business.

65. No order of assessment, re-assessment or re-computation shall be made u/s 147 after the expiry of **9 months** from the end of the financial year in which the notice u/s 148 was served. ***However, where the notice u/s 148 is served on or after 1.4.2019, the provisions of this section shall have effect, as if for the words***

"9 months", the words **"12 months"** ***had been substituted.*** **[Section 153(2)]**

It is assumed that notice in given question is issued after 1.4.2019 and hence Option (C) is treated as correct answer.

67. Payment of rent by certain individuals or HUF [Section 194-IB]

Who is responsible to deduct tax at source: Any person, being an individual or HUF *(other than those referred to in the second proviso to Section 194-I)*, responsible for paying to a resident any income by way of rent exceeding ₹ **50,000** for a month or part of a month during the previous year.

Rate of tax deduction: 5%

When to deduct: Income Tax shall be deducted on such income at the time of credit of rent, for the last month of the previous year or the last month of tenancy, if the property is vacated during the year, as the case may be, to the account of the payee or at the time of payment thereof in cash or by issue of a cheque or draft or by any other mode, *whichever is earlier.*

In a case where the tax is required to be deducted as per the provisions of Section 206AA, such deduction shall not exceed the amount of rent payable for the last month of the previous year or the last month of the tenancy, as the case may be.

75. Delhi and Puducherry have their own legislatures and hence both are States for the Purpose of GST. A registered person buying and selling goods in Delhi and Puducherry will be governed by CGST Act and State GST of Delhi and Puducherry. None of the given option contains "CGST Act and State GST Act" and hence MCQ is wrong itself.

81. Though correct answer is **"Custom Co-operation Council of Belgium"** [Option (C)] but know it is known as **"World Custom Organization"**.

90.

Particulars	CGST	SGST	IGST
Output GST on Product X @ 20%	54,000	54 000	1,44,000
(-) Input CGST	(30,000)	–	–
(-) Input CGST	–	(20,000)	–
Net GST payable	24,000	34 000	1,44,000

24,000 + 34,000 + 1,44,000 = 2,02,000. None of the given option contains figure of 2,02,000 and hence MCQ itself is wrong.